SOCIAL POLICIES IN TIMES OF AUSTERITY AND POPULISM

Featuring the latest research by Brazilian-based scholars previously inaccessible to an English-speaking audience, this book is a timely, authoritative, multidisciplinary overview of social policies in Brazil during the Temer austerity and the Bolsonaro populist presidencies. The breadth of policies studied herein provides clues on the political agenda, preferences, and strategies during this tumultuous period in Brazil's history.

Divided into four parts, Part I is a contextualization: it brings basic understanding of Brazilian social policies, explains the trajectory of the Brazil political landscape, including the growth of a populist right-wing movement, the economic crisis and the increase in poverty and inequality in Brazil prior, and the threat to democracy brought about by the disinformation ecosystem. Part II discusses social security, social assistance, conditional cash transfers, and healthcare. Part III analyzes the neoliberal strategies to social investment policies, specifically labor, family, and education. In Part IV, the authors turn their attention to non-conventional topics that are not typically included in research on welfare state retrenchment, including the environment and indigenous rights, and police violence and gun control.

Social Policies in Times of Austerity and Populism is unhesitatingly recommended to all those who teach welfare state politics, comparative public policy, development studies, Brazilian politics, and right-wing politics.

Natália Sátyro is Associate Professor of Political Science at Federal University of Minas Gerais, Brazil. She was also the coordinator of Asociación Latinoamericana de Ciencia Política (ALACIP) Public Policy Research Group (GIPP, 2013–2024) and she is the Convener of International Political Science

Association (IPSA, 2023–present) Research Committee on Welfare State and Developing Societies (RC39). Her research interests include welfare state, welfare policy, income transfer programs, income inequality, and political institutions. She teaches and researches in the field of public policies, with emphasis on institutional analysis and social policies in Brazil and Latin America.

SOCIAL POLICIES IN TIMES OF AUSTERITY AND POPULISM

Lessons from Brazil

Edited by Natália Sátyro

Routledge
Taylor & Francis Group

NEW YORK AND LONDON

Designed cover image: © Shutterstock

First published 2025
by Routledge
605 Third Avenue, New York, NY 10158

and by Routledge
4 Park Square, Milton Park, Abingdon, Oxon, OX14 4RN

Routledge is an imprint of the Taylor & Francis Group, an informa business

Library of Congress Cataloging-in-Publication Data
Names: Sátyro, Natália Guimarães Duarte, author.
Title: Social policies in times of austerity and populism : lessons from Brazil / edited by Natália Sátyro.
Description: New York, NY : Routledge, 2024. | Includes bibliographical references and index. |
Summary: "Featuring the latest research by Brazilian-based scholars previously inaccessible to an
English-speaking audience, this book is a timely, authoritative, multidisciplinary overview of social
policies in Brazil during the Bolsonaro populist presidency. The breadth of policies studied herein
provides clues on the political agenda, preferences, and strategies during this tumultuous period in
Brazil's history. Divided into four parts, Natália Sátyro and her team of experts begin by explaining the
trajectory of the Brazil's political landscape, including the growth of a populist right-wing movement,
the economic crisis and the increase in poverty and inequality in Brazil prior, and the threat to democracy
brought about by disinformation. Part Two discusses social security, social assistance, conditional cash
transfers and healthcare. Part Three analyses the neoliberal strategies to social investment policies,
specifically labor, family, and education. In Part 4, the authors turn their attention to non-conventional
topics that are not typically included in research on retrenchment, including the environment, indigenous
rights and police violence and gun control. Social Policies in Times of Populism and Austerity is
unhesitatingly recommended to all those who teach welfare state politics, comparative public policy,
development studies, Brazilian politics, and right-wing politics"– Provided by publisher.
Identifiers: LCCN 2024007146 (print) | LCCN 2024007147 (ebook) |
ISBN 9781032784137 (hardback) | ISBN 9781032758374 (paperback) |
ISBN 9781003487777 (ebook)
Subjects: LCSH: Brazil–Social policy–21st century. | Brazil–Politics and government–2003– |
Populism–Brazil–History–21st century. | Bolsonaro, Jair, 1955–
Classification: LCC HN283.5 .S28 2024 (print) |
LCC HN283.5 (ebook) | DDC 306.0981–dc23/eng/20240422
LC record available at https://lccn.loc.gov/2024007146
LC ebook record available at https://lccn.loc.gov/2024007147

ISBN: 978-1-032-78413-7 (hbk)
ISBN: 978-1-032-75837-4 (pbk)
ISBN: 978-1-003-48777-7 (ebk)

DOI: 10.4324/9781003487777

Typeset in Times New Roman
by Newgen Publishing UK

CONTENTS

CONTRIBUTORS

Pedro M. R. Barbosa is a post-doc researcher at the Center for Metropolitan Studies (CEM, University of São Paulo). His research focuses on comparative studies of welfare states, the politics of social policies, and the link between social policies and political behavior.

André Borges is Associate professor of Political Science at the University of Brasília. His research focuses on elections, parties and party systems, federalism and coalition politics. His recent research has appeared in the *Journal of Politics in Latin America, Party Politics and Government and Opposition*.

Regina Coeli Moreira Camargos is a labor relations consultant and she holds a PhD in Political Science. Formerly an economist at the Inter-Union Department of Statistics and Socioeconomic Studies-DIEESE (1993–2018), she has also held a visiting professorship at DIEESE School of Labor Sciences.

Eleonora Schettini Martins Cunha is a retired professor formerly at the Department of Political Science at the Federal University of Minas Gerais (UFMG) and guest professor at the Legislative School of the Legislative Assembly of Minas Gerais. Her main areas of research include public policy studies, social policy, welfare policy, and democratic theory.

Marco Flávio da Cunha Resende is a full professor at the Center for Regional Development and Planning, Federal University of Minas Gerais, Brazil as well as a Researcher Brazilian National Council for Scientific and Technological

Development (CNPQ). He has published extensively on macroeconomic policy and post-keynesian economics.

Alexandre Diniz is a professor in the Geography Department at the Pontifical Catholic University of Minas Gerais (PUC Minas). He has held visiting professorships at McGill University; Université de Lille; Curtin University; and Texas State University.

Pedro H. G. Ferreira de Souza is a researcher in the Poverty and Inequality unit at the Brazilian Institute for Applied Economic Research (IPEA). His first book, *Uma História de Desigualdade* (2018), won the Prêmio Jabuti for "Book of the Year" – the most prestigious literary prize in Brazil. He conducts academic and policy-oriented research on poverty, inequality, and related issues.

Sandra Gomes is a professor at the Public Policy Institute from the Federal University of Rio Grande do Norte (UFRN)/Brazil. She is also CNPq Research Productivity Scholar and Associate Editor of the *Brazilian Political Science Review* (BPSR). Her research interests and publications revolve around social policies, decision-making processes, and intergovernmental relations.

Mauro Lúcio Jerônymo has a PhD in Political Science from UFMG (2021). His areas of interest cover topics related to political institutions and strategic interaction between institutional actors, intergovernmental relations, legislative process, Constitution of 1988, public policies and inequality, research methodologies, survey, statistic, Python and R languages.

José Angelo Machado is Associate Professor at the Department of Political Science at the Federal University of Minas Gerais (DCP / UFMG), having been Head of Department in the periods 2013–2015 and 2021–2023. He was sub coordinator of the Graduate Program in Political Science in the period 2019–2020. He is a researcher at the Center for Studies in Management and Public Policy (PUBLICUS-UFMG) and member of the Interinstitutional Center for Social Policy Analysis (CIAPSoc).

Ana Luiza Martins de Medeiros is a PhD candidate in Political Science at the Federal University of Minas Gerais (UFMG), Belo Horizonte, Brazil. She has a scholarship from CAPES (Coordenação de Aperfeiçoamento de Pessoal de Nível Superior). Member of the Research Group Interinstitutional Center of Social Policies (CIAPSoc) since 2020 and the extension project Curadoria Pública (UFMG/UFABC) since 2021.

Isabele Mitozo is an Assistant Professor in the Political Science Department/ Faculty of Philosophy and Human Sciences of the Federal University of Minas Gerais (UFMG), in Brazil, and coordinates the Research Group on Democracy, Communication and Digital Engagement (DECODE/UFMG). She is an associate researcher at the Brazilian National Institute of Science and Technology in Digital Democracy (INCT.DD), and the International Parliament Engagement Network (IPEN).

Joana Mostafa is an economist, a civil servant, and a researcher of Brazilian Institute for Applied Economic Research (IPEA). With top management experience in the line ministry of Social Development, she directed Brazil's Single Registry as well as collaborated in diverse international cooperation regarding social protection policies and their corresponding managerial and IT developments. Her current works focuses on gender and social protection policies.

Valéria Oliveira is an adjunct professor in the Department of Sciences Applied to Education (DECAE) and a researcher in the Center for Crime and Public Safety Studies (CRISP) and in the Research Center on School Inequalities (NUPEDE), all of them at the Federal University of Minas Gerais (UFMG). She researches on school violence, neighborhood effects and violence, and school inequalities and public safety policies in peripheral areas.

Gabriel Penna holds a master of arts in political science from the Federal University of Minas Gerais, Brazil. He is currently an attorney for Itabira, a municipality in the Brazilian state of Minas Gerais. His main research interests include human rights policies, gender roles, family policies, and social policies

Fernanda Pernasetti is a postdoctoral researcher funded by the Brazilian National Council for Scientific and Technological Development (CNPq) at the Institute of Urban and Regional Planning of the Federal University of Rio de Janeiro (Ippur-UFRJ). She is affiliated with the research groups Espaço e Poder (Space and Power) (CNPq/Ippur-UFRJ) and Futuros da Proteção Social (Future of Social Protection) at the Center for Strategic Studies from Oswaldo Cruz Foundation (CEE-Fiocruz). Her research interests lie within social policies, focusing on social security and pensions; welfare states; rounds of neoliberalization; and transformations in the redistributive capacity of states in Brazil and Latin America.

Bruno R. Pinheiro is Analyst at Quaest Consultoria, where he utilizes his expertise in research methodology, analytical thinking, and policy evaluation to provide data-driven solutions across various industries. His research interests include public opinion, electoral behavior, and institutional design Through his work, he is committed to contributing to the development of effective public policies using evidence-based methods and rigorous research.

Arnaldo Provasi Lanzara is Professor of Political Science at the Fluminense Federal University (UFF) and researcher at the National Institute of Science and Technology in Public Policies, Strategies and Development (INCT/PPED) and the "Futures of Social Protection" Group at the Center for Strategic Studies of the Oswaldo Cruz Foundation (CEE/FIOCRUZ).

Alexandre Queiroz Guimarães is Professor and Researcher at the João Pinheiro Fundation and Pontifical Catholic University – PUC at Minas Gerais. He is the author of many articles on comparative political economy and development studies.

Ludmila Ribeiro is an associate professor in the Department of Sociology and a researcher in the Center for Crime and Public Safety Studies (CRISP), both at the Federal University of Minas Gerais (UFMG). She has also held visiting positions at the University of Florida, University of Groningen and Texas State University. During her career, she has coordinated several research projects on how the criminal justice system operates in Brazil. Nowadays, her research interests are focused on police violence, gender violence, and management of the criminal justice system.

Rafael Rocha is a researcher at the Instituto Sou da Paz (I am in Peace Institute) and an affiliate researcher at the Center for Crime and Public Safety Studies (CRISP), at the Federal University of Minas Gerais (UFMG). He holds a bachelor degree in social sciences (2006) and got his master (2012) and PhD (2017) in sociology at UFMG.

Eliara Santana is a journalist, PhD, and MA in Linguistic Studies. She is an associate researcher at CLE/Unicamp. She is a member of the research groups Media, Public Opinion and International Relations (MOPRI/UEPB) and Multilingualism and Interculturality in the Digital World (CLE/Unicamp); co-organizer of "Elections 2022 and the reconstruction of democracy in Brazil". In 2019, she was a visiting student at Teachers College, Columbia University, in NY, developing research activities at MASClab (Media and Social Change), focusing on fake news research, addressing structure, language, and ways of working with student audiences. She is one of the creators of the Disinformation Observatory (www.observatoriodadesinformaçao.org)

Catarina Ianni Segatto is Information Analyst at the Regional Center for Studies on the Development of the Information Society (Cetic.br/NIC.br), researcher at the Center for Metropolitan Studies (CEM), and professor at the Graduate Program in Public Policy at the Federal University of ABC (UFABC). She holds a PhD in Public Administration and Government at Fundação Getulio Vargas's Sao Paulo School of Business Administration (FGV EAESP) and worked as a Houston Family Postdoctoral Fellow at Johnson Shoyama Graduate School of Public Policy (University of Regina).

Fernanda Silva is a PhD student in political science at the Federal University of Minas Gerais-UFMG. She has a master in social work from the Federal University of Juiz de Fora. She is a specialist in public health policies and research and multidisciplinary residency in family health. She currently works as a social worker at the Federal University of Minas Gerais and is a member of the Interinstitutional Center for Social Policy Analysis at UFMG. She has experience in the areas of public policy, focusing on social assistance, health, education, political culture, and street-level bureaucracy.

Maria Dolores Lima da Silva is PhD of Political Science at the IUPERJ. She has been a professor at the Faculty of Social Sciences of the Federal University of Para UFPA since 1996. Since 2009, she is a professor of the Graduate Program of Political Science at the UFPA, in Belém, Brazil. Dolores coordinates the activities of research group Policies for Environment in Amazon (Políticas para o Meio Ambiente na Amazônia), registered by CNPq. Her main research interest is related to environmental policies and legislative production.

1

INTRODUCTION

Elements to reflect on dismantling of social policies in Brazil

Natália Sátyro[1]

1.1 Introduction

Brazil has been the scenario for a socio-political experiment throughout recent years. In 2016, a right-wing coalition brought Michel Temer (PMDB, per its Portuguese name, Brazilian Democratic Movement Party[2]) to power after the impeachment of President Dilma Rousseff (PT, per its Portuguese name, Worker's Party). This put an end to 13 years of administration by the Worker's Party. Temer, who was Rousseff's vice president, took over and began implementing a political project that was the opposite of the one his ticket had won with at the polls two years before (Sátyro, 2021). Brazil was facing one of its worst economic crises, which had already been foreseen in 2014 (the year of Rousseff's re-election). In addition to Dilma Rousseff's political inability, her economic policy cost her a lot (Pérez-Liñán, 2007). The process that removed her from power followed all rites and procedures within the law and with the approval of the Supreme Federal Court, under the supervision of Supreme Minister Enrique Ricardo Lewandowski. However, the process was based on a fallacy, namely the Portuguese term "pedalada fiscal," referring to the practice of taking out loans from state banks to cover for a budget deficit, and it is a well-known fact that it was the absence of political support that caused the greater trouble. Whether her impeachment was a coup or not, as well as what was the contribution of different political and institutional actors, is not the subject of this book. The fact is that this political movement rearranged the articulation between the Legislative and Executive branches. Historically, the Brazilian Congress had always been more to the right than the Executive (Power and Rodrigues-Silveira, 2019).

DOI: 10.4324/9781003487777-1

According to Kershe and Marona (2022), in the morning of March 17, 2014, the beginning of Operation Car Wash (*Operação Lava a Jato*), mentioned in the press as the "strongest action for fighting corruption in history" (quote from the authors), occurred. It was a spectacular launch, with over 400 federal police officers, 81 search and seizure warrants, 18 warrants for pre-trial detention, and 19 for coerced conveyance, distributed over 17 municipalities (Kershe and Marona, 2022). It became stronger in the following years and, in parallel to its actions, opinion polls showed the corrosion of the Brazilian party system and the disbelief aimed at democratic institutions, especially parties. Thus, we come into 2018, the year of presidential elections, when the main candidate Luís Inácio Lula da Silva (PT) was arrested, and this, along with many other reasons, led to the election being won by a candidate from the populist ultra-right. That is, in 2018, by direct election, Jair Messias Bolsonaro (PSL, per its Portuguese name, Social Liberal Party) was elected in Brazil, with a campaign based on authoritarian speech, support of a military dictatorship, and an ultra-right position regarding social issues. His anti-system discourse organically fit in with the anti-corruption banner of Operation Car Wash. Along with that, the Brazilian Congress steered further to the right. The Social Liberal Party, which had only one seat prior to 2018, won 52 seats in the Chamber of Deputies, and grew to reach 99 seats in 2022. And the left was entrenched while facing a majority composed by the center-right and the ultra-right. During this period, which began in 2016 and lasted until the end of the Bolsonaro government (December, 2022), a systematic process of retrenchment of social welfare policies was carried out, as well as a programmatic one, as we will see ahead (Pierson, 1994). The purpose of this book is to bring together studies that analyze the drivers and the scope of the changes and reforms in the Brazilian system of social protection over those seven years to understand how we came from the Brazilian "golden era" of social protection to the dismantling of these systems by two consecutive right-wing administrations in the head of the executive branch, one of them an ultra-right government.

From the point of view of the evolution of well-being in Brazil, what happened during this period? Was there a retrenchment of social policies? It is important to note that the well-being of the population was already declining in the face of the economic crisis, which can be seen by the increase in poverty, as we will see in Chapter 6. After a period of continuous decline in poverty and extreme poverty rates, they grew again in 2014 (Chapter 6), a year in which the economy was already showing clear signs of the severity of the crisis that effectively exploded in 2015. A reversal of the previous trajectory of decrease in poverty rates took place. There was a recrudescence of the social situation and a very quick return to the situation of 10 years prior (Vinhaes et al., 2022; Jannuzzi and Sátyro, 2023). With the covid-19 pandemic, which devastated the planet, there was a break in this negative evolution due to the Emergency Aid payments – a cash transfer program (Chapter 10) that, being temporary, also had temporary effects. Despite the well-being of the population being only a proxy for what interests us, it allows us to have an idea of the dimension of what had been happening.

In the face of a more critical crisis between 2014 and 2015, there was a cost for the poorer population. In 2020, due to the federal response to the covid-19 pandemic with the Emergency Aid payments, there was an increase in well-being with a decrease in poverty. However, such investment only took place in the most critical period of the pandemic, and in a scenario of deregulation, financial withdrawal, and other extremely restrictive institutional changes to the protection system, as it will be shown in this book; there is the return of economic growth, but Brazil is back in the map of hunger. To make it worse, inequalities of every kind remain, leaving us with a very heterogeneous country in term of well-being (Sátyro and Cunha, 2018b).

In case the reader does not already know (it will be described in detail on Chapter 4), Brazil had already been coming from a scenario of fiscal austerity and entered a severe economic crisis (2014–2015) that claimed its costs. What followed was the end of a 13-year long period of left-wing governments based on a broad coalition of support, an impeachment process, two years of a government that we can describe as mainstream right-wing, followed by the election of a president from a populist radical right party (PRRP) who was not re-elected in 2022 but who received 58 million votes against the winner's 60 million. Half of Brazilian society actually did support his re-election, a fact that needs to be taken seriously when analyzing the country`s current political life. From a social point of view, in this same period, an accentuated worsening of conditions can be observed and, for the two right-wing governments, many reforms, re-regulations, and deregulations of social policies can be mentioned. Assuming that after CF88 there was a paradigm shift in Brazilian social protection and was the construction of a system in which the set of policies have a universal vocation and that the State assumed a leading role, being able to speak of a welfare state (Chapter 2). The basic questions are: Are we facing a dismantling of the Brazilian social welfare regime? Are we facing a dismantling of the Brazilian social welfare state? How has this regime changed? In which direction?

Ferragina (2022) proposed to analyze high-income countries using a double movement between compensatory policy spending and favor of employment-oriented policies. The central questions that guided him were: "To what degree are different welfare regimes and countries moving away from compensatory policy spending and in favor of employment-oriented measures? Is the reduction of compensatory policy spending prevailing over the expansion of employment-oriented policy spending, or are we facing an equilibrium?" A secondary question of this book is that, faced with the ultra-right in the presidency, which drinks both from the waters of neoconservatism and neoliberalism at once (Brown, 2006; 2015; Cooper, 2017), are these questions the best ones?

The ultra-right does not fit into a taxonomy that only considers mainstream parties; they have created a different *modus operandi*. Nunes and Traumann (2023) show that, in Brazil, people's perception of proposals from the political left and right were very similar in terms of social and economic policies. After the electoral success of Bolsa Família, even the right-wing parties understood the importance of serving the most vulnerable part of the population and the left needs to convince them of fiscal responsibility. Santos and Traumann show that the extreme right understood this and differentiated itself from conservative agendas.

And this ultra-right, in an era of fake news on large digital platforms, leads us to argue that it could even have a different way of dealing with the classic strategies of blame avoidance and credit claiming. Studies on the ultra-right already have a certain density, but for the most part, it had been present in the political scene as a supporting actor. Przeworski showed the strong presence of such parties in Austria, France, Switzerland, and Denmark (Przeworski, 2020: 118–119). If we think about the last few years on the global stage, we have had a spread of the radical ultra-right as a phenomenon that gains strength in countries of different expressions on the global stage, making it to presidency or representing the state as prime ministers, or simply with strength in parliament: Donald Trump in the USA (2017–2021); the permanence of Viktor Mihály Orbán in Poland in his fourth term; the victory of Giorgia Meloni's far-right party in Italy in 2022; Ulf Kristersson, Prime Minister of Sweden, in a coalition of three center-right parties that rely on the support of the ultra-right Sweden Democrats; the 42% votes that Marine Le Pen received in 2022; Bolsonaro in Brazil (2019–2022); the growth of the far-right in Spain; the Freedom Party of Austria (FPO) in government with the Christian Democratic-Conservative Austrian People's Party (OVP) from 2000 to 2006 and from 2017 to 2019; to pinpoint a few.

Have these governments prioritized certain areas? Has there been stability in any social policy arenas? Has there been a greater retrenchment of compensatory policies, in favor of employment-oriented measures or universal policies? In the case of Brazil, was there a project for the dismantling or refocusing of social policies? According to Rathgeb and Busemeyer (2022), the literature on party politics and voting behavior as well as the literature on comparative political economy and welfare state research are neglecting the role of populist radical right parties (PRRPs) in terms of their association with the welfare state itself and, as it is known, missing variables create biases. This is certainly due to the fact that only very recently the PRRPs have grown electorally to the point of being specifically researched. The contribution of this book takes place in this particular point for this field of research. A basic question that the book addresses is whether, in Brazil, PRRPs are really different from the mainstream right, and, if so, in what ways?

In order to shed light on this phenomenon, a collective effort was carried out that resulted in a large multifaceted case study. A collective project with researchers from different institutions and academic backgrounds made it possible to deeply analyze what happened within nine different sectorial arenas. Among the *classic compensatory policies*, the project analyzed **social security**, **social assistance**, **conditional cash transfer**, as well as policies for **healthcare**, which in Brazil is a universal right. As for policies considered as *social investment*, such as those for the **labor market** and **family policies**, the latter shows a movement that is completely opposite to what had been seen in the literature by the Organisation for Economic Co-operation and Development (OECD), for there was explicit reinforcement of gender roles due to the neoconservative stance of the ultra-right, with a return to the idea that care should be provided within the family unit, the "traditional" one. As for **education policies**, the basis for social investment in human capital as well as a constitutional right in Brazil, access is paradoxically so unequal that the educational heterogeneity directly impacts citizens' insertion in the labor market and income, which makes it the bedrock for the high levels of inequality in the country. The reader will also find *two other policies* that are not usually part of the analyzed set within social welfare regimes, such as **environmental policies** and **public safety** and **gun control policies**. The authors were urged to consider in their analyses, as far as possible, four moments in time: first, the effects of the 2015 economic crisis, still under Rousseff's government; second, Temer's actions, especially Constitutional Amendment N 95 of 2016 considered a New Fiscal Regime (see Chapter 2); third, Bolsonaro's agenda and actions; and, finally, the pandemic. The way in which the Brazilian ultra-right dealt with these agendas will give us clues to better understand their preferences and strategies, but we need to compare them with the mainstream right to understand their peculiarities. The breadth of policies will allow for looking beyond the impact of the pandemic specifically.

Before reading about each of the policies, the reader will be given a contextualization within five dimensions: The structure of the welfare regime from the Federal Constitution and the Temer and Bolsonaro`changes with a break in the trajectory from 2016. The *political arena*, with the growth of a populist ultra-right, and the *economic situation* unfolding since the 2000s. Added to this, an analysis of the trajectory of *poverty and inequality* in the country since the 1990s. The book also makes a contribution to the debate with an analysis of the *disinformation ecosystem* and why it represents a threat to democracy, in an attempt to begin to understand how the spreading of fake news works as a kind of macro-strategy for obfuscation (in Piersean terms), as well as the concept of blurring (Rovny, 2013; Rovny and Polk, 2020), in a fixture that mixes credit claiming with blame avoidance.

We will bring a conceptual discussion of what this dismantling means, its strategies, as well as some general hypotheses of what led to such process. At this point, the authoritarian and neoliberal values of the PRRPs will be discussed, as well as their adaptation to countries outside Europe. After that, the plan of the book is presented with the organization of the chapters and their contents. This will allow the reader to be prepared to understand the analysis of each of the arenas and their idiosyncrasies within a complex federative system.

1.2 Defining dismantling as a multi-dimensional concept

Institutional changes are always in the agenda for the research field of public policies, even if the debate on institutional changes is much wider (North, 1993; Mahoney and Thelen, 2010; Tang, 2017). Specifically within changes in public policies or the systems of social protection, there is a more restricted debate on expansion, adaptation, retraction, or dismantling of social policies. Ferragina (2022) suggests the existence of a continuum between retrenchment and expansion and organizes the literature on "retrenchment" and "dismantling" into three main interpretations on the changes in welfare state (2022:706). According to the author, the first one considers welfare state change as retrenchment. This approach focuses on the political battle against protection from old risks, basically the reduction of transfers for poor individuals and families. From that perspective, there are several solutions to deal with new risks, from neoliberal strategies to social investment policies. The second group focuses mostly on continuity over change insofar as welfare states are rooted in old historical and political legacies. The strength of path dependency and of organized groups for the protection of rights halts major structural changes. The third one focuses on the ability/capacity of the welfare state to adapt to times of "permanent austerity," that is, to the new political economy context (2022:706). In this last interpretation, the retrenchment concept and the cost-containment idea are joined. In some way, this variation connects to the same line of thought of Green-Pedersen (2004) when he affirms that "much of the disagreement about the dependent variable actually originates from scholars having different theoretical perspectives and not always being fully aware of the implications of their theoretical approaches to welfare state retrenchment" (2004:4). This literature holds many approaches and interpretations of what retrenchment is or what dismantling actually means.

By taking stock of existing research on the retrenchment/dismantling of welfare regimes, this book aims to be a case study, a collective work drawn from the mixed approaches related to the concepts as well as the methodologies. Here, the debate brought up by Green-Pedersen on the dependent variable within the study of welfare state retrenchment is key. According to Green-Pedersen (2004), the "dependent variable problem" is about defining the object of the entire retrenchment debate. This involves such questions as which changes to welfare states should be classified as retrenchment; how one can separate retrenchment from reform and reconstruction; and which data are most appropriate for empirical investigations of retrenchment outcomes. (2004:3–4). That is, when we deal with the idea of dismantling, we may be dealing with an array of phenomena and strategies which can encompass "policy termination, welfare state retrenchment, deregulation, etc." and these strategies, according to Jordan et al. (2013), are instruments which will be strongly determined by each specific arena of social policy being analyzed (Jordan et al., 2013:796).

In fact, although it is known that concepts usually change the focus of the analysis, we will be working complementarily with the concepts instead of being exclusionary when we analyze the Brazilian social protection system. According to Bauer and Knill (2014), policy dismantling is "a change of a direct, indirect, hidden or symbolic nature that either diminishes the number of policies in a particular area or reduces the number of policy instruments used, and/or lowers their intensity. It can involve changes to these core elements of policy and/or it can be achieved by manipulating the capacities to implement and supervise them" (2014:35). This is our point of departure. When analyzing high-income countries, there is resistance to use the term "retrenchment" (Jordan et al., 2012). Jordan, Green-Pedersen, and Turnpenny (2012) are questioning whether governments terminate, deregulate, or retrench policies, because those are different strategies for policy dismantling. The Brazilian case encompasses reforms, cutbacks, (de)regulation, and efforts to contain and reduce social expenditures, and when they are observed all together, there is no doubt we are dealing with welfare retrenchment and policy dismantling, as noted by Pierson (1994) and Bauer and Knill (2014).

To this end, there are analyses presented in ten different arenas. Some of them are not in the usual scope of social well-being analyses, as is the case for environmental policies or public safety policies. However, they will help build an argument regarding a broader process of dismantling. Looking at the whole system, we are not dealing with a simultaneous expansion and reduction policy. The findings show dismantling/retrenchment because we are demonstrating a set of arenas and the use of most of the strategies together. The book's proposal is to give the whole picture, or at least a broad set of social arenas and their "reforms," to allow us to deeply observe the extension of the changes implemented in Brazil, as a country case study. This does not mean a change in the focus, as pointed out by Green-Pedersen, by comparing different studies with different set of policies, but, on the contrary, it guarantees the affirmation that distinct strategies occurred and that we can sustain that in fact there was systemic retrenchment as well as programmatic retrenchment in the terms of Pierson (1994). Moreover, the ways of implementing such changes to policy are diverse, and take the form of reforms, regulations, de-regulation, termination, among others.

The need for a broader framework is present when we consider the distinction of the rules in the different policy sectors analyzed in this book, as well as that each of them has a different legacy. That is, their institutionality is distinct, and even within each arena there will be differences. For example, within the conditional cash transfers (assistance/non contributive), the Continuous Cash Benefit is a benefit that has a constitutional guarantee, while the Bolsa Família Program, not being constitutionalized, does not have the same guarantee and becomes more vulnerable to reforms (Chapter 10). In terms of different legacies: Social Security, a system that is 90 years old, should be more resistant than Social Assistance, a teenage policy. That is why this book proposes to analyze different policies and will work with different concepts of welfare state changes as well as distinct dismantling strategies. The work in its entirety will assess the *commitment to equality*, as the utlimate measure of social justice commitment sought by the welfare state, a conceptual concern brought by Green-Pedersen (2004), with which this book is aligned.

The entire work will allow us to use analytical categories developed by Bauer and Knill (2014) when they propose the dimensions of policy density and policy intensity in the conceptualization of policy dismantling. It will also be possible to observe the use of *retrenchment as cutbacks* which, according to Green-Pedersen, "is a question of cuts in people's welfare entitlements. (…) [and that] such changes are cuts in benefit levels, stricter eligibility criteria or shorter duration of benefits." (2004:7) as seen in the Social Security Reform of 2019 (Chapter 7). However, as noted by the author, the concept is too restricted to handle changes that go beyond budgeting. Thus, even though in times of fiscal austerity, budgeting is a central axis and mandatory in the analysis, there will also be areas in which the concept of *retrenchment as institutional changes* will be more appropriate, as it is understood as "qualitative changes, that is, a break with basic institutional principles" (2004:9). Yet, the author's own conclusion is that the cuts are actually a type of institutional change (Green-Pedersen, 2004).

In theoretical terms, each analytical category among all those can have different weights in the different worlds of welfare capitalism we are focusing on. This perspective is even more compelling given our concern with analyzing the commitment to equality and the fact that, according to Sátyro and Cunha (2018b), there are different regimes of well-being co-existing in the Brazilian territory, which is another way to demonstrate the institutionalized inequality that is characteristic of Brazil.

1.3   Under what conditions do politicians engage in policy dismantling?

A question the book tries to answer is: Are we facing a retrenchment or dismantling or just a moment of fiscal and economic crisis? Considering that, in fact, we are facing a case of dismantling, the unfolding questions are: Under what conditions do politicians engage in policy dismantling? Why do politicians dismantle?

First, it is necessary to understand the coalition presidentialism in Brazil and how the political arena is organized. Currently, Brazil has 31 political parties registered at the Superior Electoral Court and 23 with representatives at the House of Representatives, elected in 2022. In 2018, the House was formed with representatives from 30 different parties, but Bolsonaro ruled with about 15 effective parties at the Chamber, which means a very fragmented Legislature. And to govern in Brazil there is the need to dialogue with the Legislature, which means presidents need to build cross-party coalitions because their parties always control a minority of seats. Added to that is the fact that Dilma Rousseff's impeachment rearranged the playing board. Power and Rodrigues-Silveira (2019) showed at least three things: That the Legislature was always more to the right than the Executive, that there was an equilibrium between a left-wing Executive and a more right-wing Legislature throughout all of the PT administration, and that the impeachment did change the composition of the Chamber to an extremely conservative one, worse than the time before the PT administration. Adding two other facts to that, one cyclical, as with Bolsonaro's election, a more right-wing House composition in Brazilian history was also elected, and another structural, that the Federal Constitution of 1988 gave presidents strong proactive and reactive powers, meaning that they have sweeping constitutional powers. However, with a highly fragmented party system, it will always be necessary to build coalitions in order to form governments, even informal ones. Despite the executive presidential power, they need to be closely related with the Legislature (Mainwaring, 1997). According to Guimarães and Braga (2019), before Rousseff's impeachment, there was a deterioration of the way the coalition occurred within the "coalition presidentialism" which culminated with the removal of President Rousseff. Since then, more changes have been reported regarding the way decisions are made within the parliament, with a centralization of power, changes in the budgetary process, in the distribution of positions, and in the President's power to dictate the agenda, which changed the rules of the game.

Secondly, the ideology of governments is a central analytical factor explaining the phenomenon, what Bauer et al. (2012) call *political preferences*. After years of expansion of the welfare state, this was proven to be one of the main factors (Hibbs, 1977; Korpi, 1983; Schmidt, 1996), and time brought about the questioning of its strength; going through the conceptually and methodologically dense literature, it becomes clear that the loss of the ideological element could be an explanatory factor. The presence of institutional constraints, and more specifically the times of austerity induced both the right and the left to adjust to the center. This occurs even within a single country, as is the case with Brazil (Sátyro, 2013). It is possible to think that, to some extent, parties tend to the center when facing institutional constraints and austerity. However, this is all part of a dynamic debate. In a recent study on social policies in Latin America, Niedzwiecki and Pribble (2022) suggest that the right-wing parties are more engaged in retrenchment, and partisanship is an analytical factor that needs to be considered to explain variation, even though it is not a sufficient category in itself. That is, the debate goes on, and when it concerns far-right parties, Chueri affirms that "recent studies suggest that PRRPs' distributive preferences go beyond the clash between simply expanding or retrenching welfare" (2022:383).

There is no doubt that the analytical lens suggested by Kitschelt and McGann (1997) coming from the *winning formula* they attributed to right-wing populist parties, which is cultural authoritarianism along with an economic neoliberalism as the space for action and definition of preferences, is still in the agenda. This positioning of the PRRPs served to attract an electorate previously mobilized by the left in permanent austerity times. Since then, from Mudde (2007) to more recent authors, many assume that there is an ideological core of the PRRPs, which is constituted by the categories of nativism, authoritarianism, and populism, which guide their preferences and actions with respect to social and economic policies. Coming from these three analytical categories, Rathgeb (2020) developed his argument that they guide the PRRPs to choose which electorate/citizen groups are considered as "deserving or undeserving of welfare support" (2020:640). According to Rathgeb (2020), each of these three analytical categories brings a dimension to the analyses of deserving vs. undeserving groups. Thus, for him the "nativism leads PRRPs to exclude non-citizens from welfare support." The authoritarianism allows for the classification between the "hard-working" vs. the "lazy free-riders" in such a way that the informal and unemployed are associated with a lack of deservingness. And the populism is based on the rhetoric of the "corrupt elite" from whom we have to withdraw privileges (2020:640).

However, recent studies argue that the analytical categories in the *winning formula* became insufficient for understanding the strategies and preferences regarding the view of the PRRPs on the welfare state. The focus of the analysis should also be on what they classify as "descrving" and "undeserving" (Röth, Afonso and Spies, 2018; Lefkofridi and Michel, 2014; Rathgeb and Busemeyer, 2022; Abou-Chadi and Immergut, 2019; Enggist and Pinggera, 2022; Bergmann et al., 2021; Busemeyer et al., 2022; Chueri, 2022; Rathgeb, 2020). Rathgeb (2020) develops the "distributive deservingness" line brought by Hausermann and Kriese (2015:206) and the "deserving benefit recipients" that can be found in Busemeyer et al. (2022).

According to Chueri (2022), this refers to the promotion of a "dualistic" welfare state: On one side, protectionism for the "deserving" and, on the other side, a neoliberal focus for those classified as "undeserving." Chueri (2021; 2022), Ennser-Jedenastik (2020), Abts et al. (2021), Otjes et al. (2018), and Rathgeb (2020) suggest that the confluence between the narratives of nativism, authoritarianism, and populism are fertile soil to develop the rhetorical classification of the "groups deemed 'benefit deserving'." In fact, Chueri (2021; 2022), Enggist and Pinggera (2022), Otjes et al. (2018), and Rathgeb (2020) suggest a dual situation in which, on the one hand, there is a "selective universal" provision of benefits for the "deserving," and, on the other hand, a neoliberal welfare logic is applied to the "undeserving" groups. It is clear that this classification is subjective and, according to Otjes (2019), there is a feeling and a perception that these groups are untrustworthy and parasitic, and any support given to them has to be in very similar terms to those of the liberal/ residuals regimes, even if this is not a characteristic of the welfare regime of the country being analyzed (Otjes, 2019).[3]

In the same way, Enggist and Pinggera (2022) suggest that the PRRPs mobilize more socio-cultural agendas, to which we would add the adjective "moral," that are not related to class perspective or economic questions. The authors counterpoint the mainstream literature (which does not refer directly to the PRPPs), developing the point of view that says the imbroglio is not over the size of the welfare state and its objectives, principles, or what needs should be addressed (investment in human capital or basic protection, for example). According to the authors, the PRRPs have preferences and "priorities" that go beyond the debate between investment vs. consumption or recalibration, as far as they introduce as priority a moral agenda with cultural issues from a neoconservative perspective. For Enggist and Pinggera, the PRRPs differentiate themselves from the center and the left by making very clear what type of welfare regime they prefer for each populational group.

We must now add other dimensions to this discussion, such as the fact that different governments had different risks of being punished electorally, while we also assume that they want to remain in power. Right-wing administrations can benefit electorally from retrenchment of the welfare state (Persson and Svensson, 1989; Klitgaard et al., 2014; Bonoli, 2012; Giger and Nelson, 2011; Schumacher et al., 2013; Elmelund-Præstekær et al., 2015). This means that the idea of systemic and, mainly, programmatic retrenchment can be attractive to right-wing governments. In contrast, one would expect that left-wing governments would be punished for it (Giger and Nelson, 2011; Schumacher et al., 2013; Elmelund-Præstekær et al., 2015; Wenzelburger, 2014). Based on this, it is necessary to also think about strategies to implement distributive preferences and about who would be affected by the interventions; after all, regardless of the party, politicians want to preserve their chances of re-election, even when they want to implement policy-dismantling agendas. So there is a need to focus on which strategies are chosen by politicians and what segments of the population are chosen to lose something (Bauer and Knill, 2014:30–31). What strategies were used, who was affected by the reform, the extent "to which the costs and benefits of dismantling are distributed across the affected actors; and the extent to which these actors were able to organize and mobilize for or against it" (Bauer et al., 2012:41). Thus, it is key to answer the question of who will be affected. In this case, we consider Jordan et al. (2013), questioning "who gets less, when and how" (2013:4), paraphrasing Laswell (1936 – apud Jordan et al., 2013), revising his political concept of "who gets what, when and how" and suggesting a version for policy dismantling. This takes us directly to the rhetoric between deserving and undeserving groups. According to Otjes (2019), there is a skepticism regarding the so-called undeserving groups and a perception that they should not be treated equally. Moreover, the fact that the "undeserving" groups, in general, are groups of people who are less likely to have veto power, they are less politically organized, with less capacity to mobilize support in Parliament, such as immigrants, informal workers, and people who are poor or extremely poor (Bonolli, 2012:107; Palier, 2001:103). Therefore, it is easier to place the weight of retrenchment on them. This, in turn, goes with the strategy of the "path of least resistance" (Bonolli, 2012).

As for the strategies themselves, policy dismantling needs to be a combination of blame avoidance and politically feasible options (Wenzelburger 2014), even when the politician wants to credit claim. And, in times of fake news at systemic levels, this has become a strong strategy (Chapter 5). Especially because, for PRRP governments, the idea of systemic retrenchment is perfectly consistent with their general preference of less taxing and government spending. Therefore, even when they have the option to claim the credit, they will pursue strategies.

Over the last few decades, three analytic proposals stood out regarding the understanding of the strategies used by politicians interested in dismantling social policies. In a seminal study, Pierson (1994) shed light on this debate by emphasizing three strategies for dealing with retrenchment: obfuscation strategies, which consist on the conscious manipulation of information related to the retrenchment. In this case, politicians give less emphasis to the negative effects, be it because of the spreading of the consequences over time or because of their diffuse distribution, *decrementalism*. It is also possible to create difficulties for the average reader in being able to connect the negative effects to the policies or for them to even be capable of tracking the consequences of such changes. Another strategy would be the division of the benefit recipients, of the constituencies, which means implementing reforms and changes that are perceived differently by different communities, making it difficult to collectively act against such reforms. Lastly, the technique of offering compensation to the groups with more organizational capacities, leaving the greater costs to those who have less ability to organize and pressure.

This is rational action, we could say, abstract strategies, that can take place in different ways of instituting change. Mahoney and Thelen (2010) developed a typology for institutional change that helps put the Piersonean abstraction into more concrete terms. For them, there are basically four ways of instituting change: displacement, layering, drifting, and conversion. That is, a policy or program that is completely replaced by another in a radical change that presents in a moment of punctual balance, *displacement*; or there is a series of new layers instituted within a policy through new rules, amendments, additions, or subtractions done to a policy in such a way that it changes its initial characteristics to another proposal, *layering*; another possibility is when, coming from externalities and external shocks a given policy has its capacity altered, so even when its instruments remain the same it starts fulfilling other purpose, *drifting*; finally, the authors highlight that it is possible to change and not change at the same time. Through new formal interpretations, the instruments and procedures can remain unaltered, but the implementation starts happening in a different way, *conversion* (Mahoney and Thelen, 2010).

After that, Bauer and Knill (2014) proposed a new concept of dismantling based on the number of objectives and instruments in the policy, what they call density, as well as one based on the type, quality, and configuration of the instruments used, what they call intensity, as we have seen. They propose ideal types constructed based on two dimensions: if the decision to dismantle is a decision taken actively or by inaction, and if the politician intends to give visibility or to hide the negative consequences of the reforms undertaken. Based on these two dimensions they propose the following types: 1) *dismantling by default* when there is no active decision for dismantling (No Dismantling Decision) and when there is the intention to minimize the visibility of the effects (Low Visibility); 2) *dismantling by arena-shifting* when there is an active decision to dismantle (Active Dismantling Decision), but there is no intention to make neither its authorship nor its effects visible (Low Visibility); 3) *dismantling by symbolic action* for the cases in which there no concrete action for dismantling (No Dismantling Decision), while using the strategy of giving visibility to the intention even if it does not follow an action (High Visibility); and, lastly 4) the *active dismantling* type, in which there is the intention of and concrete actions for dismantling (Active Dismantling Decision) and they want credit for it, therefore openly sharing it (High Visibility) (Bauer et al, 2012; Bauer and Knill, 2014). That is, these authors somehow incorporated the concern brought by Pierson, which led to the debate on blame avoidance and credit claiming and to the development of obfuscation, division, and compensation strategies. However, the concern with commitment to equality, brought by Green-Pedersen, which for us is central to the debate, was still secondary.

On March 17, 2019, in a meeting with eight businesspeople from the United States, Bolsonaro made the following statement: "Brazil is not an open terrain where we intend to build things for our people. We actually have much to unbuild, much to undo. So that we can then do things. If I serve at least as an inflection point, I'll be happy."[4] This statement holds symbolic content that brings us back to the concepts and strategies of symbolic dismantling from Bauer and Knill (2014), but mostly a discursive construction typical of what Lynch and Cassimiro (2022) call reactionary populism, with a messianic tone of salvation that appears in many of his statements. Also, it shows more than the credit claiming strategy, in a clear intention of being "the" great leader in this endeavor.

1.4   Structure and contents of book

The book is divided into two parts. In the first, the objective is to offer the reader information that contextualizes and helps us find part of the explanatory factors for the phenomenon analyzed, that is, the changes that were imposed on the Brazilian social protection system between 2015 and 2022. In Chapter 2, "Social policies in Brazil: an introduction," Natália Sátyro shows the basis of social protection in Brazil ever since the Federal Constitution of 1988 (CF88), which enshrines the return of democracy in 1985. The author brings forth the constitutional principles that enable the understanding of the paradigmatic change that the Letter meant, and added to this there are notions of how intergovernmental relations are articulated in the Brazilian Federation. Next, the author presents the main change undertaken by Temer's administration and analyzes Bolsonaro's Government Plan, presented for the 2018 elections. In Chapter 3, "Political Parties, Ideological Preferences and Social Policy: Accounting for right-wing strategies in Brazil after the left turn," André Borges carries out an analytical mapping of the political scenario, including relations between the Executive and the Legislative in recent years, with a focus on the advance of the right. Following that, in Chapter 4, "The political economy of the Brazilian economic crisis (2014–2022) – economic policy, ideas and the limits of neoliberal austerity measures," Alexandre Q. Guimarães and Marco Flávio da C. Resende offer a longitudinal analysis of the economic and fiscal choices from Rousseff's administration to Bolsonaro's, showing the immediate consequences of the policies undertaken. In a scenario where fake news became a (mis)governance strategy, this subject is mandatory. Eliara Santana and Isabele B. Mitozo, in Chapter 5, "Disinformation and democracy," discuss the use of disinformation as a political strategy of obfuscation and how much of a threat this is to democracy and, more specifically, to social policies. Currently, in PRRP analysis, no assessment can do without understanding fake news as intentional actions, with means to ends. Finally, in Chapter 6, "Poverty and inequality over the last 30 years," Pedro H. F. Souza presents a longitudinal analysis of poverty and income inequality rates, focusing on how the reversal of the trajectory that prevailed until the mid-2010s had negative consequences for the population.

This informs the reader in advance of what is to come and enables the authors of the second part to focus on the analyses of social policies without having to explain the political and economic processes that influenced each of them in every chapter. Given the complexity of such phenomena, there was a need for further investigation. In other words, it is from this panorama that the reader reaches the second part of the book, prepared to better understand what happened between 2015 and 2022. And, as stated throughout this introduction, the authors were urged to consider four events in their analysis: the economic crisis (2014–2015), the entry of Temer and the New Fiscal Regime approved, the arrival of Bolsonaro, and then, the covid-19 pandemic.

In the second part, this book presents a set of nine policy analyses of different natures. Initially, the reader will find four chapters that analyze compensatory policies, called Social Welfare (*Seguridade Social*) in the CF88. In Chapter 7, "Authoritarian populism and fiscal austerity: the dismantling of social security in Bolsonaro's government," Arnaldo P. Lanzara and Fernanda Pernasetti analyze the pension reform debated during Temer's administration and approved in November of 2019, the first year of Bolsonaro's government. The authors show that despite having failed to capitalize on the system, the new regulation induced a migration to the private sector. In Chapter 8, "The Unified Health System in danger and the sequelae of the Bolsonaro era," Jose Angelo Machado and Mauro Lúcio Jerônymo analyze the Unified Health System. In this chapter we also recognize health policies as the great locus for science denialism. Finally, social assistance policies are divided into two chapters. In Chapter 9, called "Socio-assistance services: One dies of starvation and no one sees," Natália Sátyro, Eleonora S. M. Cunha, Bruno R. Pinheiro, and Fernanda C. da Silva specifically analyze the provision of social assistance services, demonstrating that there was an inflection that began in 2015, for budgetary reasons, but which was later reinforced through regulation, resulting in a reduction in the provision of basic services. The Bolsa Família Program and the Continuous Cash Benefits are analyzed by Joana Mostafa in Chapter 10, "Non-contributive cash transfers: borderline social protection," which shows the different patterns of dismantling of the two main programs, but the greater fragility of the PBF and its massive instability during this period.

Moving on, the reader will find an analysis of three policy sectors that are considered classics for social investment: education, family policies, and the labor market. In Chapter 11, "Credit-claiming and nondecision-making as an ideological agenda: did Bolsonaro succeed in changing education policies in Brazil?," Sandra Gomes and Catarina Segatto show the strength of the symbolic strategy. Then, in "Brazilian family policies under the neo-conservatism rhetoric of Bolsonaro," Gabriel P. P. Andrade and Natália Sátyro demonstrate how family policies constituted a symbolic locus for Bolsonaro, becoming one of the major pieces of evidence of the former president's conservative bias. In Chapter 13, "Labor market from 2015 to 2022: heightened risks and dismantling policies,"

Regina C. Camargo and Pedro R. M. Barbosa, regarding labor market policies, demonstrate the neoliberal tone of the reforms undertaken.

Finally, in a last moment, two policies outside the traditional scope of welfare regimes are brought to the reader. In Chapter 14, "Opportunities and strategies of the process of dismantling of Brazilian environmental policy," Maria Dolores Silva and Ana Luiza M. de Medeiros analyze environmental policies, showing the liberal desire through deregulation, but not only. The chapter written by Ludmila Ribeiro, Valéria C. Oliveira, and Alexandre M. A. Diniz, "Police violence in Brazil: how was Bolsonaro's government involved?," bring forth a debate that is one of Bolsonaro's central interests: public security, specifically gun control.

Finally, in the "Conclusion: policy dismantling and system retrenchment," I take stock of what was developed in the book in a comparative analysis, showing the social policy-dismantling processes and the similarities between the mainstream right and a PRRP.

Notes

1 Although I am responsible for all content, I want to thank Eleonora Schettini Martins Cunha, Joana Mostafa e José Angelo Machado who provided me with encouragement, and useful criticisms that improved the text a lot. I also need to thank the Conselho Nacional de Desenvolvimento Científico e Tecnológico (CNPq) funding via the Productive Researcher Grant.
2 In 2017 PMDB changed its name and is now simply Brazilian Democratic Movement (MDB).
3 In many moments in Bolsonaro's speeches such construction becomes clear, to the point of dehumanizing certain groups. In one of his weekly live streams in April, 2020, the president spoke of indigenous populations in a tone that may have been complimentary: "The Indigenous have changed, they are evolving... Ever more so each day, the Indigenous is a human being like us." www.youtube.com/watch?v= WX7Xrs2Y3QY
4 See on Twitter the video of Jair Bolsonaro's son, Eduardo Bolsonaro: https://twitter. com/BolsonaroSP/status/1107596301133406209
    Or in the news article: https://veja.abril.com.br/politica/temos-de-desconstruir-muita-coisa-diz-bolsonaro-a-americanos-de-direita

References

Abou-Chadi, T., & Immergut, E. M. (2019). Recalibrating social protection: Electoral competition and the new partisan politics of the welfare state. *European Journal of Political Research, 58*(2), 697–719.

Abts, K., Dalle Mulle, E., Van Kessel, S., & Michel, E. (2021). The welfare agenda of the populist radical right in Western Europe: Combining welfare chauvinism, producerism and populism. *Swiss Political Science Review, 27*(1), 21–40.

Bauer, M. W., & Knill, C. (2014). A conceptual framework for the comparative analysis of policy change: Measurement, explanation and strategies of policy dismantling. *Journal of Comparative Policy Analysis: Research and Practice, 16*(1), 28–44.

Bauer, M. W., Green-Pedersen, C., Héritier, A., & Jordan, A. (Eds.). (2012). *Dismantling public policy: Preferences, strategies, and effects*. OUP Oxford.

Bergmann, J., Hackenesch, C., & Stockemer, D. (2021). Populist radical right parties in Europe: What impact do they have on development policy? *JCMS: Journal of Common Market Studies*, *59*(1), 37–52.

Bonoli, G. (2012). Credit claiming and blame avoidance revisited. In: David Natali and Giuliano Bonoli (Eds.), *The politics of the new welfare state*. pp. 93–110. Oxford University Press.

Brown, W. (2006). American nightmare: Neoliberalism, neoconservatism, and de-democratization. *Political Theory*, *34*(6), 690–714.

Brown, W. (2015). *Undoing the demos: Neoliberalism's stealth revolution*. MIT Press.

Busemeyer, M. R., Rathgeb, P., & Sahm, A. H. (2022). Authoritarian values and the welfare state: the social policy preferences of radical right voters. *West European Politics*, *45*(1), 77–101.

Chueri, J. (2021). Social policy outcomes of government participation by radical right parties. *Party Politics*, *27*(6), 1092–1104.

Chueri, J. (2022). An emerging populist welfare paradigm? How populist radical right-wing parties are reshaping the welfare state. *Scandinavian Political Studies*, *45*(4), 383–409.

Cooper, M. (2017). *Family values: Between neoliberalism and the new social conservatism*. MIT Press.

Elmelund-Præstekær, C., Klitgaard, M. B., & Schumacher, G. (2015). What wins public support? Communicating or obfuscating welfare state retrenchment. *European Political Science Review*, *7*(3), 427–450.

Enggist, M., & Pinggera, M. (2022). Radical right parties and their welfare state stances–not so blurry after all? *West European Politics*, *45*(1), 102–128.

Ennser-Jedenastik, L. (2021). What drives partisan conflict and consensus on welfare state issues? *Journal of Public Policy*, *41*(4), 731–751.

Ferragina, E. (2022). Welfare state change as a double movement: Four decades of retrenchment and expansion in compensatory and employment-oriented policies across 21 high-income countries. *Social Policy & Administration*, *56*(5), 705–725.

Giger, N., & Nelson, M. (2011). The electoral consequences of welfare state retrenchment: Blame avoidance or credit claiming in the era of permanent austerity? *European Journal of Political Research*, *50*(1), 1–23.

Green-Pedersen, C. (2004). The dependent variable problem within the study of welfare state retrenchment: Defining the problem and looking for solutions. *Journal of Comparative Policy Analysis: Research and Practice*, *6*(1), 3–14.

Guimarães, A., & Braga, R. J. (2019). Prefácio. In: Giovanna Perlin and Manoel Santos (Eds.), *Presidencialismo de coalizão em movimento*. Edições Câmara, pp. 25–59.

Hibbs, D. A. (1977). Political parties and macroeconomic policy. *American Political Science Review*, *71*(4), 1467–1487.

Januzzi, P. M., & Sátyro, N. (2023). Social policies, poverty, and hunger in Brazil: The social and institutional legacy of the Lula/Dilma governments. In: Richard Bourne (Org.), *Brazil After Bolsonaro: the comeback of the Lula da Silva*. 1ed. Routledge, v. 1, pp. 67–79.

Jordan, A., Green-Pedersen, C., & Turnpenny, J. (2012). Policy dismantling: An introduction. In: *Dismantling public policy: preferences, strategies, and effects*. Oxford University Press, pp. 3–29. Oxford University Press.

Jordan, A., Bauer, M. W., & Green-Pedersen, C. (2013). Policy dismantling. *Journal of European Public Policy*, *20*(5), 795–805.

Kerche, F., & Marona, M. (2022). *A política no banco dos réus: a Operação Lava Jato e a erosão da democracia no Brasil*. Autêntica Editora.

Kitschelt, H., & McGann, A. J. (1997). *The radical right in Western Europe: A comparative analysis*. University of Michigan Press.

Klitgaard, M. B., & Elmelund-Præstekær, C. (2014). The partisanship of systemic retrenchment: Tax policy and welfare reform in Denmark 1975–2008. *European Political Science Review*, *6*(1), 1–19.

Korpi, W. (1983). *The Democratic Class Struggle*. Routledge and Kegan Paul.

Lefkofridi, Z., & Michel, E. (2014). Exclusive solidarity? Radical right parties and the welfare state. *Radical Right Parties and the Welfare State (December 2014). Robert Schuman Centre for Advanced Studies Research Paper* (2014/120).

Lynch, C., & Cassimiro, P. H. (2022). *O populismo reacionário: ascensão e legado do bolsonarismo*. Contracorrente.

Mahoney, J., & Thelen, K. (2010). *Explaining institutional change: ambiguity, agency, and power*. Cambridge University Press.

Mainwaring, S. (1997). Multipartidarism, robust federalism and presidentialism in Brazil. In: Scott Mainwaring and Matthew Soberg Shugart (Eds.), *Presidentialism and Democracy in Latin America*. Cambridge University Press, pp. 55–109.

Mudde, C. (2007). *Populist radical right parties in Europe*. Cambridge University Press.

Niedzwiecki, S., & Pribble, J. E. (2022). *Social policy expansion and retrenchment after Latin America's commodity boom*. Helen Kellogg Institute for International Studies.

North, D. C. (1993). Institutions and credible commitment. *Journal of Institutional and Theoretical Economics (JITE)/Zeitschrift für die gesamte Staatswissenschaft*, *149*(1), The New Institutional Economics Recent Progress; Expanding Frontiers (Mar. 1993), 11–23.

Nunes, F. & Traumann, T. (2023). *Biografia do abismo como a polarização divide famílias, desafia empresas e compromete o future do Brasil*. Rio de Janeiro HarperCollins Brasil.

Otjes, S. (2019). What is left of the radical right. *Politics Low Countries*, *1*, 81.

Otjes, S., Ivaldi, G., Jupskås, A. R., & Mazzoleni, O. (2018). It's not economic interventionism, stupid! reassessing the political economy of radical right-wing populist parties. *Swiss Political Science Review*, *24*(3), 270–290.

Palier, B. (2001). Beyond retrenchment. CES Working Paper no. 77, 2001.

Pérez-Liñán, A. (2007). *Presidential impeachment and the new political instability in Latin America*. Cambridge University Press.

Persson, T., & Svensson, L. E. (1989). Why a stubborn conservative would run a deficit: Policy with time-inconsistent preferences. *Quarterly Journal of Economics*, *104*(2), 325–345.

Pierson, P. (1994). *Dismantling the welfare state? Reagan, Thatcher, and the politics of retrenchment*. Cambridge University.

Power, T. J., & Rodrigues-Silveira, R. (2019). Mapping ideological preferences in Brazilian elections, 1994–2018: A municipal-level study. *Brazilian Political Science Review*, 13(1), e0001. Epub February 7, 2019. https://doi.org/10.1590/1981-38212 01900010001

Przeworski, A. (2020). *As crises da Democracia*. Editora Zahar.

Rathgeb, P. (2020). Makers against takers: the socio-economic ideology and policy of the Austrian Freedom Party. *West European Politics*, *44*(3), 635–660.

Rathgeb, P., & Busemeyer, M. R. (2022). How to study the populist radical right and the welfare state? *West European Politics*, *45*(1), 1–23.

Röth, L., Afonso, A., & Spies, D. C. (2018). The impact of populist radical right parties on socio-economic policies. *European Political Science Review*, *10*(3), 325–350.

Rovny, J. (2013). Where do radical right parties stand? Position blurring in multidimensional competition. *European Political Science Review*, *5*(1), 1–26.

Rovny, J., & Polk, J. (2020). Still blurry? Economic salience, position and voting for radical right parties in Western Europe. *European Journal of Political Research*, 59(2), 248–268.

Sátyro, N. (2013). Institutional constraints, parties and political competition in Brazilian States, 1987–2006. *Revista de Ciencia Política*, *33*(3), 583–605.

Sátyro, N. (2021). The paradigmatic radical reform in Brazil's social policies: The impact of the Temer administration. In: Natália Sátyro, Eloisa Del Pino, and Carmen Midaglia (Eds.), *Latin American Social Policy Developments in the Twenty-First Century*. Palgrave Macmillan, pp. 317–340.

Sátyro, N. G. D., & Cunha, E. S. M. (2018a). The transformative capacity of the Brazilian federal government in building a social welfare bureaucracy in the municipalities. *Revista de Administração Pública*, *52*, 363–385.

Satyro, N. G. D., & Cunha, P. S. (2018b). The coexistence of different welfare regimes in the same country: a comparative analysis of the Brazilian municipalities heterogeneity. *Journal of Comparative Policy Analysis: Research and Practice*, *21*(1), 65–89.

Schmidt, M. G. (1996). When parties matter: A review of the possibilities and limits of partisan influence on public policy. *European Journal of Political Research*, *30*(2), 155–183.

Schumacher, G., Vis, B., & Van Kersbergen, K. (2013). Political parties' welfare image, electoral punishment and welfare state retrenchment. *Comparative European Politics*, *11*, 1–21.

Tang, S. (2017). *A general theory of institutional change*. Routledge.

Vinhais, F., Dick, P., & Jannuzzi, P. (2022). Desigualdade, Pobreza e os efeitos do mercado de trabalho e das políticas de transferência e garantia de renda no Brasil: evidências da década de 2010. In: Fernando Augusto Mansor de Mattos (Eds.), *Desigualdade no Brasil*. Hucitec, pp. 126–139.

Wenzelburger, G. (2014). Blame avoidance, electoral punishment and the perceptions of risk. *Journal of European Social Policy*, *24*(1), 80–91.

PART I
Contextualization

2

SOCIAL POLICIES IN BRAZIL

An introduction[1]

Natália Sátyro

2.1 Introduction

This chapter has the objective of presenting the reader with introductory notes on the trajectory of social protection in Brazil. The intent is to provide basic notions on two moments. First, starting at the Federal Constitution of 1988 until the end of PT's administration (PT, per its Portuguese name, Worker's Party). Here we will address the paradigmatic changes made as of the 1988 Federal Constitution and emphasize the complexity of a federative arrangement with that many veto points. Consequently, we will demonstrate the centrality of the coordinating role of the federal government with regards to reaching national goals, as well as the participation of the three federate bodies in social spending. In this way, the reader can understand the importance of the state capacity of the federal government in relation to the subnational bodies, especially regarding the capacity for financing social policies. Second, when right-wing parties took on the National Executive Power. The goal is to draft what it meant to remove an elected president, and the fact that her vice-president implemented a political project very different from the one approved by vote in the ballot boxes. Next, the proposal for a social arena mentioned in the government program of the Bolsonaro administration. It is possible to affirm that there was a breakage of the former trajectory with Temer's entrance, who in six months managed to impose a heavy fiscal austerity measure on federal administrations, valid for 20 years (2017–2037). Bolsonaro's entrance, after that, reinforced his neoliberal agenda for the economic arena and, therefore, for social policies.

DOI: 10.4324/9781003487777-3

2.2 Return to democracy: The 1988 Federal Constitution brought back the right to vote and social protection for all

The end of 21 years of military dictatorship in Brazil, with the indirect election of a civilian in 1985, was anchored three years later, in 1988, with the enactment of the Federal Constitution of 1988, following two years of National Constituent Assembly carried out with intense participation of the civil society (1986–1987). In 1989, the first presidential election by direct, secret, and universal voting took place, the first moment of political participation of every man and woman over 18 years of age, including illiterate persons, in the history of Brazil. This means Brazil's democracy is quite recent if we think, in Robert Dahl's terms, of the incorporation of all adults in the political community.

2.2.1 The professed protection system

In Brazil, the first state intervention toward any social protection occurred in 1919, with a bill on labor safety, which in the end was not implemented. The second, the Eloy Chaves Bill, from 1923, obliged companies to create Pension and Retirement Funds (CAPs, *Caixas de Aposentadorias e Pensões*). This bill made history as the first state intervention of such kind, even if it the payments were not provided by the State. It was in the 1930s, under Getúlio Vargas' government, which started with a coup, that the Institutes for Retirement and Pensions (IAPs, *Institutos de Aposentadorias e Pensões*) were founded, public and organized by professional categories, agglutinating workers employed by various companies, unlike the CAPs, which were private, restricted to, and organized by companies. According to Oliveira and Teixeira (1986), in 1939 there were 98 CAPs and 5 IAPs: the Maritimes' (1933), the Traders' (1943), the Banking Clerks' (1934) (the most generous one), the Industrials' (1936) (the largest one in number of beneficiaries), and the Transportation and Cargo Workers' (1938). The IAPs were under the Ministry of Labor, Industry, and Trade, and were only allowed formally recognized professional categories. It was the government, on its turn, who made the categorization and acknowledgement of such professions (Oliveira and Teixeira, 1986). Therefore, it was up to the Ministry to determine which categories of workers would receive social protection. Plus, the whole system was developed with formal workers in mind (Oliveira and Teixeira, 1986). It is important to mention that each IAP had its own path for the negotiation of benefits with the government, which led to an extremely stratified system, Bismarckian in nature.

Therefore, a kind of "regulated citizenship" arose from "a system of occupational stratification in which, furthermore, the stratification system is defined by the legal norm" (Santos, 1979). For Santos, the people considered citizens, that is, those who had access to rights and social protection, were only those who had occupations that were recognized and defined by law. According to Santos (1979), "the extension of citizenship is thus done through the regulation of new professions and/or occupations, firstly, and through the expansion of the scope of the rights associated to these professions, first by expanding the inherent values for the concept of a member of the community" (Santos, 1979, p.75). Therefore, first, for the case of Brazil we need to invert Marshall's sequence of rights, for we see the birth of social rights without the previous outreach of political rights, as was the case in England. One possible reading suggests that the benefits were used to demobilize and stratify the working class (Malloy, 1979). Second, since there never was anything remotely close to full employment in Brazil and since informality rates have been historically high, for decades only part of the population had access to social rights. Informal workers were destined to non-citizenship, to the absence of social and political rights. This has its historical roots in the way slavery was abolished, where most black and mixed-race people were never properly absorbed by the liberal/bourgeois/democratic economy or society. Brazil was the country that received the largest number of enslaved Africans during colonial rule in the American continent, double that of the USA, and it was one of the last countries in the world to end slavery. Until the 2000s, the Brazilian government had not yet deployed any policies for reparation, compensation, or affirmative action in favour of black and mixed-race people, which comprise 54% of the population today. Furthermore, also hereditary to Portuguese colonial rule, the Brazilian society is extremely conservative regarding gender and family relations, imposing most of the care work onto the household, for example, to unpaid women. Reconciling unpaid care work with the labour market requires informal arrangements. Thus, most of the informal labour market is comprised of black and mixed-race women in Brazil.

This did not change in the democratic period (1945–1964) during which voting was considered "universal" but excluded illiterate people and soldiers. Added to that is the fact that during the military dictatorship (1964–1985) there was a second moment of coverage expansion, incorporating into the pension system workers such as housekeepers (1972), soccer players (1973), and mine workers (1974), and establishing maternity leave (1974), to name a few, while still leaving out informal workers, which constituted most of the population (Oliveira and Teixeira, 1986). It is also important to emphasize that it was in 1966 that the CAPs and the IAPs were brought together to form the National Institute for Social Security, unified into a single system. This led to a system that could be understood as a residual/liberal regime, for it promoted a dualization of the population between those who received social protection and those who did not, or a corporative regime insofar as the part that accessed the protection were stratified in the terms of Esping-Andersen (Santos, 1979).

As already mentioned, in 1985 the first civilian president, elected by indirect vote (José Sarney, 1985–1990[2]), took office and summoned elections for the National Constituent Assembly, thus consecrating the resuming of democracy with the FC88, which changed the paradigm for social protection in Brazil. The FC88 established a set of public policies with universal voting, imputing solidarity into the system, as well as a sense of social justice that was previously absent.

As far as the social security system (this term should be understood as retirements and pensions) went – which was well matured by then – rural workers, for the first time, received the same rights as urban workers, regardless of their contributive capacity, placed under family agriculture activities. To get a sense of the importance of this change, currently, 70% of the food consumed by Brazilian families comes from small farmers. Up to that point, rural workers had less benefits, worth smaller amounts than urban workers (Oliveira and Teixeira, 1986). The unemployment insurance, created in 1986, became a right for formal workers. Adding to that, the FC88 bound the amounts paid for all basic social security benefit to the minimum wage, which equalized urban and rural workers. With this binding of basic social security benefit amounts to the minimum wage, a consistent step was taken to ensure protection, since inflation rapidly undermined the protective capacity of the benefits.

Healthcare became a universal right, and therefore non-contributive. It is important to note that the Healthcare Department was created alongside the Social Security System, which means it had been contributive up to that point. It was the FC88 that determined the creation of Brazil's Unified Public Health System (SUS, *Sistema Único de Saúde*), which currently assists virtually the whole of the Brazilian population – the same constitution allowed for the parallel supplementary private practice of medicine, which now covers around 30% of the Brazilian population. However, any person who goes to a hospital, Brazilian or not, with or without income, will receive care. For instance, even though the middle-class and the rich in Brazil use private health services, the entire population is vaccinated through SUS, and, to mention higher complexity, organ transplants in the country are only made via SUS. All free of charge.

Solidarity was imputed into the social security system, and healthcare was ensured for all, regardless of contributive capacity; and another highlight is the acknowledgement of social assistance as a public policy. The FC88 determined that all citizens including the poor and extremely poor (positively discriminated) should receive protection regardless of contributive capacity, both as benefits and as services. It further determined that elderly persons and people with disabilities living under extreme poverty, incapacitated for independent life and for work (defined in subsequent legislation), should receive a minimum wage as social benefit. This was not to be considered a retirement pension, but a welfare benefit, non-contributive, regarded as a constitutional right. This was only regulated in 1996, under Fernando Henrique Cardoso's[3] administration (1995–2002), when it was called the Continuous Cash Benefit (BPC, *Benefício de Prestação Continuada*) (see chapter 10). The recommendation for the primacy of state responsibility in protecting the needy and the acknowledgement of such protection as a right was a substantial change. Up until that moment, only charity and philanthropy shaped the social actions aimed at the well-being of the general population, the state bearing no social responsibility.

Social Security, Healthcare, and Social Assistance became the tripod for the Brazilian Welfare System (*Seguridade Social*), that is, a set of protective measures that the international literature calls compensatory. These policies function as immediate protection against social risks, be it lack of employment, illnesses, or bearing the need for services or social benefits to fight social vulnerability and poverty (Morel and Palier, 2011, p. 92).

However, the FC88 also prescribed the development of policies for social investment, those that ensure the qualification of the human capital over time, that is, in the future. In that matter, the great highlight was that education became mandatory for children from 7 to 14 years of age. Under Cardoso's administration, the admission of children and teenagers in elementary school became mandatory. Results were so positive that Lula, in 2006, extended the requirement to reach children from 6 to 14 years of age and, three years later, from 4 to 17, securing a complete Basic Education, with consistent effects (Chapter 13).

But the set of policies recognized as social rights in the FC88 is much larger, encompassing public security and labor, further incorporating other areas, formally acknowledging them as social rights, such as habitation, recognized as a social right as of Constitutional Amendment 26/2000, transportation, recognized as a social right as of Constitutional Amendment 90/2015, and food safety, recognized as a social right as of Constitutional Amendment 64/2010.

This construction led to a system of policies meant to be universal, but that deliver different patterns of well-being depending on territory and populational subgroups. Despite the advances registered until 2014, seen in Chapter 6 of this book, Sátyro and Cunha (2018b) argue that there are six regimes for social well-being existing concomitantly in the Brazilian territory. The authors analyze private and public data regarding social security, education, healthcare, and social assistance in 5,565 Brazilian municipalities along five dimensions: expenditure, coverage, share of private spending, family structure, and poverty. According to them, the findings show highly heterogeneous institutional forms of social protection across municipalities, which are classified as social assistance, quasi-social assistance, corporative, quasi-corporative, family insurance, and intermediary welfare regimes.

2.2.2 The federative organization and its consequences for social policies

To fully grasp Brazilian social policies, it is necessary to understand the institutional basis that supports their functioning. First, the FC88 structured a federation with many veto points, giving political autonomy to all federative bodies, not only the central body but also subnational ones, which currently includes 5,570 municipalities, 26 states and the Federal District, as well as the Federal Executive Branch (the Union). Political autonomy means, by principle, that no elected ruler can be deposed by another, and that they all have the liberty to make choices regarding which public policies to implement, considering the responsibilities distributed among the different government levels as of the FC88. Added to that, on the one hand is the veto power of smaller states that are over-represented in a second legislative house, with legislative powers considered excessive, even if necessary to the federative balance. On the other hand, the need for super-majorities for constitutional amendments would mean, in practice, veto power for the minorities. This, as a compound, made Brazil an extreme case in the demos-constraining scale, with a kind of federalism in which the political institutions conform decisive processes that are strongly restrictive to the president's actions, which for the author is the manifestation of the will of the majority (Stepan, 1999). This set of characteristics had the literature of the 1990s expecting some sort of decisional paralysis, as it was assumed there would be subordination of the preferences of the federal government to those of subnational governments.

Years went by, policies were implemented, and the decisional paralysis arising from the excess of veto power and excessive fragmentation of power among federative bodies did not happen. The political regime (that is, the fact that a country is unitary or a federation) has proven to be an insufficient analytic category to explain the variation and implementation of the social policies. Therefore, Federalism itself is an insufficient explanatory factor (Arretche, 2012; Sellers and Lidström, 2007; Machado, 2023). According to Arretche (2012), what matters is how the intergovernmental relations take place and what coordination mechanisms does the central government of a country have to shape such relations (Arretche, 2012). Therefore, what many authors sustain is that the coordination capacity of the Federal/Central Executive Branch, usually measured by its normative and financial capacities, determines the way in which intergovernmental relations take place, as well as the outcomes of social policies (Arretche, 2012; Machado, 2018; Sátyro and Cunha, 2018a). The fact is that the Federal Government, using institutional mechanisms of coordination of the relations between federative bodies, showed an ability to induce that was not expected by the literature of the 1990s (Machado, 2018). The latter focused more on rival capacities and the absence of clear attributions (who oversees what in terms of implementation) regarding the social policies left by the FC88, as well as on the veto points, and less on the instruments that provided the capacity for the coordination of intergovernmental relations by the Federal Executive Branch (Arretche, 2012; Machado, 2018; Sátyro and Cunha, 2018a).

Within this new institutional framework, the decentralization of social policies was one of the main guidelines for the implementation of the new system of social protection, and it surely constitutes a very important second aspect. The FC88 determined that social policies would now be implemented and executed at the local level, to different degrees depending on the policy. This led to the launching of operational structures with incentives for the execution of services by the municipalities. Within that, there was the fear that political deliberations would be done based on a lowest common denominator due to the dispersion of authority, which would in turn affect the content of the decisions made (Pierson and Leibfried, 1995). This fear has been replaced, in recent debates, by the clarity that there is a difference between policy-making and policy-decision-making, and this is crucial when there are so many subnational bodies that are politically autonomous, that is, which are non-hierarchical. Even guaranteeing fiscal decentralization, the decision-making capacity of municipal administrators is still quite distinct, and what has been seen is that the policy-decision-making of subnational bodies can be affected by the central government's actions (Arretche, 2012). And, in Brazil, this is done systematically with the creation of incentives for the agreement and adherence of subnational governments.

Some authors (Sátyro and Cunha, 2018a; Arretche, 2012) demonstrate how the federal government, using its normative and financial capacities, showed a coordination capacity that secured results, meaning the reaching of national goals. Sátyro and Cunha (2018a) demonstrate the transformative capacity of the Federal Executive Branch in constructing municipal bureaucracy for social assistance, that is, a kind of behavior induction capacity for other federative bodies, modifying the status quo and the sheer capacity of such federative bodies to offer policies and services. However, they emphasize that this process was also based on organizational and institutional learning, regarded as incremental processes within the ministries and coming from the internal bureaucracy within other bodies and entities, such as management counsels and committees (Sátyro and Cunha, 2018a).

Third, to understand social policies in Brazil it is also important to know the rules of the game for each social policy sector, given that the roles of the federal government, municipalities, and states are different for each sector, and thus form different political arenas. That is because the instruments used as institutional mechanisms for induction and coordination will depend on the attributions of each federative body regarding each policy. In Brazil, each policy sector has spaces where the Union, the states, and the municipalities inter-relate in different scales and rules that determine their behavior beyond their attributions. These spaces determine their behavior, despite their formal attributions. For instance, in the area of Healthcare and Social Assistance, the Federal Executive Branch has greater financing capacity than the subnational entities.[4] In these two policy sectors, first, the Union is the main funder, and second, spaces have been created for participation with deliberative and monitoring characteristics in the three levels of the government; thus, there are municipal, state, and national counsels in all spheres of the federation (Arretche, 2012).[5] This means we are talking about institutional spaces for social participation that are provided by the law, with deliberative capacity to define the principles, guidelines, and priorities of the policies.

Added to that is the creation of spaces for agreement, where the guidelines defined in conferences and counsels are agreed upon by the federative bodies. At the national level there is the Tripartite Interagency Commission (CIT, *Comissão Intergestores Tripartite*), which came to be at a space for agreements within the Union, states, and municipalities, and at the states are the Bipartite Interagency Commissions (CIB, *Comissões Intergestores Bipartite*), which are spaces for agreement between the states and their municipalities. In the use of its normative attributions and financing capacities, the Federal Executive Branch managed to shape behaviors in the municipalities' sphere and ensure universality, integrity, and standardization of health assistance and social assistance services, reaching virtually all municipalities. For every policy, transfers are conditioned to previously agreed upon standardized actions. According to Machado (2018), the federal programs within every policy sector, including education, reduce agency costs by standardizing and specifying the actions taken by subnational governments. The programs condition the transfers to the subnational governments' adhesion to such standards, while revealing a structure where there are multiple "controllers" in different stages, including those of a societal nature (Machado, 2018). To look at the implementation and qualification capacity of the municipalities' own implementing bureaucracies, Sátyro and Cunha (2018a) reveal the functioning of these mechanisms regarding their incremental aspect in time. This was only possible because in both cases there was the creation of national systems: The Unified Public Health System (1990) and, later, the Unified Public Social Assistance System (SUAS, *Sistema Único de Saúde*) (2005).

Unlike with Healthcare and Social Assistance, for Education there is no unified system with centralized management, just as there are no spaces for agreement (CITs and CIBs), only deliberative spaces for social participation, while most of the financing still comes from the municipalities. This means that there are 26 state administrative networks and all of the municipal ones, independent from one another, which generates an enormous struggle for coordination. In this context, unlike with previous policy sectors, most resources come from the subnational bodies. That is the reason the Federal Executive Branch used its normative capacity and through a Constitutional Amendment in 1996 – Cardoso's administration – created the Fund for the Development and Maintenance of Elementary Education and Appreciation of Elementary Teaching Professionals (FUNDEF, *Fundo de Manutenção e Desenvolvimento do Ensino Fundamental e de Valorização do Magistério*). According to Peres et al. (2015), this was a fund of accounting nature, at the state level, constituted of various taxes and transfers bound to the education in states, municipalities, and the Federal District. Resources from all bodies were gathered in one fund and redistributed according to the number of students enrolled in each Elementary School network. Also, 60% of the amounts in the fund were to be invested in teachers, be it their qualification or their salaries. Thus, a basic inequality was topped, that is, regarding the financing capacity of federative bodies, especially municipalities. The fund established a minimum amount per student and had an interstate redistributive effect, given that it was the Union's role to pay for the difference if the base amount was not reached for all municipalities after the allocation. That way, from a scenario with rich municipalities with few children and poor municipalities with many children, equality was promoted and a minimum standard for investments was ensured for all teaching networks regardless of their initial spending capacities (Peres et al., 2015).

The results were so positive for Elementary School that, during Lula's administration, in 2006, the FUNDEF was turned into the Fund for the Development and Maintenance of Basic Education and Appreciation of Education Professionals (FUNDEB, *Fundo de Manutenção e Desenvolvimento da Educação Básica e de Valorização dos Profissionais da Educação*). Other changes also happened in 2009. While the FUNDEF helped fulfill the constitutional resolution of ensuring that children from 7 to 14 years of age had access to Elementary School, here the Constitution itself is changed, making it mandatory for children from 7 to 14 years of age to be in school, therefore aiming for Basic Education (Peres et al., 2015). In this policy sector there were also incentives to adhesion and standardization in the services offered through conditioned income transfer programs. That is, there were programs that functioned as transfer mechanisms with specifications for the destination of resources, with direct and indirect monitoring and expected sanctions in case of deviation from finality in the implementation (Machado, 2018). In 2020 the new FUNDEB was approved, now meant to be permanent, with incremental adjustments to the volume of resources transferred by the Union and to the transfer criteria, despite the opposition held by Bolsonaro's government.

For any policy sector, but especially for Education, in the absence of a unified and coordinated system, the role of each of the 26 states becomes central. The case of the state of Ceará is largely studied in the literature for it shows fast and consistent positive results in the educational performance of its children and teenagers due to an orchestration at the state level, coordinated by the State

Executive. That is, using induction strategies and a system of incentives that involved mayors with state and municipal secretaries, as well as headmasters from every school in the state, and also universities and think tanks, the state was able to place the performance of its students among the first ones in the national rankings (Segatto and Abrucio, 2016; 2018).

2.2.3   The structure of social spending within the federation

Having set the institutional, historical, and political stage in which Brazilian social policies operate, some important questions remain, such as: How much is spent on social policies in Brazil? What is the participation of each federative body in each policy sector? These are not easy questions, for we would have to consider that there are non-social expenses within policy sectors, as well as the other way around. There is the risk of double counting when considering the origin of the resource and where it is executed, for this makes it so that at some point both bodies account for the same budget. Measuring by the processed expenditures, for approximation purposes, in 2018, social policies represent around 49% of Brazil's public expenses, of this total, 55% is spent by the Union, 25% by states, and 20% by municipalities, according to Cunha and Sátyro (2023).

The Federal Executive Branch spends more on other policies than it does on social policies. In the myriad of Municipal Executives, however, the greater expenditure is on social policies (Cunha and Sátyro, 2023). The Federal Executive Branch spends 45% of its total budget on paying the public debt, which represents 90% of this body's expenses with other public policies (Cunha and Sátyro, 2023). The Federal Executive Branch has the most capacity for generating revenue, followed by the states, and then the municipalities. Of the total spending on social policies in 2018 (1.9 trillion), 88.5% is on Social Security, Health, Education, and Social Assistance policies, 11.1% on Public Security, and Transport and 0.4% with Housing, Sports, and Leisure (Cunha and Sátyro, 2023). It is also important to note the responsibility of spending between the federative bodies regarding the main social policies. Social Security holds the largest part of Brazilian expenditures, surpassing the combined spending on education, healthcare, and social assistance. However, at the local level, municipalities spend more on education than on welfare. States spend less on those four costly social policies because their expenses concentrate on public security, for states are the bodies that hold that responsibility.

And why is this important for the purpose of this book? Because it is necessary for the reader to know the weight of each federative entity in each sector of social policy in order to understand the strategies that each government used in relation to that arena. As can be seen, the Union is the main funder of most of the set of social policies (55%), which reinforces the importance of its role.

This is the framework the reader should have in mind while reading the book in order to understand what has been done over the last years in Brazil regarding social protection. It is important to highlight the strength of the federal government and the centrality of coordination for all areas. In the absence of such coordination, we are haunted by the threat of paralysis in decision-making and even of increasing inequalities, for even with all efforts toward ensuring fairness between the federate bodies through fiscal and political decentralization we still face great institutional, fiscal, and administrative heterogeneity. During the pandemic of covid-19, the absence of such coordination was blatant when states and municipalities refused to follow directions from the Federal Executive Branch (chapter 8).

For example, during the pandemic, Bolsonaro's government published national guidelines against the use of facemasks and lockdowns, as well as supporting ineffective pharmacological measures. When the states and municipalities in their political autonomy took non-pharmacological measures such as social distancing and mandatory facemasks in public places, the federal government tried to prohibit such measures on the legal field (Cepedisa, 2021). Bolsonaro adopted a centralizing and hierarchical position on national matters and abstained from the role of a national coordinator who aims at reducing territorial inequalities, using a "dualistic model" for intergovernmental relations (Abrucio et al., 2020, p. 665). The Supreme Court had to be called in on April 2020 to ban Provisional Measure 926/2000, which aimed at blocking states and municipalities from adopting non-pharmacological measures. The Court then confirmed the basic constitutional principle of autonomy of the federative bodies, apparently unknown to Bolsonaro. In this situation, as well as others, the Supreme Court was an actor with an important veto power throughout his administration. All in all, the lack of national coordination between states and municipalities rendered widely heterogenous covid-19 responses by these entities, both sanitary and political, which made Brazilians even more vulnerable. Brazil occupies the 5th place in the international rank of covid-19 mortality rate.

2.3 Political crisis and changes in the political arena: The return of the right and its consequences for social policies

Investment in social policies, added to economic growth, and to a policy of valuing of the minimum wage during PT governments led to a decrease in poverty and income inequality (see Chapter 6 in this book). However, at the beginning of Dilma Rousseff's second administration an economic crisis erupted (Chapter 4), which became the first big inflection in a trajectory of expansion of the social protection system in Brazil since the CF88. With Rousseff's impeachment, Michel Temer takes office, and with him, Constitutional Amendment No 95 (CA95).

2.3.1 The Constitutional Amendment No 95 and its consequences for social policies

A third central element to understanding what has been happening in Brazil regarding the social policies is Constitutional Amendment No 95, approved on December 15, 2016, a few months after Temer took office. Two important aspects are highlighted here: The first one refers to the speed with which the process was concluded, which shows that after Dilma Rousseff's impeachment her vice-president, Michel Temer, now president, had the majority in both Legislative Houses in record time. The second is the very nature of this amendment, called the "New Fiscal Regime" (NFR), or "Expenditure Ceiling Law."

The "New Fiscal Regime" created an absolute limit for the growth of public expenses, only adjusted by inflation, for the following 20 years, which spanned between December 2017 to 2037. This was meant to occur regardless of demographic-populational changes as well as of how much the GDP increased or decreased. Public expenses are all expenses of the public machine related to the three powers: Executive, Legislative, and Judiciary, as well as other bodies in the federal administration, and the expenses on social policies, be it Social Welfare, Social Security, Health, and Social Assistance, or any other social policy: Education, Culture, Agrarian Development, Housing, Sanitation, Science and Technology, Infrastructure, and Transportation, among others. This means, in practice, that the only expenses that do not abide to the limit are expenses with the public debt (Fórum 21, 2016; Paiva et al., 2016). The nature of the crisis taking place could have been approached through raising taxes, through spending cuts, for instance, but the main choice was fiscal austerity. However, for instance, European countries established in 2011 a limit for the growth of expenses associated to the long-term growth rate of the GDP, but a limit bound to null real growth is a Brazilian "innovation" (Fórum 21, 2016:9). The pandemic demanded measures that would implode this rule and, for that, the Chamber of Deputies approved a Constitutional Amendment Project determining a State of Emergency to allow expenses beyond the limit.

It is interesting to note that a measure as restrictive as this, which determined the policy agenda for the following five federal administrations, was approved in record time, with no setbacks. The Amendment Project fulfilled the procedural rite of approval with qualified majority, which means three fifths of the Congress in each of the two Legislative houses, two times each. This all happened in less than three months. Rousseff's impeachment process started in December 2015, she was removed from office on May 12, 2016, and had her mandate revoked on August 31, 2016. The proposal had its first approval on October 10, 2016, in the Chamber of Deputies, and by December 15 it had already gone through both houses twice, which got the Constitutional Amendment No 95 (CA95) approved. This is a parliament that would steer further to the right after

Bolsonaro's election, with the strong presence of the agribusiness, aligned to neoliberal, neoconservative thinking.

Therefore, it is possible to affirm that the arrival of the mainstream right to the Federal Executive, without doubt, inaugurates a new political agenda; it is a point of inflection for what had been being built in the first decade and a half of the 2000s. And CA95 is the very consubstantiation of the obfuscation strategy, in Piersean terms, diluting its effects in time, making it harder for the common citizen, that is, the average voter, to identify the chain and the "traceability" of policy changes (Pierson, 1994, p. 21); they will not be likely to connect such effects to an act so distant in time. However, as we will see in this book, the far-right's entrance with the figure of Jair Bolsonaro emphasizes that trend and takes it further on a symbolic and material level.

The covid-19 pandemic hits us in that context, but as the reader can observe, it is but one element among others of equal weight. We expect that the joint analyses enable us to assess what were the effects of the pandemic and what was specific to the administrations analyzed.

2.3.2 Bolsonaro's Government Plan

Lastly, in order to understand the trajectory of social policies over the last few years, we need to know what Bolsonaro's plan for social policies was when he ran for the Presidency of the Republic. Recalling that one of the key concepts for public policies is that it comprises all a government does, but also what it chooses not to do, it is important to analyze what Bolsonaro's intentions were when running for president in 2018. With that purpose, we did a brief Content Analysis of his government plan, of exploratory nature, which does not intend to be extensive. Bolsonaro's Government Plan (BGP), presented for his campaign, is comprised of 81 Powerpoint slides, nothing more.

Slide number 22 specifies three lines of action: "SECURITY AND FIGHTING CORRUPTION: Tackling crime and cutting off corruption. HEALTH AND EDUCATION: Efficiency, management, and respect for people's lives. Improving health and making the quality of education soar, with emphasis on children's, basic, and technical education, without indoctrination. ECONOMY: Employment, Income, and Fiscal Balance. Opportunities and work for all, without inflation" (capital letters as per the original). Indeed, those three lines give the tone for the whole document.

To carry out the analysis, two word-clouds without categorization were produced using Atlas TI. The first one considers the whole document, including the candidate's motto, which appears in every slide: "Brazil above everything, God above everyone," counting out only conjunctions, articles, and other Brazilian Portuguese "supporting" words. This motto gave the tone for the opening speech and continued to be recurrently uttered in public speeches during

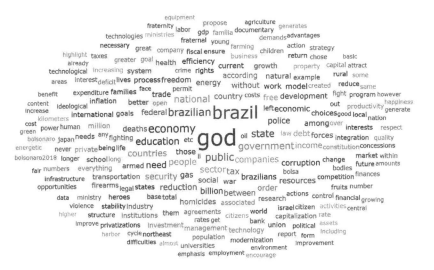

FIGURE 2.1 Word-Cloud of Bolsonaro's Government Plan presented for the 2018 campaign.

Source: Author's elaboration based on Bolsonaro's Government Plan presented for the 2018 campaign.

his administration, therefore being very representative and symbolic, which is why it was kept in for the analysis. On the same note, the first slide presents a biblical citation: "You shall know the truth, and the truth shall make you free (John 8:32)." For its systematic presence in all of the slides and its symbolic impact, Figure 2.1 shows the predominance of the word "god" (which appears 67 times in the document) next to "Brazil," both representative of the use of religion and patriotism in populist discourse. According to Borges and Vidigal (2023), one of the three major trends for the reorganization of the right, regarding the offering of conservative alternatives, is its association with neopentecostalism. This is a religious right with traditional values and Bolsonaro had the support of important neopentecostal religious leaders, which gave him, for that round (2018's election), 70% of vote intentions among evangelical people, which accounted for 29% of the Brazilian electorate (Moura and Corbellini, 2019).

However, using a filter removing the motto as well as less frequent words, the document is focuses on the three elements from slide 22 (as can be seen in Figure 2.2). The "economy" became the place from which BGP was drafted, with significant appearances of the words "companies," "development," "income," "energy," "gas," "growth," "inflation," "industry," "trade," "debt," and "economic." Next, there are the words "security," "homicides," "cops" "armed (with) forces," "guns," "war," "heroes," which appears six times, mostly praising police action against "thugs," which shows the centrality of this

FIGURE 2.2   Word-Cloud of Bolsonaro's Government Plan presented for the 2018 campaign, filtered.

Source: Author's elaboration based on Bolsonaro's Government Plan presented for the 2018 campaign.

discourse for Bolsonaro. According to some authors, it is possible to identify two right-wing populist waves in Latin America. And these two aspects represent the two waves, where the first was characterized by an economic agenda, and the second, by non-economic matters, one of them being public security (Borges and Vidigal, 2023; Weyland, 2003).

Another aspect worthy of attention is the weight of the word "corruption," central for characterizing populist discourse, when considering populism on an ideational line as a Manichean ideology that divides the society between the pure folk and the corrupt elite. In that case, the construction of corruption was placed upon the left, especially the Worker's Party. In this context, it is important to highlight the presence of the word "left" (which appears 10 times) in the *corpus* as something to be fought and which is related to "corruption," to "[in]doctrine[-ation]," "Gramsci," "cultural Marxism" which has "corrupted democracy" and is not worried about the deaths of cops. That is the tone of the document.

However, for what this chapter is due, it is necessary to identify the social policies in the 2018 proposal presented by the former candidate. It is possible to see "education" and "health" quite visible in the images. Education is addressed in seven slides, with a total of 20 occurrences, which is plenty for a document with 81 slides; Health is addressed over four slides, with a total of 18 occurrences. "Welfare" appears only in the first cloud, for it has the space of one slide, where it occurs five times.

Regarding Health, which appears before Education in BGP, is can be seen that in the four slides, two are what we call diagnostic and the other two present some propositional ideas. The first mentions an "Interconnected National Electronic Handbook" and the "Universal Physician Accreditation." The second one bears the title "Prevention is better and cheaper" and is divided into four points: one discussing the Cuban medical doctors of the "More Doctors" program, a staple of PT's governments, claiming that it would help them escape the Cuban government; a second point on the creation of a "State Physician"; and the third and fourth give examples for prevention: an idea for ensuring dental health for pregnant women, and another one for including a Physical Education professional in the Family Health Program. Thus, this is the "government program" for the Health sector.

As for Education, of the seven slides devoted to it, six are diagnoses and comparisons to other countries, and two hold proposals (there is overlap): 1) regarding school management and the educational content – "Aside from changing the management method, in Education we also need to revise and modernize the contents. This includes literacy, purging Paulo Freire's ideology (...)"; 2) bringing up the need for modernization in the universities and relating it to partnerships and researches alongside the private sector and the promotion of entrepreneurship among students, as well as emphasizing remote learning as a guideline to follow; and 3) highlighting the need to integrate the many educational systems, which, as seen before, are fragmented and do not have unified management as with Health and Social Assistance. Paulo Freire (1921–1997), mentioned by name, was a renowned philosopher and educator, even internationally, and the precursor of what is today called the pedagogy of freedom, more of a constructivist view rather than one focused on contents, having published many books on subjects such as pedagogy of the oppressed and pedagogy of outrage.[6]

Lastly, as already mentioned, "welfare" (as in social security) appears five times throughout the document. Once when addressing nominal deficit and specifying the deficit of Welfare regimes, and again on the slide addressing the Tax Reform. However, the Welfare Reform was given an exclusive slide, which basically addressed the need to capitalize the system (Chapter 8 of this book). In the absence of proposals for the social sector, the Bolsa Família program was included in the economic part of BGP, with a proposal for instituting a universal basic income based on Milton Friedman.

We can conclude by saying that the major characteristic of BGP in 2018, when referring to social protection, is its absence. That is, there is no visible intention of action, and, in this case, not even promises are made. There are no clear, structuring proposals for Health or Education, there is no mention of Housing, Social Assistance, Sports, Family Policies, and there is also no mention of the Environment, for instance. However, there is no doubt concerning the neoliberal proposal regarding economic choices and all of the centrality that the Police and Public Security have had in the candidate's agenda, which justifies the inclusion of a chapter of Public Security in this book. To the reader, we bring as an annex to this book the whole of BGP content so that they can do their own research or judge what can be extracted from there on his intentions for the social sector, which are residual, and that alone says much.

2.4 Conclusion

This chapter aimed to provide the reader with the basic knowledge needed to read the other chapters and was not meant to be extensive. Our goal was merely to provide basic tools for understanding the centrality of the federal government in federative arrangements and the change in trajectory that comes to be when right-wing governments take office as the Central Executive Power. This, along with the next four chapters, set the foundation for the reading of the chapters specific to each policy sector.

Notes

1 This chapter was significantly improved after Joana Mostafa and Eleonora Cunha's critical reading. I would also like to thank Iris dos Santos Gomes for her help with word clouds.

2 José Sarney ran for vice-president on a ticket that reconciled the right and the center. However, the head of the ticket, Tancredo Neves, who was from a centrist party and who had been known for his conciliatory disposition, fell ill and passed away before taking office. Thus, the elected vice-president became president when the ticked took office.

3 Fernando Henrique Cardoso took office as president with PSDB (Partido da Social Democracia Brasileira, the Brazilian Social Democracy Party), a party initially known to be in the center-left, and finished his term as center-right, as per the neoliberal outline of its policies; on one hand, its restrictive fiscal policies, and on the other, its focalized policies and subsidy of the third sector in the area of social assistance.

4 Different from Education, for which the union has more normative than financial capacity compared to municipalities.

5 It is important to note that on April 11, 2019, Bolsonaro launched Decree 9,759, at once extinguishing and establishing rules and limitations for all collegiates in the federal administration, defining collegiates in the same text as: councils, committees, commissions, groups, delegations, teams, boards, forums, chambers, and any other designation. Judiciary engagement was summoned to nullify much of its effect on the basis of it being unconstitutional, which still shows the strength with which, in just one act, he attacked all instances of federative agreement and social participation. However, it was only revoked on January 1, 2023, by President Lula, with Decree 11,371.

6 www.thecollector.com/paulo-freire-brazilian-philosopher/

References

Abrucio, F. L., Grin, E. J., Franzese, C., Segatto, C. I., & Couto, C. G. (2020). Combate à Covid-19 sob o federalismo bolsonarista: um caso de descoordenação intergovernamental. *Revista de Administração Pública, 54,* 663–677.

Arretche, M. (2012). *Democracia, federalismo e centralização no Brasil.* SciELO-Editora Fiocruz.

Borges, A., & Vidigal, R., eds. (2023). "Introdução: Para Entender a Nova Direita Brasileira." In: *Para Entender a Nova Direita Brasileira: Polarização, populismo e antipetismo.* 1. ed. Zouk, 426p.

Cepedisa (2021). Boletim Direitos na Pandemia. São Paulo: Centro de Estudos e Pesquisas de Direito Sanitário. Disponível em www.conectas.org/publicacao/boletim-direitos-na-pandemia-no-10/ [Consultado em April 24, 2021].

Cunha, P., & Sátyro, N. (2023). Capítulo 4: Qual ente federativo paga pelo quê e quem recebe o quê em termos de proteção social? In: Sátyro, N. and Cunha, E. (eds.), *Descomplicando Políticas Sociais no Brasil: o que, por que, como, de quem, para quem?* Editora UFMG and Editora Fino Traço, pp. 73–96.

Fórum 21; Fundação Friedrich Ebert Stiftung (FES); GT de Macro da Sociedade Brasileira de Economia Política (SEP); Plataforma Política Social. Austeridade e Retrocesso – finanças públicas e política fiscal no Brasil, São Paulo, setembro de 2016. Disponível em http://brasildebate.com.br/wpcontent/uploads/Austeridade-e-Retrocesso.pdf

Machado, J. A. (2018). Federalismo e políticas sociais: conexões a partir da Teoria da Agência. *Revista do Serviço Público, 69*(1), 57–84.

Machado, J.A. (2023). Capítulo 2: Federalismo e relações intergovernamentais nas políticas sociais: mais autonomia ou mais coordenação? In: Sátyro, N and Cunha, E. (eds.), *Descomplicando Políticas Sociais no Brasil: A Constituição Federal de 1988 e a estrutura de proteção social brasileira.* Editora UFMG and Editora Fino Traço, pp. 39–58.

Malloy, J. (1979). *Política de Previdência social no Brasil.* Editora Graal.

Morel, N., & Palier, B., eds. (2011). *Towards a social investment welfare state?: ideas, policies and challenges.* Policy Press.

Moura, M., & Corbellini, J. (2019). *A eleição disruptiva: por que Bolsonaro venceu.* Editora Record.

Oliveira, J. A. de A. & Teixeira, S. M. F. (1986). *(IM) Previdência social: 60 anos de história da previdência no Brasil.* Editora Vozes, Petrópolis. Associação Brasileira de Pós-Graduação.

Paiva, A. B. D., Mesquita, A. C. S., Jaccoud, L. D. B., & Passos, L. (2016). O novo regime fiscal e suas implicações para a política de assistência social no Brasil. *Nota Técnica,* 27. Brasília, IPEA. Avaiable in https://repositorio.ipea.gov.br/bitstream/11058/7267/1/NT_n27_Disoc.pdf

Peres, A. J. D. S., Souza, M. L. D., Alves, F. D. A., & Rodrigues, E. G. (2015). *Efeito redistributivo intraestadual do Fundeb: uma análise a partir de variáveis financeiras, socioeconômicas e educacionais dos municípios.* Instituto Nacional de Estudos e Pesquisas Educacionais Anísio Teixeira.

Pierson, P. (1994). *Dismantling the welfare state? Reagan, Thatcher, and the politics of retrenchment.* Cambridge University Press.

Pierson, P., & Leibfried, S. (1995). The dynamics of social policy integration. In: Leibfried, S., & Pierson, P. (eds.), *European Social Policy: Between Fragmentation and Integration*. The Brookings Institution, pp. 432–465.

Santos, W. G. D. (1979). Cidadania e Justiça. Rio de Janeiro: Ed. *Campos*.

Sátyro, N. (2021). The paradigmatic radical reform in Brazil's social policies: The impact of the Temer administration. In: Sátyro, N., del Pino, E., & Midaglia, C. (eds.), *Latin American Social Policy Developments in the Twenty-First Century*. Palgrave Macmillan, pp. 317–340.

Sátyro, N. G. D., & Cunha, E. S. M. (2018a). The transformative capacity of the Brazilian federal government in building a social welfare bureaucracy in the municipalities. *Revista de Administração Pública, 52*, 363–385.

Satyro, N. G. D., & Cunha, P. S. (2018b). The coexistence of different welfare regimes in the same country: a comparative analysis of the Brazilian municipalities heterogeneity. *Journal of Comparative Policy Analysis: Research and Practice, 21*(1), 65–89.

Segatto, C. I., & Abrucio, F. L. (2016). A cooperação em uma federação heterogênea: o regime de colaboração na educação em seis estados brasileiros. *Revista Brasileira de Educação, 21*(65), 411–429.

Segatto, C. I., & Abrucio, F. L. (2018). Os múltiplos papéis dos governos estaduais na política educacional brasileira: os casos do Ceará, Mato Grosso do Sul, São Paulo e Pará. *Revista de Administração Pública, 52*, 1179–1193.

Sellers, J. M., & Lidström, A. (2007). Decentralization, local government, and the welfare state. *Governance, 20*(4), 609–632.

Stepan, A. (1999). Para uma Nova Análise Comparativa do Federalismo e da Democracia: Federações que Restringem ou Ampliam o Poder do Demos. *Dados, 42*(2), 197–251.

Weyland, K. (2003). Neopopulism and Neoliberalism in Latin America: How much affinity? *Third World Quarterly, 24*(6), 1095–1115.

3

POLITICAL PARTIES, IDEOLOGICAL PREFERENCES AND SOCIAL POLICY

Accounting for right-wing strategies in Brazil after the left turn

André Borges

3.1 Introduction

Previous research has argued that disagreement over the role of the state in the economy and in society is the primary axis of party competition in Latin America. Different from Western Europe, where increasing levels of economic security led to the rise of post-materialist values, Latin America's highly unequal societies did not create the conditions necessary for the emergence of a cultural axis of competition (Zanotti and Roberts, 2021).

Despite the centrality of the state-market divide, there is evidence that noneconomic issues pertaining to the liberal-conservative divide are far from being irrelevant for party competition in Latin America. These issues oppose traditional and religious values, on the one hand, and progressive and secular views on gender roles, reproductive rights and sexuality on the other (Wieschomeier and Doyle, 2014; Alcántara and Rivas, 2007). The cultural dimension of party competition has become more salient in the recent years, as increasing secularization and progressive policy changes have fostered greater involvement of religious groups and, especially, of the rapidly growing evangelical churches, in electoral politics (Boas, 2020).

Cultural backlash and voters' resentment toward the political establishment have created an environment favorable to the rise of far-right alternatives all over the region. Far-right populist leaders have taken advantage of rising crime, corruption scandals and stagnant economies to mobilize voters' discontent with traditional parties and present themselves as the "true" representatives of the people (Luna and Rovira Kaltwasser, 2021; Kaltwasser, 2020; Rennó, 2020).

DOI: 10.4324/9781003487777-4

The case of Brazil is exemplary of these trends, as evangelical churches and their representatives in Congress, in alliance with conservative catholic groups, have succeeded in politicizing previously dormant cultural issues. Moreover, Brazil's far-right has obtained extraordinary success in recent years. Authoritarian populist Jair Bolsonaro was elected president in 2018 and was defeated in his re-election bid for a tiny margin, winning almost 50% of the national vote in 2022.

This chapter explores the main policy differences between left and right, in view of the changing landscapes of Brazil's polity and society. More specifically, the chapter intends to assess: i) to what extent parties' preferences on state intervention in the economy and on redistribution and social policy-making distinguish the left from the right in Brazil; and ii) how the populist radical right differs from the traditional right in what concerns economic, cultural and social issues.

While the political right in Brazil and elsewhere in Latin America has more often than not embraced neoliberal economic policies that are inimical to the expansion of social services, conservative parties in the region face substantial electoral challenges due to extreme levels of inequality. According to Luna and Kaltwasser (2014a, p. 9–10), if voters in unequal societies vote according to their "true" economic interests and parties compete on a one-dimensional divide, then we should expect left-wing parties with a redistributive agenda to fare systematically better than the political right. Throughout the 2000s, indeed, the Latin American left took advantage of voters' discontent with the market-oriented reforms of the previous decade to politicize inequality and defeat right-of-center incumbents (Baker and Greene, 2011, Wiesehomeier and Doyle, 2013; Levitsky and Roberts, 2011, Roberts, 2014a, Luna and Kaltwasser, 2014a). As leftist incumbents relied on redistributive social policies to build or strengthen linkages to poor voters, conservative parties found themselves in a position of relative electoral weakness (Luna and aKaltwasser, 2014a, Bowen, 2011).

In Brazil, the left turn witnessed the rise of moderate center-left governments. Prior to the election of Jair Bolsonaro in 2018, the Workers' Party (PT) had governed the country for 13 years (2003–2016) forming large and ideologically heterogeneous coalitions comprised of parties of virtually all ideological orientations. Notwithstanding the potential veto power exerted by the large right-wing bloc in Congress, the PT's presidential administrations delivered consistent economic growth and low inflation, in addition to an unprecedented reduction in inequality, at least until Dilma Rousseff's first presidential term (2011–2014). Thanks to these social and economic achievements the PT was able to mobilize the lower strata of Brazilian society to obtain successive victories in presidential elections (Samuels and Zucco Jr, 2016, Zucco, 2008).

Considering the successful politicization of inequality by the PT governments, how did rightist actors position themselves with regard to the expansion or retrenchment of the welfare state in the recent period? Moreover, to what extent have the emerging anti-system, radical right forces distinguished themselves from the traditional right in what concerns redistribution and the provision of social policies, as well as regarding cultural grievances that have become increasingly salient?

This chapter explores these questions by relying on data from the Parliamentary Elites in Latin America (PELA) project. The 2019 PELA survey with Brazilian federal deputies covers a large number of economic, social and cultural issues. I utilize a set of questions extracted from this elite survey to estimate legislators' mean policy positions by ideological bloc. I divide the political right into two groups – populist radical right (PRR) and mainstream right – and rely on descriptive and multivariate statistical analysis to assess whether the PRR differs from the rest of the right on economic, social and cultural issues.

3.2 Conservative parties, redistribution and electoral mobilization in Latin America

The conception and ideal of equality are the central issues separating left from right. Building on this central assumption taken from Bobbio (1996), Luna and Kaltwasser (2014b) define the right as a political position characterized by the belief that social inequalities are natural and outside the purview of the state. By contrast, they define the left as a political position distinguished by the idea that the main inequalities between people are socially constructed and should therefore be counteracted by active state involvement (p. 4). Borges, Lloyd and Vommaro (forthcoming) have refined this definition, by arguing that the notion that social inequalities are natural does not necessarily lead to a blanket rejection of social policy. Instead, what distinguishes the political right is the adoption of a "thin," market-oriented conception of social justice (Kerstenetzky, 2006), according to which social policies should be devised to address market failures and/or to provide individuals with insurance for maintaining their living standards in the face of age, sickness, or any other condition negatively affecting one's ability to earn income in the market. More broadly, the "thin"conception of social justice that separates the left from the right is characterized by the rejection of inequality as a major justification for state intervention. The political left, by contrast, is strongly associated with a "thick" conception of justice, which is based primarily on the goals of promoting political liberty and economic equality. Given the core differences between left and right, it follows that right-wing parties should find it harder to attract lower-class voters in highly unequal societies by relying solely on programmatic appeals.

Consistent with the definitions proposed by Luna and Kaltwasser and Borges, Lloyd and Vommaro, right-wing parties in contemporary Latin America have distinguished themselves from both the left and the center in that they are much more likely to defend neoliberal reforms such as privatization and market deregulation and a smaller role of the state in the economic realm (Wiesehomeier, 2010). Moreover, because of the strong connections that exist between these parties and prominent members of the upper classes (large landowners, bankers and industrialists), the Latin American right has been much more likely to defend the status quo and the existing social hierarchies as compared to left-of-center parties (Bowen, 2014, Cannon, 2016, Roberts, 2014b).

Comparative research has indicated that conservative parties' responses to the challenge of mobilizing mass electorates in unequal societies have been of three sorts. First, rightist actors can de-emphasize economic issues and class identities to forge multiclass coalitions. In this scenario, conservatives may opt for campaigning on noneconomic issues that cross-cut social classes (Giraudy, 2015; Kaltwasser, 2014). By politicizing ethnic, territorial or religious identities, right-wing parties can more easily build electoral coalitions made up of segments from different social strata and thus compete more effectively against their opponents on the left (Eaton, 2011; Kaltwasser, 2014).

With regard to this strategy, the Latin American right has been successful in politicizing religious identities and traditional values. These processes are directly related to the expansion of evangelical churches in several countries in the region, such as Brazil, Colombia and Costa Rica. Trends such as the secularization of societies and changes in values and legislation around issues such as LGBT rights, abortion and gender identity in many countries in the region created incentives for the organization and mobilization of conservative religious groups who saw progressive cultural and political changes as a threat to traditional values and ways of life (Boas, 2020; Villazón, 2014).

When cultural, noneconomic issues come to the forefront, parties' positions on redistribution and welfare tend to lose importance accordingly. Thus, the politicization of noneconomic identities and issues may allow right-wing parties to obfuscate conflict over distinct models of social policy provision and financing.

PRR parties in Western Europe seem to have adopted this latter strategy to obtain electoral success. Because these parties mobilize voters with distinct social profiles and preferences on redistribution (e.g., working class and petty bourgeois voters), they have an incentive to project vague, contradictory or ambiguous positions on economic issues. Consequently, radical right parties emphasize and take clear ideological stances on issues such as immigration and law and order, while at the same time avoiding precise economic placement (Rovny, 2013, Rovny and Polk, 2020).

In Latin America, PRR parties have been less successful in mobilizing lower class voters and, thus, they might have weaker incentives to adopt mildly centrist economic positions (or blur their positions on welfare policies). Still, recent comparative research indicates that, similarly to their Western European counterparts, PRR parties and candidates in Latin America tend to emphasize cultural as opposed to economic issues (Tanscheit and Zanotti, 2023).

A second response of conservative parties to the challenge of building multiclass coalitions involves the partial moderation of ideological appeals, partly incorporating the social policy agenda of the left. This goal may be achieved either through the rebranding of existing conservative parties or through the creation of new ones. While this strategy is well-suited to the task of attracting centrist voters, it entails the risk of losing the support of core voters (Kaltwasser, 2019).

Note, however, that right-wing parties may combine centrist positions on economic issues while at the same time adopting more extreme positions on the liberal-conservative divide. Thus, the incorporation of leftist, pro-redistribution agendas does not necessarily imply the abandonment of the party's core ideological values altogether. Right-wing parties may pursue strategic positioning along distinct policy dimensions to more effectively appeal to distinct segments of the electorate (Röth et al., 2018).

Finally, conservative parties may choose to maintain their ideological positions in the left-right economic dimension, while building clientelistic ties with lower-class voters through the provision of material rewards. According to these explanations, rich and middle-class voters will support conservative parties because of their identification with those parties' economic and ideological preferences, whereas poor voters will do so in exchange for material benefits provided by the party (Luna, 2010, Thachil, 2014). In this scenario, to the extent that party competition is not solely based on programmatic appeals, right-wing parties may advocate welfare policies that are less generous than those preferred by the median voter and yet succeed in mobilizing mass support among the lower strata of society.

The main disadvantage of this latter strategy is that it requires parties to have continued access to patronage resources that can be distributed among party brokers and voters. For instance, during the left turn in Latin America, right-wing elites remained, most often, in opposition to the central government and, thus, were cut off from access to pork and patronage resources. This likely explains the electoral decay of many traditional right-wing parties that had built clientelistic linkages with voters (Bowen, 2014; Roberts, 2014b).

To sum up, conservative parties may succeed in mobilizing mass electorates in unequal societies by pursuing three main strategies: they may campaign on issues that are orthogonal to the economic left-right dimension and/or they may politicize identities that cross-cut social class; they may opt for moderating their positions on redistribution and state intervention; they may rely on clientelism to obtain the support of poor voters. While strategy number two – ideological moderation – necessarily requires that parties alter their positions on social policy, this is not the case of strategy number three – cultivating clientelistic linkages. Strategy number one – campaigning on noneconomic issues – will usually lead parties to de-emphasize the economic left-right dimensions. In this case, even if parties do not moderate their overall positions on state intervention and redistribution, they will tend to adopt positions that are vague or inconsistent across distinct issues. For instance, parties may advocate privatization and market deregulation while at the same time defending generous welfare schemes.

3.3 The case of Brazil: From the decay of the traditional right to the rise of the populist radical right

Brazilian conservative parties have arguably relied on all three types of strategies to mobilize multiclass electoral constituencies. Throughout time, the particularistic, patronage-seeking right, which had relied to a substantial extent on clientelistc linkages to mobilize voters has lost ground to anti-establishment and ultraconservative alternatives. Cultural backlash throughout the 2010s was followed by the increasingly salience of cultural grievances that have been purposefully politicized by new right forces (Borges, 2021; Rennó, 2022; Rocha, 2021). There is also evidence of right-wing parties and politicians seeking to obfuscate and moderate their ideological positions by presenting themselves as "centrist." Tim Power (2000) created the term "direita envergonhada" (abashed right) to account for conservative politicians' tendency to deny their own ideological orientations. He noted that some of Brazil's major right-wing parties up to the early 2010s adopted policy positions in party programs and manifestos that were substantially more progressive than parties' ideological positions according to elites' perceptual data (Power, 2018).

Prior to the left turn of the early 2000s, the major parties of the right were mostly secular organizations that had been founded by the former supporters of the dictatorship (1964–1985): the PFL (Liberal Front Party) and the PDS (Social Democratic Party).[1] Both parties descended directly from the authoritarian ruling party, the ARENA, and they inherited the organizational structure and clientelistic networks built by military-appointed state governors (Ferreira, 2002; Power, 2000). As the partisan right fragmented across a myriad of small, particularistic organizations, an anti-system, anti-political right emerged in the mid-2010s, organized around conservative and liberal social movements that would later support the election of extreme-right populist Jair Bolsonaro in 2018.

The ideological classification of parties utilized in this chapter relies to a large extent on the ideology scores estimated by Zucco Jr and Power (2021) based on legislators' responses to several editions of the Brazilian Legislative Surveys (BLS) from 1990 to 2017. Due to the lack of information on various small-sized and recently created parties, I opted for complementing the BLS ideology scores with those obtained from two expert surveys, the V-Party and Political Representation, Presidents and Parties Expert Survey (PREPPS). Ideology scores were averaged both across sources and periods.[2] I rescaled the ideology scores obtained from the Brazilian Legislative Survey and from the V-Party to ensure consistency with the 20-point scale utilized in the PREPS survey (1= extreme left; 20 = extreme right).

The left- and the right-wing blocs were defined by creating 7-point intervals at the extremes of the 20-point ideology scale. The center was defined as the remaining 6-point interval, ranging from 8 to 13. Right-wing parties were thus defined as those parties that obtained an average ideology score higher than 13 in the 20-point ideology scale.

The major party of the right until the late 2000s – the PFL/DEM – was created by a dissident faction of the pro-military party comprised of governors and other senior politicians from the Northeast region and it absorbed most of the territorial organization and party cadres of the ARENA (Ferreira, 2002; Ribeiro, 2014; Power, 2000). Arguably, the PFL/DEM was the most successful party of traditional right. By 1998, the party had the largest delegation in the lower chamber. Since 1998, however, the partisan right has rapidly fragmented, whereas the PFL/DEM experienced rapid electoral decline. By 2018, the party had the support of only about 5% of voters, as compared to 17% in 1998.

In what concerns voter-politician linkages, the traditional right depended to a very substantial extent on subnational political machines that connected local brokers to state and national executives. Programmatic appeals played at best a marginal role in the mobilization of voters (Mainwaring et al., 2000; Montero, 2014). The PT governments broke down the territorial bases of the traditional right, and especially so in Brazil's poorest regions – the North and the Northeast – by federalizing social policies and promoting large-scale redistribution through a major cash-income transfer program that bypassed state and local-level intermediaries. Moreover, as the PT and its left allies had the opportunity to benefit from policy and patronage at the national level, this created a more even playing field in previously conservative-dominated states (Borges, 2011).

Different from other instances of conservative party decline in Latin America, however, the shrinking of the traditional right did not necessarily result in poor electoral performances for the right-wing bloc as whole. Figure 3.1 shows right-wing parties' aggregate vote shares in elections for the Senate and Chamber of Deputies, from 1990 to 2018.

Interestingly, the worst performance ever of the PFL/DEM in lower chamber elections (5% of the national vote in 2018) coincides with the best performance of the right-wing bloc since 1990: 50% of the vote. Thus, the decline of the major and most successful right-wing party before the left turn did not prevent the political right from maintaining and even surpassing levels of popular support observed prior to Lula's election in 2002. Figure 3.1 shows a decrease in the total right-wing vote in lower chamber races held in 2002 and 2006, followed by small increases in 2006 and 2010, and large increases in the last two elections

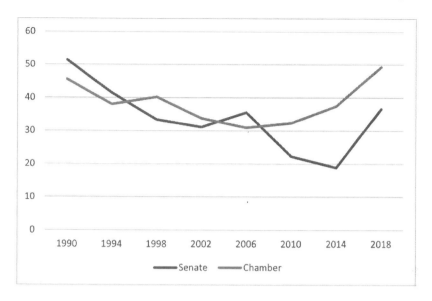

FIGURE 3.1   Right-wing parties' share of the vote, Chamber of Deputies and Senate elections, 1990–2018.

Source: High Electoral Court Database (www.tse.jus.br), Brazilian Legislative Surveys (various waves), V-Party 2020 and PREPSS (waves 2006, 2011, 2015 and 2019).

of the series. The curve for Senate elections shows a slightly different trend between 2006–2014, with a steep decline in conservative's share of the vote. The figure indicates that the political right suffered heavier electoral losses in the upper chamber, but, still, there was a very rapid and impressive recovery in 2018, which is consistent with the performance observed in elections to the Chamber of Deputies.

3.3.1   The rise of the anti-system and evangelical rights

The successful response of the Brazilian conservatives to the challenges brought about by PT rule has depended on a major reorganization of the political right. This reorganization involved the emergence of a new right, divided in two major wings: the evangelical right and the anti-political right.

The rise of the evangelical right is related to major changes in the religious affiliation of Brazilian voters. The enormous success of neo-Pentecostal churches in the competition for adherents, amidst a decrease in the size of the once overwhelming Catholic majority, created both incentives and opportunities for the politicization of religious cleavages. Between 1980 and 2010, the percentage of Brazilians self-identifying as evangelical increased from 6.5% to 22% (Smith,

2019). Compared to the Catholic majority, evangelicals are much more likely to attend worship service regularly. This implies that evangelical voters are much more susceptible to the influence of the clergy than Catholics (Rodrigues and Fuks, 2015).

On average, evangelicals have more conservative positions than both Catholic and secular voters on issues such as marriage, traditional gender roles, homosexuality and abortion. In particular, evangelicals' strong opposition to gay rights clearly differentiates them from other religious groups (Bohn, 2004; McAdams and Lance, 2013). In the left-right economic dimension, however, religious affiliation has no relevant effect on voters' attitudes (Smith, 2019).

The evangelical caucus in the lower chamber increased from 4% of the total seats in 1990 to 14.4% in 2014 (Quadros and Madeira, 2018). Note, however, the major evangelical churches such as the UKCG (Universal Kingdom of the Chuch of God) and AG (Assembly of God) did not care to coordinate around a major confessional party that might represent Protestants from different denominations. Rather, evangelical churches have taken advantage of Brazil's open-list PR system with high district magnitudes to scatter church-sponsored candidates across several different parties (Reich and dos Santos, 2013). More recently, evangelical churches have established stronger connections to confessional right-wing parties such as the PRB (Brazilian Republican Party), the PSC (Social Christian Party) and the PR (Party of the Republic).[3] By 2015, 40% of the federal deputies in the evangelical caucus were affiliated with these parties (Quadros and Madeira, 2018).

Despite the growing importance of confessional parties for the electoral strategies of Protestant churches, the highly pragmatic and nonideological behavior of evangelical clergy and politicians during most of the recent democratic period has prevented the organization of party competition around religious cleavages. It is worth noticing that some of the major evangelical churches supported Lula in the 2002 election and in his re-election bid in 2006. As the evangelical right participated in electoral and governing coalitions that included leftist parties with progressive agendas that conflicted with traditional religious views, the saliency of the liberal-conservative divide remained low, at least until the early 2010s.

This scenario of low polarization would radically change in view of a nonpartisan cultural backlash that was triggered by progressive shifts in Brazil's polity and society. Decisions such as the high court's legalization of same-sex marriage in the 2010s motivated a conservative reaction led by the evangelical clergy. In the absence of strong right-wing parties, conservatives relied on nonpartisan organizations and forms of action to wage a cultural war against progressive values (Smith, 2019). Increasing polarization led to an unavoidable conflict between the evangelical caucus in Congress and the PT's progressive agendas (Quadros and Madeira, 2018). Evangelical churches gradually took distance from the PT and the left. This movement culminated with their enthusiastic support to the presidential candidacy of extreme-right populist Jair Bolsonaro in 2018.

The other arm of the new right organized, in part, around liberal-conservative social movements that emerged throughout major political and economic crises that led to the impeachment of president Dilma Rousseff and to the discrediting of all major parties. The anti-political new right also included a populist, radical branch that coalesced around Jair Bolsonaro in 2018.

Several of these right-wing movements were founded by young activists that felt that their ideas were not adequately represented due to the cultural hegemony of the left in the academia and the media (Rocha, 2021). Although they were very small initially, movements such as the MBL (Free Brazil Movement) experienced rapid growth in the wake of major pro-impeachment protests in 2015. Street protests against president Dilma Rousseff were motivated by a deep economic contraction in 2015–2016 and a series of corruption scandals uncovered by a major federal investigation started in 2014. The Lava Jato (Car Wash) operation emerged as an investigation of a bribery scheme in the Petrobrás state oil company, but gradually expanded and revealed several corrupt schemes involving other public companies, construction firms and politicians affiliated with virtually all the major parties. The operation led to the conviction and imprisonment of several key PT figures. In addition to economic mismanagement and stagflation during Rousseff's administration, corruption scandals led to a major anti-incumbent wave that resulted in growing rejection of the Workers' Party. Rousseff's successor, Michel Temer of the PMDB fared no better: his economic team delivered poor economic growth and Temer himself was caught up in a corruption scandal.

Later on, leaked conversations between judges and prosecutors would reveal that the Car Wash operation had relied on extra-constitutional strategies to deliberately discredit parties and politicians and gain popular support in favor of the "cleansing" of the political system.[4] The "Vaza-Jato" scandal made clear that prominent judges and prosecutors had deliberately manipulated the due legal process to convict politicians charged of corruption, including former president Lula.[5] Federal judge Sérgio Moro who gained national prominence for this leading role in the Car Wash operation would be later appointed as Bolsonaro's minister of Justice. Moro soon became a potential presidential candidate, which was yet another evidence that the operation had been used in favor of the personal political ambitions of judges and prosecutors.

Despite substantial variation in their agendas and modes of organization, new right movements were all strongly critical of traditional parties and party politics, and they sided with the Car Wash operation and its moralistic crusade against corruption. Moreover, they presented themselves as nonpartisan, "apolitical" movements, in spite of their connections to the center-right opposition to the

PT (Dias et al., 2021; Tatagiba, 2018). In this sense, the grassroots right adhered to an anti-political, anti-system rhetoric that was also present in the presidential project of radical right populist Jair Bolsonaro. Indeed, Bolsonaro built his campaign, to a large extent, on the condemnation of traditional, corrupt party politics, claiming that effectively fighting corruption required leaders with high moral standards ("homems de bem"), recruited among political outsiders with no previous connections to the traditional political system (Almeida, 2019).

The radical populist variant of the anti-political right represented by *bolsonarismo* differed from its grassroots variant in what concerns the commitment to basic democratic values. Consistent with his affiliation to the military extreme right, Bolsonaro relied on openly undemocratic rhetoric during he campaign: he glorified the dictatorship (1964–1985) and known torturers, and spoke of shooting leftist opponents. The grassroots new right was less keen to defend overtly anti-democratic positions (Tatagiba, 2018), although several of these movements supported Bolsonaro in the runoff presidential election in 2018.

The radical populist right is, undoubtedly, the most important new right force that emerged in the recent period. In addition to being elected president in 2018 and almost re-elected in 2022, Bolsonaro was able to boost the performance of radical right candidates in lower-level races. In 2018, Bolsonaro's personal electoral vehicle, the PSL (Social Liberal Party), elected the largest delegation in the lower chamber (11% of the seats). Four years later, Bolsonaro switched parties and joined the PL (Liberal Party) to dispute re-election. Thanks to the incumbent president's coattails, the PL elected almost 20% of federal deputies, an impressive feat given Brazil's abnormally high levels of party system fragmentation.

In the following section, I analyze the policy positions of right-wing parties in comparison with left-wing and center parties, on a set of economic, social and cultural issues. I also explore differences and similarities between the radical populist right and the mainstream right.

3.4 Political parties, ideology and social policy in Brazil

I utilize the 2019 PELA survey applied to Brazilian federal deputies to assess variation in legislators' policy positions by ideological bloc. The survey was conducted by the Center for Legislative Studies of the Federal University of Minas Gerais between December 2019 and March 2020. A total of 125 deputies, from over twenty different parties, agreed to participate in the research.

I explore the sources of the left-right divide in Brazil by analyzing a set of PELA survey questions included in the wave 2016–2020 and which were applied to parliamentary elites across a large number of Latin American countries. The first two of these questions capture legislators' preferences on the state-market economic divide, utilizing a 10-point Likert scale.[6] Question 1 (*market economy*) taps on disagreement over the role of the state and the private sector in economic production. Lower scores indicate a preference for greater state control over the economy and higher scores a preference for a deregulated market economy. Question 2 (*public services provision*) deal with disagreement over the adoption of private as opposed to public provision of public services. Lower scores indicate a stronger preference for market models of provision.

Four other PELA survey questions capture disagreement over the state's role in redistribution and in social policy provision. The original scales ranging from 1 to 7 were inverted and converted into a 10-point scale, to facilitate comparison with the measures of economic and cultural policy preferences. With the inversion of the scale, higher scores indicate greater opposition to state redistribution and provision of social policies. *Social security* measures the extent to which legislators are in favor or against a state-owned and state-administered pension system. Higher values indicate lower agreement with a major role of the state in social security and, thus, greater support for market provision. *Higher education* measures legislators' support for private provision of postsecondary education. A third measure accounts for market vs. state provision of health services. Finally, *redistribution* accounts for legislators' agreement/disagreement with the view that the state should implement effective policies to fight inequality and reduce income differences between rich and poor. Higher values indicate lower support for state redistribution.

The four remaining questions account for parliamentarian elites' views on various non-economic issues on a 10-point scale. *Abortion* measures legislators' opposition to women's right to interrupt an undesired pregnancy. *Gay marriage* accounts for opposition to the legalization of same-sex marriage. Two additional survey questions, on legislators' approval of the death penalty and drug decriminalization, complete the list of questions dealing with cultural issues.

I explore variation across these ten policy dimensions using simple descriptive statistics grouped by country and ideological bloc. Political parties were classified as center, left or right on the basis of the ideology scores obtained from both expert (V-Party, PREPPS) and elite survey data (BLS), as explained in the previous section.

Table 3.1 shows the mean and standard deviation of legislators' responses to the six questions dealing with the social and economic role of the state. Recall that the data was rescaled in some cases, to make sure that responses always vary across a 10-point scale, with higher (lower) values indicating typical right-wing (left-wing) positions. I utilize the standard deviation of legislators' responses to the survey questions as a proxy for polarization. The issues are ordered from the highest to the lowest standard deviation.

TABLE 3.1 Standard deviation of Brazilian legislators' responses to selected PELA survey questions

	Mean	*SD*
Gay marriage	4.70	2.97
Abortion	6.94	2.89
Drug decriminalization	6.42	2.80
Death penalty	3.56	2.78
Public service provision	5.34	2.70
Market Economy	5.88	2.67
Higher education	5.13	2.41
Social Security	5.20	2.33
State Redistribution	5.04	2.31
Health policy	3.04	1.80

Source: PELA 2019 Brazil survey.

Table 3.1 indicates that gay marriage is the issue that most clearly divides Brazilian legislators. It is also noteworthy that noneconomic issues – gay marriage, abortion and drug decriminalization – obtained the three highest standard deviations. Questions dealing with social policy issues such as social security, redistribution and health policy, for their part, do not seem to generate substantial disagreement among Brazilian parliamentarians. Table 3.1 also indicates that the questions on market-oriented models of public management (*public service provision*) and on the scope of state intervention in the economy (*market economy*) are more divisive than those dealing with the state's role in redistribution and in the provision of social services.

Moving forward, I now examine the association between the left-right dimension and the ten issues included in the analysis. Table 3.2 shows mean scores by ideological bloc and left-right mean differences. Issues were rank ordered from the highest to the lowest left-right difference. The last column of Table 3.2 reports the F statistics obtained from a simple analysis of variance utilizing ideological blocs as the grouping variable. F values provide a proxy measure of issue polarization. Conceptually, polarization is associated with the formation of opposing groups comprised of individuals with homogeneous preferences, at the same time the divergence in opinions among the typical individual affiliated to each of the competing groups increases (Fiorina and Abrams, 2008). The F statistic captures well this notion, because it divides the variance across groups by the within-group variance. As the opinions of legislators affiliated with each ideological bloc become more homogeneous (and thus within-group variance decreases), while differences among ideological blocs increase, the size of the F statistic should increase accordingly.

TABLE 3.2 Brazilian legislators' mean positions on economic and cultural issues, by ideological bloc, and left-right differences

	Left	Center	Right	Left-Right Diff.	F statistic
Drug decriminalization	4.58	6.47	7.69	3.11	**17.31**
Gay Marriage	2.89	4.71	5.92	3.03	**13.59**
Abortion	4.86	8.24	7.81	2.95	**16.82**
Public services provision	3.47	5.82	6.40	2.93	**16.33**
Market economy	4.19	6.59	6.67	2.48	**11.59**
Death Penalty	2.25	4.29	4.06	1.81	**5.84**
Higher education	4.43	4.71	5.75	1.32	**3.81**
Social security	4.39	5.24	5.60	1.21	3.06
Health policy	2.61	2.35	3.63	1.02	**5.33**
State redistribution	4.79	4.78	5.35	0.57	0.46

Source: PELA 2019 Brazil survey.

Note: Statistically significant F tests are in bold.

As seen in the table, cultural issues pertaining to the liberal conservative divide are the issues that most clearly divide left and right in Brazil. Mean differences in the responses of left-wing and right-wing legislators to the PELA questions on abortion, drug decriminalization and gay marriage are substantially larger than the mean differences estimated for economic and social policy issues. When we utilize the proxy measure of polarization (F statistic), we find that drug decriminalization, abortion and public services provision are the most divisive issues. We also find substantial differences between left and right in what concerns the scope of state intervention (market economy).

Overall, Table 3.2 indicates that the differences between left and right are rather small in what concerns social policies and redistribution. Ideology is more strongly correlated with policy positions regarding preferences for state control over the economy and state provision of public services.

To evaluate differences of opinion between the PRR and the mainstream right, I created a dummy variable to separate PRR deputies from the rest. One difficulty involved in the classification of PRR deputies is that partisan labels alone are insufficient to distinguish deputies aligned with radical right agendas from the rest of the political right. While parties are typically the primary entities articulating the PRR ideology in Western Europe, in Brazil and elsewhere in Latin America, far-right populist alternatives have emerged as loose electoral coalitions organized around charismatic presidential candidates (Gamboa, 2019; Rennó, 2020). Thus, identification with far-right leaders tend to constitute an important element in the construction of the mainstream right/PRR divide in national legislatures. Indeed, throughout his term president Jair Bolsonaro counted on a loyal following beyond his own party, the PSL (Social Liberal Party). Some of the most controversial measures sponsored by the president and his closest allies had the support of legislators scattered around various other right-wing parties, including Podemos, Novo and PP (Progressive Party).[7]

I define the PRR bloc in Congress as being comprised of two groups: deputies affiliated with Bolsonaro's party and deputies affiliated with other right-wing parties that strongly identified with the president. To distinguish *Bolsonarista* deputies not affiliated with the PSL from other right-wing legislators, I utilized a question on deputies' evaluation of Bolsonaro as a political leader. Note that the question demanded that respondents evaluate the president's personal leadership, and not his performance in government. The scale ranges from 1 (terrible) to 10 (excellent). I defined as right-wing Bolsonaristas the deputies that, in addition to being affiliated with a right-wing party, attributed to Bolsonaro either of the two highest values in the 10-point scale utilized to evaluate political leaders. As expected, most of Bolsonarista deputies according to this definition were affiliated with the president's party (8 out of 21). To evaluate whether identification with the president is indeed associated with ideological and policy preferences, I ran a set of tests to compare Bolsonaristas with the rest of the political right. I found that Bolsonarista deputies are more ideologically extreme and adopt substantially more conservative positions on cultural issues than the rest of the right-wing cohort. This suggests that deputies' evaluation of Bolsonaro's leadership provides a good proxy for identification with the president's ideas and agendas.

The PRR delegation was defined by summing the PSL cohort in the lower chamber with the Bolsonarista delegation affiliated to right-wing parties other than the PSL. Using these procedures, I obtained a total of 24 PRR deputies and 28 mainstream right legislators.

Table 3.3 evaluates differences in policy positions between PRR and mainstream right legislators.

As seen in the table, the only relevant differences between the two strands of the Brazilian right are found on cultural issues: abortion, death penalty and drug decriminalization. PRR deputies are significantly more culturally conservative than their mainstream right counterparts (the question on gay marriage is the only exception to this pattern). Issues related to the role of the state in the economy, redistribution and social policy do not distinguish clearly between the PRR and the mainstream right.

One important limitation of the descriptive analyses presented so far is that they only explore bivariate relationships between ideology and various issue dimensions. Moreover, because legislators' positions across issues tend to be correlated, analyzing separate means for each survey question does not allow one to deal with the potential dimensions formed by different types of issues.

TABLE 3.3 Mean positions of PRR and mainstream right-wing legislators on economic and cultural issues, and mean differences by issue

	Populist Rad. Right	*Mainstream right*	*Difference*
Drug decriminalization	9.00	6.57	**2.43**
Death penalty	5.17	3.11	**2.06**
Abortion	8.75	7.00	**1.75**
Market economy	7.21	6.21	0.99
Social security	5.13	6.01	0.88
Redistribution	4.91	5.73	0.82
Health policy	3.38	3.86	0.48
Higher education	5.55	5.91	0.36
Gay Marriage	6.08	5.79	0.30
Public services provision	6.42	6.39	0.02
Observations	24	28	

Source: PELA 2019 Brazil survey. Author's elaboration.

Note: Statiscally significant differences are in bold.

TABLE 3.4 Factor analysis of legislators' positions on cultural and economic issues

	Dimension 1	*Dimension 2*
Public services provision	0.50	0.40
Market economy	0.55	0.38
Redistribution	0.70	0.08
Social Security	**0.78**	0.06
Health	**0.82**	0.12
Abortion	0.06	**0.84**
Gay marriage	0.15	**0.45**
Drug decriminalization	0.12	**0.76**
Death penalty	0.04	0.32
Higher education	**0.86**	0.13
Eigenvalue	4.05	1.82
Variance explained	0.31	0.19
% total variance	0.61	0.38

Source: PELA 2019 Brazil survey. Author's elaboration.

Note: Three largest factor loadings in each dimension are in bold.

I relied on factor analysis to reduce the ten survey questions utilized in the descriptive analyses to a smaller number of dimensions. I found that over 80% of the variation on the data is explained by two dimensions. Factor loadings for each dimension are reported in Table 3.4. I opted for varimax rotation, which seeks to maximize the differences among dimensions, by obtaining factors that are orthogonal.[8]

Dimension 1 loads highly on social security, health, higher education and redistribution. Dimension 2 correlates strongly with legislators' positions on abortion and drug decriminalization, and, to a lower extent, with gay marriage. Overall, dimension 2 fits rather well the notion of a liberal-conservative dimension that opposes traditional and religious values to secularism and post-material values. For its part, dimension 1, which explains most of the variance in the data, taps on the left-right economic divide.

I relied on factor scores obtained for each dimension to create measures of economic liberalism and cultural conservatism. Raw scores were normalized to create measures varying between 1 and 10. I then used the economic liberalism and cultural conservatism scores as dependent variables in multivariate regression models in which the main explanatory factors are the party categories presented earlier (left, center, PRR and mainstream right). Left-wing legislators were set as the reference category.

I rely on standard linear regressions to evaluate how important is party ideology and party family to "predict" legislators' positions on cultural and economic dimensions, in the presence of appropriate controls. Since legislators' positions on distinct issues may reflect their connections to specific constituencies and social groups, regardless of party affiliation, I include controls for the support of unions, business organizations and churches. These measures were created by utilizing a battery of questions on the importance of the support of social groups for the legislators' election. In all cases (unions, business organizations and churches), a scale ranging from 1 to 4 was utilized to measure the importance of obtaining support from each particular group.

Business lobbies in the Brazilian Congress have tended to align with the defense of orthodox economic policies and liberalizing reforms. Thus, I expect deputies that counted on the support of business organizations during their electoral campaigns to be more willing to adopt neoliberal agendas. Support from unions and peak labor organizations should push legislators' preferences in the opposite direction, leading to greater willingness to advocate market regulation and state intervention. Finally, support from churches is likely to increase the saliency of cultural issues.

In Brazil, evangelical churches are extremely active in electoral politics and the reliance on church organizations during the electoral campaign is much more common among evangelical candidates, and especially so among those evangelical candidates affiliated with Pentecostal denominations (Reich and dos Santos, 2013). Since the evangelical clergy has embraced an ultraconservative reaction against progressive agendas on LGBT and reproductive rights, I expect support from the church to be correlated with right-wing positions on the cultural conservatism scale.

TABLE 3.5 Regressions for economic liberalism and cultural conservatism

	Economic liberalism		Cultural conservatism	
	B	SD	B	SD
Intercept	***4.19	0.88	***3.38	0.67
Center	−0.42	0.72	***2.65	0.54
Pop. Rad. Right	−0.18	0.68	***3.88	0.52
Mainstream Right	0.72	0.64	***1.47	0.48
Evangelical	0.40	0.70	***1.42	0.53
Group supp.: Church	0.16	0.25	*0.35	0.19
Group supp.: Unions	***−0.79	0.27	−0.33	0.20
Group supp.: Business	*0.56	0.29	0.07	0.22
N		93		93
R2		0.11		0.52

Source: PELA 2019 Brazil survey. Author's elaboration.

Notes: *** $p<0.01$, ** $p<0.05$, * $p<0.10$.

As an additional control for the effects of religion and church politicking, I include a dummy for deputies who identified themselves as evangelicals. Again, the theoretical expectation is that evangelical legislators will be more conservative than nonevangelical legislators, all else being equal.

Regression models are reported on Table 3.5.

As shown in Table 3.5, the model for the economic left-right divide has a low R^2 (0.11) and the effects of the main explanatory variables are small and lack statistical significance. The second model, which utilizes the cultural conservatism score, has an R^2 of 0.52 and all the dummies for party ideology/ party family exhibit positive and statistically significant coefficients. Populist radical right legislators are substantially more conservative than the reference category (leftist legislators). The effects for the mainstream right and center dummies are similarly positive, albeit smaller than those estimated for PRR legislators.

Model 1 returned a strong negative effect for union support and a positive effect of business support on the economic left-right dimension, as expected. However, none of the other covariates seem to have a relevant effect on this dimension. When the controls for business and union support are excluded from the model, the dummy for mainstream right-wing legislators returns a positive and statistically significant coefficient, but no relevant effect is found for the PRR dummy. Moreover, this alternative model explains very little of the total variance ($R^2=0.02$).

Overall, model results reinforce the descriptive findings of this chapter. There are larger differences between left and right in the cultural dimension than in the economic dimension. Moreover, the PRR and the mainstream right differ clearly in what concerns the cultural dimension, whereas no such differences seem to exist in the economic left-right divide.

3.5 Conclusion

This chapter explored the main policy differences between left and right in Brazil, following the emergence of the far-right. While previous research on Latin American party systems has argued that the state-market divide continues to structure party system competition throughout the region to a large extent (Martínez-Gallardo et al., 2023), the Brazilian case indicates that cultural issues are the ones that distinguish most clearly between left and right. To a large extent, elite polarization on issues such as abortion and drug decriminalization reflects the rise of populist radical right (PRR) forces. Indeed, PRR deputies stand out among right-wing parliamentarians due to their ultraconservative positions on the cultural dimension. Similarly to Western European cases, Brazil's far-right has emphasized cultural as opposed to economic issues. This likely explains why far-right deputies' positions on the economic left-right divide do not differ significantly from mainstream right parliamentarians' preferences.

This is not to say that the PRR and the mainstream right will necessarily adopt similar positions on social policies. The strong preferences of the PRR for the maintenance (or restoration) of traditional values and social hierarchies is likely to shape social policy-making to a substantial extent. For instance, policies that seek to empower minority groups and expand their rights tend to be reformed or replaced by alternative social programs that are more consistent with the radical right's traditional worldview.

It is noteworthy that the overall differences between left and right on social policy and redistribution are rather small. The distribution of responses to the 2019 PELA survey indicates that most Brazilian deputies, regardless of their ideological positions, tend to be in favor of state provision of health services. There is less support for state involvement in the provision of social security and higher education, but, still, the typical right-wing deputy places himself in the middle of the scale on these issues. Income redistribution is the least divisive of the ten issues analyzed in this chapter: the mean difference between left and right is equal to 0.46 and lacks statistical significance.

Within the left-right economic dimension, the economic roles of the state as well as the mix of public and private provision of public services are issues that most clearly distinguish the right from the left. Right-wing deputies are more likely to support the privatization of state-owned companies and the provision of public services by NGOs and private firms. It seems, therefore, that right-wing parliamentarians and their parties are in favor of a smaller and more flexible state that leaves greater room for markets and private providers, at the same time they are mostly supportive of redistribution and state funded and administered social services.

These results are not too surprising considering the electoral constraints faced by conservative parties in highly unequal societies. Since the median voter in Brazil's unequal democracy is a low-income individual that would be better off with extensive redistribution and massive state provision of social services, advocating welfare retrenchment is hardly a wining strategy from the point of view of vote-seeking politicians. Such electoral constraints tend to be even stronger for parties that ambition the presidency, because presidential candidates must necessarily win the vote of a broad national constituency to get elected. It is noteworthy that the cap on public expenditures approved in 2016 and which severely restrained social policy expenditures was proposed and approved during an interim government that was not elected by the popular vote. President Michel Temer (2016–2018) made clear in various public statements that he did not intend to dispute the 2018 presidential election. Thus, because Temer was not concerned with gaining an additional term, he did not refrain from moving ahead with unpopular reforms that contributed to his record low levels of popularity.

For his part, far-right populist Jair Bolsonaro sought to de-emphasize economic issues during his electoral campaign in 2018, focusing instead on corruption, public security and moral issues. By the end of his term, as it became clear that his re-election bid was under threat due to Lula's strong showing in the polls, Bolsonaro and his economic advisers opted for dismantling the expenditure cap put in place by Temer, rapidly expanding income transfer expenditures during the election year. This is yet more evidence of the ambiguous (or inconsistent) policy positions of the far-right regarding economic and social policy issues.

In the following chapters, these aspects are further explored through the in-depth analyses of social policy stability and changes during the Temer (2016–2018) and Bolsonaro (2019–2022) governments.

Notes

1 The PFL went through rebranding in 2007 to become the Democrats (DEM). The PDS experienced a series of fusions with other right-wing parties before it adopted its current name in 2003: Progressive Party (PP). Throughout the article, I use the original names followed by the most recent denominations to refer to these two parties (e.g., PFL/DEM).
2 First I calculated an average of party's ideology score on all available sources for each election year. Then I utilized these average scores to calculate parties' mean ideological position for the whole period for which there existed available data. For the oldest and largest parties, there existed ideological ratings since the 1990s. In other instances, the data covers a much shorter time span ranging from the early 2010s to 2018.
3 The PRB was founded by the Universal Church of the Kingdom of God in 2006 to serve as an electoral vehicle to church-sponsored candidates.
4 https://theintercept.com/series/mensagens-lava-jato/.

5 After being imprisoned in April 2018, Lula lost his political rights and could not run for president although he was ahead in the polls at the time. Thus, it is likely the case that his controversial conviction and imprisonment ended up benefiting extreme-right populist Jair Bolsonaro. Lula's condemnanetions were annulled by the Supreme Court on April 2021.

6 The original PELA survey questions are coded as ROES1, ROES2 and ROES3.

7 For instance, several legislators affiliated to Novo and Podemos voted in favor of constitutional amendment 135/2021, which stated that electronic ballots utilized in Brazil should provide each individual voter with a printed confirmation of their vote. This amendment was part of Bolsonaro's campaign to undermine the credibility of the electoral process and allow for a parallel vote count during the 2022 election, thus constituting a clear example of the illiberal and anti-system agenda of the far-right.

8 This is justified because when I utilize oblimin rotation, I find that the correlation among the dimensions is low (r = 0.29).

Bibliography

ALCÁNTARA, M. & RIVAS, C. 2007. Las dimensiones de la polarización partidista en América Latina. *Política y gobierno,* 14(2), 349–390.

ALMEIDA, R. D. 2019. Bolsonaro presidente: conservadorismo, evangelismo e a crise brasileira. *Novos estudos CEBRAP,* 38, 185–213.

BAKER, A. & GREENE, K. F. 2011. The Latin American left's mandate: free-market policies and issue voting in new democracies. *World Politics,* 63, 43–77.

BOAS, T. C. 2020. The Electoral Representation of Evangelicals in Latin America. *In: Oxford Research Encyclopedia of Politics.* Oxford, Oxford University Press, pp. 1–26.

BOBBIO, N. 1996. *Left and right: The significance of a political distinction,* Chicago, IL, University of Chicago Press.

BOHN, S. R. 2004. Evangélicos no Brasil: perfil socioeconômico, afinidades ideológicas e determinantes do comportamento eleitoral. *Opinião Pública,* 10, 288–338.

BORGES, A. 2011. The political consequences of center-led redistribution in Brazilian federalism: The fall of subnational party machines. *Latin American Research Review*, 46(3), 21–45.

BORGES, A. 2021. The Illusion of Electoral Stability: from party system erosion to right-wing populism in Brazil. *Journal of Politics in Latin America,* 13, 161–191.

BORGES, A., LLOYD, R. & VOMMARO, G. *The Recasting of the Latin American Right: Polarization and conservative reactions.* Cambridge University Press, forthcoming.

BOWEN, J. D. 2011. The Right in "New Left" Latin America. *Journal of Politics in Latin America,* 3, 99–124.

BOWEN, J. D. 2014. The Right and Nonparty Forms of Representation and Participation. *In:* LUNA, J. P. & KALTWASSER, C. R. (eds.) *The resilience of the Latin American right.* JHU Press, pp. 94–116.

CANNON, B. 2016. *The Right in Latin America: Elite power, hegemony and the struggle for the state,* New York, NY, Routledge.

DIAS, T., VON BÜLOW, M. & GOBBI, D. 2021. Populist framing mechanisms and the rise of right-wing activism in Brazil. *Latin American Politics and Society*, 63(3), 1–24.

EATON, K. 2011. Conservative autonomy movements: territorial dimensions of ideological conflict in Bolivia and Ecuador. *Comparative Politics,* 43, 291–310.

FERREIRA, D. P. 2002. *PFL x PMDB: marchas e contramarchas (1982–2000).* Goiânia, Editora Alternativa.

FIORINA, M. P. & ABRAMS, S. J. 2008. Political polarization in the American public. *Annual Review of Political Science,* 11, 563–588.

GAMBOA, L. 2019. El reajuste de la derecha colombiana. El éxito electoral del uribismo. *Colombia Internacional* (99), 187–214.

GIRAUDY, M. E. 2015. *Conservative popular appeals: The electoral strategies of Latin America's right parties.* Berkeley, CA, UC Berkeley.

KALTWASSER, C. R. 2014. La derecha en América Latina y su lucha contra la adversidad. *Nueva Sociedad,* 254, 34–45.

KALTWASSER, C. R. 2019. La (sobre) adaptación programática de la derecha chilena y la irrupción de la derecha populista radical. *Colombia Internacional,* 99, 29–61.

KALTWASSER, C. R. 2020. El error de diagnóstico de la derecha chilena y la encrucijada actual. *Estudios Públicos,* 158, 31–59.

KERSTENETZKY, C. L. 2006. Políticas Sociais: focalização ou universalização? *Brazilian Journal of Political Economy,* 26, 564–574.

LEVITSKY, S. & ROBERTS, K. M. 2011. *The resurgence of the Latin American left.* Baltimore, MD, JHU Press.

LUNA, J. P. 2010. Segmented party-voter linkages in Latin America: the case of the UDI. *Journal of Latin American Studies,* 42(2), 325–356.

LUNA, J. P. & KALTWASSER, C. R. 2014a. Introduction. *In:* LUNA, J. P. & KALTWASSER, C. R. (eds.) *The resilience of the Latin American right.* Baltimore, JHU Press, 1–24.

LUNA, J. P. & KALTWASSER, C. R. 2014b. *The resilience of the Latin American right.* Baltimore, JHU Press.

LUNA, J. P. & ROVIRA KALTWASSER, C. 2021. Castigo a los oficialismos y ciclo político de derecha en América Latina. *Revista Uruguaya de Ciencia Política,* 30, 135–156.

MAINWARING, S., MENEGUELLO, R. & POWER, T. J. 2000. *Partidos conservadores no Brasil contemporâneo: quais são, o que defemdem, quais são suas bases.* Rio de Janeiro, Paz e Terra.

MARTÍNEZ-GALLARDO, C., CERDA, N. D. L., HARTLYN, J., HOOGHE, L., MARKS, G. & BAKKER, R. 2023. Revisiting party system structuration in Latin America and Europe: Economic and socio-cultural dimensions. *Party Politics,* 29, 780–792.

MCADAMS, E. S. & LANCE, J. E. 2013. Religion's impact on the divergent political attitudes of Evangelical Protestants in the United States and Brazil. *Politics and Religion,* 6, 483–511.

MONTERO, A. 2014. Brazil: Explaining the Rise and Decline of Conservatives. *In*: LUNA, J. P. & KALTWASSER, C. R. (eds.) *The Resilience of the Latin American Right.* Baltimore, JHU Press, pp. 294–318.

POWER, T. 2018. The Contrasting Trajectories of Brazil's Two Authoritarian Sucessor Parties. *In:* LOXTON, J. & MAINWARING, S. (eds.) *Life after dictatorship: authoritarian successor parties worldwide.* Cambridge, United Kingdom; New York, NY, Cambridge University Press, pp. 229–254.

POWER, T. J. 2000. *Political right in postauthoritarian Brazil: elites, institutions, and democratization,* University Park, Penn State Press.

QUADROS, M. P. R. & MADEIRA, R. M. 2018. Fim da direita envergonhada? Atuação da bancada evangélica e da bancada da bala e os caminhos da representação do conservadorismo no Brasil. *Opinião Pública,* 24, 486–522.

REICH, G. & DOS SANTOS, P. 2013. The rise (and frequent fall) of Evangelical politicians: organization, theology, and church politics. *Latin American Politics and Society,* 55, 1–22.

RENNÓ, L. 2020. The Bolsonaro Voter: Issue Positions and Vote Choice in the 2018 Brazilian Presidential Elections. *Latin American Politics and Society,* 62, 1–23.

RENNÓ, L. 2022. Bolsonarismo e as eleições de 2022. *Estudos Avançados,* 36, 147–163.

RIBEIRO, R. L. M. 2014. Decadência longe do poder: refundação e crise do PFL. *Revista de Sociologia e política,* 22(49), 5–37.

ROBERTS, K. M. 2014a. *Changing Course in Latin America.* New York, NY, Cambridge University Press.

ROBERTS, K. M. 2014b. Democracy, free markets and the rightist dilemma. *In:* LUNA, J. P. & KALTWASSER, C. R. (eds.) *The resilience of the Latin American right.* Baltimore, MD, JHU Press.

ROCHA, C. 2021. *Menos Marx, mais Mises: o liberalismo e a nova direita no Brasil.* São Paulo, Todavia.

RODRIGUES, G. A. & FUKS, M. 2015. Grupos sociais e preferência política: o voto evangélico no Brasil. *Revista Brasileira de Ciências Sociais,* 30, 115–128.

RÖTH, L., AFONSO, A. & SPIES, D. C. 2018. The impact of populist radical right parties on socio-economic policies. *European Political Science Review,* 10, 325–350.

ROVNY, J. 2013. Where do radical right parties stand? Position blurring in multidimensional competition. *European Political Science Review,* 5, 1–26.

ROVNY, J. & POLK, J. 2020. Still blurry? Economic salience, position and voting for radical right parties in Western Europe. *European Journal of Political Research,* 59, 248–268.

SAMUELS, D. & ZUCCO JR, C. 2016. Party-Building in Brazil. *In:* LEVITSKY, S., LOXTON, J., VAN DYCK, B. & DOMÍNGUEZ, J. I. (eds.) *Challenges of party-building in Latin America.* New York, Cambridge University Press, pp. 331–355.

SMITH, A. E. 2019. *Religion and brazilian democracy: Mobilizing the people of God.* Cambridge, Cambridge University Press.

TANSCHEIT, T. & ZANOTTI, L. 2023. A ascensão da ultradireita na América Latina: Brasil e Chile em perspectiva comparada. *In:* BORGES, A. & VIDIGAL, R. (eds.) *Para Entender a Nova Direita Brasileira: Polarização, populismo e antipetismo.* Porto Alegre, Editora Zouk, pp. 361–392.

TATAGIBA, L. 2018. Entre as ruas e as instituições: Os protestos eo impeachment de Dilma Rousseff. *Lusotopie,* 17, 112–135.

THACHIL, T. 2014. Elite parties and poor voters: Theory and evidence from India. *American Political Science Review,* 108(2), 454–477.

VILLAZÓN, J. C. 2014. Viejas y nuevas derechas religiosas en América Latina: los evangélicos como factor político. *Nueva Sociedad,* 254, 112–123.

WIESEHOMEIER, N. & DOYLE, D. 2013. Discontent and the left turn in Latin America. *Political Science Research and Methods,* 1, 201.

WIESEHOMEIER, N. & DOYLE, D. 2014. Profiling the electorate: Ideology and attitudes of Rightwing voters. *In*: LUNA, J. P. & KALTWASSER, C. R. (eds.) *The resilience of the Latin American right.* JHU Press, pp. 48–74.

WIESEHOMEIER, N. 2010. The Meaning of Left-Right in Latin America: A Comparative View *Kellogg Working Paper* 370.

ZANOTTI, L. & ROBERTS, K. M. 2021. (Aún) la excepción y no la regla: La derecha populista radical en América Latina. *Revista Uruguaya de Ciencia Política,* 30, 23–48.

ZUCCO, C. 2008. The President's 'New' Constituency: Lula and the Pragmatic Vote in Brazil's 2006 presidential elections. *Journal of Latin American Studies,* 40, 29–49.

ZUCCO JR, C. & Power, T. J. 2021. Fragmentation without cleavages? Endogenous fractionalization in the Brazilian party system. *Comparative Politics* 53(3), 477–500.

4

THE POLITICAL ECONOMY OF THE BRAZILIAN ECONOMIC CRISIS (2014–2022)

Economic policy, ideas and the limits of neoliberal austerity measures

Alexandre Queiroz Guimarães and
Marco Flávio da Cunha Resende

4.1 Introduction

This chapter deals with the factors behind economic policy and economic adjustment adopted in Brazil from the 2015s. It intends to understand the political and economic elements behind the decision to limit public expenditure and adopt neoliberal measures such as labor and pension reforms. In order to accomplish that, the focus is mainly on economic policy under the Workers Party (PT) governments from 2003 to 2016, intending to understand the economic policy main lines and also the factors which led to the serious economic crisis of 2015 and 2016, essential to understand the ascendance of the right and the economic policy directions which followed.

Policies are in large part influenced by political variables and interests, mediated by national institutions. Some groups are more influent and have privileged channels of access into state apparatus (Hall, 1986). Economic policy involves much more than technical decisions; they are influenced by ideas which, also politically induced, provide an interpretation and a path to tackle the main challenges (Blyth, 2002).

However, the policies' economic results also tend to be very important, given the impact on government's political support and chances to achieve their objectives. Economic performance affects employment, an important way how people obtain incomes and access to subsistence. Although the improvement of social conditions is not possible without the appropriate social policies, it is also hard to achieve it in a context of negative economic performance. Thus, it is also

DOI: 10.4324/9781003487777-5

necessary to understand the elements which affect economic performance, given its relevance to economic policy decisions.

Constraints to economic policy increased with the changes which marked the new phase of capitalism initiated in the 1970s. The consolidation and growth of an international private financial market, marked by the instantaneous flows of short-term capital among national borders, significantly constrained national governments autonomy. The risks of massive outflows of capital, provoking instability, made national governments very concerned to inflation control and, consequently, to public expenditure and monetary supply.

Another important point is the form how Brazil defeated a very high and resilient inflation, leading, from 1999, to a model of economic policy marked by inflation target regime (IT), primary budget surplus target and floating exchange rate regime. According to mainstream literature, IT is considered a superior framework of monetary policy, having positive impacts on inflationary expectations. Government sound finance is also seen as central for macroeconomic stability, while flexible exchange rate regimes improve the management of balance of payments transactions and enable foreign reserves accumulation (French-Davis, 2003; Flassbeck, 2018; Arestis and Sawyer, 2008). This regime, nevertheless, significantly mitigated the economic policy degrees of freedom.

The point defended in this chapter is that economic policy, although very influenced by interests and ideas, has also an economic rationality, critical for the chances of success. Thus, the macroeconomic policies adopted in Brazil are analyzed in order to point out their merits and errors, as well as to highlight the alternatives that would be possible in the face of the aforementioned macroeconomic constraints. The objective is to do it in a very didactic way, attempting to show to those which do not have a background in economics why certain directions of economic policy need to be respected. By making clear the relevant economic issues, the chapter also aims to highlight the political issues which tend to be "hiden" behind certain economic policy proposals.

The chapter is organized as follows. The second and third sections provide brief historical interpretations of facts related to changes in capitalism and to past Brazilian trajectories which help to situate and understand the context which marked the Workers Party (PT) governments and the period in analysis. Section four deals with the economic policy's main decisions under the two Lula's governments (2003–2010). Sections five and six deal with Rousseff's two mandates, focusing on the direction followed by economic policy and on the main consequences. Section seven deals with the two right-wing governments which followed Rousseff and to the evolution and limits of neoliberal policies. Finally, section eight highlights the chapter's main conclusions and several points which need to be observed by the present Lula government (2023–2026).

4.2 The golden age, economic deceleration and rise of neoliberalism

The post-war period (1947–73) was the golden age of capitalism, marked, particularly in developed countries, by substantial rates of economic growth and improvement in social conditions. Citizens obtained civil, social and political rights, in a process also characterized by the consolidation and strengthening of democracy. The period was also marked by the improvement and diversification of consumption patterns, increasing access to education and improvement in health services and life expectancy (Judt, 2007).

Those results were only possible due to the extraordinary performance of the economy. Economic and industrial growth was substantial and continuous for more than two decades; international trade significantly expanded. Investment expanded at very high rates, a result of the emergence of new sectors and the opportunities to conquer new consumers. Growth was also pushed by the substantial increases in productivity, a consequence of fordism dissemination, new forms of productive organization and the transfer of workers from agriculture to industry. In addition, the Welfare State expansion, Keynesian policies and wage increases strengthened demand, consolidating a virtuous cycle, while financial regulation reduced the risks of bubbles and crises.

Another important component was the international dimension. The Bretton Woods Agreement, firmed in 1944, provided a new exchange rate regime and rules for capital flows control, while the creation of the General Agreement for Trade and Tariffs substantially stimulated international trade. The new fix exchange rate regime provided stability, without reducing governments autonomy in the pursuit of national objectives, which was also favored by the strict regulation over short-term capital flows. As a result, international integration was mainly based on productive investments (Frieden, 2008).

Prosperity lasted for two and a half decades (Judt, 2007). It was interrupted, nevertheless, in the 1970s, a decade marked by a deep economic crisis and profound transformation in capitalism trajectory. The factors behind deceleration and crisis were in large part inherent to capitalism. The sectors which had led the expansion lost vigor, once a significant part of the demand had been fulfilled. In addition, productivity increases decelerated. Thirdly, full employment and wage increases compressed profit margins, also affected by strengthening in international competition (Judt, 2007).

The crisis was also very influenced by international events. The United States' incapacity to keep the convertibility between the dollar and gold and the abandon of the exchange rate regime had deep impacts. In that moment, economic deceleration was responded to with expansionist monetary policies, followed by exchange rate devaluation. It was in that context, marked by high international liquidity, that the first oil shock took place in 1973, throwing developed countries into a deep recession (Gamble, 1988).

Another key factor was the constitution of an unregulated international financial market, also influenced by the excess of dollars in the international economy. This created the opportunity for international banks to supply credit in dollars for enterprises and governments, which was only possible through changes in regulation, motivated by the high profit opportunities. As a consequence, operations in dollars through national borders marked a rupture with the previous mechanisms of regulation and control. Later, further deregulation was promoted by the U.S. government, motivated also by the opportunities of capital accumulation in the financial sector.

The consequence was the emergence of an unregulated international financial market, able to move considerable amount of resources among national borders.[1] This put substantial constraints on governments' capacity to pursue domestic objectives, since countries with balance of payments problems and inflationary pressures tended to suffer massive outflows of capital and instability. As a consequence, control of inflation became the key economic objective, in contrast to the low unemployment rates pursued in the anterior decades. Those changes also had very significant impacts on developing countries and on the macroeconomic regimes adopted.

The 1970s were so marked by a new phenomenon, the combination of economic deceleration, unemployment and inflation. Inflation was nurtured by both expansive monetary policies and the fiscal deficits produced by economic deceleration, since tax became unable to finance the high social expenditure which marked the new social contract.

The impacts were more serious in the face of previous prosperity, provoking disillusion and skepticism (Judt, 2007). Strikes and demonstrations skyrocketed, increasing political instability. The governments, nevertheless, did not know how to react; previous economic policies were impotent to deal with the new challenges. It was in this context that neoliberalism gained force, offering a new interpretation and a political package to deal with economic problems.

Neoliberal ideas had lost relevance in the post-war period, but they never completely disappeared (Gamble, 1988). From the 1960s, business unsatisfaction with the post-war arrangement increased, resulting in the strengthening of political action. Billions of dollars were channeled into think tanks and universities in order to produce new interpretations and theories able to provide alternatives to the post-war consensus (Blyth, 2002).

Neoliberalism found its ideas and pillars in a different set of theories. The first one was monetarism, which emphasized the negative effects of inflation, responsible for creating uncertainty and deteriorating savings, investments and entrepreneurship. Its main prescription was a controlled and predictable monetary policy.

The second pillar was *supply-side economics*. According to this theory, high tax and excess of regulation damaged savings, investment and productivity, resulting in stagnation and unemployment. The reduction in tax, by increasing real wages and profits expectations, would stimulate both labor supply and investments. The third economic pillar was rational expectations, which argues that economic agents are not deceived by economic policy, making some policies not only wasteful, but also ineffective (Blyth, 2002).

Economic interpretation was complemented by a theory about the state and the policy-making policies. According to Public Choice Theory, public agents were not disinterested actors, but selfish actors aimed at increasing their chances of promotion and re-election. Thus, they are not necessarily concerned with promoting the public good. Consequently, policies tend to favor interest groups which have more resources and privileged forms of access into the state apparatus. Thus, state intervention is criticized in moral terms, followed by the defense of the insulation of organs and agencies from politicians and bureaucrats (Gamble, 1988).[2]

Thus, neoliberalism found in those theories a new path to tackle economic problems, defending the retreat in state intervention. The main prescription was to contain inflation, reduce tax and transaction costs, guarantee private property and provide the conditions to stimulate savings, investment and business in general. Those ideas, it is important to emphasize, supplied a group of politicians with a political program which allowed them do dispute and win elections.

In the United Kingdom, Margareth Thatcher embraced this narrative to gain the elections in 1979. Once in power, she promoted a strong monetary control which threw the economy into a deep recession. Inflation decreased, but she became the most unpopular prime minister in national history. Her government, nevertheless, was saved by the expansionist policies adopted in the United States and by the Malvinas (Falkland) Islands War, providing the support to go further with her economic program (Gamble, 1988).

Thatcher also reduced tax and subsidies, privatized state enterprises and retreated the state in several areas. Expenditure was cut in a dogmatic way, causing damages in several sectors. Segments of industry suffered from the reduction of state support and the lack of policies aimed at facing the main challenges.

In addition, labor rights were cut and a strong offensive was centered over trade unions. Deregulation of the labor market resulted in stimulus to business and substantial fall of unemployment, but it was accomplished through the reduction of labor and social rights. The jobs created were mainly part time and for a temporary contract, without social rights. Pension conditions also deteriorated and cuts were made in social assistance. As a consequence, inequality substantially increased. The most vulnerable public, including families with children and handicap persons, single mothers and ethnical minorities were those which most suffered (Kerstenetzky, 2012).

A similar movement took place in the United States, in which a neoliberal narrative supplied a political program which allowed business interests to reach power (Blyth, 2002). Billions of dollars were spent to fund research and interpretations and channeled to more radical politicians which opposed the post-war consensus. Once in power, Ronald Regan adopted policies to contain inflation, reduce tax and state intervention and weaken the trade unions. Billions of dollars were cut from tax over the wealthiest segments, accompanied by billion dollar cuts in welfare policies and pensions. Supply-side ideas were employed to argue that reduction in tax and benefits would stimulate economic recovery, solving the problems which had justified Welfare States creation. The astonishing result was the transfer of hundreds of billions of dollars from the poorest to the wealthiest segments (Blyth, 2002).

As Streeck (2012) concludes, conciliation between democracy and capitalism was a very hard task, achieved in the post-war period due to a very rare confluence of factors. The 1970s and the economic crisis led to a very different scenario. In the effort to create conditions for capital accumulation, neoliberalism adopted a range of measures to weaken the welfare state. Although international constraints increased and the governments lost autonomy in the pursuit of their objectives, national responses widely differed. Neoliberalism, as adopted in the United Kingdom and in the United States, was clearly a political program which promoted substantial changes in the economy at the costs of the trade unions and the most vulnerable groups. The responses in continental Europe and Scandinavia were very different (Guimarães, 2015).

4.3 Brazil: Antecedents – from rapid industrialization to the neoliberal reforms

From 1950 to 1980, a rapid process of import substitution industrialization substantially changed the structure of Brazilian economy. GDP grew 5.72% a year, per capita GDP increased 3.03% a year and productivity substantially expanded (Maddison, 2001). Brazil became an exporter of a range of manufactured goods.

This process, shared by other Latin American countries, was nevertheless also marked by distortions and difficulties. Industry in general became very dependent on state incentives and failed to conquer foreign markets. In addition, macroeconomic unbalances, including inflation and deficits in foreign accounts, impeded a continuous process of economic growth. Thus, changes were necessary to balance the process, but most of them were blocked by interest groups. The state, although a key actor, depended on business support and was not strong enough to induce industrialists to become more competitive and directed to the external market. The process was also marked by increasing inequality, very precarious social policies and serious deficiencies in the educational system.

Despite the domestic deficiencies, the crisis which led to the exhaustion of the development model was in large part internationally induced. The 1970s, as seen, were marked by a deep international economic crisis, amplified by two oil shocks. In that context, Latin America was captured by the wide supply of financial resources at negative interest rates. Macroeconomic adjustments were not adopted and those countries employed cheap international credit to preserve expansionist policies. As a consequence, Latin American imports grew substantially, while foreign debt duplicated between 1976 and 1981, reaching US$ 544 billion (Guimarães and Gambi, 2022).

The problem came when the United States unilaterally changed its monetary policy and substantially increased interest rates. As a consequence, international real interest rates, which in 1977 were negative in 11.2%, achieved 22.1% in 1981, leading many countries to bankruptcy.

The problem was that the foreign debt crisis was also transformed into a fiscal crisis, once policies were adopted to protect private investors from the risks of exchange rate devaluation. Consequently, public finances critically deteriorated, increasing inflation and reducing state capacity to deal with the new challenges. As a consequence, the 1980s was a lost decade in most Latin American countries.

In Brazil, different attempts were adopted, unsuccessfully, to defeat inflation. Stabilization was only achieved when, in the 1990s, the United States promoted a wide program of foreign debt renegotiation.

Debt renegotiation and the supply of financial recourses, nevertheless, were conditioned to the adoption of policies such as the opening of the economy, privatization, a new foreign capital law, changes in labor legislation and financial deregulation. National governments, very indebted, had little capacity to resist. This does not mean that liberal reforms were imposed, once economic problems were huge and there was strong domestic support for measures able to control inflation. Nevertheless, international institutions' influence was substantial in shaping features of the process (Panizza, 2013).

As a result, the measures provided high gains for foreign banks and enterprises, which bought many national enterprises at favourable conditions. The measures, nevertheless, were not consistent enough and failed to provide sustainable conditions for economic development (Panizza, 2013; Guimarães and Gambi, 2022). Since the reforms, Latin American countries have presented low investment rates, very low public investment and a slow path of productivity increase. This happened in strong contrast to other countries, mainly in Asia, which has preserved high investment capacity and high rates of economic growth (Palma, 2011)

The control of inflation in Brazil was a very positive achievement, producing significant social gains and giving the incumbents substantial support. However, the way stabilization was achieved also had negative consequences. The adoption of a narrow crawling band exchange rate system as an anchor, combined with high interest rates to attract foreign capital and contain demand, resulted in problems in the balance of payments and increase in public debt. In addition, overvalued exchange rates led many enterprises to bankruptcy, many of them bought by foreign enterprises. The negative performance of many sectors had impacts on the labor and on social conditions. In addition, financial deregulation brought flows of speculative capital and risks of crisis (Guimarães and Gambi, 2022).

In brief, liberal reforms promised too much and delivered too little, failing to produce sustainable conditions for national development. Economy deteriorated in the second half of the 1990s and poverty significantly increased, reversing the positive effects brough by stabilization. Dissatisfaction with neoliberal reforms is crucial to explain the emergence of center-left governments in many Latin America countries, including the PT in Brazil.

This trajectory is important to understand key questions and directions which marked PT governments. Lula was elected with the promise of tackling deindustrialisation, creating employment, improving social conditions and reverting certain neoliberal reforms. On the other hand, he had to deal with a more open and deregulated economy, which suffered with speculative capital flows destabilising impacts. Lula inherited positive features, such as consolidation of price stabilization, more stable relations with the states' governments and a very favourable external scenario. However, he also inherited negative aspects, such as the substantial increase in domestic debt and very high interest rates.

Thus, Lula faced an institutional and international context which implied substantial constraints and limited the economic policy degrees of liberty. Campello (2015) very well summarizes the constraints which resulted from financial capital volatility. The greater the current account deficits, as happened in Latin American countries, the larger the dependency on the flows of financial capital, pressuring countries to adopt the macroeconomic policies necessary to attract foreign capital. According to Campello (2015), this tends to approximate center-left and center-right governments; only in very favorable international contexts, marked by low international interest rates and boom of commodities, do domestic governments have higher autonomy to promote heterodox policies.

Those constraints help to understand the macroeconomic regime adopted in Brazil by Cardoso and preserved by PT governments, marked, as mentioned, by the combination of inflation target regime (IT), primary budget surplus target and floating exchange rate regime. The preservation of this regime is critical to understanding economic policy in this period.

The next sections investigate the economic policy during PT governments. In order to understand the decisions, it is necessary, firstly, to make some considerations about the impacts of economic policy on investment, a key variable to explain economic performance.

4.4 Economic policy during the two Lula governments (2003–2011)

Investment is marked by a high degree of uncertainty, since its yields cannot be known with certainty at the moment one decides to invest. Consequently, the investment decision is very influenced by expectations and the factors which affect confidence in it. Instability of markets, inflation, economic slowdown and balance of payment crisis tend to negatively impact it.

Agent's expectations for the future are formed upon conventions, beliefs that are shared by economic agents (Keynes, 2013; Aretis et al., 2019). Other agents' opinions are observed in order to conjecture on the economy's path, since the latter is affected by decisions made by the set of economic agents. Thus, conventions are also a tool to coordinate expectations, informing each investor about what others would expect as an outcome of determinate policies (Carvalho, 2014; Fraga and Resende, 2022). Thus, the greater other economic agents' adherence to a given optimistic (pessimist) convention, the greater the confidence in its continuity and the stronger (weaker) the decision to invest, in a self-fulfillling prophecy. In this way, conventions reduce uncertainty and "play a crucial role in shaping private agents' expectations and their decision to invest." It is "a powerful device to induce investment in an uncertainty world" (Resende, 2023, p. 37).

Regarding government finances, a balanced government budget and a stable public debt trajectory tend to produce a favorable convention and stimulate businessmen to go ahead with their investments. By contrast, a public debt trajectory that seems out of control may mitigate investment. Thus, there are two main ways a balanced fiscal policy may influence conventions. Firstly, budget under control indicates higher government capacity to adopt economic policies to boost demand in periods of deceleration, crisis and recession. Secondly, when debt is increasing without control, it signals to economic actors that inflation will grow and tax will increase, thus having negative impacts on investments. Thus, governments should chase a stable debt-to-GDP ratio, the main point being not its level, but the truth in its stability.

The months before Lula's inauguration as president were marked by uncertainty and outflows of capital, explained by PT's previous radical positions regarding economic issues. Thus, a conservative economic policy was first adopted to conquer market confidence. Fiscal surplus target was increased in an attempt to demonstrate commitment to macroeconomic stabilisation. The first years were marked by low economic growth, pushed by exports. From 2005, nevertheless, economic growth significantly expanded, propelled mainly by consumption increase (Guimarães, 2022).

From 2004 to 2010, the Brazilian economy experienced a period of high annual growth rates, 4.5% a year (Figure 4.1), as well as poverty and income

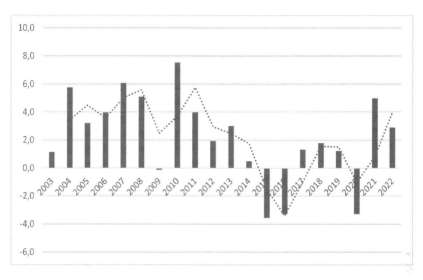

FIGURE 4.1   Brazilian GDP growth, 2003–2022.

Source: Author's elaboration based on Institute of Applied Economic Research (Ipeadata).

inequality reduction. Economic recovery was favoured by the low level of installed industrial capacity utilization and by favorable exports performance, due to strong international demand and the increase in commodity prices. The expansion was led mainly by family's consumption, a result of income transfer policies, minimum wage valorisation and the large increase in the credit-to-GDP ratio, which rose from 25.5 percent of GDP in 2002 to 40.0 percent in 2008 and 49.2 percent in 2012 (Serrano and Summa, 2015; Carvalho, 2018). Private consumption was also fostered by continuous appreciation of the real exchange rate. Although the annual average investment rate was only 17.0 percent of GDP in 2003–2005 years and 18.8 percent over 2006–2010 (Ipeadata, 2023), it did not impede growth, due to the low level of installed industrial capacity utilization.

Fiscal expansion took place from 2005 onwards, prioritizing policies such as increases in the minimum wage, civil servant wages increases and income transfer policies. The period was marked by substantial improvement of social programs. The number of people benefiting from social programs substantially increased, and also the benefits' values. Further, the expansionary fiscal policy was enlarged by the rise in public investment, mainly from 2006 to 2010. There was an increase in central government investment of 27.6 percent in real terms and the general government investment rate (central government plus federal state-owned companies) grew from 2.6 percent of GDP in 2005 to 4.6 percent in 2010 (Carvalho, 2018; Orair and Gobetti, 2017). Tax exemptions also increased and were extended to other sectors. These results were reached without a fiscal

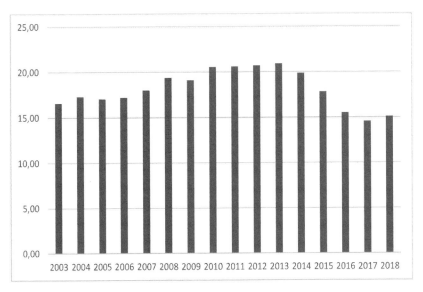

FIGURE 4.2 Gross fixed capital formation in Brazil, 2003–2018 (percent of GDP).

Source: Author's elaboration based on Brazilian Institute of Geography and Statistics (IBGE).

deterioration, since tax revenue kept up with economic growth and the increasing commodity prices (Orair and Gobetti, 2017).

The consolidation of stabilization and other factors, including the abundant international liquidity and, later, the impacts of the international financial crisis, also enabled the reduction in interest rates from 20% in 2003/2004 to 9.83% in 2009. In the face of economic recovery and exhaustion of idle capacity, private investment also recovered and the aggregate investment rate rose from 17.2 percent of GDP in 2006 to 20.5 percent in 2010 (Ipeadata, 2023; Guimarães, 2022 – figure 4.2).

Nonetheless, as highlighted by Resende and Terra (2020), there were contradictions in the mix of the policies adopted. It means that an overvalued real makes imports cheaper, which is positive. But on the other hand makes exports more expensive, and damage them. As a consequence, the continuous appreciation of the real, although helping to mitigate inflation, damaged industrial performance. Thus, after almost ten years of continuous exchange rate appreciation, there was a reprimarization of the Brazil's industrial structure and of the range of manufacturing exports (Rossi and Mello, 2016).

Secondly, the low investment rate impeded aggregate supply to meet demand in the long run, tending to provoke inflationary pressures.[3] Moreover, it mitigated technological progress and productivity gains, which, in turn, are a necessary condition for the rise in real wages without inflationary pressures (Gala, 2008;

Bresser-Pereira et al., 2015). In addition, in a context marked by continuous real exchange rate appreciation, the policies adopted to boost consumption provoked leakage of demand abroad. As a consequence, the current account of the balance of payments ranged from a surplus of US$ 8.9 billion in 2004 to a deficit of US$ 35.6 billion in 2008 (Ipeadata, 2023).

In addition, Brazilian economy was significantly affected by the outbreak of the international financial crisis in 2008. GDP fell in 2009 and, despite a substantial recovery in 2010 – pushed by China's imports and fiscal stimulus – economic growth decelerated in the following years (2011–2014). The main reason was the exhaustion of the factors which had pushed growth in the previous period, in particular the increase in consumption credit, given the very high indebtedness levels. In addition, exports suffered in the less favorable international context. It was thus necessary to strengthen private investment and rise it to another level. Attempts by the following government to do it revealed, nevertheless, a strong failure.

4.5 The first Rousseff government (2011–2014) – economic policy and the road to economic crisis

At the beginning of Rousseff's first term (2011–2014), the external scenery had changed; there was a high level (84.8%) of installed industrial capacity utilization (Ipeadata, 2023) and no more room for rises in credit-to-GDP ratio (Serrano and Summa, 2015). Consequently, the drive for growth would have to shift to investment.

From 2011 to 2014, expansionary fiscal and monetary policies and greater intervention in the foreign exchange market were adopted. Nonetheless, economic policy mistakes were committed, resulting in a pessimistic convention and in disarray in terms of expectations. Investment rates remained stagnant over 2011–2013 and fell from 2014 onwards (Figure 4.2), throwing the economy into a very deep crisis.

The beginning of the term was marked by the reinforcing of orthodoxy in an attempt to gain stability. A primary budget surplus target of 3.1 percent of GDP was fulfilled through a reduction in public investment. Central government and federal state-owned companies investments dropped 17.9 and 7.8 percent (in real terms), respectively, in 2011 (Serrano and Summa, 2015). Further, the central bank increased the base interest rate (Selic) and implemented macroprudential measures for credit control.

However, in the face of the slowdown of economic activity, the policy significantly changed from the end of 2011. At that moment, the economic team elected, as key priorities, to reduce interest rates and devalue exchange rate, intending to promote both investment and exports.

Thus, from September 2011 to October 2012, Selic was reduced from 12.5 percent per year to 7.25 percent, only 1 percent in real terms. In addition, commercial public banks (Banco do Brasil and Caixa Econômica Federal) cut their spreads to force private banks to lower their interest rates[4] (Resende and Terra, 2020). At the same time, measures to contain speculative actions on the foreign currency future and spot markets were adopted. As a result, the Brazilian real depreciated 42 percent between January 2011 and December 2013 (Cagnin et al., 2013).

Those economic policies, nevertheless, did not bring growth, but rather inflation. The economic growth rate dropped, reaching 3.9 percent in 2011 and 1.9 percent in 2012, while the inflation rate reached 6.5 percent in 2011 and 5.84 percent in 2012 (Figures 4.1 and 4.3). The reason is that a lower interest rate is not a sufficient condition to boost investment, since it is critically influenced by aggregate demand and expectations. Demand was weakened by both the restrictive policies adopted in early 2011 and the increase in household debt, which prevented the credit-to-GDP ratio from continuing to grow, while expectations had been negatively influenced by the conflicting signals given by economic policy, restrictive in 2011 and very expansive in 2012 and 2013. This scenario produced a pessimistic convention and private investment did not increase.

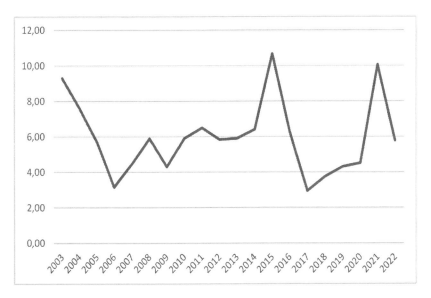

FIGURE 4.3   Inflation rate consumption index (%).

Source: Author's elaboration based on Brazilian Institute of Geography and Statistics (IBGE).

The signals sent by the fiscal policy did not help either. As seen, a contractionary fiscal policy, launched at the end 2010, remained active in 2011, centered on the reduction of public investment. This happened, nevertheless, at the same time that long-term government investment program, the Growth Acceleration Plan (PAC), was supposed to be running, sending contradictory signals (Resende and Terra, 2017). In addition, from 2011 the government gave up the role of public investment as one of growth devices; in the following years, it significantly fell[5] (Carvalho, 2018).

Meanwhile, the government substantially strengthened tax relief and subsidised credit policies. It was expected that the enlargement of profit margins would boost private investment. Some manufacturing sectors (automobile, household appliances, building material, basic basket goods, etc.) gained tax allowances, which were also extended to the taxes on the wage bill (payroll taxes). Those initiatives, initially centered on few sectors, were spread to other sectors following lobby pressures. In addition, a huge plan of subsidised credit was implemented, followed by a plan for concessions in infrastructure and a reduction in electricity tariffs, contributing to deteriorate fiscal accounts. Those initiatives did not follow a strategy, being lobby guided and confusedly implemented, jeopardizing optimistic conventions (Resende and Terra, 2017).

Government's intention was to promote an anti-cyclical policy centered on the private sector as the main investment driver (Orair and Gobetti, 2017; Carvalho, 2018). However, without a perspective of demand growth, Brazilian firms just widened their profit margins and paid or restructured their debts. A much better alternative would have been to reduce tax cuts and subsidised credit and strengthen public investment, which has a higher multiplier effect on the economy and positive impacts on logistic and externalities (Orair and Gobetti, 2017). The problem was aggravated by the government attempts, in the face of a deteriorated fiscal scenery, to hide the problem through creative forms of accounting. Following Arestis et al. (2019, pp.193–194):

(1) fiscal expansion was carried out in a manner that lacked credibility, using devices that inspired mistrust (among them the "creative accounting" or the use of non-recurrent funds, such as selling oil fields, which are State owned by law); (2) the efforts to communicate fiscal policy measures to public opinion were particularly poor and limited to an insistence on announcing unrealistic revenue expansion and primary surplus goals (…).

Inasmuch as government waived tax revenues and beared the cost of subsidised credit policy, in a context marked by lowering revenues due to the economy slowdown, its primary budget surpluses continuously went down. In addition, the Central Bank, due to inflation acceleration, strongly raised the base interest rate (Selic) from mid-2013, resulting in an increase of government debt (Arestis et al., 2019).[6]

Thus, the deterioration of primary fiscal results is explained mainly by the drop in tax revenues due to the slowdown of the economy and the policy of tax exemption and subsidised credit policy. As stated by Orair and Gobetti (2017), this scenario does not corroborate the conventional wisdom that government's fiscal deterioration was due to its spending growing in an irresponsible way.

Due to the failure of fiscal policy in stimulating growth and its harmful effects on government accounts, the anticyclical fiscal policy proposed by Rousseff revealed a huge failure and became under increasing attack from the market agents and other sectors of the society, including the mass media. As a consequence, a convention that fiscal austerity is key for growth was strengthened and the idea of "expansionary fiscal austerity" became predominant (Alesina et al., 2006). The pressure for a huge cut in government spending strengthened and reached its peak at the beginning of 2015.

4.6 Rousseff's second government

The last year of President Rousseff's first term, 2014, was marked by factors and decisions which contributed to explain the deep two-year Brazilian recession in 2015 and 2016: i) lack of fiscal control – government primary results saw their first deficit in 16 years; ii) high inflation level and contractionary monetary policy; iii) sharp drop in commodity prices; iv) the "Operation Carwash" lawsuit, an "anti-corruption" operation which directly affected Brazil's largest corporation, Petrobras (which alone accounted for 8.9 percent of aggregate investment in 2013; see Loural, 2016), and major contractors responsible for building infrastructure investments; and v) political polarization and the emergence of a pessimistic convention, given the drop in confidence index both of businessmen and consumers (Figure 4.4).

After a GDP growth of only 0.5 percent in 2014 and amid pressures to adopt an austere fiscal policy of spending cuts, president Rousseff made a complete turn and brought back a tighter version of the NCM tripod in 2015. A huge short-term fiscal adjustment was implemented, grounded upon the hypothesis that a controlled debt-to-GDP ratio would inspire confidence in the private sector and then, as a (mechanic) consequence, private investment would grow up (Alesina et al., 2006; Reinhardt et al., 2012).

Thus, following the "expansionary fiscal austerity" guidelines, Rousseff's administration announced in January 2015 a drastic adjustment in public accounts of 1.4 percent of GDP based mainly on cuts in government expenditures. At the end of that year, however, the cuts in public expenses were actually less than intended because of Congress resistance, amid the political crisis, in approving

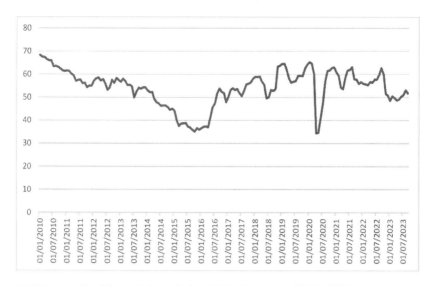

FIGURE 4.4 Confidence index – industrial businessmen, 2010–2023.

Source: Author's elaboration based on National Confederation of Industry (CNI).

some measures. The announcement of a huge cut in government expenditures, coupled with the deep economic slowdown in 2014, produced expectations toward decreases in aggregate demand, reinforced by a further contraction of 36.7% in public investment (Orair and Gobetti, 2017). A pessimistic convention means that actors believe that the situation is not good. As a consequence, they decide cut investment (Resende and Terra, 2017). They were followed by other contractionary measures, including the increase in taxes on financial loans, company financial revenues, manufactured goods and automotive exports; reduction of subsidies for companies; cuts in social benefits (unemployment and sickness insurances, for instance); and dramatic increases in public and administered prices (fuel and electrical energy).

At the same time, the Brazilian currency weakened dramatically, from an average exchange rate of R$ 2.36 per US dollar in 2014 to R$ 3.33 in 2015, very influenced by a robust drop in commodity prices. The exchange rate depreciation, coupled with the increase in administered prices, resulted in high consumer inflation in 2015 (10.67 percent). This triggered the increase in the Selic base rate, which reached 14.25 percent per year in December 2015, further deteriorating the government debt trajectory.

This was too much for expectations and, as stressed, a pessimistic convention became predominant among economic agents, while Brazilian GDP was falling by 3.3 percent and aggregate investment declining by 13.9 percent in real terms

(Figures 4.1 and 4.2). The unemployment rate increased from 4.8 percent in 2014 to 6.8 percent by the end of 2015 (Arestis at al., 2022).

The fiscal consolidation program based on spending cuts revealed a disaster. A much better economic alternative would have been to reorganize accounts by increasing personal income and property taxes and replacing government current spending with public investment. Contractionary fiscal policy, by increasing unemployment, negatively affected consumption, while exports were also negatively affected by the fall of commodity prices. All those factors, combined with political instability and the effects of the "Operation Carwash" lawsuit, led the economy to a very hard recession.

In brief, fiscal adjustment and measures to change expectations were very necessary. But they were wrongly done, guided by a set of ideas centered on "expansionary austerity." As Keynes (2013) had shown almost one century ago, cut of government expenditure in a recession is a bad response, since lower public spending further deteriorates economic activity and demand, failing thus to induce businessmen to increase investments. Meanwhile, as the government's own revenue also falls, the results tend to be the increase in public debt-to-GDP ratio and further deterioration of expectations. This was exactly what happened in Brazil, with the public sector primary deficit achieving 1.88 percent of GDP at the end of 2015, the highest for three decades, and the financial deficit achieving 7.2 percent of GDP. As a consequence, the combination of increase in interest rates, heavy government indebtedness, a solvency crisis in the private sector (households and companies) and the contraction in the credit supply led the economy to a collapse.

Economic crisis was not produced by austerity. It was mainly a result of the badly conceived policies adopted by Rousseff's governments, unable to deal with the negative international context. The key issue in economy is not more or less state intervention, but the way this intervention takes place. Fiscal policy, as argued, was done in the wrong way, since public investment, which has a higher multiplier effect, was cut, while the hundreds of billions of reais transferred to businessmen failed to induce investment. Meanwhile, public debt substantially increased and further depressed expectations, negatively affecting private investment.

However, neoliberal austerity ideas had a role in the response, leading to policies which not only aggravated the recession, but prevented the government from tackling the real issues and contributed to putting the onus on the workers and the most vulnerable segments. This is what in large part neoliberal ideology is about, as originally developed to adjust the welfare states, putting the emphasis on the reduction of wages and other costs to recover the conditions for capital accumulation (see Section two).

4.7 Crisis, fiscal austerity and other steps towards the liberal agenda

On August 2016, Vice-President Temer became president as a result of the controversial process of impeachment which removed Rousseff from power. The "expansionary fiscal austerity" proposal was renewed, combined with a liberal-oriented process of structural reforms. In December 2016, the Brazilian Congress approved a bill establishing a constitutional amendment that created the "New Fiscal Regime" (NFR), called "Expenditure Ceiling Law." It was designed to achieve a very tight fiscal consolidation, since the primary expenses of the federal budget from 2017 to 2037 could only grow in as much as the annual variation of the consumer price index. The idea was that fiscal consolidation would be reached by government's revenues growth *pari passu* with GDP growth, whereas expenditure would be fixed in real terms. The idea was to constrain public spending growth, including investment, and interrupt the trajectory of social expenditures growth.

In addition, the labour law reform was approved in July 2017 by Congress, radically changing Brazil's 1943 Consolidated Labour Laws (see Chapter 13). The goal was the flexibilization of work contracts aimed at raising the level of employment.

Meanwhile, tight monetary policy continued to be applied in order to make inflation rate converge to the target. In such a context, the aggregate investment declined by 10.3 percent in real terms (Figure 4.2). in addition, government revenues were damaged by the economic recession and primary deficit reached 2.5 percent of GDP in 2016. GDP went down 3.3 percent and unemployment rate rose to 11.5 percent. Over 2013–2016, the net debt increased from 32.6 percent to 45.9 percent of GDP (Arestis et al., 2022; Orair and Gobetti, 2017).

From the monetary police side, inflation lost strength and reached 2.95 percent in 2017. The Central Bank thus lowered the base interest rates, but did it very slowly, so that Selic reached its lower level of 6.5 percent per year in March 2018. In a context of huge economic recession over 2015–2016, high interest rates were unnecessary to contain demand (Resende and Terra, 2020). Thus, the Central Bank excess of conservatism damaged economic recovery.

As an attempt to revive the economy, the government, in 2017, released withdrawals from the Guarantee Fund for Length of Service (FGTS – *Fundo de Garantia por Tempo de Serviço*).[7] Thus, demand was boosted in a context of decreasing interest rates and low level of installed industrial capacity utilization. Investment rate, nevertheless, remained at low levels of 15.0% and 15.8% in 2017 and 2018. The GDP grew respectively 1.3 and 1.8 percent, very little after a recession, which provoked a GDP contraction of 7 percent in 2015 and 2016.

In 2018, Jair Bolsonaro, embracing a far-right discourse, was elected president. He promised to implement a radical liberal agenda, based on structural reforms, privatization and government expenditures reduction. Once more, the "expansionary fiscal austerity" proposal was renewed, combined with liberal-oriented structural reforms. A social security reform, designed in large part by the previous government, was approved by Congress in 2019 (see Chapter 7). In the same year, the government implemented an *Economic Freedom Law* and more public expenditures were cut. In February 2021, the Central Bank gained autonomy through a law passed by Congress.

In 2020 the world was hit by the Covid-19 pandemic. Economic policy was substantially changed, especially due to the social programs adopted to protect people and enterprises from lockdowns and the paralisation of the economy. The new economic context also allowed a substantial reduction in interest rates. In the following years, public expenditure increased and the government found ways to flexibilize the "Expenditure Ceiling law." From 2021, economic policy became centered on increasing the chances of the president's re-election and all possible measures were adopted to increase its popularity, in a package which combined populist and even illegal measures.

In general, the Bolsonaro government was marked by very poor public policies, mainly in social areas, while his voluntarism and unpredictability also had negative effects on the economy. The way the pandemic was combatted was especially negative, having very negative effects on the president's popularity. In addition, nothing was done to tackle and correct the negative impacts on education, while his environmental policies were disastrous. Bolsonaro demonstrated both lack of capacity and lack of will to govern. His only aim became to stay in power. The poor policies and the negative effects on job creation and social conditions played important roles in his electoral defeat in 2022.

4.8 Final considerations

Brazil has been, since the 1980s, in a trajectory marked by low economic growth. Investment rates have been low and have never returned to the levels achieved during previous import substitution industrialization period. Productivity has been stagnated, raising very slowly. The 2000s were marked by important advances, especially in social policies, which had positive effects on the economy. However, the necessary structural reforms were not done. Lula achieved high economic growth and improvement in social conditions without tackling politically difficult reforms, which would have faced strong opposition in Congress. In addition, his economic policies were also marked by contradictions, which came to the fore when the international context changed and the consumption led growth founds its limits.

Rousseff's attempts to deal with those challenges resulted in a huge disaster. She lacked the political abilities to deal with delicate issues and her economic response was inconsistent. Her conduct led Brazil to a very deep recession, a context (situation) which increased the chances that the right and, later, the extreme right achieved the presidency. In her second term, Rousseff critically adhered to neoliberal ideas, including terrible decisions which contributed both to reduce her political support and aggravate the economic situation.

Liberal ideas provided the interpretation and the justification for a political response which imposed the costs of adjustment in the vulnerable groups, while the richer groups, as usual, found forms to protect their income and wealth, including the huge financial gains provided by high interest rates. Inequality and poverty increased as a consequence. However, in contrast to what happened in Britain four decades ago, this process failed to put the economy in a new economic growth path. The combination of political difficulties, economic structural problems, bad policies and international events limited the economic achievements of neoliberal economic policies. This was not a surprise in the face of the results generally achieved by "expansionary fiscal austerity policies" around the world.

This is the scenery which marked the return of Lula to power in 2023. Even before taking office, President Lula declared his commitment to the strengthening of social expenditure, changing environment policy and abandoning austerity. In the first months in office, a new fiscal rule was approved aimed at both indicating the government's commitment to fiscal responsibility and giving more leverage to public spending, with the intention to frame a positive convention. In addition, the government succeeded in approving a tax reform which, despite several restrictions and proposals of changes by Congress, is a critical reform and has many chances to stimulate investment and contribute to economic recovery.

In brief, important lessons were learned from Brazilian trajectory in the two decades discussed here. The mistakes committed by Rousseff tend (we hope) not to be repeated and the government's financial minister has shown the disposition to keep fiscal conditions under control and provide favorable macroeconomic conditions for capital accumulation. Investments, in a capitalist economy, are mainly done by private businessmen and any economic program needs their "support" in order to be successful. Meanwhile, the government is also aware of the necessity to avoid the excesses and inconsistencies inherent in neoliberal ideology. One of the contributions of this chapter is to make clear in which sense fiscal control is important and why excessive austerity measures are mainly motivated by political and ideological concerns, failing to produce positive economic results. In this sense, we believe the government is ready to avoid those claims and to adopt a wider range of economic policy options, with much higher chances of success.

The challenges of economic development in Brazil are considerable and go much further than macroeconomic policies. They imply the adoption of successful industrial policies, the stimulus to technological development, the improvement in business environment, the radical improvement in education and in labour force skills and a wide range of measures to improve productivity, among other policies and reforms. This requires a wide political capacity to deal with a hostile Congress and the opposition from conservative political groups. This tends to be a long process, to be followed with patience and high capacity of articulation. The lessons from previous periods, including those summarised in this chapter, tend to be very helpful.

Notes

1 Capital available in international financial markets increased from US$ 160 bilhões in 1970 to US$ 1.5 trillion in 1980 and US$ 5 trillion at the beginning of the 1990s (Frieden, 2008, p. 405).
2 According to this interpretation, the main difference between public and private agents is that the last ones are permanently subject to competition.
3 As calculated by Oreiro (2013), it was necessary an investment rate of 24 percent of GDP in order to produce a sustainable annual average economic growth rate of 4.5 percent.
4 Interest rates on private banks fell, but the credit offered by them also decreased.
5 In 2014 central government investment was 1.4 percent lower (in real terms) than in 2010.
6 The ratio of the federal interest payments to GDP went up from an average of 3.05 percent in 2013 to 6.07 percent in 2015
7 The FGTS is a compulsory fund and is fed every month with a percentage of the wages. It was created in the 1960s aimed at protecting workers in case of dismissal.

References

Alesina, A, Ardagna, S, Trebbi, F. 2006. Who adjusts and when? The political economy of reform. *IMF Staff Papers* 53, special issue, International Monetary Fund.

Arestis, P, Sawyer, M. 2008. New consensus macroeconomics and inflation targeting: Keynesian critique. *Economia e Sociedade*. 17, special number: 629–653.

Arestis, P, Ferrari-Filho, F, Resende, MF, Terra, FB. 2019. Brazilian monetary and fiscal policies from 2011 to 2017: conventions and crisis. *Challenge*. 62: 187–199.

Arestis, P, Ferrari-Filho, F, Resende, MF, Terra, FB. 2022. A critical analysis of the Brazilian "expansionary fiscal austerity": why did it fail to ensure economic growth and structural development? *International Review of Applied Economics*. 36 (1): 4–16.

Blyth, M. 2002. *Great transformations: Economic ideas and institutional change in the twentieth century*. New York: Cambridge University Press.

Bresser-Pereira, LC, Oreiro, JL, Marconi, N. 2015. *Developmental macroeconomics*. Londres: Routledge.

Cagnin, RF, Prates, D, Freitas, MC, Novais, LF. 2013. A gestão macroeconômica do governo Dilma (2011 e 2012). *Novos Estudos*. 97: 169–185.

Campello, D. 2015. *The politics of market discipline in Latin America: Globalization and democracy*. Cambridge: Cambridge University Press.

Carvalho, FJC. 2014. *Expectativas, Incerteza e convenções*. BNDES-Biblioteca Digital. Available at: https://web.bndes.gov.br/bib/jspui/bitstream/1408/2281/3/Expectativas_incerteza_conven percentc3 percenta7oes_P.pdf. Acess in 27/03/2023.

Carvalho, L. 2018. *Valsa brasileira: Do boom ao caos econômico*. São Paulo: Todavia.

Flassbeck, H. 2018. Exchange rate determination and the flaws of mainstream monetary theory. *Brzazilian Journal of Political Economy.* 38 (1): 99–114.

Fraga, JS, Resende, MC. 2022. Infrastructure, conventions and private investment: An empirical investigation. *Structural Change and Economic Dynamics.* 2: 351–361.

French-Davis, R. 2003. Financial crises and national policy issues: an overview. In French-Davis, R. & Griffith-Jones, S. eds. *From capital surges to drought: Seeking stability for emerging economies.* New York: Palgrave Macmillan, pp. 20–42.

Frieden, J. 2008. *Capitalismo global: História econômica e política econômica no século XX.* Rio de Janeiro: Zahar.

Gala, P. 2008. Real exchange rate levels and economic development: theoretical analysis and empirical evidence. *Cambridge Journal of Economics.* 32: 273–288.

Gamble, A. 1988. *The Free economy and the strong state: the politics of Thatcherism.* Durham: Duke University Press.

Guimarães, AQ. 2015. Economia, instituições e estado de bem-estar social: respostas à nova configuração do capitalismo pós-1970. *Dados – Revista de Ciências Sociais.* 58 (3): 617–650.

Guimarães, AQ. 2022. The political economy of the Workers' Party governments in Brazil (2003–2014): Institutions, ideas and the main determinants of economic policy. *Nova Economia.* 32 (1): 37–62.

Guimarães, AQ, Gambi, T. 2022. Dependência, instituições e variedades de capitalismo: uma análise dos constrangimentos político-institucionais para o desenvolvimento da periferia. *Revista de Economia.* 43 (81): 372–404.

Hall, P. 1986. *Governing the economy: The politics of state intervention in Britain and France.* Cambridge: Polity Press.

IPEADATA. 2023. www.ipeadata.gov.br

Judt, T. 2007. *O pós-guerra: Uma história da Europa desde 1945.* Rio de Janeiro: Objetiva.

Kerstenetzky, C. 2012. *O Estado do bem-estar social na idade da razão: A reinvenção do Estado social no mundo contemporâneo.* Rio de Janeiro: Campus/Elsevier.

Keynes, JM. 2013. *The general theory of employment, interest and money/ the collected writings of John Maynard Keynes, VII.* Cambridge: Cambridge University Press.

Loural, MS. *Investimentos Industriais no Brasil: Uma análise setorial do período 1999–2013* (PhD thesis). Campinas: Universidade Estadual de Campinas. 2016

Maddison, A. 2001. *The world economy: A millennial perspective.* Paris: OECD.

Orair, R, Gobetti, SW. 2017. Brazilian Fiscal Policy in Perspective: From Expansion to Austerity. In: Arestis, P., Troncoso Baltar, C., & Prates, D. eds. *The Brazilian Economy since the Great Financial Crisis of 2007/2008.* Palgrave Macmillan, Cham, pp. 219–244. https://doi.org/10.1007/978-3-319-64885-9_9

Oreiro, JLC. 2013. *Por que a taxa de investimento no Brasil é tão baixa?* https://jlcoreiro. wordpress.com/2013/01/13/por-que-a-taxa-de-investimento-no-brasil-e-tao-baixa. Acesses in 03/07/2023.

Palma, J. G. 2011. *Why has productivity growth stagnated in most Latin American countries since the neo-liberal reforms?* Cambridge Working Papers in Economics (CWPE), n. 1030.

Panizza, F. 2013. *Contemporary Latin America: Development and democracy beyond the Washington Consensus.* London: Zed Books Ltd.

Plihon, D. 1995. A ascensão das finanças especulativas. *Economia e Sociedade.* 5: 61–78.

Reinhardt, CM, Reinhard, VR, Rogoff, KS. 2012. Public debt overhangs: Advanced-economy episodes since 1800. *Journal of Economic Perspectives*. 26(3): 69–86.

Resende, MF. 2023. Conventions and the Brazilian fiscal policy to face the aftermath of COVID-19 economic crisis: A Post Keynesian view. *Economic Issues*. 29(1): 31–52.

Resende, MF, Terra, FB. 2017. Economic and social policies inconsistency, conventions and crisis in the Brazilian economy, 2011–2016. In Arestis, P, Baltar, C, & Prates, D. eds. *The Brazilian economy since the Great Financial Crisis 2007/2008*. London: Palgrave Macmilan, pp. 245–272.

Resende, MF, Terra, FB. 2020. Ciclo, crise e retomada da economia brasileira: avaliação macroeconômica do período 2004–2016. *Economia e Sociedade*. 29: 469–496.

Rossi, P, Mello, G. 2016. Componentes macroeconômicos e estruturais da crise brasileira: o subdesenvolvimento revisitado. *Brazilian Keynesian Review*. 2(2): 252–263.

Serrano, F, Summa, R. 2015. Aggregate demand and the slowdown of Brazilian economic growth in 2011–2014. *Nova Economia*. 25: 803–833.

Streeck, W. 2012. As crises do capitalismo democrático. *Revista Novos Estudos Cebrap*. 92: 35–56.

5

DISINFORMATION AND DEMOCRACY

The strategies for institutional dismantle in Brazil (2018–2022)

Eliara Santana and Isabele Mitozo

5.1 Introduction

The realm of political discourse has always revolved around a contest of framing, such that engaging in sociopolitical struggles transpires by means of rhetoric, which means that it "involves more than words" (Mendonça et al., 2022, p. 157). Consequently, the caliber of information consumed by a society is a pivotal determinant of the quality of democracies (Dahl, 1998; Downs, 1957), including trust in institutions (Przeworski, 2019).

However, the current context of democracies is permeated by an informational disorder, or as Bennett and Livingston (2018) prefer to call it, a "disinformation order." These scholars employ this term to denote the establishment of a network for the creation and dissemination of questionable veracity content, conspiracy theories, and an institutionalization of falsehood, primarily (but not exclusively) employed by radical right-wing movements. This has propelled individuals to the highest echelons of power in nations by nurturing a personal "human brand" of salvation ("superhero"), spontaneity, and supposed honesty, facilitated by digital social media use (Schneiker, 2019). This phenomenon has engendered a pronounced crisis in the public sphere (Mendonça & Sarmento, 2023), as it has generated factors previously identified by Przeworski (2019) as triggers of democratic crises: erosion of trust in institutions and the breakdown of public order.

Brazil is a unique case in this context, as it experienced the establishment of this new "order" starting with the 2018 electoral campaign, which saw the election of the far-right candidate Jair Bolsonaro. During his government and, notably, in 2020 with the Covid-19 pandemic, there was a strengthening of

DOI: 10.4324/9781003487777-6

what we will refer to as a coordinated disinformation ecosystem, as it was not only highly organized but also aligned with the federal government structure (Avritzer et al., 2022; Massuchin et al., 2021). This structuring had severe impacts on democracy in the country because, in addition to undermining the regime itself, it constituted an institutional strategy to garner popular support for the dismantling of social policies, the subject of this book.

In this scenario, it is imperative to comprehend the phenomenon through a reflection on the complex Brazilian political disinformation system in recent years, which is the objective of this chapter. Thus, we discuss different perspectives on so-called fake news, which is not always entirely false (Wardle & Derakshan, 2017; Dourado & Salgado, 2021; Santana, 2022), contrasting with the premise of the high quality of information for the consolidation of robust democracies. Lastly, we address the case of electoral disinformation and the network of discrediting social instances and public institutions in Brazil (Journalism, Electoral System, Supreme Federal Court, and Science) through online platforms, reflecting on how this context has provided a fertile ground for the distortion of public policies in the country.

5.2 Disinformation and politics

Disinformation is a multifaceted and wide-reaching phenomenon that has become increasingly prevalent in contemporary societies, with profound impacts on social, political, economic, and other contexts. The surge in disinformation significantly affects the public sphere (Mendonça & Sarmento, 2023). Therefore, it is not limited to mere rumors or inconsequential falsehoods; rather, it is a complex and impactful phenomenon, capable of reshaping aspects of reality (Wardle & Derakshan, 2017), leading to new constructions of meaning that prompt citizens to question, for instance, scientific and historical principles.

Commonly referred to as fake news, false and distorted content that ranges from causing comprehension errors to complete distortions of reality are more intricate than simple lies or rumors. This is because, at times, these contents are taken out of context or selectively edited to fit the desired argumentation. Wardle and Derakshan (2017) discuss an information disorder consisting of three levels: *disinformation*, understood as information deliberately created to harm individuals, social groups, or countries – a set of information based on reality that is intentionally reframed to produce meaning and benefit certain groups (Santana, 2022); *misinformation*, which is false information but not intentionally created, meaning its dissemination is not intended to cause harm; and *mal-information*, which is genuine information based on reality but spread to inflict harm on organizations, groups, or individuals, often involving the circulation of old news as if it were freshly released. Consequently, it can be observed that deceptive and/or manipulated content does not always originate from entirely false information or are crafted with the intention to deceive the public. However, this represents their most detrimental aspect as it can lead to irreparable damage to what their creation aims to combat.

The appropriation of such content has been extensively carried out in political contexts, and although not exclusive, it has seen widespread use by the far-right. Bennett and Livingston (2018) discuss the formation of a disinformation order based on episodes involving Donald Trump's first presidential campaign in the United States and the beginning of his presidency (2016–2017). Bluffing about alleged violent actions by non-white immigrants, specifically Muslims in Europe, insinuating that they could occur in the United States (anti-immigration agenda), as well as the dissemination of false and manipulated content in favor of Trump (four times more than such content in favor of his opponent, Hillary Clinton), spread not only through social networks but also by the journalistic company Fox News, characterized the tone of this period (Allcott & Gentzkow, 2017).

Therefore, it is evident from this case that investment in disinformation (adopting here the specific concept by Wardle and Derakshan, 2017) is connected to campaign proposals that will be developed during the tenure of the then-candidate, which is a crucial factor in capturing an audience based on their beliefs and perceptions about lesser-known situations, such as the case of alleged violence by immigrants against white natives. In other words, disinformation is not a random occurrence, simply the spread of inconsequential rumors, but is part of a political project that engages with the complexity of societal structures. Thus, "[s]olving these problems requires more than just fact-checking and setting the record straight and goes to deeper issues of repairing political institutions and democratic values" (Bennett & Livingston, 2018, p. 123).

Given that politics is an ongoing contest of framing and, at this moment, of facts (consider the "alternative facts" of Trump, which gives its name to the US far-right – Alt-Right), it is undeniable that information is intrinsically linked to democracies. Ensuring access to high-quality information is an inherent value of this political system, highly important for its maintenance and consolidation in society. According to Dahl (1998), the right to access multiple sources of information and freedom of expression are some of the fundamental guarantees of democracies. Dahl, who argues for the non-existence of contemporary democracies but rather "polyarchies" (non-autocratic regimes with power concentrated in a few individuals, not the "people"), places such importance on information, primarily because among the factors determining the maintenance of a political regime are the beliefs of people involved in the political sphere, "a key stage in the complex processes by which historical sequences or subcultural cleavages, for example, are converted into support for one kind of regime or another" (Dahl, 1998, p. 124). Downs (1957), a researcher of the Economic Theory of Democracy, similarly argues that the existence of uncertainty in the voting decision-making process (which can be caused by a lack of party identification) leaves the voter susceptible to external influences, such as the dissemination of dubious news about candidates or causes.

Hence, disinformation harms democracies because ill-informed citizens may, among other factors, fail to recognize the errors committed by political actors and isolate themselves within comfortable echo chambers that propagate supposed news aligning with these individuals' worldviews, because they are fueled by a lack of faith in traditional and trustworthy sources of information such as journalism. In the dissemination of content through digital networks, there are no "significant external filters, fact-checking, or editorial judgment, and an individual user, without any prior history or reputation, can reach as many readers as Fox News, CNN, or The New York Times" (Allcott & Gentzkow, 2017, p.2). The formation of these echo chambers and filter bubbles would thus be detrimental to the quality of democracies by restricting citizens' access to a diversity of information (Dahl, 1998) and, consequently, to framing.

Thus, it is natural that a recurring strategy of political actors and anti-democratic governments is to capitalize on the undermining of media credibility and "subvert democratic institutions without openly questioning the principles of democracy" (Curato & Fossati, 2020, p. 1006). In this context, leaders rise to political prominence through this approach, as seen with figures like Rodrigo Duterte (Philippines), Vladimir Putin (Russia), and Viktor Orban (Hungary). Furthermore, it is common to observe in the discourse of these political actors the reconfiguration and reversal of democratic characteristics, leading citizens to profess their support for the regime while simultaneously advocating for the return of dictatorships, as seen in the Brazilian case. This is a distinctive feature of Populist Radical Right Parties (PRRPs), particularly because actors associated with these parties consider as freedom of speech supporting publicly the issues on their agenda such as "stricter immigration controls, tougher law and order policies, and restrictive welfare provision" (Röth, Afonso & Spies, 2017, p. 326).

It is worth noting that politicians with the above-mentioned characteristics quickly rise to prominence as anti-establishment celebrities. According to Schneiker (2019), the focus of these individuals, who establish a "human brand" as a political strategy, is politically disillusioned citizens, which aligns well with the strategy of discrediting institutions and presenting themselves as what the researcher terms an "antipolitical superhero." Therefore, the ideal spaces for these individuals are social media platforms, where they isolate themselves and persistently say what they consider

[...] to be "the truth," without allowing for deliberation. In this sense, the concept of celebrity politicians is not "a source for reinvigorating democracy" (Wood et al., 2016, p.582), but decreases the democratic quality of politics.

This is even more relevant if one considers that [their posts on social media] […] are sometimes further distributed by traditional media and become news.
(Schneiker, 2019, p.6)

This point becomes quite evident with the phenomenon of "infodemic," a term referring to the rampant spread of disinformation like a disease amidst the Covid-19 pandemic, as described by Posetti and Bontcheva (2020) in a report prepared for the United Nations Educational, Scientific and Cultural Organization (UNESCO). The research emphasizes that "Covid-19 disinformation creates confusion about medical science with immediate impact on every person on the planet, and upon whole societies. It is more toxic and more deadly than disinformation about other subjects" (Posetti & Bontcheva, 2020, p. 2).

In Brazil, the production and dissemination of lies and false news (with the endorsement of the government and some media outlets) about the disease have significantly impacted the behavior of the population and the methods for combating the new virus (as can be seen in Chapter 8 of this volume). The encouragement of non-compliance with virus prevention measures – social isolation and mask-wearing – prior to the availability of a vaccine was facilitated by the support of a public figure of authority, the President of Brazil, Jair Bolsonaro. This situation is reinforced by institutional actions and communication proposals, such as the weekly live broadcasts conducted by him, during which he openly opposed the recommendations of the World Health Organization (WHO) regarding virus prevention and advocated for the use of medically proven ineffective drugs against the virus, such as hydroxychloroquine.

In the realm of the quality of democracies, counteracted by the phenomenon of fake news and its derivatives, and considering the examples presented above, the development of public policies cannot be overlooked. Since cutting public resources from essential societal domains is not an easy task to justify, it is common for governments to employ "strategies to avoid and/or deflect responsibility" for this action (Jordan et al., 2014, p. 6). In this regard, Pierson (1994) argues that there are three steps followed by public administrators to disguise the consequences of dismantling policies: obfuscate, divide, and compensate. The first step involves precisely playing with the limits of citizens' access to information and the potential opposition to a desired policy. In this context, tactics used to garner popular support for contingency policies through obfuscation would involve reducing the real impact of their adverse consequences by diminishing the visibility of government policies, showcasing only the indirect effects of decisions, and reducing the public's knowledge about the actual extent of the government's responsibility for the consequences (Pierson, 1994, pp. 20–21). Among these strategies would be to shift the blame for the damages to other entities, such as local governments. The second move would involve dividing opposition to a decision by reinforcing a discourse that pits social groups against each other, given that "The constituencies of all public programs are to some extent heterogeneous. In the case of income-transfer programs, a wide range of distinctions can be exploited, including differences in household composition, income level, age, geographic location, and gender" (Pierson, 1994, p. 22). Finally, the last step to solidify a controversial policy would be to offer some benefit to the targets of contingency policies, which could mitigate opposition attacks.

Despite the researcher making clear that the relationship with access to public information is only the first step, what can be observed from the disinformation crisis is that all these strategies involve control over this access. In the context existing at the time of Pierson's text (1994), characterized by vertical communication, where information would flow only from political institutions or traditional journalism to citizens, the author found in institutional political spaces the arenas for these disputes with the opposition. However, with the establishment of the new media convergence environment, especially through digital social networks, where consumers have become content producers and institutions lose space and followers to their members, it is necessary to observe how the recurring informational disorder of this new configuration can be added to the strategies of dismantling public policies. Thus, an emblematic case is what happened in Brazil in recent years, which will be discussed in the next section.

5.3 The Brazilian case: The dismantling of the credibility on institutions

In the Brazilian context, we can speak of a kind of institutionalization of disinformation, fostered by the support of governmental entities and the President of the Republic himself between 2019 and 2022. It is true that the distribution of forged or invented facts has always been present, especially during election campaigns, as engaging in politics involves contesting framings. However, there are particularities that arise with the appropriation of the digital environment for this purpose.

The fact that, between 2019 and 2021, two Parliamentary Inquiry Committees (CPI)[1] were established in the National Congress, namely the CPIs on Fake News and Covid-19, as a consequence of harmful lies that, in the former case, impacted democratic processes and, in the latter, directly affected citizens' lives and survival, propagated by the Federal Government, suggests that the systematic and systematized spread of disinformation has become a fundamental part of a power project. In this sense, the following outlines the process that ranges from discrediting various political and social institutions to the consolidation of the dismantling of public policies in the country, based on the phenomenon discussed earlier.

Therefore, we will consider the configuration of two moments: the construction of a structured network of political disinformation, which solidifies itself from the 2018 elections; and the process of discrediting institutions, from journalism to science, especially from the Covid-19 pandemic, but also with impacts on the 2022 electoral process, with the Federal Government and the president and candidate for re-election, Jair Bolsonaro, overtly utilizing this disinformation structure.

5.3.1   The construction of a (hidden) network: The role of social media

In the electoral year of 2018, we witnessed the organization of a new model of political campaign, with a significant rise in the use of social media for political propaganda, but especially through online private messaging services. Even at the beginning of that year, when Jair Bolsonaro was not yet a presidential candidate for Brazil, political discussion groups in favor of the then-federal deputy were already identified on WhatsApp (Chagas et al., 2021). At that time, the organization of these groups via social media was still portrayed by the press as spontaneous and random expressions, without constituting an orchestrated organization.

In October, on the eve of the second round of elections, an important piece of information was revealed in a report published by the Brazilian newspaper *Folha de S. Paulo*, written by journalist Patrícia Campos Mello, who later published a book on the case.[2] According to the report, several companies associated with the then-candidate Jair Bolsonaro purchased packages for mass messaging on WhatsApp, preparing for a large-scale operation – hundreds of millions of messages – in the period leading up to the second round of the election.[3] Despite the gravity of the allegations, which included a possible connection of the campaign with Steve Bannon – a central figure in the Facebook-Cambridge Analytica scandal during the Trump campaign – the issue did not gain significant political repercussion at that time. However, this case indicated how the far-right disinformation network in Brazil was established and managed to undermine the trust in traditional institutions, such as journalism, and gain the unquestioning support of a significant portion of Brazilian society, which, according to the *Digital News Report* 2021 from the Reuters Institute, was more open to consuming information that aligned with their worldview (Newman et al., 2021).[4]

The results of the study by Mont'Alverne and Mitozo (2019) on 213 support groups for presidential candidates in Brazil in 2018 on the WhatsApp platform reveal that in all analyzed groups, social networks predominated as the main sources of content, namely: YouTube, Facebook, WhatsApp, Instagram, and Twitter, respectively. In other words, the data illustrate the information sources for these groups and the extent to which they focus on those outside traditional media. With WhatsApp itself being among these sources, it is further evident that there is a feedback loop within the groups with the contents they produce themselves.

Regarding Bolsonaro's winning campaign, it was observed that his supporters used, in a significantly higher proportion compared to other groups, the following sources from which the shared information originated: 1) YouTube, 2) their own WhatsApp groups, and 3) the *Jornal da Cidade Online*. The latter is one of the disinformation outlets investigated by the Parliamentary Inquiry Committee on Fake News in the National Congress later, in 2021. It is worth noting that the *Jornal da Cidade Online* was a source almost exclusively used by groups in favor of the then-elected candidate, yet it appeared among the 15 most shared information channels with links among all analyzed groups, confirming the numerical superiority of pro-Bolsonaro groups (Mont'Alverne & Mitozo, 2019).

Another information channel that deserves attention among the most activated ones is the *Pesquisa Eleitoral 2018*, which directed users to a supposed survey about voters' voting intentions. However, it did not belong to any recognized opinion research institute, nor was it registered with the Superior Electoral Court, a requirement for serious polling institutes – thus, it was not valid. Nevertheless, it was considerably shared in the analyzed groups, particularly leading in groups supporting Jair Bolsonaro, as it consistently indicated that this candidate would be elected in the first round with over 60% of the votes. Therefore, it was natural that it would be more widely shared in groups that desired this outcome.

The existence of this channel of supposed surveys fueled the narrative of electoral fraud and the perceived need for printed voting receipts due to the alleged lack of trust in electronic voting machines. The discourse was ready to reinforce the questioning of the electoral system if Jair Bolsonaro failed to legitimately defeat his opponent, Fernando Haddad of the Workers' Party (PT). In 2022, this narrative would support (alongside other nationally registered polling agencies such as *Paraná Pesquisas* and *Futura*) an attempt to criminalize polling institutes regarding voter intention, claiming results significantly discrepant from those agencies.[5] Additionally, there was uncertainty about the incumbent's re-election, which did not occur. Thus, directly attacking electronic voting machines would incite supporters of the then-president to protest the election result, as happened with the attack on 8 January 2023, in Brasília, a topic we will revisit later in this chapter.

Still within the context of the 2018 elections, there is a significant example of disinformation that had a major impact on the country's political scene during the electoral period: the so-called "gay kit,"[6] a material supposedly to be distributed in early childhood education schools. The then-candidate Bolsonaro and his supporters spread the idea that the former Minister of Education in the Lula and Dilma Rousseff governments (from 2005 to 2012), Fernando

Haddad, also a presidential candidate in 2018, had authorized the production of material for six-year-old children in early childhood education to have lessons on homosexuality.[7] This falsehood was constructed by reinterpreting a real fact: during Dilma Rousseff's government in 2009, the National Plan for the Promotion of Citizenship and Human Rights for LGBTQ+ individuals was produced as part of the strengthening actions of the "Brazil Without Homophobia Program," implemented since 2004.

This narrative strongly appealed to moral values, especially those of evangelical Christians, linking the then-candidate Fernando Haddad to a perspective of degradation of family values, which had a significant impact. However, it is essential to note that this was not a false content originating from those elections: it had been a recurring theme in Bolsonaro's conservative discourse for many years, since Fernando Haddad's election as mayor of São Paulo in 2012. During the electoral period, misinformation about this issue resurfaces as an element of the so-called anti-PT (Workers' Party) sentiment, a movement that had already been established earlier, starting with the "Car Wash" investigation in 2014, reinforced by Dilma Rousseff's re-election and her impeachment process, events that contributed to the rise of Populist Radical Right Parties and actors, especially Jair Bolsonaro.

From the campaigns, it can be observed that this deliberately created and intentionally transmitted production of false content, with a systemic reach, has distinctive influences in the macropolitical scenario and in the restructuring of the role of instances such as the press, which has dedicated itself to fact-checking or denials since then. On the other hand, disinformation channels on social media, camouflaged as informative sites, spread false content in the guise of news and can constitute the process of obfuscation by playing with the citizens' limited information about the topics under discussion (Pierson, 1994). This strategy, which also involves controlling the means of information during elections, intensifies in the elected government, as will be seen later.

5.3.2 The informational crisis over institutions: The disinformation strike

5.3.2.1 Consolidation of distrust in traditional journalism and attacks on science

Following Jair Bolsonaro's inauguration as the president of Brazil, the process of consolidating distrust in traditional journalism begins, strongly associated with the informational conflict surrounding the Covid-19 pandemic. Following the steps of Donald Trump in the United States (Bennett & Livingston, 2018, the then newly elected president in Brazil accused the entire national press of being "leftist" and only spreading fake news. This goes entirely against the findings of research indicating the alignment of the Brazilian corporate media with certain power groups in recent historical moments, such as the impeachment of President Dilma Rousseff (2016) and the arrest of President Lula (2017), to persecute and hinder experiences of popular governments in Brazil (Santana, 2022). Meanwhile, Bolsonaro-supporting networks on WhatsApp and Telegram strengthened, becoming more than mere content repositories. These spaces were fueled by increasingly numerous sources of (dis)information, taking on the forms and even the names of journalism to legitimize themselves as reliable sources.

Studying Bolsonaro-supporting groups on WhatsApp between August and December 2020, a period marked by a peak in the pandemic in the country with no available vaccine, Massuchin and colleagues (2021) observed a shift in information sources compared to the 2018 campaign. While social networks still played a role in legitimizing information, the prevalence, except for YouTube (shared as a source in 5% of messages in the studied groups), was allegedly journalistic websites with questionable credibility (11 sites with links present in 27% of messages). These sites, such as the *Jornal da Cidade Online* identified by Mont'Alverne and Mitozo (2019) in 2018, are noteworthy, and it is important to mention that the names of these sites simulated well-known traditional media outlets in the country, often criticized by the far-right.[8]

Therefore, it is evident that the scenario is different from that of 2018 when social networks played a prominent role as sources in these groups (Mont'Alverne & Mitozo, 2019), leaving room for the rapid proliferation of supposed journalistic outlets. This would be the conducive scenario for, in 2020, a concerning situation of disinformation to take hold in Brazil during the pandemic caused by the SARS-COV-2 virus.

Disinformation about the disease spread again through groups in mobile instant messaging services, where "the mean frequency of sending unscientific messages to government supporter groups on WhatsApp was 416.1 messages per day" (Massuchin et al., 2021, p.166). From this universe, researchers selected a representative sample of 908 messages for qualitative content analysis. The results showed that, concerning the denial of the severity of the situation, nearly 30% of the analyzed messages focused on criticisms of representative institutions and political actors in general, especially those who opposed the president Bolsonaro's view that Covid-19 was just "a little flu." Following that, one can highlight the recurrence of criticisms of the vaccine, China, scientific recommendations, and the traditional press. It is also worth mentioning the use of conspiracy theories, including the claim that the Chinese vaccine intended to implant a microchip in Brazilians or transmit AIDS, and not infrequently were cited by the president himself.[9]

The institutional promotion of content supposedly scientific but false or manipulated caused a societal loss of control regarding the understanding and adherence to scientifically defined rules, as the pronouncements of the nation's leader contradicted the communication of the Ministry of Health itself (Pinto et al., 2020). The overt denial of premises established by the World Health Organization (WHO) regarding pandemic control (social isolation, mask use outdoors, maintenance of social distancing, and avoidance of gatherings) from the center of the National Executive also contributed to the systematic worsening of the health situation in the country, shifting responsibility to state and local governments. This can be considered another strategy of obscuring its decisions (Pierson, 1994), as well as blame avoidance, claiming that it was prevented from working by the Supreme Court when it defeated its unconstitutional action of rendering these governments inoperative (Arretche, 2022) – they utilized the federal model to function. This was the case with the creation of the Northeast Consortium for Covid-19, formed by the states of the Northeast region of the country to purchase vaccines and other health supplements independently of the Federal Government, in defiance of the unconstitutional Provisional Measure No. 926, of March 20, 2020, which established "parameters for the operation of economic activities during the pandemic [...] directly challenging the autonomy of federated entities in their social distancing measures" (Rossi & Silva, 2020, p. 11).

5.3.2.2   The battle against the Judiciary

In this context, we come to another institution strongly contested by the Bolsonarist movement: the Judiciary. In April 2020, democratic acts took place in Brasília calling for Jair Bolsonaro's "civic-military intervention" in conjunction with the Brazilian Armed Forces, involving the closure of the Supreme Federal Court and the National Congress. Following these acts, during which protesters launched fireworks at the STF building, some of them being arrested, a judicial inquiry was initiated. This inquiry aimed to investigate financiers and the government's relationship with alleged communication channels and participants in the movement, as the president had already incited supporters in various speeches, including one on 7 September 2019, Brazil's Independence Day from Portugal.

This inquiry was archived. However, in 2021, the (dis)information ecosystem behind this movement gained official representation through another inquiry, the one about antidemocratic digital militias, opened on the 1st of July by one of the Justices of the Supreme Federal Court, Alexandre de Moraes. The judge ordered investigations focused on the nuclei of production, publication, and financing of fake news. According to him, the investigations "pointed to strong evidence of the existence of a criminal organization aimed at promoting various conducts to destabilize and, why not, destroy the Legislative and Judiciary Powers from an insane logic of absolute prevalence of a single power in the decisions of the State."[10]

Still regarding investigations into the mobilizations of the disinformation ecosystem, a survey conducted by the Federal Police in June 2021, within the inquiry into antidemocratic acts in 2020, showed that the YouTube platform had paid almost 7 million reais – from 2018 to 2020 – to 12 channels supporting Bolsonaro suspected of involvement in protesting the Supreme Federal Court and the National Congress in 2021.[11] The Judiciary's actions that highlighted the functioning of that ecosystem also revealed a *modus operandi* of disinformation management with clear objectives of institutional destabilization and threats to the Powers.

Another aspect that gained prominence in the disinformation scenario in Brazil, especially from the previously mentioned Covid-19 Parliamentary Inquiry Committee (CPI), concluded in October 2021, was the operation of the so-called "Hate Cabinet" – a term initially referring to a group formed by public servants and political aides associated with Carlos Bolsonaro, son of Jair Bolsonaro. This structure expanded and encompassed the president's office, serving to disseminate disinformation, undermine institutions, and fuel "a network of Bolsonaro-supporting blogs and social media profiles that spread misinformation and attacks against journalists, politicians, artists, and media outlets critical of the president."[12]

The discussion about the integrity of the Brazilian electoral process through electronic voting machines was revived, leading to a process of discrediting the Judiciary, especially the Superior Electoral Court (TSE), which began investing in a fact-checking platform (*Fato ou boato*[13]), and the Supreme Federal Court (STF). However, the distrust in electronic voting machines was not a new phenomenon. A study led by Ruediger and Grassi (2020) had already noted that since 2014, pieces of disinformation expressing doubt about the integrity of the voting machines circulated on social media platforms. A total of 103,542 pieces were found on Facebook and YouTube, with continuous circulation but heightened publicity during election years.

The incumbent's insecurity regarding his reelection created a scenario that intensified the distribution of content advocating for printed votes against electronic voting machines, the Supreme Court, and the Superior Electoral Court, almost materialized in the figure of its president at the time, Justice Alexandre de Moraes. After Bolsonaro's defeat, the tension seemed to dissipate, but his supporters, still informed through misinformation bubbles, were already preparing a protest in Brasília. On 8 January 2023, vandals invaded and vandalized the buildings of the *Palácio do Planalto* (the official Executive branch building), the National Congress, and the Supreme Federal Court (STF), supported even by military personnel who had formally been part of Bolsonaro's government. The following day, dozens of participants were arrested, some already indicted for the act, and currently, a CPI is underway to investigate the involvement of institutional actors in the attempted attack on Brazilian democracy, as well as the financiers of the movement.

5.3.2.3 Connection between disinformation strategies and public policies

In addition to the misinformation surrounding the pandemic and the other conflicts presented above, the Federal Government also utilized its network of (dis)information to move toward what Pierson (1994) refers to as a strategy of division. As economic policies became more austere, especially for the most vulnerable population, cuts were made in key areas, such as higher education, one of the most targeted during that period (which had already been undergoing significant cuts since 2015, still under Dilma Rousseff's government – Côrtes & Santos, 2022). To garner popular support, it was argued that universities did not need investment, as they had a high cost to the taxpayer and produced nothing.[14]

Because of high inflation and with the approaching elections, the Government resorts to the third strategy presented by Pierson (1994): compensation. In this context, we can highlight the dispute for the approval of the *Auxílio Brasil* (see Chapter 10), an emergency financial assistance program for the population, which passes with Constitutional Amendment Project No. 15/2022, known as the PEC of Emergency Aids (Côrtes & Santos, 2022). This law, which increased the values of social programs (emergency aid and gas voucher) and created benefits for truck drivers and taxi drivers, at a total cost of R$ 41.2 billion, would be unlikely not to gain opposition support, as it would bring benefits to the needy population. Voting against this project could entail an electoral failure, although the project was filled with unfavorable highlights, disguised in any content distributed by the government about them, including the duration of the emergency aids, which were planned only until December 2022. It demonstrated a clear electoral interest in the proposal, as the budget law sent by the Executive to Congress to be voted on and approved in October 2022 did not allocate any funds for it.

It is important to mention that disinformation also permeated this political move, as the content circulating in Bolsonaro's networks and the statements of this president in electoral debates attributed the discontinuity of the program to Luís Inácio Lula da Silva's government, if elected, which also constituted Bolsonaro's re-election campaign platform. Note that, in this context, there is no fake news, but rather the manipulation of content. First, the policy would be allegedly dismantled by the competitor, but in practice, it was already scheduled to end before his mandate. Moreover, concerning the fact that Lula intended to reactivate the previous program, *Bolsa Família*, it was rarely mentioned by the incumbent, when he argued that Lula would revert the aid to the old value (two hundred reais) from Lula's second term, which ended in 2010.[15]

The Brazilian disinformation ecosystem consolidates itself based on the experience of the so-called *Bolsonarism* and the government of Jair Bolsonaro, anchoring in the country's communication macro-scenario, characterized by high media concentration, limited information access plurality, conservative religious groups with extensive access and control over media, lack of broadcasting regulation, and intensive use of social media, especially WhatsApp and Telegram (Santana, 2022). Thus, it can be understood through key elements such as the professional production of intentionally false content, funding from both public and private sectors, support from neopentecostal church groups, backing from military-affiliated groups, and support from sectors of corporate media. These elements contribute to the ecosystem by disseminating false content widely, both on social media and within churches and institutions.

The professional scheme of false content production also engages in a process of transforming messages into media products. All these groups revolve around intentionally reinterpreted and recreated facts that possess significant political reach, proving especially effective in recent years (Santana, 2022).

Based on the presented data, it becomes apparent that there is an organized network that no longer relies solely on encrypted messaging groups. It has moved beyond these confines to establish itself as an independent "informational" network, constituting the daily information intake for those primarily informed through links shared in groups on the messaging service WhatsApp. This accounts for over 50% of the platform's users in Brazil, as reported by Rossini and colleagues (2020). It cannot be asserted, however, that this phenomenon developed solely through "alternative" means, as the funding of certain journalistic outlets, such as Jovem Pan[16] and Rede Record,[17] provided spaces within traditional media for disseminating disinformation by government agents.

Thus, there is a connection between the government and strategies of legitimation and seeking popular support for governmental measures since the 2018 elections. This connection is established through the creation of disbelief in various institutions and the formation of a nationally coordinated network of disinformation. The point to be observed in Brazil, therefore, is not "just" the widespread dissemination of rumors or fake news. The phenomenon should be seen as a systemic issue of redefining reality, involving the governmental appropriation of this network: a well-structured process of intentionally producing and disseminating false or manipulated content to legitimize a process of institutional dismantling.

5.4 Conclusion: *Quo vadis?*

The discussion developed in this chapter demonstrates that information is a source of power, and consequently, the informational disorder prevalent in current times, systematized as a political project by the far-right, directly undermines the health of democracies (Bennett & Livingston, 2019). In Brazil, this process brought to power a political group that institutionally appropriated a network of disinformation, contributing significantly to its creation and, therefore, proving crucial for its consolidation. This systematized process, organized as a powerful disinformation ecosystem orchestrated by authoritative public figures, especially the President of the Republic, managed to establish itself as a constant in the informational diet of citizens (Rossini et al., 2020), strengthening a kind of parallel reality where, for example, the nation's leader denied the existence of an ongoing pandemic.

This context shows that, more than inventing lies, the disinformation process developed to undermine the credibility of institutions and even democracy, although without directly questioning the principles of this political regime (Curato & Fossati, 2020), stems from a reconstruction of reality based not only on lies but also on the distortion of true information, as in the case of the termination of the *Auxílio Brasil* with the inauguration of the new Federal Government, in 2023.

The discredit of reliable sources of political information and even the erasure of traditional information channels, such as journalism and state institutions, including the Supreme Court, for a significant portion of the population, opened the door to what is discussed in this book: the support to the attempts of dismantling of public policies. In this sense, disinformation is used to develop the strategies of obfuscation, division, and compensation presented by Pierson (1994), with the recurrent use of blame avoidance (Arretche, 2022), aiming to secure support for decision-making unfavorable to the population, which has called into question the Brazilian federalist model.

The process, which began in an unprecedented manner during the 2018 electoral period through digital media, especially private messaging platforms (WhatsApp and Telegram), continued until 2022, and remains ongoing, given the attack on institutional buildings in Brasília on 8 January 2023,[18] and the persistence of groups advocating for a coup. To gauge its power, it is enough to remember that, even in the face of the dismantling of public policies, the deterioration of living and health conditions, etc., Jair Bolsonaro, the president who used official channels and his authoritative voice to disseminate disinformation, almost secured reelection in 2022.

As in other cases, as presented earlier in this chapter (Bennett & Livingston, 2019; Curato & Fossati, 2020; Schneiker, 2019), disinformation has thus been a political strategy that found very fertile ground in the country due to various factors. It is a structure supported by the coordination of various stages: production, circulation, consumption, reproduction (Santana, 2022). In this context, it is worth mentioning the involvement of ordinary individuals in the production and circulation of content, which, instead of democratizing access to information, has become a dangerous factor due to the reach that content without verified sources can have (Allcott & Gentzkow, 2017), and the consequences that this circulation can generate.

With all this power to reinterpret themes and agendas and mobilize public opinion, disinformation in Brazil does not come to an end with Jair Bolsonaro's defeat in the 2022 elections. Therefore, it is still necessary to go through a long period until a reconstruction of the public sphere occurs. This stage needs to involve, as can be observed from the data presented here, rebuilding credibility in institutions and restoring credibility of reliable sources of information, as well as more effective efforts to combat fake news networks that reach individuals grouped in the bubbles created around this phenomenon. It is worth emphasizing, finally, that the restoration of informational order is crucial to constrain new attempts to use disinformation as a power strategy to promote institutional dismantling.

Notes

1 Parliamentary Inquiry Committees are bodies established in the Brazilian National Congress, formed based on allegations submitted to one of the Houses (Senate and Chamber of Deputies), and they serve the purpose of overseeing the Executive, as represented by the parliament.
2 A review of the book can be found at https://link.springer.com/content/pdf/10.1057/s42984-021-00034-1.pdf
3 Available at www.bbc.com/news/technology-45956557
4 According to the mentioned report, 42% of Brazilians preferred to consume news from outlets that published content aligned with their worldview.
5 There are other factors to be considered in the realm of polling institutes, but they fall outside the scope of this discussion.
6 This link contains the main element of the so-called kit, the penis-shaped baby bottle (literally translated in Brazil as "cock baby bottle"): https://pt.wikipedia.org/wiki/Mamadeira_de_piroca
7 More information on this fake news available at www.newamerica.org/weekly/how-false-news-haunted-brazilian-elections/
8 An example of this is *Folha de S. Paulo*, a traditional newspaper widely criticized by the Bolsonaro movement, which inspired names like *Folha Política* e *Folha do Brasil*, disinformation outlets.
9 Available at www.nbcnews.com/news/latino/facebook-yanks-bolsonaro-video-claiming-vaccines-cause-aids-rcna3771
10 Available at www.cnnbrasil.com.br/politica/ministro-do-stf-abre-novas-investigacoes-contra-deputadas-bolsonaristas/ and www.bbc.com/portuguese/brasil-63990040
11 Available at www.intercept.com.br/2021/06/08/youtube-paga-milhoes-canais-bolsonaristas-stf/
12 Available at www.nytimes.com/pt/2020/08/04/opinion/international-world/bolsonaro-gabinete-do-odio.html
13 Available at www.justicaeleitoral.jus.br/fato-ou-boato/#
14 In the early months of the government in 2019, the second Minister of Education in Bolsonaro's administration set out to deny the merits of public universities, accusing them of being spaces of "disorder" and "large marijuana plantations" (see https://theconversation.com/brazilian-universities-fear-bolsonaro-plan-to-eliminate-humanities-and-slash-public-education-budgets-117530). These accusations from the head of the ministry were used as justification for the subsequent budget constraints and cuts to these institutions, which only intensified in the following years.

15 Available at: www.metropoles.com/brasil/politica-brasil/bolsonaro-rebate-lula-sobre-fim-do-auxilio-brasil-e-mentira
16 Jovem Pan is a Brazilian journalistic group that has taken a stance in favor of the far-right, openly expressing support for Jair Bolsonaro since the 2018 elections.
17 Rede Record is a group owned by Edir Macedo, the leader of the Universal Church of the Kingdom of God, and it was one of the conglomerates of information with one of the largest shares of the advertising budget of the Bolsonaro government.
18 Available at https://edition.cnn.com/2023/01/09/americas/brazil-congress-attack-explained-intl/index.html

References

Allcott, Hunt, and Gentzkow, Matthew (2017), "Social media and fake news in the 2016 election," *Journal of Economic Perspectives*, v. 31, n. 2, pp. 211–236.

Arretche, Marta (2022). Para onde vamos? Federalismo, relações intergovernamentais e políticas públicas. In: Inácio, Magna, and Oliveira, Vanessa Elias de (Eds.), *Democracia e eleições no Brasil: para onde vamos?* 1st ed., Hucitec, São Paulo, pp. 270–288.

Avritzer, Leonardo, Santana, Eliara, and Bragatto, Rachel C. (Eds.) (2023), *Eleições 2022 e a reconstrução da democracia no Brasil,* Autêntica, Belo Horizonte, Brazil.

Bennett, W. Lance, and Livingston, Steven (2018). "The disinformation order: Disruptive communication and the decline of democratic institutions," *European Journal of Communication*, v. 33, n. 2, pp. 122–139.

Chagas, Viktor, Mitozo, Isabele, Barros, Samuel, Santos, João Guilherme, and Azevedo, Dilvan (2021), "The 'new age' of political participation? WhatsApp and call to action on the Brazilian Senate's consultations on the e-Cidadania Portal," *Journal of Information Technology & Politics*, v. 19, n. 3, pp. 253–268. DOI: 10.1080/19331681.2021.1962779

Côrtes, Soraya Varga, and Santos, Priscilla Ribeiro dos (2022), "Políticas sociais do governo Bolsonaro e a promoção da descoordenação e da desigualdade: políticas de saúde e de assistência social," in: Inácio, Magna, and Oliveira, Vanessa Elias de (Eds.), *Democracia e eleições no Brasil: para onde vamos?* 1st ed., Hucitec, São Paulo, pp. 289–316.

Curato, Nicole, and Fossati, Diego (2020), "Authoritarian Innovations: Crafting support for a less democratic Southeast Asia," *Democratization*, v. 27, no. 6, pp. 1006–1020.

Dahl, Robert A. (1998), *Polyarchy: Participation and Opposition*, Yale University Press, New Haven and London.

Dourado, Tatiana, and Salgado, Suzana (2021), "Disinformation in the Brazilian pre-election context: probing the content, spread and implications of fake news about Lula da Silva," *Communication Review*, v. 24, n. 4, pp. 297–319.

Downs, Anthon (1957), *An economic theory of democracy*, Harper, New York, NY.

Jordan, Andrew, Green-Pedersen, Christoffer, and Turnpenny, John (2014), "Policy dismantling: An introducint," in: Bauer, Michael et al. (Eds.), *Dismantling public policy: Preferences, strategies, and effects*, Oxford University Press, Oxford.

Massuchin, Michele G., Tavares, Camilla Q., Mitozo, Isabele B., and Chagas, Viktor. (2021), "A estrutura argumentativa do descrédito na ciência: Uma análise de mensagens de grupos bolsonaristas de WhatsApp na pandemia da COVID-19," *Revista Fronteiras – estudos midiáticos*, vol. 23, n. 2, pp. 160–174.

Mendonça, Ricardo F., and Sarmento, Rayza (Eds.) (2023), *Crises da democracia e esfera pública: Debates contemporâneos*. Ed. UFMG/Incipit, Belo Horizonte, MG.

Mendonça, Ricardo F., Ercan, Selen A., and Asenbaum, Hans. (2022), "More than words: A multidimensional approach to deliberative democracy," *Political Studies*, v. 70, n. 1, pp. 153–172.

Mont'Alverne, Camila, and Mitozo, Isabele (2019), "Muito além da mamadeira erótica: As notícias compartilhadas nas redes de apoio a presidenciáveis em grupos de WhatsApp, nas eleições brasileiras de 2018," *Proceedings of the 8th COMPOLÍTICA*, Brasília-Brazil, pp. 1–25.

Newman, Nic et al. (2021). *Reuters Institute Digital News Report*, 10th Edition, Reuters Institute for the Study of Journalism.

Pierson, Paul. (1994), *Dismantling the Welfare State? Reagan, Thatcher and the Politics of Retrenchment*, Cambridge University Press, Cambridge.

Pinto, Pamela, Antunes, Maria João, and Almeida, Ana Margarida (2021), "Public Health on Instagram: an analysis of health promotion strategies of Portugal and Brazil," *Proceedings of the CENTERIS – International Conference on Enterprise Information Systems / ProjMAN – International Conference on Project Management / HCist – International Conference on Health and Social Care Information Systems and Technologies*, Algarve, Portugal, pp. 231–238.

Posetti, Julie, and Bontcheva, Kalina (2020), *Disinfodemic: deciphering COVID-19 disinformation*, UNESCO, Paris.

Przeworski, Adam (2019), *Crises of democracy*, Cambridge University Press, Cambridge.

Rossi, Rinaldo de Castilho, and Silva, Simone Affonso da (2020), "O Consórcio do Nordeste e o federalismo brasileiro em tempos de Covid-19," *Espaço e Economia: Revista brasileira de geografia econômica*, v. 18, pp. 1–16.

Rossini, Patricia, Stromer-Galley, Jennifer, Oliveira, Vanessa Veiga de, and Baptista, Erica Anita (2020), "Dysfunctional information sharing on WhatsApp and Facebook: The role of political talk, cross-cutting exposure and social corrections," *New Media & Society*, v. 23, n. 8, pp. 2430–2451.

Röth, Leonce, Afonso, Alexandre, and Spies, Dennis C. (2017), "The impact of Populist Radical Right Parties on socio-economic policies," *European Political Science Review*, v. 10, n. 3, pp. 325–350.

Ruediger, Marco Aurélio, and Grassi, Amaro. (Coord.) (2020), *Desinformação on-line e processos políticos: a circulação de links sobre desconfiança no sistema eleitoral brasileiro no Facebook e no YouTube (2014–2020)*, Policy paper, FGV DAPP, Rio de Janeiro-RJ.

Santana, Eliara (2022), *Jornal Nacional, um ator político em cena. Do impeachment de Dilma Rousseff à eleição de Jair Bolsonaro: as bases da construção da narrativa jornalística que legitimou processos políticos na recente história brasileira*, 1st ed., Meraki, Andradina, Brazil.

Schneiker, Andrea (2019), "Telling the story of the superhero and the anti-politician as president: Donald Trump's branding on Twitter," *Political Studies Review*, v. 17, n. 3, pp. 1–14. DOI: 10.1177/1478929918807712

Wardle, Claire, and Derakshan, Hossein (2017), *Information Disorder: Toward an interdisciplinary framework for research and policy making*, Council of Europe Report.

6

INCOME INEQUALITY AND POVERTY IN BRAZIL SINCE RE-DEMOCRATIZATION

An overview

Pedro H. G. Ferreira de Souza

6.1 Introduction

The electoral successes of radical right-wing populists in recent years have stoked fears of democratic backsliding across the globe. Brazilian democracy underwent its own stress test when prolonged political and economic crises culminated in the election of President Jair Bolsonaro in 2018. While Bolsonaro's failed reelection bid in 2022 assuaged fears for the moment, it is unlikely that his substantial political base will disperse anytime soon. In the words of Levitsky (2018, p. 102), Brazilian democracy has survived, but it is hardly thriving.

The time is ripe to take stock of the accomplishments and shortcomings of the New Republic, and this chapter places its focus on the distribution of income since re-democratization. To begin, I document trends and levels of income inequality and monetary poverty since 1985 alongside international comparisons. Data and measurement issues are the main challenges, often leading to conflicting results. Hence, I discuss different approaches in detail. Next, I apply decomposition methods to pinpoint the proximate determinants of distributional changes and review the prevailing explanations.

My approach emphasizes the political backdrop and the pivotal role of institutions. This framing is motivated by a puzzling dissonance in recent appraisals of Brazilian institutions. Redistribution has been a recurring theme in Brazilian politics since the end of the military dictatorship. The 1988 Federal Constitution enshrined poverty eradication and inequality reduction as fundamental goals of the New Republic, and this commitment has underpinned the political discourse for decades. While the rhetoric often rings hollow, it nonetheless expresses a profound shift in the political landscape: the institutional

DOI: 10.4324/9781003487777-7

framework established after 1988 undeniably bolstered the political incentives to promote "social inclusion" (Alston et al., 2013; Arretche, 2018).

Nevertheless, lasting progress remains elusive. Public opinion polls reveal widespread disillusionment, with most adults believing that inequality persists at excessively high levels and is unlikely to diminish in the short run (Oxfam Brasil, 2022). "Extreme social inequality" is in fact frequently mentioned as a structural cause of political dissatisfaction in Brazil and elsewhere in Latin America (Levitsky, 2018). Recent empirical evidence aligns with this pessimism: extreme poverty endures (Souza et al., 2022) and comparative studies still rank Brazil among the world's most unequal nations (e.g., Chancel et al., 2022).

This chapter contends that both sides of the argument have merit. On one hand, democratic institutions have abetted profound changes in the distribution of income. By most metrics, poverty and inequality in Brazil have markedly decreased over the past four decades. Absolute poverty declined the most, but there was also some success in reducing relative poverty and income inequality. On the other hand, progress has been bookended by substantial setbacks. The most noteworthy improvements occurred during the relatively brief period from 2003 to 2015, when a confluence of political and economic circumstances resulted in growth and redistribution among much of the population. There is little cause for celebration either before or after this period. Furthermore, even during the prosperous years of 2003–2015, the concentration of income at the top persisted unabated.

This unresolved tension underscores the dilemma facing highly unequal developing countries: democratic institutions are crucial to social progress, but not very conducive to sustaining incremental changes over a long enough period (Souza, 2018a, 2018b). Large-scale redistribution usually happens in spurts during times of massive crises and disruptions (Scheidel, 2018).

6.2 Levels and trends in income inequality

6.2.1 Interpersonal inequality

Most research on income inequality in Brazil analyzes the distribution of pre-tax, post-transfer household income per capita as reported by household surveys. Accordingly, Figure 6.1 presents the evolution of selected measures of income inequality estimated from Brazil's flagship surveys. Panel (a) charts the most popular Lorenz-consistent indicators, like the Gini coefficient, and panel (b) shows percentile ratios.

Both panels tell the same story: high inequality with no clear trend until the late 1990s, followed by a steep decline starting in the early 2000s, which came to a halt by 2015. Inequality climbed quickly between 2015 and 2019, then the

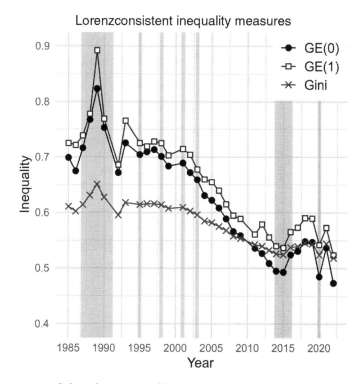

FIGURE 6.1   Selected measures of income inequality – Brazil, 1985–2022.

Notes: Results refer to pre-tax, post-transfer household income per capita. Shaded areas denote recessions. PNAD and PNADC series were harmonized by anchoring relative changes between 1985 and 2011 to observed levels in the 2012 PNADC.

Source: Author's calculations based on PNAD and PNADC microdata.

onset of the pandemic brought wild fluctuations. All series end on a positive note, though: by 2022, most measures were close to their lowest since the 1980s.

The ebb and flow of income inequality correlates with national politics and Brazil's checkered economic performance (see Chapter 4 in this volume). Transition to democracy occurred amidst rising inflation and protracted economic downturns, and income inequality fluctuated, except for a brief spike in the late 1980s. The *Plano Real* achieved macroeconomic stabilization in 1994, but most measures hardly budged, and inequality plateaued until the early 2000s. At that point, even researchers were dismayed by the "unacceptable persistence of high inequality" (Barros et al., 2000).

The fall in inequality in household surveys began around the turn of the century and took off in earnest during President Lula's first term. The Gini coefficient plunged 12% between 2003 and 2015. Other inequality measures

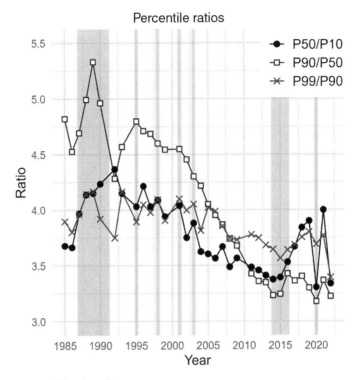

FIGURE 6.1   (Continued)

recorded even steeper declines. Unsurprisingly, all the gloom and doom turned into unabashed optimism (e.g., Alston et al., 2013; Lopez-Calva and Rocha, 2012; Neri, 2008). Soares (2008) even speculated that Brazil could reach Canadian levels of inequality in a couple of decades if income inequality kept falling at the same rate.

Alas, it was not to be. The deep recession of 2014–2016 inaugurated a period of political and economic turmoil that reversed the previous trend. Inequality increased between 2015 and 2019. The Gini coefficient grew by 4%, the GE(0) rose by 11%, and the P50/P10 ratio soared by 15%. Then the onset of the pandemic disrupted the pattern once again. Inequality fluctuated wildly owing to erratic government policy: it dipped in 2020 as the massive Covid-19 stimulus greatly expanded cash transfers to poor and vulnerable families, spiked again in 2021 as most measures expired, and finally plunged again in 2022 as President Jair Bolsonaro ramped up social spending as part of his failed reelection bid.

Figure 6.2 illustrates the association between politics, growth, and inequality more forcefully by displaying the joint evolution of the Gini coefficient (vertical axis) and average incomes (horizontal axis) under each

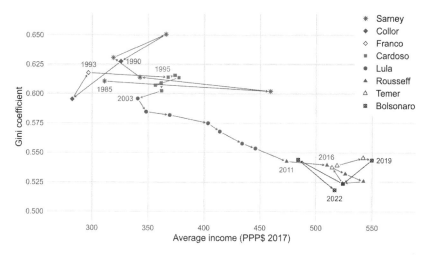

FIGURE 6.2   Gini coefficient *versus* average income per capita over Presidential terms — Brazil, 1985–2022.

Notes: Results refer to pre-tax, post-transfer household income per capita. Hollow symbols refer to vice presidents who took office after the impeachment and removal from office of their predecessors. PNAD and PNADC series were harmonized by anchoring relative changes between 1985 and 2011 to observed levels in the 2012 PNADC.

Source: Author's calculations based on PNAD and PNADC microdata.

President since re-democratization. The Lula (2003–2010) and, to a much lesser degree, the Dilma Rousseff (2011–2016) years stand out: the Workers' Party administrations were the only period of growth and redistribution. Trendless fluctuations prevailed before and afterward. Naturally, it is unwarranted to ascribe the evolution of income inequality in Brazil solely to partisanship: Figure 6.2 depicts a mere correlation, and the causal influence of national politics on the distribution of income is hard to ascertain and context-dependent (Kenworthy, 2010).

Moreover, most of Latin America also combined growth and some degree of redistribution in the 2000s. Figure 6.3 shows a similar trend for the Gini coefficient in Brazil and the rest of the region: inequality fell after the turn of the century and then tapered off in the mid-2010s, with Brazil faring worse than the unweighted average of other countries in Latin American and the Caribbean (LAC) in the years right before the Covid pandemic. In turn, upper-middle-income countries in other regions (non-LAC UMC)[1] experienced a different pattern: no significant reductions in inequality during the 2000s, followed by a slight decline after 2015. Both Brazil and LAC still grapple with much higher levels of inequality, although the gap between the series has narrowed down somewhat.

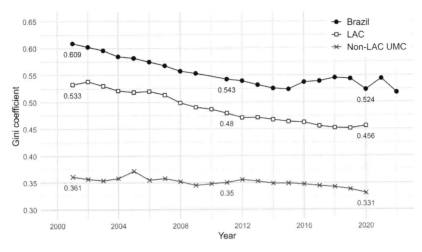

FIGURE 6.3 Gini coefficients in Brazil, Latin America and the Caribbean (LAC) and other upper-middle-income countries (non-LAC UMC), 2001–2022.

Notes: Brazilian results are the same as in Figure 6.1. LAC is the unweighted average of 11 countries in Latin America & the Caribbean (Argentina, Colombia, Costa Rica, Dominican Republic, Ecuador, Honduras, Panama, Paraguay, Peru, and Uruguay). Non-LAC UMC is the unweighted average of 12 upper-middle-income countries outside of LAC (Armenia, Belarus, Bulgaria, Georgia, Indonesia, Kazakhstan, Moldova, North Macedonia, Russia, Serbia, Thailand, and Turkey).

Source: Author's calculations based on PNAD and PNADC microdata for Brazil and World Bank (2023) for Latin America and Caribbean (LAC) and non-LAC upper-middle-income countries.

6.2.2 Top income shares

Household surveys are the standard source of statistics on poverty and inequality worldwide. However, their limitations are well-known. For our purposes, the relevant problem is that surveys struggle to capture the upper tail of the income distribution, leading to downward biased estimates of top income shares, inequality levels and, in some cases, inequality trends (Atkinson et al., 2011; Blanchet et al., 2022; Kennickell, 2017; Yonzan et al., 2022). As a response, researchers are increasingly turning to administrative records to study the concentration of income at the top, with personal income tax returns emerging as the preferred data source.

Figure 6.4 compares the income share of the top 1% according to income tax tabulations and household surveys (Souza, 2018a, 2018b). Due to data constraints, results refer to the distribution of individual incomes among adults, not household income per capita (as in the previous section). Clearly, the concentration of income at the top is severely underestimated by Brazilian household surveys. The top 1% income share is, on average, about nine percentage points (p.p.) higher in the tax data. Methodological differences notwithstanding, top shares

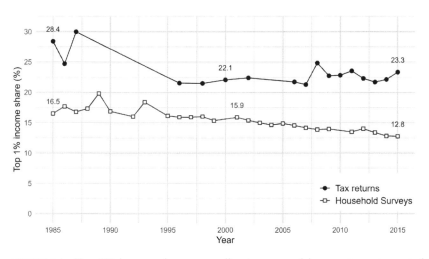

FIGURE 6.4   Top 1% income shares according to personal income tax returns and household surveys – Brazil, 1985–2015.

Notes: Results refer to pre-tax, post-transfer individual incomes among adults aged 20 or older.

Source: Souza (2018a).

in Brazil are comparable to many Latin American countries but around twice as high as in Europe (Chancel et al., 2022; Souza, 2018a, 2018b). More puzzlingly, trends differ markedly between data sources: as opposed to surveys, estimates from income tax returns show no decline in top shares after 2001. This finding is robust to wide-ranging methodological choices (Medeiros et al., 2015; Morgan, 2017) and not exclusive to Brazil, as survey and tax estimates also clash in many other Latin American countries (De Rosa et al., 2022).

The contrast between income tax data and household surveys suggests the latter may have overestimated the magnitude of distributional changes in Brazil. Souza's (2018a) "adjusted" Gini coefficients imply the decrease in inequality may have been only half as large as previously estimated. The rising concentration of property incomes and capital gains at the top is the main explanation for the divergence (Medeiros and Castro, 2018). Unfortunately, the Brazilian tax revenue agency only publishes limited data on income tax returns, making conclusions tentative.

Tax returns and household surveys also furnish conflicting evidence for the post-recession period. De Rosa, Flores, and Morgan (2022) find a slight dip in the top 1% share and no change in the Gini coefficient between 2015 and 2019, followed by a slight uptick in both indicators in 2020. In contrast, household surveys reveal rising inequality up to 2019, followed by a tumble in 2020. Differences in income concepts and units of analysis may partly account for the divergence, though much work still needs to be done to reconcile household surveys and administrative data. Presently, the accumulated evidence indicates that income concentration at the top is higher and more persistent than previously thought. Survey estimates apparently exaggerate the fall in inequality in the 2000s. The picture for recent years is still foggy, and the scarcity of studies using tax records recommends caution.

Due to data constraints, the remainder of this chapter relies exclusively on household surveys. Readers are advised to interpret all findings presented hereafter as pertaining to the "bottom 99%" of the income distribution.

6.3 Levels and trends in monetary poverty

The standard approach to poverty monitoring in Brazil is to compare pre-tax, post-transfer household income per capita to administrative poverty lines. This norm deviates from international practice due to data limitations (budget and consumption surveys are only carried out once or twice per decade) and institutional factors (means-tested social programs adopt similar definitions). None of the controversies befalling inequality researchers spill over into poverty studies, although researchers have acknowledged problems like income measurement error and the misreporting of program participation (e.g., Souza and Bruce, 2022).

Figure 6.5 tracks the evolution of poverty – as measured by the FGT(0) and FGT(2) indices (Foster et al., 1984) – according to three absolute poverty lines frequently used in international research. The PPP$ 2.15/day poverty line is the World Bank's benchmark to monitor global poverty, while the other two reflect median national poverty thresholds among lower and upper-middle-income countries ($3.65/day and $6.85/day, respectively). By this yardstick, Brazil has made great progress against poverty since re-democratization, with both measures falling by 40–60% since the mid-1980s. Improvements first came in spurts, with a very short-lived dip in 1986 during the *Plano Cruzado* and a more permanent one-off tumble when the *Plano Real* reigned in inflation in the mid-1990s. Prolonged poverty reduction only took off from 2003 onwards as economic growth resumed and inequality receded. Again, the mid-2010s recession reversed course. Real incomes collapsed in the bottom deciles of the income distribution, erasing a few years' worth of progress. Poverty rates swayed considerably during the pandemic: the uptick in 2021 was the largest year-on-year increase in poverty in three decades, raising most indicators to their worst levels since the late 2000s; conversely, the falloff in 2022 was equally steep, bringing poverty down again to similar levels as in 2014–2015. Still, extreme poverty has not been eradicated.

Conclusions are less optimistic for relative poverty lines, as expressed in Figure 6.5 by the relative threshold set at 50% of median income per capita (50% of P50). Poverty headcount rates hardly budged over time, and poverty severity

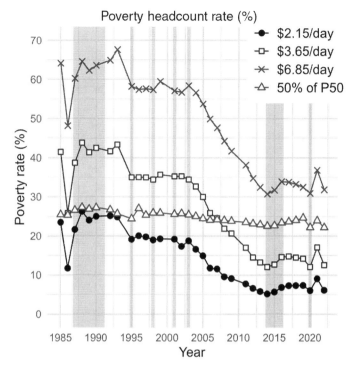

FIGURE 6.5   FGT measures of monetary poverty for absolute and relative poverty lines – Brazil, 1985–2022.

Notes: Poverty headcount and poverty severity rates are, respectively, the FGT(0) and FGT(2) measures estimated from the distribution of pre-tax, post-transfer household income per capita. Global poverty lines of $2.15, $3.65, and $6.85 calculated by Jolliffe et al. (2022) using 2017 PPP factors. Shaded areas denote recessions. PNAD and PNADC series were harmonized by anchoring relative changes between 1985 and 2011 to observed levels in the 2012 PNADC.

Source: Author's calculations based on PNAD and PNADC microdata.

rates did not fare much better, with the slight decline in the 1990s and 2000s being offset after 2015. Income inequality in the bottom half of the distribution has essentially flatlined for decades.

The Datt and Ravallion (1992) decompositions in Figure 6.6 convey the unique pattern of pro-poor growth between 2003–2015. On average, the poverty headcount rate at PPP$ 3.65/day decreased by 1.5 p.p. per year. Income growth by itself entailed a reduction of almost one p.p. per year, while falling inequality accounted for the rest. Both contributions were four to five times lower in the previous period (1985–2003). From 2015 onwards, growth and redistribution moved in opposing directions, and the latter became the main driver of changes: rising inequality contributed to increasing poverty from 2015 to 2019,

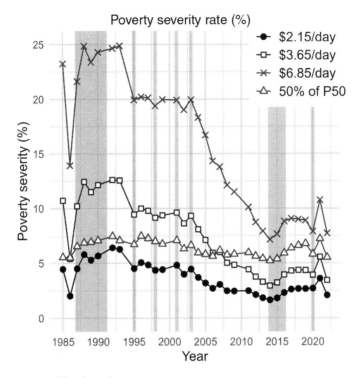

FIGURE 6.5 (Continued)

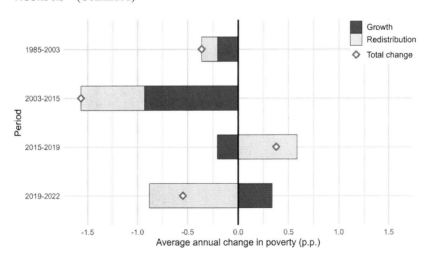

FIGURE 6.6 Datt-Ravallion decomposition of the variation in the $3.65/day poverty rate by period – Brazil, 1985–2003, 2003–2015, 2015–2019, and 2019–2022.

Notes: "Growth" measures the variation in poverty associated with changes in the mean income; "redistribution" is the shift in poverty due to changes in inequality while keeping the mean constant. See Datt and Ravallion (1992). Residual eliminated by the Shapley method.

Source: Author's calculations based on PNAD and PNADC microdata.

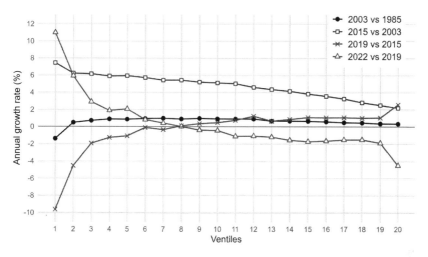

FIGURE 6.7 Growth incidence curves – Brazil, 1985–2003, 2003–2015, 2015–2019, and 2019–2022 (% per year).

Notes: Results refer pre-tax, post-transfer household income per capita.

Source: Author's calculations based on PNAD and PNADC microdata.

while redistribution between 2019 and 2022 played an outsized role in poverty reduction.

Growth incidence curves (GIC) offer valuable insights into the disparity between absolute and relative poverty trends. Figure 6.7 compares annual growth rates across ventiles of the income distribution over the same periods as in Figure 6.6. Between 1985 and 2003, average growth rates were low and flat across ventiles, except for the poorest 5%, who suffered real income losses. The GIC comparing 2015 to 2003 is completely different: income growth was fastest among the poor, but even the top 5% benefitted substantially. Hence, absolute poverty collapsed. Relative poverty did not improve as much due to the modest difference in growth rates between the bottom tail and the median.

The GICs comparing 2019 to 2015 and 2022 to 2019 mirror each other almost perfectly. The recession and its aftermath were disastrous for the bottom 20%. Real incomes among this group cratered from 2015 to 2019, and the poorest ventiles bore the worst of the crisis. No one except the top ventile experienced meaningful income growth: for the richest 5% the recession was a mere blip on the radar, with average incomes growing at a rate comparable to the prosperous years between 2003 and 2015. The pandemic upended this pattern. The poorest ventiles saw the largest relative gains during this period,

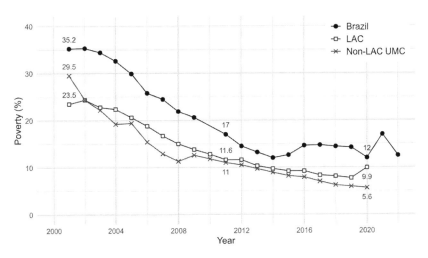

FIGURE 6.8 Poverty headcount rates at PPP$ 3.65/day in Brazil, Latin America and the Caribbean (LAC) and other upper-middle-income countries (non-LAC UMC), 2001–2022.

Notes: Brazilian results are the same as in Figure 6.5. LAC is the unweighted average of the same 11 countries as in Figure 6.3. Non-LAC UMC is the unweighted average of the same 12 countries as in Figure 6.3.

Source: Author's calculations based on PNAD and PNADC microdata for Brazil and World Bank (2023) for Latin America and Caribbean (LAC) and non-LAC upper-middle-income countries.

marking a departure from previous trends. Conversely, the upper half of the income distribution was bogged down by the economic hurdles. This time, the top 5% hurt the most.

Finally, Figure 6.8 presents the poverty headcount rate in Brazil alongside estimates for Latin America & the Caribbean and other upper-middle-income countries (non-LAC UMC). The early 21st century witnessed widespread poverty reduction. Brazil essentially converged to the (unweighted) regional average due to stronger performance in the 2000s and to the Covid-induced dip in poverty. However, this accomplishment appears less impressive when contrasted to the non-LAC UMC series. Upper-middle-income countries in other regions sustained high growth rates for a much longer period, outpacing Latin America in the 2000s. The 2008–2009 global financial crisis was a short-lived slump, and the decline in poverty resumed in the early 2010s.

Overall, Brazil has made greater strides in reducing poverty than in addressing income inequality, which aligns with Arretche's (2018) argument that the institutions that emerged after the democratic transition are geared towards the "inclusion of outsiders," rather than outright redistribution from the top.

6.4 Understanding changes in inequality and poverty in the 21st century

Brazil's journey has been marked by ups and downs. The high hopes engendered by re-democratization were dashed by the persistence of high poverty and inequality in the 1980s and 1990s. Encouraging signs of change appeared at the turn of the century, and suddenly Brazil entered an unprecedented period of prosperity. Poverty declined swiftly for about a decade and a half, and inequality among most of the population narrowed considerably. Progress stalled in the early 2010s, then reversed in the wake of the 2014–2016 recession, leading another "lost decade" (Barbosa et al., 2020). Finally, the COVID-19 pandemic ushered in another period of sharp fluctuations.

What explains the twists and turns in poverty and inequality in the 21st century? Innumerable factors affect the distribution of income, and a grand unified theory of distributional change is as elusive as cold fusion. More realistically, one common approach is to use decomposition methods as the first building block to understand how the interplay of markets and institutions shapes trends in poverty and inequality. In this section, I apply such methods to decompose distributional changes by income components and then relate the results to the accumulated evidence from previous studies.

6.4.1 Decompositions by income sources

Shapley-Shorrocks decompositions provide a coherent framework for breaking down distributional changes by income components (cf. Azevedo et al., 2013; Azevedo et al., 2012; Barros, Henriques et al., 2006; Shorrocks, 2013). Figures 6.9 and 6.10 present results for the Gini coefficient and the poverty headcount rate at the PPP\$ 3.65/day poverty line, respectively, over three periods (2003–2015, 2015–2019, and 2019–2022). Household income per capita was divided into labor market earnings (the sum of wages and salaries and self-employment income), Social Insurance benefits (retirement and survivors' pensions and unemployment insurance), Social Assistance transfers (means-tested transfers to the poor), and other sources of income. Both figures report average annual changes as the periods under consideration vary in length. All estimates are based on household survey data, so they do not reflect the persistence of top income shares registered in personal income tax returns and overstate the reduction in inequality. Nevertheless, the survey-based decompositions shed light on the fall in inequality among the "bottom 99%."

All income components typically moved in the same direction in the Gini decompositions displayed in Figure 6.9. Labor earnings were the leading driver of the downturn in inequality from 2003 to 2015, accounting for 51% of the drop in the Gini, but Social Assistance transfers (22%), Social Insurance benefits (18%), and other incomes (9%) made meaningful contributions as well. The

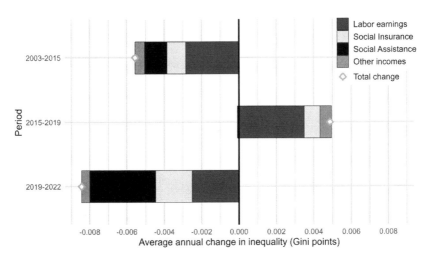

FIGURE 6.9   Shapley–Shorrocks decompositions of changes in the Gini coefficient by income sources – Brazil, 2003–2015, 2015–2019, and 2019–2022.

Notes: Results refer to pre-tax, post-transfer household income per capita. *Labor earnings* comprise wages and salaries as well as earnings of employers and self-employed workers; *Social Insurance* encompasses contributory public pensions and unemployment benefits; *Social Assistance* refers to non-contributory transfers targeted to the poor (BPC and Bolsa Família); *other incomes* include other sources of non-labor income captured in surveys. See Azevedoet al. (2012); Azevedo et al. (2013); Barros, Carvalho et al. (2006); Shorrocks (2013).

Source: Author's calculations based on PNAD and PNADC microdata.

turnaround in the mid-2010s was stark, with the average annual increase in the Gini coefficient matching the earlier decrease (roughly 0.005 Gini points per year). Once again, labor earnings were at the forefront, contributing to more than 70% of the upswing. Contributory benefits and other incomes split the difference, while Social Assistance transfers had a minimal negative contribution. Surprisingly, the Bolsonaro years (2019–2022) marked another reversal of the trend: the Gini coefficient fell at a blistering 0.008 points per year, driven by redistributive changes across all income sources. Social Assistance transfers accounted for 42% of the decline, with labor earnings (30%) and Social Insurance benefits (23%) making substantial contributions as well.

The poverty headcount decompositions in Figure 6.10 deviate slightly from this pattern. Overall, the rate of poverty reduction from 2003 to 2015 (over 1.5 p.p. per year) was not matched in subsequent periods. Labor earnings were also relatively more consequential to changes in the poverty rate compared to the Gini coefficient. Lastly, income sources moved in opposite direction during the period from 2019 to 2022: the downswing in poverty was entirely driven by Social Assistance transfers, while the other three components slowed down the rate of poverty reduction.

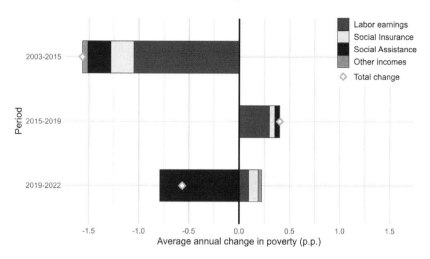

FIGURE 6.10 Shapley–Shorrocks decompositions of changes in the poverty headcount rate at the PPP$ 3.65/day poverty line by income sources – Brazil, 2003–2015, 2015–2019, and 2019–2022.

Notes: Results refer to pre-tax, post-transfer household income per capita. *Labor earnings* comprise wages and salaries as well as earnings of employers and self-employed workers; *Social Insurance* encompasses contributory public pensions and unemployment benefits; *Social Assistance* refers to non-contributory transfers targeted to the poor (BPC and Bolsa Família); *other incomes* include other sources of non-labor income captured in surveys. See Azevedo et al. (2012); Azevedo et al. (2013); Barros, Carvalho et al. (2006); Shorrocks (2013).

Source: Author's calculations based on PNAD and PNADC microdata.

Two caveats are in order. First, the decompositions are only descriptive tools that rely on counterfactual income distributions generated by modifying one income source at a time while keeping everything else constant. Second, the results for the most recent period hinge entirely on the choice of the endpoint, given the abrupt fluctuations in poverty and inequality during the Bolsonaro administration. In any case, the decompositions illuminate the relative contributions of each income source to changes in poverty and inequality, but they do not, and cannot, explain the underlying reasons for these trends. Sections 6.4.2, 6.4.3, and 6.4.4 review the prevailing explanations for each case. Given its heterogenous nature and minor contributions, I do not analyze the residual component encompassing all other income sources.

6.4.2 Labor market earnings

Labor earnings comprise 75% to 85% of total income reported in Brazilian household surveys, overshadowing all other income components. Social Insurance benefits come in a distant second, accounting for just 15–20% in recent years.[2] Thus, labor market outcomes have an outsized influence on the personal income distribution. Accordingly, the previous section showed labor earnings played a pivotal role in redistribution from 2003 to 2015, followed by an even more prominent contribution to rising poverty and inequality between 2015 and 2019.

Panel (a) in Figure 6.11 depicts the evolution of the unemployment rate alongside the breakdown by educational attainment, while panel (b) tracks percentiles ratios at different parts of the earnings distribution. Between 2003 and 2015 low- and medium-skilled workers experienced an increasingly tighter job market, and earnings inequality fell across the board. Unemployment rates soared during the 2014–2016 recession, barely dipped between 2016 and 2019, peaked again as the pandemic ravaged the country and finally plunged in 2022.

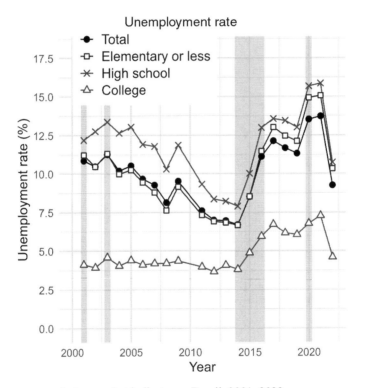

FIGURE 6.11 Labor market indicators – Brazil, 2001–2022.

Notes: results refer to adults aged 18 to 64. Percentile ratios calculated for earned income from all jobs, with the estimating sample trimmed at the 0.5th and 99.5th percentiles. Shaded areas denote recessions. PNAD and PNADC series were harmonized by anchoring relative changes between 1985 and 2011 to observed levels in the 2012 PNADC.

Source: author's calculations based on PNAD and PNADC microdata.

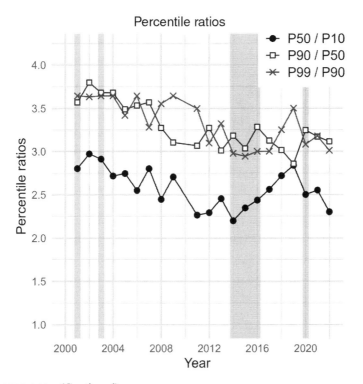

Percentile ratios

FIGURE 6.11   (Continued)

Workers with low or intermediate educational credentials bore the brunt of the recession, while top earners prospered. Correspondingly, the P50/P10 and P99/P90 ratios climbed back to levels last seen in the mid-2000 before sloping down after the onset of the Covid shock.

The strong labor market performance of the 2000s – also replicated in most of Latin America – spurred a cottage industry of academic studies (e.g., Barros, Foguel et al., 2006; Engbom et al., 2022; Ferreira et al., 2022; Firpo and Portella, 2019; Messina and Silva, 2021). Brazil and its neighbors shared a similar confluence of structural and contextual factors, leading to a virtuous interplay of market forces and institutions.

Diminishing returns to human capital played a significant role in reducing earnings inequality. Returns to education and experience saw sharp declines after 2002 (Ferreira et al., 2022; Firpo and Portella, 2019; Messina and Silva, 2021). Shifts in the relative supply of education were large enough to partially explain the narrowing of the educational premiums, with increased access to schooling translating into higher attainment and lower educational inequality among younger cohorts. The compression in returns to experience is more challenging to understand. Demographic changes do not explain the decline, which was the key driver of the reduction in earnings inequality in Brazil (Ferreira et al., 2022; Firpo and Portella, 2019). Lower returns to education compressed wages in the bottom half of the distribution, but education seemingly did not matter much for broader measures of inequality due to the so-called paradox of progress, whereby educational upgrading entails higher inequality due to the convexity of the educational premiums (Ferreira et al., 2022).

The puzzling reduction in the experience premium and the steep decline in earnings inequality within skill groups highlight the need to go beyond human capital theory. Brazil – and, again, most of Latin America – underwent demand shocks that contributed to lower inequality. Some are linked to previous policy choices: for instance, Firpo and Portella (2019) review a long list of studies trying to assess the distributional consequences of trade liberalization in the 1990s. They conclude it had muted direct effects on wage inequality but may have contributed to reducing regional, racial, and gender wage gaps.

The China-driven commodity boom of the 2000s was far more consequential. Commodity-rich countries in Latin America fared better than other countries in the region (Messina and Silva, 2021), and there are several plausible mechanisms suggesting a causal relationship instead of a spurious correlation. Precise quantification of its effects is tricky, but clearly the demand shock triggered by the commodity boom boosted growth, promoted currency appreciation, and relaxed fiscal constraints. The direct effects of the mid-2000s bonanza contributed to diminishing regional and sectoral inequalities, with greater benefits accruing to unskilled and semi-skilled workers. It may have also played a role in compressing skill premiums by encouraging the reallocation of labor across firms and sectors (Firpo and Portella, 2019; Messina and Silva, 2021). Although the exact causes are unclear, interfirm wage differentials in the formal sector have plummeted since the mid-1990s (Alvarez et al., 2018; Messina and Silva, 2021). Additionally, the volatility of earnings in the labor market declined substantially (Engbom et al., 2022).

The indirect impact of the commodity boom may have been even greater, as it provided the Workers' Party administrations the leeway to pursue expansionary policies. We will address the expansion of government benefits and transfers in the following sections, but institutional factors also shaped the earnings distribution, notably the minimum wage policy. The 1988 Constitution enshrined the federal statutory minimum wage (henceforth, MW) as binding for all (formal sector) employees and mandated regular adjustments to compensate for inflation-induced losses. The Constitution also defined the MW as the legal floor to all Social Security benefits, thereby creating a large constituency of workers and pensioners whose incomes are directly pegged to the MW. Raising the MW over and above the mandatory adjustment for inflation became an immensely popular policy, and presidents were happy to oblige after the *Plano Real* stabilized inflation in the mid-1990s.

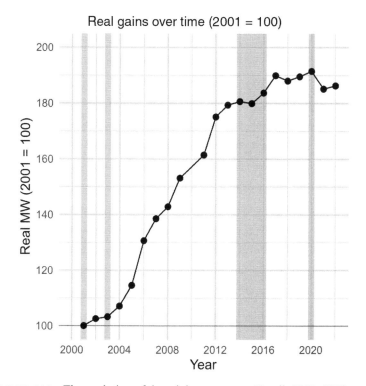

FIGURE 6.12   The evolution of the minimum wage – Brazil, 2001–2022.

Notes: Results in panel (b) refer to adults aged 18 to 64 with full-time jobs, with the estimating sample trimmed at the 0.5th and 99.5th percentiles. Shaded areas denote recessions. PNAD and PNADC series were harmonized by anchoring relative changes between 1985 and 2011 to observed levels in the 2012 PNADC.

Source: Author's calculations based on the MW law, the official consumer price index (INPC) and PNAD and PNADC microdata.

Panel (a) in Figure 6.12 depicts the real value of the MW over time using 2001 as a benchmark. The real minimum wage nearly doubled between 2001 and 2017. Most gains happened during the Lula and Dilma administrations, which leveraged economic growth to prioritize MW hikes, although the upward trend traces back to the Cardoso administration in the 1990s. Panel (b) in Figure 6.12 shows that MW adjustments outpaced earnings growth in the 2000s, with the MW rising from 50% to 65% of median earnings of full-time workers. The proportion hovered around that level in the early 2010s, and then trended upward again after 2018 due to falling labor earnings, rather than MW increases.

There is overwhelming evidence the rising MW compressed the earnings distribution and reduced overall inequality (Brito et al., 2017; Engbom and Moser, 2022; Ferreira et al., 2022). Furthermore, researchers have not

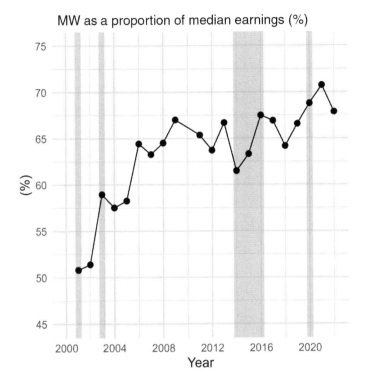

FIGURE 6.12   (Continued)

found negative employment effects nor large-scale displacement to the informal sector. These findings also apply to some extent to many other Latin American countries where "pink tide" governments also granted generous adjustments to the MW in the 2000s (Messina and Silva, 2021). As noted by Firpo and Portella (2019), the relationship between the MW, unemployment and inequality is heavily context dependent. At the turn of the century, MW levels were low across most of Latin America, and real MW adjustments were facilitated by the commodity-driven economic growth of the 2000s. Neither of these circumstances holds true in the 2020s, limiting the potential for further inequality reduction through MW hikes.

6.4.3   Social insurance benefits

Brazilian household surveys collect information on two types of Social Insurance benefits: public pensions (retirement benefits and survivors' pensions) and unemployment insurance (UI). Both are contributory benefits. Outlays on public pensions account for approximately 13% of GDP, a figure 15 to 20 times larger than annual expenditures on UI. Moreover, household surveys severely underestimate the number of UI recipients, so we can safely ascribe all the results in Section 4.1 to public pensions.

Pension spending in Brazil is high considering the country's age structure, and the combined shortfall of public pension schemes often exceeds 4% of GDP (Costanzi et al., 2018; Cuevas et al., 2018). Pundits and politicians frequently raise redistributive concerns both in favor and against pension reform. The decompositions in Section 4.1 show that public pensions were not decisive to poverty and inequality trends, but they did make meaningful, albeit ancillary, contributions to redistribution between 2003 and 2015 and between 2019 and 2022.

All pension systems tend to reproduce past labor market inequality, as refracted by population demographics and institutional design. The Brazilian case is no different. The 1988 Federal Constitution greatly expanded coverage and benefits for low-wage workers without curtailing high replacement rates and premature retirement among the upper-middle classes. At the risk of oversimplification, we may say that a three-tiered pay-as-you-go system emerged in practice: a) low-wage workers had to meet minimum age requirements to become eligible for benefits close or equal to the federal statutory minimum wage (MW), which became the binding legal floor for all Social Security benefits; b) higher-wage workers with stable jobs in the formal private sector retired at a younger age with pensions limited by a benefit cap; and c) public servants had to fulfill even less demanding eligibility criteria and their benefits were not only uncapped but also maintained "wage parity," that is, retirees and their survivors were entitled to all salary hikes associated with the public sector position from which they retired.

Pension spending ballooned following the 1988 Constitution,[3] prompting multiple rounds of reform supported by political leaders from various parties (Costanzi et al., 2018). The general thrust of these reforms was to curb expenditure growth by raising retirement ages and reducing replacement rates (see chapter seven in this volume). The most recent reform was passed by Congress in the first year of the Bolsonaro administration, but microsimulation studies suggest that the redistributive effects of this 2019 reform may be very small. In any case, the cumulative impact of these reforms will take decades to materialize.

Given these constraints, incumbents have limited policy levers at their disposal to promote redistribution through public pensions. The most salient is the federal MW policy. As discussed above, Brazil has unusual constitutional provisions that established the MW as the floor for Social Security benefits. The Cardoso and, to a greater extent, the Lula and Rousseff administrations seized this opportunity for credit-claiming with a large constituency of low-wage workers and pensioners during a period when the MW was still relatively low. The contribution of Social Insurance benefits to lower poverty and inequality between 2003 and 2015 was strongly influenced by the rising minimum wage.

Pensions above the MW were adjusted only for inflation after 2005, as mandated by the Constitution. Hence, the spread of private-sector pension benefits narrowed considerably: the cap-to-floor ratio dropped from roughly 10 in 2004 to about six in 2015.

The effectiveness of redistribution via MW adjustments faced diminishing returns in the mid-2010s. The marginal effect of MW benefits on poverty and inequality declined while the fiscal cost escalated because roughly 60% of all Social Insurance benefits for private sector workers are pegged to the MW. MW growth decelerated during Dilma Rousseff's second term due to the looming recession, slowing to a crawl under Michel Temer and Jair Bolsonaro.

Another lever for redistribution via pensions is the wage policy for public servants, especially high-level bureaucrats at the federal level. As mentioned earlier, most current retirees in the public sector scheme receive pensions that are adjusted in lockstep with wages associated with their former public sector positions. Therefore, the sizable wage increases granted by the Lula administration to public servants also accrued to retired public sector employees and their survivors, partly counteracting the redistributive effects of the MW policy (Barbosa and Souza, 2012; Medeiros and Souza, 2015). After 2014, incumbents essentially froze wages and salaries in the federal government.

Thus, the influence of pensions on poverty and inequality since the mid-2010s is more closely related to inaction than to deliberate policy decisions. Population aging dictated the evolution of the number of recipients, and benefit values grew in line with inflation. Pensioners became relatively richer when incomes for the bottom deciles cratered (2015–2019) and lost ground when these income losses turned into robust gains (2019–2022).

6.4.4   Social assistance transfers

Targeted cash transfers to poor and vulnerable families are a recent innovation in Brazilian social policy, with two prominent federal programs commanding attention. The Benefício de Prestação Continuada (Continuous Cash Benefit; hereafter, BPC) came first: it is an entitlement enshrined in the 1988 Constitution and implemented in the mid-1990s. The BPC offers unconditional, means-tested transfers to individuals with disabilities and elderly citizens who do not meet requirements for contributory social insurance pensions. Benefits are uniform and pegged to the federal minimum wage. In contrast, the Bolsa Família (Family Grant) program was launched in 2003 during the first Lula administration to streamline a patchwork of overlapping federal transfers. From its inception, Bolsa Família was an income supplement for poor families cut off from the formal labor market, paying meager benefits (in comparison to the BPC) to a broader population of low-income families who were, in turn, subject to health and education conditionalities.

Both programs underwent substantial expansion during the 2000s. The BPC catapulted from 1.7 million recipients in early 2004 to 4.2 million in 2015, and average benefits rose in alignment with the MW. As a result, the program's budget climbed from PPP$ 5.2 to 19.2 billion (in constant 2017 international dollars) between 2004 and 2015. Similarly, the number of Bolsa Família families surged from 3.6 to 14 million over the same period, with the average monthly benefit per family growing by 30% (Souza and Bruce, 2022). Federal spending on Bolsa Família increased from PPP$ 3.4 to 13.4 billion. Still, both programs combined for just 1% of GDP in 2015.

The decomposition results in Figures 6.9 and 6.10 demonstrate that the BPC and Bolsa Família punched above their weight: Social Assistance transfers account for 15% of the decline in poverty rate and 22% of the fall in inequality between 2003 and 2015, slightly outperforming Social Insurance benefits, which were 10 to 15 times larger in terms of budget size. Moreover, these outstanding results may be biased downward due to the underreporting of transfers in surveys (Souza and Bruce, 2022).

Indeed, experts lauded both programs for filling notable gaps in the Brazilian social protection system (Costa et al., 2016; Paiva et al., 2019; Souza and Bruce, 2022). Bolsa Família garnered acclaim for eschewing clientelism, promoting access to health and education, and achieving excellent targeting accuracy with no adverse side effects on fertility rates or labor supply decisions (Fried, 2012; Hunter and Power, 2007; Ribeiro et al., 2017; Souza and Bruce, 2022). The program rapidly established itself as Brazil's flagship anti-poverty initiative and one of the world's largest conditional cash transfer programs (CCTs) (World Bank, 2015, p. 12).

Following the footsteps of Brazil and Mexico, many developing countries implemented CCTs in the 2000s, particularly in Latin America (Fiszbein and Schady, 2009). Results for several outcome areas were usually positive (Bastagli et al., 2019), with CCTs making significant contributions to reduce poverty and inequality in many Latin American countries (Gasparini and Cruces, 2021). Nevertheless, most programs were much stingier than Bolsa Família and, thus, did not achieve the same level of redistribution (Souza and Bruce, 2022).

The fiscal crunch of the mid-2010s ended the period of continuous expansion of social assistance transfers. For all its merits, Bolsa Família suffered the most. The program was not an open-ended entitlement, and neither eligibility thresholds nor benefit levels were indexed to inflation or any other parameter. As such, it was an easy target for austerity measures. Incumbents essentially froze the program in place, so coverage did not respond to increased poverty and inflation-adjusted expenditures fell by 13% between 2014 and 2019 (Souza and Bruce, 2022). The BPC fared better because of its more rigidly regulated framework. The MW stopped growing in real terms from the recession onwards, but mandatory annual adjustments protected benefits from inflation. In addition, incumbents could not curtail the scope of the program because eligible individuals have legally actionable claims to participation – the number of recipients grew by 12% between 2015 and 2019. Still, social assistance transfers failed to counteract the upswing in inequality and poverty in this period (Barbosa et al., 2020).

As of late 2019, the most likely scenario was that transfers would continue to wither for the foreseeable future. However, this was not the case either. The Covid-19 pandemic marked a sea change in public spending on welfare transfers: by April 2020, Congress had passed a gargantuan relief package, including a temporary cash transfer program – the Auxílio Emergencial – that was much more generous than the Bolsonaro administration had initially signed off on. Over 68 million Brazilians benefited directly, comprising about one-third of the population. Federal spending on cash transfers climbed from 1.2% of GDP in 2019 to 4.8% in 2020. Poverty and inequality plunged, possibly hitting an all-time low around August 2020.

The Bolsonaro administration was not persuaded. The Auxílio Emergencial expired in late 2020, even though the pandemic still ravaged the country, with Covid-related deaths peaking in March 2021. In April, the federal government introduced a new, less ambitious iteration of the Auxílio. It was too little, too late: household surveys registered the largest year-on-year spike in poverty since the early 1990s (Souza et al., 2022). Inequality ratcheted up as well.

Another policy turnaround took place in 2022. The pandemic waned, but inflation crept up, and President Bolsonaro's low approval ratings endangered his re-election bid. The administration successfully negotiated with Congress an unprecedented waiver from fiscal rules, using social discontent as a pretext. The Bolsonaro administration had reformed the Bolsa Família program in late 2021, renaming it Auxílio Brasil. From the start the revamped program was already more generous than its predecessor, and both the number of recipients and average benefit levels rose considerably in 2022 just a few months ahead of the election.

Ultimately, the staunchly conservative Bolsonaro administration presided over the largest expansion of welfare spending in Brazilian history: electoral incentives to promote the "inclusion of outsiders" trumped ideology. Expenditures on the Auxílio Brasil in 2022 were nearly three times greater in inflation-adjusted terms than what was spent on Bolsa Família the year before the pandemic. This unprecedented expansion fully explains the outsized contribution of Social Assistance transfers to reduce poverty and inequality from 2019 to 2022. Once again, Figures 6.9 and 6.10 probably understate the degree of redistribution operated by transfers during this period due to underreporting and measurement error.

In early 2023, the recently inaugurated Lula administration scrapped the Auxílio Brasil moniker and reverted to the name Bolsa Família. The re-branded program cemented the expansion of transfers by making the temporary changes introduced in 2022 permanent. Additionally, the Lula administration instituted a new benefit for children, so spending on targeted cash transfers in 2023 is expected to be around 40% higher than in 2022, which is likely to lead to further reductions in poverty and inequality. Sustaining this momentum from 2024 onwards may prove challenging as it is very hard to envision additional budget expansions.

6.5 Summary and conclusions

The late historian José Murilo de Carvalho (2001, p. 229) concluded his classic book on citizenship in Brazil by glumly comparing our high levels of social inequality to a malignant tumor that, if not promptly addressed, could cause irreparable damage to the country's fledgling democracy. Hyperbole aside, the concern is still valid almost four decades after the demise of the military dictatorship. Recent threats of authoritarianism raise the need of a critical evaluation of the achievements and failures of our democratic institutions.

In this chapter, I surveyed the evolution of poverty and inequality in Brazil since the mid-1980s. Encouragingly, there was progress across both dimensions. Absolute poverty has declined steeply, regardless of the chosen poverty threshold, and most metrics also show sharp reductions in income inequality in the long run. For instance, the poverty headcount rate using the international benchmark of PPP$ 2.15/day dropped from approximately a quarter of the population in the mid-1980s to 6% in 2022, while the Gini coefficient has fallen 20% since peaking in 1989.

Political institutions were responsive to demands for better living conditions. Improved access to public education, the rising minimum wage, and the expansion of targeted cash transfer programs contributed to reducing poverty and inequality. Political incentives to promote the "inclusion of outsiders" (Arretche, 2018) were so strong that even conservative political leaders often sanctioned large increases in social spending.

Unfortunately, excessive optimism is as unwarranted as relentless pessimism. Progress has been uneven and punctuated by considerable setbacks, with economic instability often reversing previous gains. The relatively narrow period from 2003 to 2015 was the only time of prolonged improvement in poverty and inequality indicators. Worse, top income shares measured from income tax returns did not budge even during this period. Further, international comparisons reveal that poverty and inequality fell at similar rates or even faster elsewhere in Latin America and in upper-middle-income countries in other regions in the early 21st century.

In short, democratic institutions in Brazil have struggled to sustain incremental progress for long. The "lost decade" of the 2010s (Barbosa et al.,

2020) underscored this difficulty. The labor market cratered in the fallout of the 2014–2016 recession and never fully recovered. Poverty and inequality rose, and social policy did not respond effectively at first. Social indicators only improved after the Covid pandemic unleashed an unprecedented expansion of targeted cash transfers to the poor. The silver lining is that this unexpected outcome vindicates more positive views of Brazilian democracy, as political competition has made part of this expansion permanent.

Hopefully, this will serve as a building block for a new era of progress against poverty and inequality. The challenge, however, remains daunting. The low hanging fruit is gone. Fiscal constraints preclude further increases to the minimum wage or social assistance transfers, and such measures are subject to diminishing returns in any case. Budgetary and inflationary concerns hinder the capacity to induce a tighter labor market through expansionary fiscal policy, improving the quality of public education is substantially more difficult than merely promoting enrolment in public schools, and political polarization contributes to economic instability. Population ageing and technological change compound these problems. Durable, long-lasting redistribution will require a new approach.

Notes

1 Brazil is an upper-middle-income country according to the country classification by income level used by the World Bank.
2 Household surveys overstate the income share of labor earnings and public pensions due to differential unit and item nonresponse and underreporting or misreporting of other income sources.
3 The income share of pensions in household surveys doubled from 8%–10% in the late 1980s to 17%–19% in the early 2000s. It has fluctuated around that level since then.

References

Alston, Lee, Marcus Andre Melo, Bernardo Mueller, and Carlos Pereira. 2013. "Changing Social Contracts: Beliefs and Dissipative Inclusion in Brazil." *Journal of Comparative Economics* 41(1): 48–65.

Alvarez, Jorge, Felipe Benguria, Niklas Engbom, and Christian Moser. 2018. "Firms and the Decline in Earnings Inequality in Brazil." *American Economic Journal: Macroeconomics* 10(1): 149–89.

Arretche, Marta. 2018. "Democracia e Redução da Desigualdade Econômica No Brasil: A Inclusão Dos Outsiders." *Revista Brasileira de Ciências Sociais* 33(96): 1–23.

Atkinson, Anthony, Thomas Piketty, and Emmanuel Saez. 2011. "Top Incomes in the Long Run of History." *Journal of Economic Literature* 49(1): 3–71.

Azevedo, João Pedro, Viviane Sanfelice, and Minh Nguyen. 2012. "Shapley Decomposition by Components of a Welfare Aggregate." *Munich Personal RePEC Archive, MPRA Paper n. 85584.* https://mpra.ub.uni-muenchen.de/85584/1/MPRA_paper_85584.pdf

Azevedo, João Pedro, Gabriela Inchaust, and Viviane Sanfelice. 2013. "Decomposing the Recent Inequality Decline in Latin America." *World Bank Policy Research Working Paper n. 6715.* https://elibrary.worldbank.org/doi/abs/10.1596/1813-9450-6715

Barbosa, Ana Luiza, and Pedro H. G. F. Souza. 2012. "Diferencial Salarial Público-Privado e Desigualdade dos Rendimentos do Trabalho no Brasil." *Ipea, Boletim Mercado de Trabalho* 53: 29–36.

Barbosa, Rogério, Pedro H. G. F. Souza, and Sergei Soares. 2020. "Income Distribution in Brazil during the 2010s: A Lost Decade in the Struggle Against Inequality and Poverty." *CEQ Working Paper n. 103.* http://repec.tulane.edu/RePEc/ceq/ceq103.pdf

Barros, Ricardo Paes de, Mirela Carvalho, Samuel Franco, and Rosane Mendonça. 2006. "Uma Análise das Principais Causas da Queda Recente na Desigualdade de Renda Brasileira." *Econômica* 8(1): 117–47.

Barros, Ricardo Paes de, Miguel Foguel, and Gabriel Ulyssea, eds. 2006. *Desigualdade de Renda no Brasil: Uma Análise da Queda Recente.* Ipea.

Barros, Ricardo Paes de, Ricardo Henriques, and Rosane Mendonça. 2000. "Desigualdade e Pobreza No Brasil: Retrato de Uma Estabilidade Inaceitável." *Revista Brasileira de Ciências Sociais* 15(42): 123–42.

Bastagli, Francesca, et al. 2019. "The Impact of Cash Transfers: A Review of the Evidence from Low- and Middle-Income Countries." *Journal of Social Policy* 48(03): 569–94.

Blanchet, Thomas, Ignacio Flores, and Marc Morgan. 2022. "The Weight of the Rich: Improving Surveys Using Tax Data." *Journal of Economic Inequality* 20(1): 119–50.

Brito, Alessandra, Miguel Foguel, and Celia Kerstenetzky. 2017. "The Contribution of Minimum Wage Valorization Policy to the Decline in Household Income Inequality in Brazil: A Decomposition Approach." *Journal of Post Keynesian Economics* 40(4): 540–75.

Carvalho, José Murilo de. 2001. *Cidadania no Brasil: O Longo Caminho.* Civilização Brasileira.

Chancel, Lucas, Thomas Piketty, Emmanuel Saez, and Gabriel Zucman. 2022. *World Inequality Report 2022.* World Inequality Lab. https://wid.world/document/world-inequality-report-2022/

Costa, Nilson, Miguel Marcelino, Cristina Maria Duarte, and Deborah Uhr. 2016. "Proteção Social e Pessoa Com Deficiência No Brasil." *Ciência & Saúde Coletiva* 21(10): 3037–47.

Costanzi, Rogério Nagamine et al. 2018. "Reforma da Previdência Social." In *Desafios da Nação: Artigos de Apoio*, eds. João Alberto de Negri, Bruno César Araújo, and Ricardo Bacelette. Ipea, pp. 129–91.

Cuevas, Alfredo et al. 2018. "Fiscal Challenges of Population Aging in Brazil." In *Brazil: Boom, Bust, and the Road to Recovery*, eds. Antonio Spilimberg and Krishna Srinivasan. International Monetary Fund, 191–206.

Datt, Gaurav, and Martin Ravallion. 1992. "Growth and Redistribution Components of Changes in Poverty Measures: A Decomposition with Applications to Brazil and India in the 1980s." *Journal of Development Economics* 38: 275–95.

De Rosa, Mauricio, Ignacio Flores, and Marc Morgan. 2022. *More Unequal or Not as Rich? Revisiting the Latin American Exception.* SocArXiv. preprint. https://osf.io/akq89 (September 12, 2023).

Engbom, Niklas, and Christian Moser. 2022. "Earnings Inequality and the Minimum Wage: Evidence from Brazil." *American Economic Review* 112(12): 3803–47.

Engbom, Niklas, Gustavo Gonzaga, Christian Moser, and Roberta Olivieri. 2022. "Earnings Inequality and Dynamics in the Presence of Informality: The Case of Brazil." *Quantitative Economics* 13(4): 1405–46.

Ferreira, Francisco H. G., Sergio Firpo, and Julián Messina. 2022. "Labor Market Experience and Falling Earnings Inequality in Brazil: 1995–2012." *The World Bank Economic Review* 36(1): 37–67.

Firpo, Sergio, and Alysson Portella. 2019. "Decline in Wage Inequality in Brazil: A Survey." *World Bank, Policy Research Working Paper n. 9096.*

Fiszbein, Ariel, and Norbert Rüdiger Schady. 2009. *Conditional Cash Transfers: Reducing Present and Future Poverty.* World Bank.

Foster, James, Joel Greer, and Erik Thorbecke. 1984. "A Class of Decomposable Poverty Measures." *Econometrica* 52(3): 761–6.

Fried, Brian J. 2012. "Distributive Politics and Conditional Cash Transfers: The Case of Brazil's Bolsa Família." *World Development* 40(5): 1042–53.

Gasparini, Leonardo, and Guillermo Cruces. 2021. "The Changing Picture of Inequality in Latin America: Evidence for Three Decades." *UNDP LAC, Working Paper series n. 01.* www.undp.org/latin-america/publications/changing-picture-inequality-latin-america

Hunter, Wendy, and Timothy Power. 2007. "Rewarding Lula: Executive Power, Social Policy, and the Brazilian Elections of 2006." *Latin American Politics and Society* 49(1): 1–30.

Jolliffe, Dean et al. 2022. "Assessing the Impact of the 2017 PPPs on the International Poverty Line and Global Poverty." *World Bank, Policy Research Working Paper n. 9941.*

Kennickell, Arthur B. 2017. "Getting to the Top: Reaching Wealthy Respondents in the SCF." *Statistical Journal of the IAOS* 33: 113–23.

Kenworthy, Lane. 2010. "How Much Do Presidents Influence Income Inequality?" *Challenge* 53(2): 90–112.

Levitsky, Steven. 2018. "Democratic Survival and Weakness." *Journal of Democracy* 29(4): 102–13.

Lopez-Calva, Luis Felipe, and Sonia Rocha. 2012. *Exiting Belindia? Lesson from the Recent Decline in Income Inequality in Brazil.* World Bank. https://openknowledge. worldbank.org/handle/10986/12808

Medeiros, Marcelo, and Fábio Castro. 2018. "A Composição da Renda no Topo da Distribuição: Evolução no Brasil entre 2006 e 2012, a Partir de Informações Do Imposto de Renda." *Economia e Sociedade* 27(2): 577–605.

Medeiros, Marcelo, and Pedro H. G. F. Souza. 2015. "State Transfers, Taxes and Income Inequality in Brazil." *Brazilian Political Science Review* 9(2): 3–29.

Medeiros, Marcelo, Pedro H. G. F. Souza, and Fábio A. Castro. 2015. "The Stability of Income Inequality in Brazil, 2006–2012: An Estimate Using Income Tax Data and Household Surveys." *Ciência & Saúde Coletiva* 20(4): 971–86.

Messina, Julian, and Joana Silva. 2021. "Twenty Years of Wage Inequality in Latin America." *World Bank Economic Review* 35(1): 117–47.

Morgan, Marc. 2017. "Falling Inequality beneath Extreme and Persistent Concentration: New Evidence for Brazil Combining National Accounts, Surveys and Fiscal Data, 2001–2015." *World Inequality Lab, Working Paper, n. 2017/12.*

Neri, Marcelo. 2008. *A Nova Classe Média.* FGV/CPS.

Oxfam Brasil. 2022. *Nós e as Desigualdades: Percepções sobre Desigualdades no Brasil, 2022*. Oxfam Brasil. www.oxfam.org.br/um-retrato-das-desigualdades-brasileiras/ pesquisa-nos-e-as-desigualdades/pesquisa-nos-e-as-desigualdades-2022/

Paiva, Luis Henrique, Tereza Cotta, and Armando Barrientos. 2019. "Brazil's Bolsa Familia Programme." In *Great Policy Successes*, eds. Mallory E. Compton and Paul T. Hart. Oxford University Press, 21–41.

Ribeiro, Felipe Garcia, Claudio Shikida, and Ronald Hillbrecht. 2017. "Bolsa Família: Um Survey sobre os Efeitos do Programa de Transferência de Renda Condicionada do Brasil." *Estudos Econômicos* 47(4): 805–62.

Scheidel, Walter. 2018. *The Great Leveler: Violence and the History of Inequality from the Stone Age to the Twenty-First Century*. Princeton University Press.

———. 2013. "Decomposition Procedures for Distributional Analysis: A Unified Framework Based on the Shapley Value." *Journal of Economic Inequality* 11(1): 99–126.

Soares, Sergei. 2008. "O Ritmo de Queda na Desigualdade no Brasil é Adequado? Evidências do Contexto Histórico e Internacional." *Ipea, Texto para Discussão, n.* 1339.

Souza, Pedro H. G. F. 2018a. "A History of Inequality: Top Incomes in Brazil, 1926–2015." *Research in Social Stratification and Mobility* 57: 35–45.

———. 2018b. *Uma História de Desigualdade: A Concentração de Renda entre os Ricos, 1926–2013*. Hucitec, ANPOCS.

Souza, Pedro H. G. F., and Raphael Bruce. 2022. "Uma Avaliação Final da Focalização e da Efetividade contra a Pobreza do Programa Bolsa Família, em Perspectiva Comparada." *Ipea, Texto para Discussão, n.* 2813.

Souza, Pedro H. G. F., Marcos Hecksher, and Rafael Osorio. 2022. "Um País na Contramão: a Pobreza no Brasil nos Últimos Dez Anos." *Ipea, Nota Técnica Disoc/ Ipea, n.* 102.

World Bank. 2015. *The State of Social Safety Nets 2015*. World Bank. http://elibrary. worldbank.org/doi/book/10.1596/978-1-4648-0543-1 (July 18, 2021).

———. 2023. "Poverty and Inequality Platform." www.pip.worldbank.org (August 1, 2023).

Yonzan, Nishant, Branko Milanovic, Salvatore Morelli, and Janet Gornick. 2022. "Drawing a Line: Comparing the Estimation of Top Incomes between Tax Data and Household Survey Data." *Journal of Economic Inequality* 20(1): 67–95.

PART II

Compensatory policies

7

AUTHORITARIAN POPULISM AND FISCAL AUSTERITY

The dismantling of social security in Bolsonaro's government

Arnaldo Provasi Lanzara and Fernanda Pernasetti[1]

7.1 Introduction

The conventional view on policy dismantling processes poses that social protection systems are hard to transform through radical reforms. According to Paul Pierson (2001), the stabilization of voters' preferences around redistributive benefits would be proof of the "institutional inertia" of welfare policies, regardless of each government's reformist or ideological inclinations.

Although valid, such propositions seem to no longer answer to the transformations that have been marking the trajectory of social protection systems, be those consolidated or in a phase of expansion. Recent literature on the retraction of these systems shows that the underlying factors for policy dismantling are quite complex, identifying a variety of changes in social policies, usually activated through discreet actions (Streeck and Thelen, 2005; Palier, 2007; Bauer and Knill, 2014). Furthermore, the notion that retrenchment is an unpopular political alternative has also been questioned (Giger and Nelson, 2013). Pierson (2001) seems to have underestimated two aspects that, although mentioned in their theory, were not properly approached: 1) the changes in the preferences of politicians and voters in a scenario of growing ideological polarization; and 2) the severity of current fiscal austerity measures.

This chapter analyzes the dismantling of social security in Brazil. Although it supports the hypotheses that privatizing reforms in social security systems rarely happen abruptly, it highlights that the sequential and negotiated character of such reforms can catalyze changes through the gradual modification of aspects linked to the density and intensity of the policies (Bauer and Knill, 2014). In that sense, we demonstrate that the introduction of instruments that

DOI: 10.4324/9781003487777-9

weaken the robustness of public pay-as-you-go systems (PAYG), as with the complementary capitalization arrangements, enhances such changes, for they have an ambivalent nature, with functions and meanings handled according to the interpretation of the political coalitions and organized interests (Lanzara and Salgado Silva, 2023). The central hypothesis that guides this chapter is that the recent changes produced in the Brazilian social security system are symptoms of such ambivalence, and have made the (apparently resilient) system more receptive to the expansion of private pensions.

The ultraliberal governments of Michel Temer (2016–2018) and Jair Bolsonaro (2019–2022) acted deliberately to explore such ambivalence, approving reforms that weakened social security. During his turbulent administration, Bolsonaro counterbalanced two audiences, the populists and the market, in order to, amid diversionary tactics, reform central aspects of the social protection system. The preferred targets of this action were the contributive benefits, seen as "privileges" in the face of the exponential growth of informal work, which receives no protection. At the same time, these workers were lifted to the condition of "entrepreneurs" by the demagogue discourse of the president and his technocratic finance world team, a maneuver that had a strong insertion in the middle and lower classes, contributing to the conformation of a favorable environment to measures that until then were considered "unpopular." Exploring the constitutional austerity goals approved during Temer's government (Brasil, 2016), Bolsonaro managed to implement a reform in social security at the beginning of his mandate. Despite congressional opposition to the original proposal to establish a full-capitalization pension system, the measures approved in the wake of this reform are radicalized versions of previous ones, particularly arising from the unapproved proposal by Michel Temer's government (Proposed Constitutional Amendment No. 287 of 2016).

Sanctioned by the end of 2019, Jair Bolsonaro's pension reform (Brasil, 2019) deconstitutionalized the pension system, tightening the eligibility criteria for benefits. Although the capitalization regime had been previously rejected, several measures introduced with the new system benefited the expansion of private pensions, especially the possibility to privatize benefits such as those intended for sick pay, maternity leave, accident insurance; and the prohibition on the creation of new social security regimes by federative entities, which meant the further privatizing of the states and municipalities public servant's pensions. Also, the government adopted a deliberate strategy of dismantling public pension bureaucratic agencies such as the Social Security National Institute (*Instituto Nacional do Seguro Social* – INSS). Side by side with the lowering of the system's public contributive pillar, these measures represent a rather explicit movement to induce the expansion of the private pensions' market in the country.

Following this introduction, this chapter is divided into four sections. The first one presents theoretical aspects to support that the logic of austerity, added to the rise of authoritarian populist regimes across the world, represents a new scenario against to which is important to read the established literature on policy dismantling. The second section details dynamics of institutional change in PAYG systems, questioning path dependence arguments based on the analysis of the Brazilian case. The aim is to emphasize the steps through which the introduction of measures that restricted the public pension system have bolstered the expansion of private pensions in Brazil. This dismantling's evidence illustrates the theoretical questions initially raised. The third section details the most recent reform in social security, highlighting in what way the horizon of capitalization, even though rejected as a radical proposal, is now, in practice, put into effect by cumulative successive changes to the Brazilian social security system. The fourth and last section concludes the chapter by resuming the main arguments and analysis.

7.2 A new scenario for the dismantling of policies

The recent emergence of far-right populist regimes in different countries has awakened deep anxiety regarding the future of democracies. Despite its controversial character, the concept of populism requires some redefinition in order to qualify the nature of these new regimes. In this chapter we employ the concept of "authoritarian populism" such as defined by Nadia Urbinati (2019) to characterize the dismantling of policies promoted by Bolsonaro's government in Brazil.[2]

Comparative literature on democratic backsliding and public administration points to several strategies that authoritarian populist governments use to dismantle policies, highlighting the capture of bureaucratic agencies and reforms (Bauer and Becker, 2020). Bauer and Becker (2020), for instance, mobilized the policy dismantling argument to claim that the success of these governments in dismantling policies depends on the resilience of bureaucratic institutions.

However, in contexts in which social policies are weakly institutionalized, authoritarian leaders face fewer obstacles to introducing dismantling strategies. Some cases confirm that populist authoritarian governments seek to explore identity antagonisms to obfuscate their commitment to predatory economic interests and the promotion of rights-reducing reforms, as happened in the United States with Donald Trump (Hacker and Pierson, 2020).

The Brazilian variant of authoritarian populism represented by Bolsonaro's government holds similarities to those cases. Heller (2020) qualifies the authoritarian populist regimes of Brazil and India as "retrenchment populism": a populism that is centered on dismantling policies and affirming "traditional sociocultural hierarchies." In both countries, the strategies for dismantling social protection followed a project of "society's cultural transformation" in which some elements, such as entrepreneurship, the responsibility of care work within the family, religious morality, and privatization of benefits were deliberately promoted in order to replace the social protection system (Heller, 2020).

The destructive effects of the policies produced by authoritarian populist leaders survive beyond their mandates, and their long-term impact is still poorly explored in the literature. Another aspect worthy of attention is that some of these leaders, as with Bolsonaro in Brazil, share ultraliberal economic views, complying with austerity fiscal rules.

The conventional view tends to consider populism and liberalizing policies as antinomian terms, assuming that populist leaders do not have enough credibility to keep their fiscal commitments to investors and, as a corollary, that self-enforcing fiscal rules work as antidotes against them (Schultz and Weingast, 2003). Contrary to such predictions, authoritarian leaders can benefit from fiscal discipline because the costs of losing discretion in order to produce further expansionist policies are strongly compensated by the benefits of the markets "confidence" (Aaskoven and Grundholm, 2021).

According to Weaver (1986), the automatic imposition of fiscal austerity rules is the most recent manifestation of the politicians' desire to avoid the blame for adopting unpopular measures. It is worth highlighting that blame avoidance strategies have been further systematized as the governments' commitment to imposing fiscal discipline grew stronger (Wenzelburger, 2011). Despite voters' preferences, certain environments dominated by those rules already constitute "institutionalized blame-prevention arrangements" for governments to promote a spiral of cuts in social policies (Hinterleitner and Sager, 2017).

The strategy employed by Bolsonaro's government to dismantle the social protection system was to combine his authoritarian discourse with constitutional measures for fiscal austerity. It is important to highlight that his election in 2018 was the consecration of a conservative movement, with diffuse traits until then, which two years earlier had helped rush the judicial-parliamentary coup staged against president Dilma Rousseff (2011–2016). With the president's impeachment, a new conservative coalition, strongly supported by financial experts and the corporate sector, rises to power led by Michel Temer, who soon put into practice a wide program for liberalizing reforms (Boschi and Pinho, 2019). Under the claim that diminishing public debt would restore the investors' "trust," the new government established the constitutional goal of freezing public expenses for 20 years. Constitutional Amendment n. 95 from 2016 (Brasil, 2016), the backbone of the so-called "New Fiscal Regime," limited public spending directly jeopardizing the State's ability to create policies, generating a spiral of deregulation, such as with the reforms in labor laws – Law n. 13,467, from 07/13/2017 (see Chapter 11 of this volume) – and social security (Brasil, 2019).

Despite having set unrealistic goals for the fulfillment of fiscal rules, one of the immediate effects of EC n. 95/2016 was to generate a dispute between the many sectors of social policy for scarce budgeting, limiting the outreach of different policies (Rossi, Dweck, and Oliveira, 2018). In that sense, the "automatic government" (Weaver, 1986) introduced by the new spending cap became the main justification for Bolsonaro's government to dismantle policies.

However, welfare policies are not threatened only by austerity. Politicians interested in dismantling policies tend to take advantage of the new scenario of electoral realignments around controversial issues that permeate the moral dimension of social policies (Wenzelburger and Hörisch, 2016). As many studies point out, different forms of framing welfare policies as well as notions of "deserving" or "not-deserving" public assistance have been used to convince voters that the restrictive reforms of welfare policies are necessary and have inclusive goals (Green-Pedersen, 2002; Slothuus, 2007; Marx and Schumacher, 2016). Furthermore, these different forms of framing are usually channeled by the populist authoritarian discourse to spread resentment among the beneficiaries of social policies, feeding complaints that contributive benefits linked to work are insensitive to groups who are traditionally excluded from the formal sector. On the other hand, traditional beneficiaries of these policies resent the pressures coming from below. All of that, along with the income concentration in various societies, leads to a sense of spread-out disbelief among citizens towards the redistributive results of such policies (Eatwell and Goodwin, 2018).

In Brazil, where contributive social rights are traditionally fragmented, covering only part of the population, these disputes are fairly common, and usually exploited to justify rights-reducing reforms. It can be said that these discursive strategies and surreptitious mechanisms were widely used by Bolsonaro's government to weaken labor and social security benefits. With the argument that these benefits are expensive, have "low redistributive efficiency," and feed "privileges," Bolsonaro promoted a strategy of "expansionist dismantling" (Jensen et al., 2014) in which contributive benefits, essential for the maintenance of income in poor wage-earner families, suffered continuous attacks and gave way to compensatory instruments to combat poverty.

As Häusermann (2010) highlights, the mismatch between the growth of new risks and a macroeconomic environment dominated by austerity configures a scenario that is completely different from that which constituted the Welfare State. Bismarckian pay-as-you-go pension systems, built on the tripod of full employment, solidarity contributions, and collectivization of risks are in particular disagreement with the current scenario of growing austerity, dissemination of new risks, and exclusions. Therefore, "a variety of different institutional faults emerges, as a consequent variety of possible dimensions of reform" (2010, p.7).

PAYG pension systems are a privileged object of analysis when it comes to considering this wider context. They present two distinct sets of pressures, nonetheless related, which conspire against its stability, facilitating processes for rights-reducing reforms. Firstly, there is a pressure "from below" for more inclusion, which postulates the expansion of the beneficiaries. Such pressure is contained by the flattening of the average value of benefits. Secondly, and related to the first, there is a pressure "from above" that, given the average reduction in the value of public benefits, that drives groups with bigger contributive capacity towards capitalized arrangements.

Facing this scenario, any indication of inequality in the distribution of benefits in PAYG pension systems, traditionally stratified, become a problem for those who do not have any resources. It is no accident that authoritarian populist leaders tend to exploit this fact to reform welfare institutions in strong consonance with moralistic and individualistic agendas. The way out of such discomfort would be leveling the protections to a tolerable minimum or an unjustifiable return of the protections by merit and individual performance. That is why governments committed to reforming these systems can be prone to adopting dismantling strategies that are more decisive in order to not displease the majority's opinion, now centered around matters related to "beneficiaries' merit" and the scarcity of resources determined by fiscal austerity. In short, the recent changes in welfare systems seem to have produced a growing indifference in voters regarding redistributive justice and solidarity, which heavily affects the public pension systems funded on the supportive share of risks.

The recent dismantling of the Brazilian social security system carried out by Bolsonaro's government reinforces the idea that the commitment between authoritarian populism and fiscal austerity is structured to exploit divisions, deconstruct social rights, and promote interests linked to the privatization of benefits, as will be shown ahead.

7.3 Strategies for the dismantling of social security systems: The Brazilian case

Policy dismantling strategies can be classified as considering two inter-related dimensions: (1) the government's deliberate decision to dismantle policies; and (2) the visibility and costs of the dismantling actions (Jordan, Bauer and Green-Pedersen, 2013; Bauer and Knill, 2014). Such strategies vary according to the "density" of policies – the way in which they are structured by governmental activities, expressed in terms of the number of policies and policy instruments – and the "intensity" of the policies, which refers to the level of generosity and the institutionalization of social benefits (Bauer and Knill, 2014, p.33). As highlighted by Bauer and Knill (2014), dismantling is more pronounced in the intensity dimension, as calibration adjustments in the instruments that characterize public policies usually have less visibility, thus being less prone to resistance.

Since the beginning of the 20th century, social security in Brazil has developed in a very fragmented manner. Historically, the system was guided by selectivity in the granting of benefits, exempting itself from guaranteeing protection to a huge number of rural and urban workers without a formal employment relationship. Structural characteristics of the Brazilian labor market, such as the marked heterogeneity of work situations and high levels of informality, inhibited the movement towards the extension of social security protection.

The Federal Constitution of 1988, however, has breached this trajectory of selectivity in social rights and innovated by creating an integrated social security system (Fleury, 1994). It instituted rural workers as special beneficiaries of the social security system, breaking its strictly contributive character and expanding the floor of one minimum wage to all its beneficiaries. Furthermore, in the scope of Social Assistance, it created benefits targeted at groups who were vulnerable to poverty, especially with the Continuous Cash Benefit (*Benefício de Prestação Continuada* – BPC), universally paid to all people with disabilities or older than 65 years living with families with per capita incomes of up to a quarter of a minimum wage (see Chapter 10 of this volume).

This movement of expansion of rights boosted the electoral participation of the poorest and increased the political costs of not providing or dismantling these policies (Arretche, 2018). However, at the same time, certain differences were preserved for beneficiaries located in specific pillars of protection: on the one hand, there was the expansion of coverage for risks related to loss of working capacity; on the other, the emergence and consolidation of an income guarantee pillar for the poor population (Jaccoud, 2009). Therefore, policies aimed at income replacement, which integrate social security benefits, and policies for fighting poverty, targeted at specific segments, coexist. Thus, although it has important Bismarckian characteristics of "institutional resilience," the Brazilian PAYG pension system has never attained the comprehensiveness of European systems, becoming rather susceptible to reforming processes (Lanzara and Salgado Silva, 2023).

Indeed, as soon as social security expanded its horizons towards universality, social and political groups linked to economic liberalization movements claimed a "lack of feasibility" of the social security system. To those, the new legislation was excessively benevolent, encouraging early retirements and, above all, generating growing pressure on public expenses due to its indexation to the minimum wage (Giambiagi et al., 2004). De-indexing social security benefits from the reference value of the minimum wage was one of the main goals of social security reformers, representing a frontal threat to the public pillar of the system, since the average value of 98% of rural benefits and 52% of urban benefits in the country is one minimum wage (Pernasetti, 2021). In general, however, these arguments conformed the theoretical basis of justification for successive parametric changes in Brazilian PAYG pension system, accused of being structurally deficient.

Even while failing to cover informal workers, the Brazilian social security system has become crucial to the countries' social well-being because its resources integrate the family income of more than 100 million Brazilians – a little over half of the population (DIEESE, 2017). In addition, several studies confirm that rural social security is fundamental for the economy of small towns, acting as one of the main mechanisms for fighting regional inequalities (França, 2011; Pernasetti, 2021). Still, since the Federal Constitution of 1988 there was not one decade without the approval of new rights-reducing changes in the scope of social security – namely, in 1998, 1999, 2003, 2015, and more recently, 2019 – a movement which has been duly followed by the growth and strengthening of complementary private pension institutions in the country.

Palier (2007) highlights that since the 1990s, mature PAYG pension systems have undergone negative feedback processes, in which measures such as the decrease in income replacement rates and the establishment of caps for receiving public pensions have led to an expansion of the private pensions arrangements, be it for individuals or professional categories. The cumulative effects of these reforms have been gradually loosening the ties of the PAYG pension systems from the path dependence phenomena (Palier, 2007). Surreptitiously, changing the configuration of these instruments is a low-cost political alternative to operate significant changes, although not structural, making contributive social rights less generous and attractive (Green-Pedersen, 2002; Jensen et al., 2014).

The Brazilian case is exemplary of these recalibration movements. In Brazil, the first pension reform (Brasil, 1998) replaced the evidence for workers' "time of service" by "time as contributors" for calculating public pensions; eliminated proportional retirement; for benefits above the payment floor, it disassociated the adjustment of the social security benefit from that of the minimum wage; and lowered the benefits' nominal maximum ceiling (BRASIL, 1998). After three years of debate and discussion in Congress, this first reform contributed to reducing of the expenses with social security by imposing more obstacles on retirement in the scope of the General Social Security System (*Regime Geral de Previdência Social*- RGPS), which covers private sector's workers.

Along with its approval, two other retrenchment instruments were created: the Fiscal Responsibility Law (*Lei de Responsabilidade Fiscal* – LRF) and the Unbinding of Union Revenue (*Desvinculação de Receitas da União* -DRU). The first one limited spendings on social protection by determining that they should be conditioned to public revenue, while the DRU, created in 1994, authorized the deviation of 20% of the tax collection and federal contributions destined for social security towards other ends (Fagnani, 2008). Such mechanism remains active, showing that much of what was established then was consolidated into the fiscal engineering of the Brazilian state. Soon after the approval of the first reform, Law 9,876/99, also called the Social Security Factor Law (*Lei do Fator Previdenciário*), introduced a calculation that substantially lowered the RGPS replacement rates for those who opted for early retirement.

The second phase of these reforms was implemented during the governments of the center-left coalition led by the Workers' Party (PT) – Lula da Silva's (2003–2010) and Dilma Rousseff's (2011–2016) governments. Constitutional Amendment n. 41 (Brasil, 2003) was approved at the beginning of Lula's first mandate, equating social security rules for all workers in the country, specifically targeting the civil servants' Special Pension Regimes (*Regimes Próprios de Previdência Social* – RPPS). A maximum ceiling was established for the compensation in RPPS which was equivalent to that of RGPS, raising the civil servants' retirement age: from 53/48 years of age to 60/55 (for men and women, respectively). The reform also instituted the taxation of retired civil servants.

According to the literature on policy dismantling, the widespread use of social rights-reducing reform instruments arises from the advantages of its "ambiguous properties" (Palier, 2007). Palier (2007) highlights that some of those instruments are rather contradictory, and can be mobilized by governments to pursue various goals, be it the expansion of protection or its commodification. Lula's government promoted inclusion measures for social security by reducing contributory rates to stimulate workers in the informal sector to sign up for the RGPS. Besides that, between 2004 and 2012, the expansion of formal employment and the appreciation of the minimum wage had a positive impact on social security. However, despite the growth of formal employment and social security coverage, the period marked an explicit connection between complementary pension benefits, specifically pension funds, and the movement of economy's financialization (Pernasetti, 2021).

Indeed, the construction of a wide base of support for the first administration of Lula (2003–2007), which included, for instance, the growing national financial sector, involved actors willing to exploit the ambiguity of the policy instruments that structure social security sector to subvert its guidelines. According to Palier (2007), the dynamic of action regarding pension funds, in many countries, reveals a constitutive tension arising from its different ways of apprehension by the political coalitions and organized interests: sometimes operating as an instrument of financial speculation; sometimes as a mechanism to enhance productive investments; sometimes both (which is a paradox). Pensions funds can be used to expand employment and welfare; but also can be used to surreptitiously dismantle such systems (Hacker and Pierson, 2014). Furthermore, pension funds are disputed by insurance companies, banks, and corporate conglomerates; as well as by unions, bureaucracies, and mostly politicians interested in manipulating such ambiguities to pursue different goals (Lanzara and Salgado Silva, 2023).

As for complementary or private pensions in Brazil, pension funds, they all grew strongly in the period following 2003, configuring an important instrument of dispute in terms of the directing the pension savings of workers to the goals of the so-called "new developmentalism" (Santana and Fracalanza, 2019). This was based on fostering the formation of large economic conglomerates in the country in sectors considered strategic. In that sense, it is important to observe how the amounts managed by pension funds expressed an attempt to "tame, or to domesticate the national capitalism" (Jardim, 2009).

By establishing a limit on the value of civil servants' pensions, the strategy was to open the way for the creation and strengthening of supplementary pension schemes. This was a conciliatory bet that it would be possible to maintain the commitment with the generation of primary surpluses to pay high interest rates, financing public debt, as well as increase savings and promote development through the financialization of the workers' private pension – mainly public sector workers and those linked to state-owned companies. As discussed by Bonoli and Palier (1998), the level of the replacement rate of public retirement benefits (that is, the percentage of the benefit's value paid in relation to the last active salaries) is a determining variable to measure the generosity of pension systems based on PAYG model. The higher that rate, the more attractive the benefit becomes; on the other hand, the lower that rate, the more prone workers will be to migrate to different regimes – in most cases, private ones. In the Brazilian case, with the change in the rules, the workers' interest in integrating complementary private pension schemes that would compensate for the lowering in their retirement pensions would grow, generating, at the same time, several resources applicable to financial operations – thus, available to finance the national productive sector.

Exploiting the ambiguity of these instruments, therefore, meant expanding the multidimensional space of reforms, sectioning the social interests that structure the social security sector (Häusermann, 2010). It is through the direct or surreptitious appropriation of these ambiguous instruments that some organized actors, mostly bound to the financial sector, spend enough resources to exploit legal loopholes left behind by reform processes creating a variety of "hidden pathways" that end up impairing the structuring guidelines of the social protection systems (Hacker and Pierson, 2014). Indeed, incremental reforms are more transformative than they seem. Certain strategies and instruments serve to dilute the immediate perception of the public regarding the change in the policy as dismantling, obfuscating its most radical impacts. Using invisible instruments for cuts and visible instruments for expansions, changing the Welfare State can indeed be carried out without major electoral punishment (Bauer and Knill, 2014).

Although the PT governments' strategy has proven to be "feasible" it was not only ineffective for the whole of pension funds, as it was also proven to be of little sustainability in the face of the maintenance of the imperatives for an orthodox monetary policy with high-interest rates. Despite the trend for reduction between 2004 and 2013, Brazil has one of the highest interest rates in the world, discouraging pension funds from acquiring riskier assets to finance the real economy, given the guaranteed profits by short-term government bonds (Conti, 2016). From the second Dilma administration (2015–2016) – which, during a political and economic crisis, was compelled to adopt a policy of fiscal austerity – the strategy of using workers' pension savings to finance the Brazilian economy in the long term became frustrated in the face of the inability to compete with the advantages of short-term fixed income remuneration (Pernasetti, 2021).

It is worth remembering that social security reforms also forge new interests given that its distributive effects produce winners and losers who then become new actors in future rounds of negotiation (Mahoney and Thelen, 2010). In the Brazilian case, the two previous reforms, added to a national scenario of political crisis, would result in a new radicalized proposal for social security reform from 2016 onwards. Of course, the characteristics of political systems matter for the success of the establishment of any reformist coalition. Political systems that have too many veto points disperse decision power, making consensus around more radical reform proposals unlikely (Bonoli, 2000). But in "difficult times," when the dismantling of policies is a presumed priority in the governmental agenda, building new reforms over the previous ones can configure new opportunities for radical change (Häusermann, 2010).

7.4 The 2016 reform proposal and the pension reform of 2019

The year 2016 represents a milestone in the ultraliberal offensive on the legacy of the social pact enshrined in the 1988 Federal Constitution, due to the significant inflection it represented in terms of guaranteeing social rights and the provision of services and public goods by the Brazilian State.

The new pension reform proposal, presented as PEC 287/2016, became a priority in the fiscal austerity agenda in the country. Among the measures that appear in its original, most radical version, three stood out: 1) establishing one single minimum age for the retirement of men and women, ignoring the gender inequalities within the Brazilian labor market; 2) expanding the minimum contribution time to 25 years, in absolute incompatibility with the characteristics of the labor market; 3) unbinding the BPC from the minimum wage. In the reformers' strategic calculation, the proposal to unlink basic assistance benefits, such as the BPC, from the value of the minimum wage represented, in practice, the possibility of de-indexing the retirements and pensions paid by the RGPS from this reference value. However, in a context of political crisis powered by the disruptive movements made in the scope of Operation Car Wash (*Operação Lava Jato*), the National Congress preferred to avoid abrasion with its voter base rather than approving a widely unpopular reform. In the terms presented by Temer's government, the PEC 287 was not even voted by the Chamber of Deputies. However, there was a political margin to adjust the instrument in the DRU, which in 2016 was expanded from 20% to 30% of the social security budget (DIEESE, 2017).

In this crisis scenario, however, the political figure of Jair Bolsonaro managed to gather support from sectors interested in advancing the reforms, the dissatisfied middle class, and even from some popular sectors of society, immersed in insecurity and increasing unemployment. The latter latched onto the conservative points of his campaign, especially those spread using the "fake news" strategy – "hybrid war" tactics via social networks that promoted misinformation and disorientation of the public opinion. In 2018, Bolsonaro's campaign capitalized on the support of figures such as that of ultraliberal economist Paulo Guedes, his future minister of economy, decisively nodding at the financial market segments. To his authoritarian populist discourse, the "pending" social security issue was added, the most pressing distributive national conflict.

Once elected, Bolsonaro soon presented the PEC 06/2019, its own pension reform proposal, heavily based on that of 2016. This time, however, it was debated and voted on by the National Congress. Unlike the 2016 proposal, the new reform did not foresee the disentanglement of the benefits' payment floor from the minimum wage – perhaps its most controversial point – but replaced it with the end of the obligation of benefit readjustment, which was blocked by the Chamber of Deputies.

In general, it is possible to say that it was the discussions and votes at the Federal Senate that managed to soothe the most radical proposals in the reform's original project, many of which had been ratified by the Chamber of Deputies. Regarding the RPPS (the social security regime for civil servants), the adoption of new rules at the federal level was relegated to a later definition by state and municipal legislatures, subjected to the approval of the so-called "parallel PEC" (Proposed Constitutional Amendment n. 133/2019), therefore many of the most unpopular and controversial decisions regarding the social security benefits of civil servants in states and municipalities were relegated to a later moment. The important point here is that political systems with many veto points tend to compress the space available for more radical changes, pushing minimum consensuses – "ambiguous consensuses" (Palier, 2007) – towards moderation. But this moderation can be an instantaneous and apparent picture of a "soft" reform process, masking more incisive and hidden transformations, as their effects can only be measured over time.

This is what we can see when analyzing the developments of Constitutional Amendment n. 103/2019 (Bolsonaro`s pension reform). The reform established minimum age rules for retirement in the RGPS (62 and 65 years old, for women and men) and reduced replacement rates (the value of retirements will account for 60% of the average of the contribution salaries, requiring 40 years of contribution to receive the full benefit). There will be, in that sense, a substantial decrease in the pensions paid by the RGPS, which tends to discourage worker's contributions. More than that, it is important to note that the labor market in Brazil is quite unstable, characterized by a high level of informality and intermittent employment. Also, regional inequality is also expressed by variations in life expectancy, with federal states – such as Maranhão – in which they do not exceed 67 years. Thus, the requirement of 40 years of contribution imposes an inviable parameter that makes it impossible for many Brazilian workers to access full retirement benefits.

In the case of death benefits there was a substantial 50% reduction in the amount of benefits originally paid, plus 10% per dependent of the insured. For the RPPS, it is worth highlighting the establishment of staggered social security contribution rates on the salary of civil servants, which can reach 22%. In line with previous reforms, the so-called "New Social Security" opened substantial space for private pensions by prohibiting the opening of new public schemes for civil servants, obligating states and municipalities to create supplementary pension schemes offered by banks and private insurers (Brasil, 2019). In addition, it allowed some of the most important benefits provided by social security, such as sickness aid, maternity leave, and work-accident insurance, to be offered by the private sector, in competition with the public sector (DIEESE, 2017).

Despite society's resistance, reflected in the behavior of part of the National Congress, which managed to deter some points from the original proposal by the Executive, the setbacks were expressive, given that they were made easier by the general context of fiscal austerity and by the cumulative effects of the previous reforms. The "New Social Security" decreased the value of retirements and pensions above the minimum wage, bringing them closer to the constitutional minimum, as historically proposed by the defenders of more radical measures. Besides that, the rise in the minimum age for retirement added to the 15 (if women) or 20 (if men) extra mandatory contribution years may very well hinder retirement altogether for many workers, especially in states with a lower life expectancy and high intermittence of the population between formal and informal employment.

Although it was unable to approve a capitalization system, the stated objective of the then federal government, the most important consequence of the 2019 reform was the strengthening of private pensions as an alternative to the downgrading and toughening of social security for Brazilian workers. In a different sense than what was pointed out by the 2003 reform, which aimed at strengthening pension funds, the dismantling strategies of Temer's and Bolsonaro's governments directly impacted the financing mechanisms of the Brazilian economy, turning specifically to the criminalization of pension funds managed by state companies.

According to Salgado Silva (2023), such a movement started with the Pension Funds Parliamentary Inquiry Committee (2015–2016) which, using discourse against systemic corruption and the incompetence of state management, started criticizing investments in the real economy, as well as criminalizing the funds' officers, counselors, and directors, with the goal of transferring administration to banks and private insurance companies. As a result of this process, the pension funds reduced investments in the productive sector, as grew the discourse on discrediting contributive social rights and the encouraging entrepreneurship and self-protection – alternatives that were much more convenient to the strengthening of private pensions.

In the context of massive "bancarization" as of the 2000s, the connection between the money moved via checking accounts in institutions offering private pension plans was already bringing such products closer to the general population. From 1995 to 2019, the data available on the trajectory of complementary social security in Brazil point to the closed segment (pension funds) historically gathering annual amounts higher than those of the open segment (private pensions offered by insurance companies and banks). Closed Private Pension Entities (*Entidades Fechadas de Previdência Complementar* – EFPC) are the commonly known pension funds, organized by sponsoring companies for their employees or by categories of workers, from a collective perspective. These supplementary pension entities are institutional investors within a system in which workers' pension savings, which could otherwise be scattered individually, are integrated into professionally managed funds for their capitalization. On the other hand, Open Private Pension Entities (*Entidades Abertas de Previdência Complentar* – EAPC) are individual private pension plans, accessible to the general public, and administered by banks and insurance companies. However, the speed of growth of the open segment, particularly over the last decade, was much superior to that of closed entities: while pension funds grew 73% over those 10 years, almost doubling in size, open entities grew 304% – which means they quadrupled their administered assets (Pernasetti, 2021). For instance, the real growth rate of the VGBL (*Vida Gerador de Benefício Livre*), the most commercialized pension product in the insurance market, was 13.29% in 2019, falling in the following years only due to the consequences of the sanitary crisis (SUSEP, 2023).

As shown in the Integrated Report on Complementary Social Security (Sprev, 2019) from the Ministry of Economy, reproduced in Figure 7.1, the difference in terms of amounts of the assets of EFPC and EAPC resulted in a change of scenario that was already on the horizon: in 2019 the private pension assets in

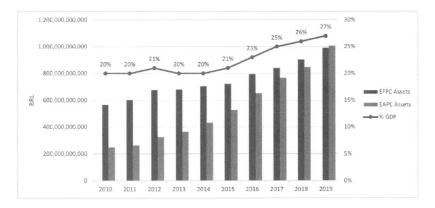

FIGURE 7.1 Assets of open and closed entities (BRL).

Source: Elaborated from Sprev (2019).

individual accounts under the administration of banks and insurance companies (1.01 trillion) surpassed the assets of closed entities (991.5 billions) for the first time in history.

Besides privileging private pensions over collective arrangements and pension funds, Bolsonaro's government also adopted a deliberate strategy of dismantling public agencies linked to the sector. The institutional weakening of the largest public social security agency in the country, the INSS, was one of the most expressive illustrations of the destruction of public services practiced by Bolsonaro's government. At the same time, the government tried to privatize the agency responsible for collecting and systematizing data on social security beneficiaries, the Social Security Technology and Information Company (*Empresa de Tecnologias e Informações da Previdência Social* – Dataprev), threatening to deliver sensitive data on all Brazilians to private companies. The pension reform made the most experienced INSS employees anticipate their retirement, which lost 50% of its employees, accumulating a national deficit of 27,000 employees and generating delays in granting benefits (Pinho and Lanzara, 2022). Adding to that, the population's access to the benefits was made difficult and, at the same time, a gradual but premeditated strategy of rights-removal was promoted through the publication of various decrees by the executive branch.

7.5 Conclusion

The most recent pension reform (2019) in Brazil was also the most radical in the sense of reducing the attractiveness of the public system, further developing policy dismantling strategies tied to the density and intensity of social security policies (Bauer and Knill, 2014).

Recovering goals from previous parametric reforms, even without directly approving the adoption of a full-capitalization system, the reform carried out during Bolsonaro's government established the reduction of benefits, added requirements for its granting, and encouraged the migration of workers to the complementary private pensions system. In this period, there was a sharp decrease in the government's commitment to maintaining the attractiveness and robustness of the contributory public pillar of the social security system.

In a cumulative manner and through the calibration of restrictive reform instruments, complementary pension schemes in Brazil opened up "exits alternatives," according to the famous analysis by Hirschman (1970), for workers with higher incomes to constitute their complementary funds in detriment of the public pension system.

In the Brazilian case, the introduction of restrictive measures promoted marginal but significant changes in the social security system. The introduction of such measures following the processes of reform directly affected the public PAYG system, producing a spiral of incremental transformations: the explicit recognition of the complementary private pension as a structural pillar of the social security; the fixation of a cap for receiving pensions in the public sector; the decrease in income replacement rates in the public subsystems of RGPS and RPPS; and, more recently, the obligation of states and municipalities to adopt private pension schemes for their civil servants.

Besides that, especially through the liberalizing reforms introduced in 2016, the declared predominant discourse in the public debate was in favor of open private pensions, aligned with the financialized trends in the national economy.

Recovering the trajectory of the approved institutional changes, this chapter demonstrated in what way the Brazilian case support the literature on policy dismantling in the sense of questioning the false resilience of public PAYG systems, especially in contexts that combine fiscal austerity and authoritarian populism.

Finally, it is worth highlighting that the process of expansion of complementary private pensions tends to accelerate as a consequence of the recently implemented package of reforms. It is always worth remembering that the Constitutional Amendment n. 95/2016 compressed the fiscal space for social security spending; and that the 2017 labor reform (Brasil, 2017), by allowing the proliferation of subcontracting and forms of intermittent work, tends to negatively affect the sources of financing for social security.

These measures, added to the harmful effects of decreasing public benefits coming from the last pension reform, may encourage expressive segments of the Brazilian population to move towards capitalization arrangements.

Notes

1 This study was partially supported by CNPq process n°152309/2022-5
2 According to Urbinati (2019), these new regimes, although legitimized by the vote, manifest authoritarian traits, aiming at undermining representative democracy.

References

AASKOVEN, L.; GRUNDHOLM. A. T. (2021), Stability through constraints: The impact of fiscal rules on autocratic survival. *Democratization* 28 (8): 1564–1562.

ARRETCHE, M. (2018), Democracia e redução da desigualdade econômica no Brasil: a inclusão dos outsiders. *Revista Brasileira de Ciências Sociais* 33 (96): 1–22.

BAUER, M.; BECKER, S. (2020), Democratic backsliding, populism, and public administration. *Perspectives on Public Management and Governance* 3 (1): 19–31.

BAUER, M.; KNILL, C. (2014), A conceptual framework for the comparative analysis of policy change: Measurement, explanation and strategies of policy dismantling. *Journal of Comparative Policy Analysis: Research and Practice* 16 (1): 28–44.

BONOLI, G. (2000), *The politics of pension reform. Institutions and policy change in Western Europe*. Cambridge: Cambridge University Press.

BONOLI, G.; PALIER, B. (1998), Changing the politics of social programs: innovative change in British and French welfare reforms. *Journal of European Social Policy* 8(4): 317–330.

BOSCHI, R.; PINHO, C. E. S. (2019), Crisis and austerity: the recent trajectory of capitalist development in Brazil. *Contemporary Politics* 25 (3): 292–312.

BRASIL. (1998), Emenda Constitucional n° 20, 15-12-1998. Retrieved June 28, 2023, from www.planalto.gov.br/ccivil_03/constituicao/emendas/emc/emc20.htm

BRASIL (2003), Emenda Constitucional n° 41 de 19 de Dezembro de 2003. Retrieved April 12, 2024, from www.planalto.gov.br/ccivil_03/constituicao/emendas/emc/emc41.htm.

BRASIL (2016), Emenda Constitucional n° 95 de 15 de Dezembro de 2016. Retrieved April 12, 2024, from www.planalto.gov.br/ccivil_03/constituicao/emendas/emc/emc95.htm.

BRASIL (2017), Lei n° 13467 de 13 de Julho de 2017. Retrieved April 12, 2024, from www.planalto.gov.br/ccivil_03/_ato2015-2018/2017/lei/l13467.htm.

BRASIL. (2019), Emenda Constitucional n. 103, 12-12-2019. Retrieved June 28, 2023, from www.planalto.gov.br/ccivil_03/constituicao/emendas/emc/emc103.htm

CONTI, Bruno de. (2016), Previ, Petros e Funcef: uma análise da alocação das carteiras das três maiores entidades brasileiras de previdência complementar. *Texto para discussão n° 2216*. IPEA, Brasília: Rio de Janeiro. Retrieved July 02, 2023, from https://repositorio.ipea.gov.br/bitstream/11058/6874/2/TD%202216_Sumex.pdf

DIEESE. (2017), Previdência: reformar para excluir? Contribuição técnica ao debate sobre a reforma da previdência social brasileira. Brasília, Dieese/Anfip. Retrieved July 2, 2023, from www.dieese.org.br/livro/2017/previdenciaSintese.pdf

EATWELL, R.; GOODWIN, M. (2018), *National populism: The revolt against liberal democracy*. London: Pelican.

FAGNANI, E. (2008), Direitos sociais no fio da navalha. In F. T. Vaz.; J. S. Musse.; R. F. Santos (Org.), *20 anos da Constituição Cidadã: avaliação e desafios da Seguridade Social*. Brasília: ANFIP, pp. 23–44.

FLEURY, S. (1994), *Estado sem cidadãos: Seguridade social na América Latina*. Rio de Janeiro: Editora Fiocruz.

FRANÇA, A. S. de. (2011), *A previdência social e a economia dos municípios*. Brasília: ANFIP.

GIAMBIAGI, F.; MENDONÇA, J. L. O.; BELTRÃO, K. I.; ARDEO, V. L. (2004), Diagnóstico da Previdência Social no Brasil: O que foi feito e o que falta reformar? *Repositório IPEA*. Retrieved July 4, 2023, from https://repositorio.ipea.gov.br/bitstr eam/11058/4344/1/PPE_v34_n03_Diagnostico.pdf

GIGER, N.; NELSON, M. (2013). The welfare state or the economy? Preferences, constituencies, and strategies for retrenchment. *European Sociological Review* 29 (5): 1083–1094.

GREEN-PEDERSEN, C. (2002), *The politics of justification: Party competition and Welfare State retrenchment in Denmark and the Netherlands from 1982 to 1998*. Amsterdam: Amsterdam University Press.

HACKER, J.; PIERSON, P. (2014), After the `master theory`: Downs, Schattschneider, and the rebirth of policy-focused analysis. *Perspectives on Politics* 12 (3):643–662.

HACKER, J.; PIERSON, P. (2020), *Let them eat tweets: How the right rules in an age of extreme inequality*. New York: Liveright Publishing.

HÄUSERMANN, S. (2010), *The politics of welfare state reform in Continental Europe: modernization in hard times*. New York: Cambridge University Press.

HELLER, P. (2020), The age of reaction: Retrenchment populism in India and Brazil. *International Sociology* 35 (6): 590–609.

HINTERLEITNER, M.; SAGER, F. (2017), Anticipatory and reactive forms of blame avoidance: Of foxes and lions. *European Political Science Review* 9 (4): 587–606.

HIRSCHMAN, A. O. (1970), *Exit, voice, and loyalty. Responses to decline in firms, organizations, and states*. Cambridge: Harvard University Press.

JACCOUD, L. (2009), Pobres, pobreza e cidadania: os desafios recentes da proteção social. *Texto para Discussão n. 1372*. Rio de Janeiro: IPEA. Retrieved July 7, 2023, from https://repositorio.ipea.gov.br/bitstream/11058/1598/1/TD_1372.pdf

JARDIM, M. A. C. (2009), `Domesticação` e/ou `moralização do capitalismo` no governo Lula: inclusão social via mercado e via fundos de pensão. *Dados* 52 (1): 123–159.

JENSEN, C.; KNILL, C.; SCHULZE, K.; TOSUN, J. (2014), Giving less by doing more? Dynamics of social policy expansion and dismantling in 18 OECD countries. *Journal of European Public Policy* 21 (4): 528–548.

JORDAN, A.; BAUER, M. W.; GREEN-PEDERSEN, C. (2013), Policy dismantling. *Journal of European Public Policy* 20 (5): 795–805.

LANZARA, A.P.; SALGADO SILVA, B. (2023), As reformas previdenciárias no Brasil e a expansão da previdência complementar. *Revista Brasileira de Ciências Sociais*, 38 (111): 1–20.

MAHONEY, J.; THELEN, K. A. (2010), A theory of gradual institutional change. In J. Mahoney; K. A. Thelen (Eds.), *Explaining institutional change: Ambiguity, agency, and power*. Cambridge: Cambridge University Press, pp. 1–37.

MARX, P.; SCHUMACHER, G. (2016), The effect of economic change and elite framing on support for welfare state retrenchment: A survey experiment. *Journal of European Social Policy* 26 (1): 20–31.

PALIER, B. (2007), Tracking the evolution of a single instrument can reveal profound changes: the case of funded pensions in France. *Governance* 20 (1): 85–107.

PERNASETTI, F. (2021), Miragens do amanhã: Previdência e rodadas de neoliberalização no Brasil pós 1988. Tese de Doutorado. Rio de Janeiro: IPPUR/UFRJ. Retrieved July 3, 2023, from http://objdig.ufrj.br/42/teses/933404.pdf

PIERSON, P. (2001), Introduction: investigating the welfare state at century's end. In P. Pierson (Ed.), *The new politics of the welfare state*, Oxford: Oxford University Press, p. 1–16.

PINHO, C. E. S.; LANZARA, A. P. (2022), Democracia vilipendiada, privatização e desmonte de políticas públicas sob o governo Bolsonaro. In R. Marques; J. C Cardoso Jr (Eds.), *Dominância financeira e privatização das finanças públicas no Brasil*. Brasília: Fonacate, pp. 347–382.

ROSSI, P.; DWECK, E.; OLIVEIRA, A. L. (org.). (2018), *Economia para poucos: impactos sociais da* austeridade *e alternativas para o Brasil*. São Paulo: Autonomia Literária.

SALGADO SILVA, B. (2023), Fundos de pensão no Brasil: uma alternativa para o financiamento do desenvolvimento econômico. Tese de doutorado apresentada ao Programa de Pós-graduação em Ciência Política da Universidade do Estado do Rio de Janeiro.

SANTANA, M. U.; FRACALANZA, P. S. (2019), Fundos de pensão como fonte de financiamento: A experiência dos fundos de pensão brasileiros na estratégia de desenvolvimento econômico dos governos do PT. *Pesquisa & Debate* 31: 136–166.

SCHULTZ, K.; WEINGAST, B. (2003), The democratic advantage: Institutional foundations of financial power in international competition. *International Organization* 57 (1): 3–42.

SLOTHUUS, R. (2007), Framing deservingness to win support for welfare state retrenchment. *Scandinavian Political Studies* 30 (3): 323–344.

SPREV. (2019), Relatório Gerencial da Previdência Complementar, Dezembro, 2019, Ministério da Economia. Retrieved June 28, 2023, from www.gov.br/previdencia/pt-br/acesso-a-informacao/dados-abertos/previdencia-complementar/surpc_relger_19.12b.pdf

STREECK, W.; THELEN, K. (2005), Introduction: Institutional change in advanced political economies. In W. Streeck; K. Thelen (Eds.), *Beyond continuity: Institutional change in advanced political economies*. Oxford: Oxford University Press, pp. 1–39.

SUSEP. (2023), Painel de Inteligência do Mercado de Seguros. Retrieved June 28, 2023, from www2.susep.gov.br/safe/menuestatistica/pims.html

URBINATI. N. (2019), *Me the people. How populism transforms democracy*. Cambridge, London: Harvard University Press.

WEAVER, R. K. (1986), The politics of blame avoidance. *Journal of Public Policy*, 6(4): 371–98.

WENZELBURGER, G. (2011), Political strategies and fiscal retrenchment: Evidence from four countries. *West European Politics* 34 (6): 1151–1184.

WENZELBURGER, G.; HÖRISCH, F. (2016), Framing effects and comparative social policy reform: Comparing blame avoidance evidence from two experiments. *Journal of Comparative Policy Analysis: Research and Practice* 18 (2): 157–175.

8

THE UNIFIED HEALTH SYSTEM AT RISK AND THE SEQUELAE OF THE BOLSONARO ERA

José Angelo Machado and Mauro Lúcio Jerônymo

8.1 Introduction

How did the process of institutional corrosion and attack on the structures guaranteeing social rights established by the 1988 Federal Constitution, which occurred in the second half of the last decade, affect the Unified Health System (*Sistema Único de Saúde – SUS*), "the most democratic of institutions"[1] in the words of the President Lula when he took office? How would this process have affected the various dimensions of this public policy, which so well represents the effort to universalize and equalize the social guarantees promised in this same Constitution? Would its effect on the health policy financing system, a frequent victim of austerity policies, have been accompanied by significant changes in service coverage? Such effects could be exclusively attributed to the Bolsonaro government or, even if intensified during the latter, would they have begun earlier?

These are crucial questions to consider when analyzing to what extent the dismantling of the public policy enshrined in ensuring the right to health in Brazil has advanced. When searching for answers, we are aware of the methodological challenge involved of doing so under the conditions inherited by a management that deliberately restricted the transparency of information about government acts and their results at the same time as it spread misinformation. But this challenge becomes even greater when dealing with multidimensional and complex issues which require academic investment, the achievement of which will require significant effort and time from the research community. Nevertheless, it is our purpose to make an initial contribution here, and to this end, we use the triangulation of available documentary and bibliographical sources, as well as

DOI: 10.4324/9781003487777-10

using secondary data sources which express the analytical dimensions expressed in the questions formulated above.

Our objective in this work is to therefore describe the evolution of selected dimensions of the Brazilian health system based on their potential sensitivity to the process of dismantling this public policy, contributing to delimiting the very temporality of the trends identified based on the general hypothesis that the Bolsonaro government was the outcome of a process which had already begun with economic crisis in the early 2010s, and which deepened in the second term of President Dilma Rousseff (2010–2014/2015–2016) and the rise of Michel Temer (2016–2018).

In addition to this introduction and conclusion, this work is divided into three parts. In the next section, we introduce the inflection process that occurred in the last decade based on the features which mark the innovative character of the *SUS* and its achievements and limitations, with emphasis on the impeachment of President Dilma Rousseff and the formation of the Temer government. In the second section we map some of the main characteristics of the Bolsonaro Administration (including his reaction pattern to the Covid-19 Pandemic), which led to deepening of this inflection. At this point we locate the problem to be addressed herein, namely what were the effects effectively produced from this change in *SUS* operation, as conceived in the Federal Constitution of 1988. Finally, in the third section we analyze evidence based on three selected analytical dimensions – government spending on health, local financial capacities and vaccination coverage – which, even if only partially, points to the questions proposed at the beginning of this Introduction.

8.2   The Unified Health System (*SUS*): From the 1988 Constitution to fiscal austerity

The *SUS* was one of the pillars of the social protection system that emerged from the 1988 Federal Constitution, and was an institutional invention born from the convergence between two historical vectors. On the one hand, the theoretical criticism directed at the private pension model (Oliveira & Teixeira 1989) and the traditional discourse of preventive medicine (Arouca 2003). On the other hand, reflection on experiences of institutional integration that began in the 1970s, such as the Montes Claros Project (Teixeira 1995), the Program for the Internalization of Health Actions (*Programa de Interiorização das Ações de Saúde – PIASS*) and the Integrated Health Actions (*Ações Integradas de Saúde – AIS*) (Stralen 1996). Based on this convergence, the constitution of a new health movement was successful in incorporating two trends strongly present in the redemocratization process and which have been manifested in the Constituent Congress since its installation in 1987: decentralization and local participation.

Despite the clashes in the Constituent Congress and the necessary concessions, such as those made to the municipalist movement that became an important ally of the health movement against privatist interests (Stralen 1996), a bold universalist project was born and was based on the institutional articulation of a social security subsystem and a public subsystem as a strategy to enable equal access and comprehensive services provided to Brazilian citizens. In fact, under the attribute of comprehensiveness, the *SUS* was committed to the "priority for preventive actions without prejudice to care services," articulating activities of an individual and collective nature, expanding care to citizens by simultaneously incorporating health promotion, protection and recovery.

The *SUS* was supported by an advocacy coalition articulated at the three levels of government. It was mobilized from formulation to implementation to the point of achieving strong capillarity on a national scale, and was a precursor among Brazilian social policies organized as a system, generating institutional innovations that included health funds and participatory councils at the three levels of government, in addition to internal control and organizational structures for core activities that have multiplied throughout the country. The incremental development of various practices in the field of healthcare was then added to this diffusion of an organizational model articulated federatively, pursuing implementation of the principles of comprehensiveness and equity in access. The dissemination of national programs and strategies – among which Community Health Agents (*Agentes Comunitários de Saúde – ACS*) and Family Health (*Estrategia de Saúde da Família – ESF*), Psychosocial Care Centers (*Centros de Atenção Psicossocial – CAPS*) and the Mobile Emergency Care Service (*Serviço de Atendimento Móvel de Urgência – SAMU*) are examples – reinforced regional and local capabilities to respond to population health problems.[2]

Its implementation, even under severe funding limitations (Araújo 2017, Servo et al. 2021, Cunha 2021) and under a predominantly negative framing by traditional media vehicles which profoundly affected its perception in public opinion (Oliveira 2000), inserted Brazil as a regional and global reference for health policies. The innovations in HIV/AIDS care policy (Portela & Lotrowska 2006) and immunization were notable, as well as the significant improvements in the primary care model offered in a comparative perspective (Giovanella & Almeida 2017). Mortality from unknown or poorly defined causes – an indicator that represents both the quality of the information system and the health care provided – fell from 14.3% to 5.7% between 2000 and 2015, while coverage of prenatal care with four or more consultations rose from 79.3% to 90.9%in the same period.[3] In addition, immunization coverage against Polio grew from 78% to 98% between 1995 and 2015, while it was 81% to 97% for DPT (triple vaccine which covers Diphtheria, Pertussis (whooping cough), and Tetanus).[4]

But the *SUS*'s financing problems deserve special attention. Their origin dates back to the beginning of the 1990s in the first years of implementation, during which they were aggravated by the austerity policies that were already embedded in the State reforms at that time promoted on the Latin American continent under the sponsorship of international organizations. And here is a paradox which marks this moment: on the one hand, the generosity of the constitutional promise to set up a universal, comprehensive and egalitarian health system in a developing and deeply unequal country; on the other, the prolonged lack of definition regarding the financing sources to support this policy, which lasted until the approval of Constitutional Amendment 29/2000, as well as the budget restrictions that crossed several governments and show lower government spending than that of Latin American countries with non-universal healthcare systems (Machado 2021).

Regarding this last aspect, even though the 1988 Federal Constitution had included health in the Social Security Budget, competition for resources with Social Security generated a financing crisis that was only alleviated by creating the Provisional Contribution on Financial Transactions (*Contribuição Provisória sobre Movimentação Financeira – CPMF*) in 1996, but extinguished in 2007 (Cunha 2021). During this period, Constitutional Amendment 29/2000 was approved, which shared the responsibility for applying constitutional minimums for their own revenues between entities at the three government levels. But what we saw was a progressive reduction in the Union's participation in public health financing while the states maintained their share, spending close to the 12% minimum, and the municipalities significantly increased it, spending on average well above the 15% minimum (Piola et al. 2018). Regarding budgetary restrictions, considering the three largest federations and the three largest unitary countries in Latin America in 2016, Brazil had the lowest proportion of the national government budget allocated to health, as well as occupying fourth place in the proportion of Gross Domestic Product (GDP) allocated by the government to the sector and only third in per capita spending in dollars (Machado 2021). Considering that the *SUS* is the only universal coverage system among the six countries studied, the relative position of health spending in Brazil does not present a reasonable justification.

But if this issue has been present since the beginning of its history, a very relevant moment in the trajectory of the *SUS* was the beginning of the Temer Government after the impeachment of President Dilma Rousseff. From then on, there was an enthusiastic adherence to fiscal austerity policies with the adoption of the Spending Ceiling established by the approval of Constitutional Amendment 95, of 12/15/2016. This Amendment created a new fiscal regime in which public expenses and investments would be limited to the same amounts spent in the previous year, only adjusted for inflation (see Chapters 2 and 4). The impact on the already weakened *SUS* financing would be even more dramatic, both due to restrictions generated by possible pressure for spending in other areas of government and due to the way in which the federal floor for expenses with Public Health Actions and Services (*Ações e Serviços Públicos de Saúde – ASPS*) is calculated. From then on, it was estimated that health spending would remain at a value equivalent to 15% of net current revenue (NCR) in 2017 for a long period, ranging from 2018 to 2036 (Vieira et al. 2018).

Still regarding the Temer Government, it is worth highlighting that the Ministry of Health (MoH) was handed over to the Progressive Party (PP) in the person of the deputy Ricardo Barros,[5] which remained there between May 2016 and April 2018. The change in political orientation in the direction of the MoH marked a significant turn in its trajectory, breaking dialogue with the coalition that supported the *SUS* over the previous decades. Thus, while on the one hand the influence of entities and personalities from the health movement was blocked, on the other the MoH opened up to intensify dialogue with the medical corporation and with representations of supplementary medicine. Statements by the Minister himself clearly pointed towards greater porosity to these interests when he stated that it was necessary to "review the size of the *SUS*," proposing the creation of "accessible health" plans, which would relieve the State of the need to provide healthcare for a portion of the population.[6] Another political approach to the MoH took place in the direction of municipal public managers with a localist orientation, led by the National Council of Municipal Health Secretaries (*Conselho Nacional de Secretários Municipais de Saúde – CONASEMS*), accepting proposals to remove conditions for the use of financial transfers from the *SUS* in a clear centrifugal movement by which the MoH gave up an important federative coordination mechanism through suppressing *SUS* financing blocks through the Ordinance of MS No. 3.992/2017.

8.3   Then on the way there was a pandemic...

The 2018 elections were marked by the surprising rise of the extreme right to the Executive Branch, opening a new window of opportunities to unlock the changes within the *SUS* that had been desired and outlined during the Temer government.

Prepared under the coordination of Luís Henrique Mandetta, Jair Bolsonaro's first Minister of Health, the "government plan" for the sector was based on the premise that spending on this policy was already sufficient, something that was translated as "do more" with the available resources. The few topics mentioned in the document delivered as a "plan" were: (1) Creation of the national electronic medical record, although without any mention of its necessary integration with the systems already existing within the scope of *DATASUS*, as well as any reference to the various systems with medical records already implemented in several municipalities across the country; (2) Universal accreditation of doctors and creation of a State medical career in the *SUS*, which welcomed this corporation, the first being an old flag and the second a proposal more recently adopted by this category; (3) Ideological criticisms of the More Doctors (*Mais Médicos*) Program; and finally; (4) Some vague proposals to improve the Family Health Strategy, such as incorporating physical education professionals into the teams, although without indicating in the slightest how this would happen.

Mandetta, a doctor and federal deputy who was not re-elected in 2018, was the former municipal health secretary of Campo Grande – in the state of Mato Grosso do Sul, Central West region of the country – but he had also been former president of Unimed[7] in this municipality (2001–2004) and one of the creators of the Parliamentary Front for Medicine in the Chamber of Deputies, when he led the opposition to the *Mais Médicos* Program and opening more spots in medicine courses. Thus, two priorities stood out in the first months of his tenure at the MoH; the first being to reformulate the national policy for basic care, expressed in the *Previne Brasil* Program, established by Ministerial Ordinance 2,979 of November 12, 2019. This Ordinance established a new form of financing this care level based on the number of registered users and linked to the Family Health teams, breaking the idea of universalization in exercising responsibility for the population present in the territory. Furthermore, the Ordinance incorporated payment for performance, although its implementation was postponed with the start of the Pandemic, as well as taking into account the estimated large loss of resources for a significant part of the municipalities when the new evaluation criteria were applied (Mendes et al. 2022). The second visible change in this first year of government was a reorientation of the National Mental Health Policy (*Política Nacional de Saúde Mental – PNSM*), which once again refinanced psychiatric beds and valued therapeutic communities, to the detriment of the Psychosocial Care Networks (*Redes de Atenção Psicossociais – RAPS*), which had been established in the *SUS* as a care strategy for patients in mental distress, articulating services at different levels of technological complexity in order to ensure social reintegration and monitoring for these patients.

However, the emergence of the Covid-19 Pandemic brought to light what was one of the main hallmarks of the Bolsonaro administration in the Presidency of the Republic: the dissociation between health policy and the technical and scientific guidelines adopted by national and international health authorities. According to the COVID Parliamentary Inquiry Commission Report, the Bolsonaro Government chose to deliberately expose the population to the risk of contagion in the name of supposed "natural immunity" and disseminate the use of ineffective medicines – including ordering the manufacture, acquisition and distribution through official means – in addition to deliberately delaying the acquisition of vaccines (Federal Senate 2021). These measures were taken over by the so-called "parallel cabinet" formed informally around the President, which generated tensions since the beginning of the Pandemic in relations with the then Minister Mandetta, publicly disapproved by Bolsonaro.

Although aligned with a marketing proposal to reformulate the *SUS*, Mandetta refused to give in to the denialist view of the Pandemic, which ended up leading to his dismissal. But the President went further by seeking, through Provisional Measure 926/2000, to disallow state and municipal governments from adopting non-pharmacological measures to contain the virus spread; this was only not accomplished due to a contrary decision by the Federal Supreme Court in April 2020, which reinforced the autonomy of states and municipalities to take measures to protect the collective health of their populations, in accordance with the institutional design established by CF88. In fact, the topic of federative relations in the Bolsonaro government deserves at least two highlights here.

The first is due to the expression of tensions in intergovernmental relations in the face of the President's leading role in the (lack of) national management in the face of the pandemic, moving them from a sectoral arena with equal representation of managers linked to the three levels of the federation and institutionalized for decades – the Tripartite Intermanagers Commission (*Comissão Intergestores Tripartite – CIT*)[8] – for the public confrontation between the Federal Executive and the Governors' Forum[9] (Almeida 2021). Varying between a simple majority and two-thirds of the heads of state governments, the letters from this Forum became more vehement and frequent in defending the prerogatives and resources to combat the Pandemic as it worsened. The first of them, dated March 25, 2020, asked for the Federal Government's collaboration in adopting fiscal measures that would create conditions for states to organize themselves to combat the virus. The second, on April 18, expressed solidarity with the presidents of the Senate and Chamber, verbally attacked by the President of the Republic when they made moves to make the fight against the Pandemic in its various dimensions viable in against the inaction of the Federal Executive. The governors confronted the President several times in the following letters, contesting false information released by him about state revenues or demanding acquisition of immunization agents, for example. The President's confrontational strategy undid a long cooperative tradition in intergovernmental relations within the *SUS* and reduced the scope of activities technically coordinated by its national leadership.

The second highlight refers to such activities under the weak presence or even absence of the MoH, which began to depend on initiatives from the states themselves using two instruments. The first was the National Council of Health Secretaries (*Conselho Nacional de Secretários de Saúde – CONASS*), which played a role in disseminating information to the press and general population, as well as technical cooperation between state governments (Almeida 2021). However, its role was limited by the predominantly technical and consensual nature of its decisions which gave strong veto power to representatives aligned with the President. A second instrument was regional cooperation, the best-known experience being that of the Northeast Consortium, through which there was a movement of technical collaboration in producing and disseminating information, guidance for adopting non-pharmacological measures and the acquisition of inputs and equipment (Almeida 2021). However, despite their importance these initiatives produced limited benefits in the absence of the coordinating role of the Federal Executive.

The second minister, Nelson Teich, spent less than a month in office and requested his resignation after realizing the lack of autonomy to formulate and implement measures technically guided by Science to contain the Pandemic. It was up to Eduardo Pazuello, an active General who had temporarily taken over the MoH in May, with Teich's departure, and who only took office in September 2020 (four months later), to carry out the policy adopted by the Bolsonaro government until March 2021.

With regard to the MoH, Pazuello's management was completely aligned with the President's purposes,[10] amplifying problems that seriously affected the *SUS* operation: lack of transparency of information available to the public (including disclosure of cases and deaths amid the Pandemic) and of a communication policy that guided the population's conduct; confrontation with subnational government entities and lack of federative articulation; militarization of the composition of MoH staff; interference in the work of eminently technical commissions, such as the National Commission for the Incorporation of Technologies into the Unified Health System (*Comissão Nacional de Incorporação de Tecnologias – Conitec*); contempt for public control mechanisms and decades-old institutional learning on the operation of the epidemiological surveillance system in confronting crisis situations. Such problems left a tragic institutional legacy: evasion of highly qualified technicians from the MoH; loss of confidence regarding the reliability of official data from the Ministry of Health on the Pandemic;[11] a delay in the purchase of immunization agents, negotiations for which were already taking place between suppliers and countries;[12] or even degradation in institutional relations, both horizontally (National Congress and Federal Supreme Court) and vertically (states), among other aspects.

Cardiologist Marcelo Queiroga took over the MoH from March 2021 to December 2022, and with the installation of Covid Parliamentary Commissions of Inquiry (*Comissões Parlamentares de Inquérito – CPI*) from April 2021, he began to act under the pressure of public opinion, assuming an ambiguous policy: sometimes he reproduced the President's denialist positions, and sometimes publicly made commitments to immunizing the population. Faced with demands for consistency, he essentially leaned in favor of the Bolsonaro government's position: he opposed the requirement for a vaccination card and the mandatory use of masks, going so far as to declare that it was "better to lose your life than freedom."[13]

In retrospect, there are strong reasons to believe that the emergence of the Pandemic provided great visibility for public health policy and opened a front of negative reactions to the conduct of the Bolsonaro government which paralyzed the selective and gradualist setbacks originally intended by Minister Mandetta, and which would probably have led us to the inclusion of supplementary medicine in the *SUS* as a substitute line for a considerable part of the public served. Thus, if on the one hand the reaction of public opinion produced a loss of credibility for the MoH, on the other hand it hindered advancement of the ongoing reformist agenda, which does not mean that other institutionally destructive actions of the Bolsonaro administration were not put into practice and left a legacy of serious consequences for the Brazilian health system. In this chapter we ask ourselves, exactly, under what dimensions these processes of change – whether gradualist or acute in nature – managed to effectively alter the trajectory taken by the *SUS* since its creation in the Federal Constitution of 1988, as well as where to more precisely identify the beginning of these changes.

With the election of President Lula in 2022 for a term that would begin in 2023, the installation of the government transition commission formulated a preliminary vision which pointed to two major sets of problems: (1) generalized worsening of health indicators, such as those related to vaccination coverage; (2) institutional, budgetary and regulatory setbacks, such as the disruption of successful national policies and programs that have been maintained for decades, in addition to worsening of *SUS* financing problems. The report also records more urgent challenges such as the recovery of the health and technical authority of the MoH, as well as its budgetary capacity and federative articulation, in addition to rescuing the role of participatory collegiate bodies that were discredited and marginalized in the previous administration (Gabinete de Transição Governamental 2022).

In the next section, we bring together a set of data extracted from public databases to construct an answer to the questions presented herein.

8.4 The consequences of *SUS*

Given the opacity and lack of transparency of the acts carried out by the Federal Executive Branch throughout the Bolsonaro Government, as well as the lack of updated information on various components of the system relating to capabilities, processes and results, we chose to select some relevant dimensions to answer our question base. They were government spending on health, intergovernmental transfers in the formation of local financial capacities and vaccination coverage. Government spending on health directly points to the dimension of expenditure allocation, expressing the government priority level attributed to public policy, and it is expected that austerity policies or policies which work towards its dismantling will produce important inflections in terms of its restriction over time. Intergovernmental transfers in the formation of local financial capacities constituted an important instrument of federative coordination for organizing the national health system, given the role of municipalities as a basis for forming care networks, and it is expected that dismantling policies will also affect this mechanism, especially in its redistributive character. Finally, we take vaccination coverage as a proxy for a possible inversion of priorities towards a care model focused on individual medical care to the detriment of collective health prevention actions. In this sense, it would be possible that the changes in guidance from the Ministry of Health described in the previous section could have affected the priority level of immunization actions and consequently their results in terms of coverage.

The information collected was organized descriptively into a historical series in order to identify patterns over time and build inferences about the decisions made, even when not declared.

8.4.1 Government spending on health

Researchers in Health Economics, even before the Bolsonaro Government, predicted that the approval of EC 95/2016 would negatively affect government spending on health (Vieira et al. 2018). One of the ways to measure this effect in the years following the promulgation of the aforementioned EC would be to take health spending as a proportion of the Gross Domestic Product (GDP). Graph 8.1 suggests that this measure varied between 2000 and 2014 between values close to 3.5%, rising until 2016, when it reached close to 4%, and then showing a slight drop until 2019 and an abrupt rise in 2020, due to the Pandemic. However, the interpretation regarding the evolution of this indicator requires caution, considering that variations in GDP may eventually mask ongoing trends

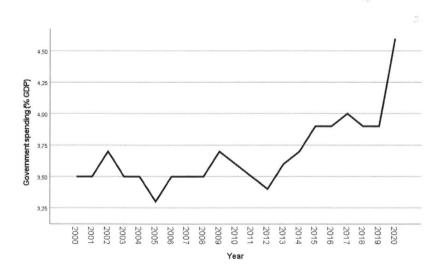

GRAPH 8.1

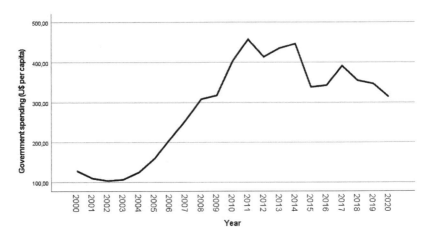

GRAPH 8.2

if this indicator is taken in isolation. As an example, the years in which the curve showed the sharpest rises (2014, 2015 and 2020) were exactly those in which GDP showed negative growth, which suggests that there may not have been real growth in government spending in the period. On the other hand, the slight decrease in the percentage of GDP invested in health between 2017 and 2019, years in which GDP grew close to 1%, suggests the constraint of government spending on health in the period at the end of the Temer government and the first year of the Bolsonaro government.

These constraints become clearer when examining government spending as a per capita value allocated by the government to health (in US$), presented in Graph 8.2. There is strong growth between 2002 and 2011, reaching a level that (remained with some fluctuation) until 2014. From then on there was a drop in 2015, still under Rousseff, with a brief recovery in 2017, and a subsequent consistent drop from then on, including in the first year of the Pandemic, in 2020. The fiscal austerity measures initiated at the end of Dilma Rousseff's administration, but constitutionally crystallized in the Temer Government with the "Spending Ceiling" and deepened in the Bolsonaro Government, affected the growth curve of health spending designed in the 2000s, even though such growth had already been interrupted between 2011 and 2014, when it became stagnant.

Concomitant to this reduction in government spending on health, it is noted that the relative participation of the public sector in health financing in Brazil declined after 2014, after a stable growth trajectory that began at least since 2001 (after the Constitutional Amendment 29/2000), as seen in Graph 8.3. On the other hand, the private sector grew more consistently in the second half of the decade while monitoring fiscal austerity measures, with the growth of its participation in health spending only declining with the Pandemic outbreak.

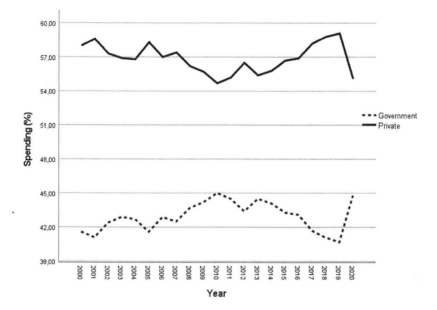

GRAPH 8.3

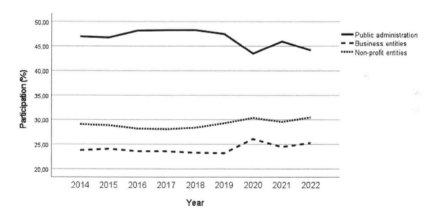

GRAPH 8.4

Finally, it is worth mentioning an aspect of a different nature, but which adds to the perception of the weakening role of public services in health policy, even among *SUS* providers. Graph 8.4 points to reduced participation of public providers in the total number of outpatient procedures approved for payment in the *SUS*, concomitantly with an increase in the participation of the non-profit private sectors and mainly of business entities. This trend began more clearly in 2019 and was consolidated from 2020 onwards. It is possible, and this is an aspect to be further explored in future studies, that this movement can be credited to restrictions in the financing of health policy in recent years, leading to a loss in the capacity to invest in expanding its own service network.

From the indicators analyzed above, it is clear that both stagnation in the growth curve of health spending and the reduction in the public sector's participation in its financing precede the Temer and Bolsonaro governments. However, these trends suffer a more severe inflection from these governments, including an introduction of important restrictions in the *SUS* organization. On the one hand, they reduce the capacity to invest in technologies and innovations which are important for improving the health system, affecting everything from the absorption of new procedures and medicines to the introduction of innovations in the field of information technologies. These trends also reduce the ability to value, develop and retain professionals specialized in health careers whose training is generally time-consuming. Then on the other hand, they also reduce the capabilities of the Federal Executive to coordinate the *SUS*, which is necessary to induce service provision and organize healthcare networks in order to ensure equality and completeness in access to services since the 1988 Constitution, leaving municipalities to their own devices regardless of their decision-making capacity.

The next dimension selected also relates to constraints in financing the *SUS*, but more specifically on the formation of municipal revenues via national conditional transfers and on the execution of local health expenditures, since municipalities constitute the basis for the organization of services and management of providers in the constitutional and legal arrangement of the SUS..

8.4.2 Intergovernmental transfers and local health expenditures

The analysis of intergovernmental transfers for forming local financial capacities focuses on one of the main mechanisms of federative coordination under the *SUS*: the conditioned transfers of resources, fund to fund, from the Union to states and municipalities (Arretche 2012, Baião et al. 2017,). Such transfers were fundamental for local governments to organize themselves as the nodes that would constitute healthcare networks. Transfers from the MoH to municipalities represented something around 45% of the resources allocated to public actions and services in the first years of the 2010s, while direct execution by the Ministry accounted for 33% and transfers to states for 20%, in addition to transfers to other entities (Piola 2017). The transfers had an important compensating effect on forming local revenues available for health given the inequalities between the municipal revenue bases, even if regulated by the constitutional floor of at least 15% to be allocated to the sector (Machado et al. 2021).

Taking the national per capita of *SUS* transfers by the Union as a reference to compare the amounts allocated by region, Graph 8.5 points to a change in pattern

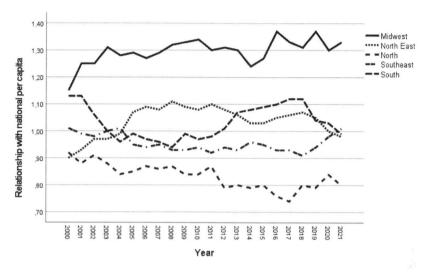

GRAPH 8.5

when we keep our attention on the Southeast and Northeast regions. The annual per capita value transferred to the Northeast starting in 2000 and remaining until 2011 showed a growth trajectory in relation to the national per capita, surpassing the value for the Southeast between 2004 and 2005, and then surpassing the latter region from then on, suggesting an effort to reduce inequalities. However, the annual amount per capita for the Northeast began to decrease from 2012 onwards. The Southeast region maintained a downward trend until 2018, then began to grow sharply from 2019 onwards, exactly in the period in which the Northeast region showed its sharpest drop, having surpassed the latter region in 2021 after maintaining it a decade and a half ago. Remembering that these are the two most populous regions of the country, one being the richest and the other the poorest, and the identified inversion suggests a decrease in the redistributive effect of *SUS* transfers which was intensified from 2019 onwards under the Bolsonaro government. It is important to note here that the Northeast is a strong base for Lula and that Bolsonaro made several discriminatory speeches about Northeasterners and publicly and notoriously harassed the Northeast Consortium.

It should not be forgotten that data relating to *SUS* transfers, fund by fund, do not include discretionary allocations from the national government such as those possible through Voluntary Union Transfers (*Transferências Voluntárias da União – TVU*), which open up the possibility for the Federal Executive to reward supporters and retaliate against opponents, as could be the case with the governors of the Northeast. It is also worth considering that *SUS* transfers during the pandemic may account for part of this effect of inverting fund-to-fund

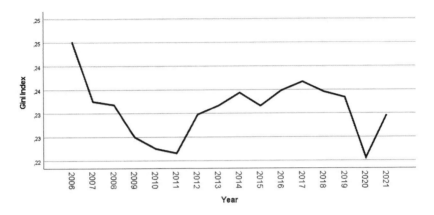

GRAPH 8.6

resources from the poorest to the richest region of the country, something which could be better described and explained in future studies that cover programs such as *Previne Brasil* and the change dynamics in financing the various healthcare components in the period.

Directly examining the level of inequality between local financial capabilities tells us a lot about the performance of the national government. Even though economic crises, such as the one that occurred in the last decade, have a different impact on the capacity to collect and generate their own revenues between municipalities, pushing towards an increase in inequality, national governments have instruments to mitigate this effect, as is the case of intergovernmental transfers (Oates 1999, Silva 2005). However, in analyzing the period between 2006 and 2021 (Graph 8.6), what can be seen is inequality between these expenditures has grown again since 2012 (already during the mandate of President Dilma) after an equalization period of per capita municipal expenditure between 2006 and 2011, and then went to even higher levels, except in 2020 when the Pandemic emerged and there was a change in the pattern of *SUS* transfers. The increase in inequalities between municipal expenditures per capita occurred while the Union reduced and municipalities increased their relative participation in public health financing (Piola 2017).

The data in Graph 8.6 were constructed from calculating the Gini Index between the per capita values of total municipal expenditure on health and converge with the previous graph (8.5) in order to point out that not only regional inequalities between per capita values transferred by the *SUS* for municipalities increased again from 2012, as they did and in the same year for total per capita health expenditure in Brazilian municipalities.

Thus, if the economic crisis increased territorial inequalities in local health expenditure, *SUS* transfers lost their equalizing power even before the Temer government. However, this increase intensified under the Spending Ceiling created by the latter and under the attack by the Bolsonaro government on the coordinating role of the MoH (and remember here the "*Mais Brasil, Menos Brasília*"[14] and the proposal to delink the constitutional minimum for health). The country was thus missing a great opportunity to reformulate the transfer scheme so that it could assume an equalizing role in facing the concentrating effects of the economic crisis.

8.4.3 Vaccination coverage

Considering the wide range of care modalities that can be analyzed in this third and final dimension given that the *SUS* proposes comprehensive healthcare, we pay attention to item II of article 198 of the Federal Constitution, which refers to "priority for preventive activities," as a criterion for selecting vaccination coverage as a proxy for these latter activities.

From Graph 8.7, it is preliminarily worth highlighting that the National Immunization Program (*Programa Nacional de Imunização – PNI*) earned Brazil international recognition, as in the case of the Pan-American Health Organization (PAHO), which considered it one of the best in the world for several aspects such as free vaccines, the quality of immunobiologicals and the high vaccination coverage achieved.[15] Thus, we selected three immunizers among the most important in the vaccination calendar (BCG, Hepatitis B and Polio) to analyze this modality of action, and considering a broad historical series covering almost three decades. The coverage curves illustrate that there

GRAPH 8.7

was clear growth until they reached high levels in 1999 and reached levels close to 100% from 2004 onwards. However, vaccination coverage began a period of consistent decline from 2016, the year the Temer administration began, which remained in the Bolsonaro government until reaching worrying levels in 2022, all of them below 80%.

The denial of immunization throughout the Bolsonaro administration was therefore not restricted to the case of the Covid-19 Pandemic, but deepened the inflection trend in the *PNI*'s previous success trajectory, leaving one of the saddest marks of the *SUS* management in recent years. This situation is still representative of a loss in priority for preventive and collective actions in favor of a model of individual care centered on the medical act. But what would be Brazil's relative position in the evolution of vaccination coverage in Latin America in the last decade compared to larger countries in this region? The World Data Bank, produced by the World Bank,[16] presents data relating to two vaccines – Measles and DPT (Diphtheria, Pertussis and Tetanus) – for all countries.

Graph 8.8 shows vaccination coverage for Measles. It is noticeable that the curve for Brazil had a slight drop between 2013 and 2016 after having maintained close to 100% vaccination coverage for many years, even ahead of other countries in the Region, but then fell dramatically from 2019 to the point of finishing the series as last placed in 2021. Only Argentina showed a clear drop in the historical series analyzed from 2018 onwards, but recovering in 2021, while Chile and Colombia maintained stable coverage curves. The trends for the vaccination coverage curves for DPT, in Graph 8.9, were relatively

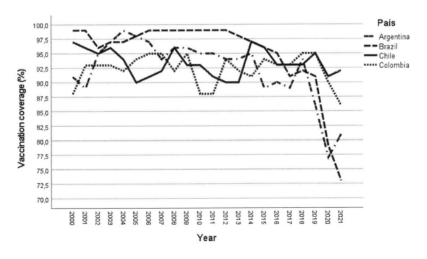

GRAPH 8.8

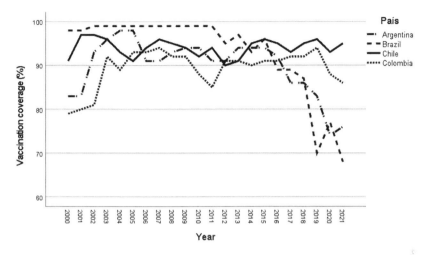

GRAPH 8.9

similar: Brazil led or remained among the highest in coverage until 2015, but after 2016, it began a clear decline among the other countries, finishing in last place. Both graphs show that what happened with the vaccination coverage curves in Brazil clearly differs from the cases in Chile and Colombia, as well as the drop in Argentina, which mainly occurred in 2019 and 2020, but culminated in a beginning of recovery in 2021.

Although the drop in vaccination coverage is clear under the Temer Government, it was further intensified under the Bolsonaro Government, and it is implausible to attribute such effects to the pandemic for at least two reasons: first, such trends were already underway in 2019, before the pandemic; second, medium and high complexity procedures only showed a reduction in 2020, having resumed in 2021 to levels very close to those found in 2019.[17] The governmental choices of both presidents contributed to dismantling immunization actions in the country, as opposed to individual curative care, but the data suggest a more intense movement in this direction in the last government.

8.5 Conclusions

Recent history has taught (with great difficulty) that one cannot take the statements made by former President Bolsonaro as metaphors or inconsequential performances only intended to mobilize his support base. Not that words cannot fulfill these functions in the mouths of other political leaders and in other circumstances, but Bolsonaro has sent clear signals of his preferences and intentions since the beginning of his career as a parliamentarian. At the beginning of his term as President, in March 2019, he categorically stated at a dinner at the Brazilian embassy in Washington that he intended to "deconstruct" or "undo" a lot of things before starting to "remake."[18] His four years in office generated a strong process of institutional corrosion and collected a series of attacks on the structures guaranteeing social rights established by the 1988 Federal Constitution. On the other hand, before Bolsonaro, some movements had already been rehearsed based on austerity measures and the political realignment of the Federal Executive, which even led to a disjunction between the guidance of the Ministry of Health – the coordinating body at the national level – and the actors who historically supported the *SUS*.

In this work we have outlined a representation of how political changes in the Federal Executive in the second half of the last decade would have affected fundamental aspects of the Unified Health System (*SUS*), "the most democratic of institutions," based on references and available data. To this end, aware of the complexity and limitations of our intention, we selected three dimensions to be considered: health spending, the configuration of local financial capacities based on intergovernmental transfers and vaccination coverage.

With regard to spending on health, it was clear that government funding for health had already been declining (already during the crisis of President Dilma Rousseff's second term and the beginning of Michel Temer's administration), with government participation reducing while it was increasing the relative share of private spending. If we saw a national government with the financial capacity to coordinate the *SUS* and induce provision of structuring services for the healthcare network in different corners of the country until the first half of the last decade, this trend was reversed in the second half and combined with growth in the weight of the private sector in the provision of health services, including among *SUS* providers themselves.

In this scenario, even the fund-to-fund transfers from the Union to the municipalities – the basis of the organization of the healthcare network and managers of *SUS* services in the first instance – lost their redistributive capacity by reversing the trend of privileging the Northeast over the Southeast in the second half of the decade. But it was not just inter-regional inequalities that increased: inequalities between per capita municipal expenditures have increased since 2012. If government spending on health fell, that fraction consumed through intergovernmental transfers from the Union to municipal governments underwent a change in orientation to be even better analyzed in subsequent studies. Given this situation, the fact is that local financial capacities in health have become more asymmetrical over the last decade, compromising equality and completeness in access to services.

From the point of view of vaccination coverage, a downward trend began since the Temer government which was intensified during the Bolsonaro administration; this phenomenon was only noticed among the large Latin American countries with less intensity and with signs of recovery at the end of the period in Argentina. The political choices were clear in the sense of contradicting section II, of article 198 of the Federal Constitution, of "priority for preventive activities, without prejudice to care services" as a qualifier of the comprehensiveness promised by the *SUS*.

The axes selected for analysis in this work are obviously limited and must be complemented by other dimensions in future work, but they already point to consequences whose reversal will not only have a budgetary cost, but also a political one. Resuming the redistributive nature of *SUS* transfers and equalizing local financial capacities requires greater centralization and strengthening of the national government, and will largely depend upon a resumption of its coordination capacity. This is about reversing a centrifugal trend that has marked intergovernmental relations in the health sector in recent years and that has met the preferences of a significant number of municipal health secretaries, especially those most strongly aligned with private interests. Likewise, reversing the low priority given to preventive actions will not be a simple task, nor will reversing the weakening of the public sector's ability to directly offer services, which will contradict private sector sectors whose supply has grown in recent years.

The remnants of dismantling carried out in recent years based on the information systematized in this work suggests that the health sector has operated more like retrenchment as cutbacks than, strictly speaking, a retrenchment as institutional changes (Green-Pedersen 2004). The institutional changes detected in our research were restricted to certain spaces that, although relevant such as primary care financing mechanisms or national mental health policy, were not capable of creating structuring inflection points that introduced stable institutional changes. It is possible that the emergence of the Pandemic created conditions for interrupting the right-wing reformist agenda in the MoH, which does not mean that the reductions in sectoral financing, in the redistributive nature of *SUS* transfers or in vaccination coverage, have not produced serious consequences in the system functioning.

Thus, the reversal of the legacy left in the health sector by the Temer government and mainly by the Bolsonaro government will require more than good diagnoses and a good design for technically adequate solutions. It will also depend on the political capacity to reassemble a broad coalition which supports reconstructing the foundations of what made the *SUS* one of the greatest innovations, and perhaps "the most democratic of the institutions" created by the Federal Constitution of 1988.

Notes

1 Upon taking office as the Presidency of the Republic, on January 1, 2023, President Lula declared *"The SUS is probably the most democratic of the institutions created by the 1988 Constitution. That is certainly why it has been the most persecuted since then, and it was also the most harmed by a stupidity called the Spending Ceiling, which we will have to repeal"* (Source: https://conselho.saude.gov.br/)

2 For more information about the Community Health Agents Program, we suggest: DA SILVA, Joana Azevedo; DALMASO, Ana Sílvia Whitaker. Agente comunitário de saúde: o ser, o saber, o fazer. SciELO-Editora FIOCRUZ, 2002. For more information about the Family Health Strategy, we suggest: PINTO, Simone Nunes. Estratégia Saúde da Família – Londrina: Editora e Distribuidora Educacional S.A., 2016. For Psychosocial Care Centers, we suggest: BRASIL. Ministério da Saúde. Secretaria de Atenção a Saúde. Departamento de Ações Programáticas Estratégicas. Saúde mental no SUS: os centros de atenção psicossocial. Brasília: Ministério da Saúde, 2004.

3 Data accessible at: <https://opendata.paho.org/>.

4 Data accessible at: <https://tabnet.datasus.gov.br/>.

5 The Progressives Party is a center-right party formed from personalities who were historically linked to the party that supported the military regime, a *Aliança Renovadora Nacional* (*ARENA*).

6 www1.folha.uol.com.br/cotidiano/2016/05/1771901-tamanho-do-sus-precisa-ser-revisto-diz-novo-ministro-da-saude.shtml.

7 Unimeds constitute a system of medical cooperatives created in Brazil from the end of the 1960s and which are part of the subsistence of supplementary medicine in Brazil. For more information, see: DUARTE, Cristina Maria Rabelais. UNIMED: história e características da cooperativa de trabalho médico no Brasil. Cadernos de Saúde Pública, v. 17, p. 999–1008, 2001.

8 Palotti, Filgueiras & Testa (2023) found that the CIT did not intensify its activities during the pandemic, holding only nine ordinary meetings in 2020, in addition to not prioritizing the Covid-19 issue on its agenda, contributing to weakening or suppressing intergovernmental coordination mechanisms.

9 The National Forum of Governors is an arena that brings together the heads of state executive powers to debate common agendas, from which collective positions or initiatives are proposed to combat them.

10 Minister Pazuello's statement after meeting with Bolsonaro to address issues related to management in the face of the Pandemic was symbolic: "it's that simple, one commands and the other obeys" (Source: https://g1.globo.com/politica/noticia/2020/10/22/e-simples-assim-um-manda-e-o-outro-obedece-diz-pazuello-ao-lado-de-bolsonaro.ghtml)

11 According to Covid's CPI Final Report: "Due to changes in the way data is disseminated by the Ministry of Health, reducing the transparency of information about the pandemic, several press vehicles came together and created the consortium of press vehicles, which became the main disseminator of information consistent with interest of the Brazilian population." (Federal Senate 2021).

12 The same Report recorded that "...there were 81 correspondences from Pfizer to the Brazilian government, sent from March 17, 2020 to April 23, 2021, of which 90% received no responses" (Federal Senate 2021).

13 https://g1.globo.com/saude/noticia/2021/12/07/melhor-perder-a-vida-do-que-a-liberdade-diz-queiroga-veja-analise-de-frases-e-medidas-sobre-viajantes.ghtml.

14 Bolsonaro's government program for the 2018 presidential elections adopted the motto "More Brazil, Less Brasilia" by proposing less Union action in public policies, reducing the importance of federative coordination and widening regional inequalities (Abrucio et al. 2020).

15 Source:https://agencia.fiocruz.br/programa-nacional-de-imuniza%C3%A7%C3%B5es-pni-reconhecimento-nacional-e-internacional.

16 Accessed at the World Data Bank: https://data.worldbank.org/indicator.

17 Data on the amount of approved outpatient procedures linked to the medium and high complexity block show that their amount grew consistently until 2019, having an abrupt drop in 2020, and resuming in 2021 at a level close to that of 2018, according

to information from Datasus (https://datasus.saude.gov.br/acesso-a-informacao/producao-ambulatorial-sia-sus/).

18 https://veja.abril.com.br/politica/temos-de-desconstruir-muita-coisa-diz-bolsonaro-a-americanos-de-direita/.

References

Abrucio, F L, Grin, E J, Franzese, C, Segatto, C I, & Couto, C G 2020, 'Combate à Covid-19 sob o federalismo bolsonarista: um caso de descoordenação intergovernamental', *Revista de Administração Pública*, vol. 54, no. 4, pp. 663–677.

Almeida, L F 2021, 'Federalismo, Ação Coletiva e Governos Estaduais: Uma análise das relações interestaduais durante a crise sanitária da Covid-19', Monografia, Belo Horizonte.

Araujo, C E L 2017, 'Estado e mercado, continuidade e mudança: A dualidade da política de saúde nos governos FHC e Lula' Tese de Doutorado, Belo Horizonte.

Arouca, S 2003, *O dilema preventivista*, UNESP, São Paulo.

Arretche, M 2012, *Democracia, Federalismo e Centralização no Brasil*, FGV / FIOCRUZ, Rio de Janeiro.

Baião, A, Cunha, A, & Souza, F 2017, 'Papel das transferências intergovernamentais na equalização fiscal dos municípios brasileiros', *Revista Do Serviço Público*, vol. 68, no. 3, pp. 583–610.

Cunha, J R A 2021, 'O (Des) financiamento do direito à saúde no Brasil: uma reflexão necessária', *Revista de Direitos Sociais, Seguridade e Previdência Social*, vol. 7, no. 1, pp. 59–77.

Federal Senate 2021, *Relatório Final – Comissão Parlamentar de Inquérito da Pandemia*, Senado Federal, Brasília.

Gabinete de Transição Governamental 2022, *Relatório Final*, Brasil / Governo de Transição, Brasília.

Giovanella, L, Almeida, P F 2017, 'Atenção primária integral e sistemas segmentados de saúde na América do Sul', *Cadernos de Saúde Pública*, vol. 33, no. 2, acesso em 24 Abril 2023, https://doi.org/10.1590/0102-311X00118816

Green-Pedersen, C 2004, 'The dependent variable problem within the study of welfare state retrenchment: Defining the problem and looking for solutions', *Journal of Comparative Policy Analysis: Research and Practice*, vol. 6, no. 1, pp. 3–14.

Machado, J A 2021, 'Universalidade e equidade em saúde na América Latina: federalismo importa?', in Aziz T S, Dawisson B L & Manoel L S (org.), *Desafios globais (vol. 3)*, Editora UFMG, Belo Horizonte, pp. 57–85.

Machado, J A, Gonçalves, G Q, Jeronymo M L, & Araújo C E L 2021, 'Financiamento da Saúde e Despesas Municipais com Receitas Próprias: Fazendo a diferença?', *Novos estudos CEBRAP*, vol. 40, pp. 281–299.

Mendes, A, Melo, M A & Carnut, L 2022, 'Análise crítica sobre a implantação do novo modelo de alocação dos recursos federais para atenção primária à saúde: operacionalismo e improvisos', *Cadernos de Saúde Pública*, vol. 38, no. 2, acesso em 24 Abril 2023, https://doi.org/10.1590/0102-311X00164621

Oates, W E 1999, 'An essay on fiscal federalism', *Journal of Economic Literature*, vol. 37, no. 3, pp. 1120–1149.

Oliveira, J A & Teixeira, S M F 1989, *(IM) Previdência social: 60 anos de história da previdência no Brasil*, Editora Vozes, Petrópolis.

Oliveira, V C 2000, 'A comunicação midiática e o Sistema Único de Saúde', *Interface-comunicação, saúde, educação*, vol. 4, pp. 71–80.

Palotti P, Filgueiras, F & Testa, G G 2023, 'Desmobilização institucional e estilos de governança multinível: o caso da CIT da saúde no Governo Federal Brasileiro na pandemia de Covid-19', in Gomide A A, Silva M M S & Leopoldi M A (eds.), *Desmonte e reconfiguração de políticas públicas (2016–2022)*, IPEA, Brasília, pp. 529–555.

Piola, S F 2017, *Transferências de Recursos Federais do Sistema Único de Saúde para Estados, Distrito Federal e Municípios: os desafios para a implementação dos critérios da Lei Complementar No 141/2012*, IPEA, Brasília.

Piola, S F, Benevides, R P S & Vieira, F S 2018, *Consolidação do gasto com ações e serviços públicos de saúde: trajetória e percalços no período de 2003 a 2017*, IPEA, Brasília.

Portela, M C & Lotrowska, M 2006, 'Assistência aos pacientes com HIV/Aids no Brasil', *Revista de Saúde Pública*, vol. 40, pp. 70–79.

Servo, L M S, Santos M A B, Oliveira F S & Benevides R P S 2021, 'Financiamento do SUS e Covid-19: histórico, participações federativas e respostas à pandemia', *Saúde em Debate*, vol. 44, pp. 114–129.

Silva, M S 2005, 'Teoria do federalismo fiscal: notas sobre as contribuições de Oates, Musgrave, Shah e Ter-Minassian', *Nova Economia*, vol. 15, no. 1, pp. 117–137.

Stralen, C J 1996, *The Struggle over a National Health Care System: the "movimento sanitário" and health policy-making in Brazil*, FSW / RUU, Utrecht.

Teixeira, S M F 1995, *Projeto Montes Claros: A utopia revisitada*, Abrasco, Rio de Janeiro.

Vieira, F S, Piola, S F & Benevides, R P S 2018, *Controvérsias sobre o Novo Regime Fiscal e a apuração do gasto mínimo constitucional com saúde*, IPEA, Brasília.

9

SOCIO-ASSISTANCE SERVICES

One dies of starvation and no one sees

Natália Sátyro, Eleonora Schettini Martins Cunha,
Bruno R. Pinheiro and Fernanda Silva

9.1 Introduction

Social protection for the most vulnerable groups in Brazil was built over the first 15 years of the 21st century, structuring the Unified System of Social Assistance (SUAS). SUAS offers socio-assistance protection to individuals and families facing vulnerable situations and social risks and is now present in all 5,570 Brazilian municipalities. Over the course of these 15 years, the number of services has steadily increased. This growth underscores the consolidation and institutionalization of a system dedicated to addressing poverty across its various dimensions. However, given the multidimensionality of poverty and the high level of income inequality in Brazil, it would be naive to assume that poverty and inequality could be tackled only through income transfer. The importance of the social assistance policy lies in offering services that address other dimensions of poverty that characterize the vulnerability and social risks of part of the Brazilian population. This chapter is dedicated to the social assistance policy, particularly socio-assistance services that focus on a range of circumstances, from vulnerabilities arising from insufficient income to situations of risk, when rights are violated, and family ties are strained or broken. Examples include families where there is child labor, sexual exploitation of children and adolescents, and abandonment of children, elderly people, or people with disabilities, among others. The next chapter addresses conditional cash transfers.

This policy sector offers us an interesting opportunity to analyze the actions of a government linked to a populist radical right party (PRRP) because this policy deals with social groups that are seen by these parties as unworthy of state

DOI: 10.4324/9781003487777-11

social protection. As several authors suggest in the introduction to this book, the notion of social protection promoted by PRRPs is dualistic in the sense that it has protectionist positions for "deserving" groups and a neoliberal perspective when considering "undeserving" groups (Chueri, 2022; Otjes, 2019). From the perspective of PRRPs, undeserving groups do not deserve equal treatment as compared to deserving groups. In general, they are characterized as poor people with diffuse interests, who are less politically organized, have little veto power, and rarely take part in political action beyond voting. The PRRP's authoritarian perspective, according to Rathgeb (2020), classifies this group – informal workers and the unemployed – as the "lazy free-riders" that lack deservingness, as opposed to "hard-working citizens'" (2020, p. 640). While in European countries immigrants are classified as undeserving, in countries of the Global South such a label is more frequently associated with the very poor, who are subject to moral judgments reinforced by intrinsic racial and gender discriminations/hierarchies. However, it remains to be seen whether, in practice, this translates into different actions when compared to the mainstream right.

In 2014, during the presidential government of Dilma Rousseff (affiliated with the Workers' Party, or PT, and who was in office between 2011 and 2016), Brazil faced an economic crisis that led to a period of austerity. The country's political crisis thus further deteriorated, culminating in Rousseff's impeachment and removal from office in August 2016. Michel Temer, affiliated with the Brazilian Democratic Movement, or MDB, succeeded Rousseff and held the presidential office between 2016 and 2018. Constitutional Amendment No. 95 (EC95) was promulgated on December 15, 2016, establishing a new fiscal framework and limiting the federal government's social spending. Subsequently, in 2018, Jair Messias Bolsonaro (affiliated with the Social Liberal Party, or PSL, and who was in the presidential office between 2019 and 2022) was elected president, establishing a populist far-right government. During his administration, the country was devastated by the Covid-19 pandemic. These are the key points and the context of our analysis: austerity policies and budget restrictions imposed by EC95, presidential choices for a PRRP in the federal government, and the Covid-19 pandemic.

In line with international trends, since the 1990s Brazil has been making substantial changes to its frameworks, with varying degrees depending on the municipality and legislature. That is particularly true for fiscal austerity policies and, consequently, spending and investment cuts. The pace of such changes, however, was intensified with the approval of the new fiscal framework. EC-95 established a spending ceiling to limit the federal government's spending until 2036. This amendment determined that primary expenditures can only be increased according to the previous year's expenditures updated by inflation (Sátyro, 2021; Soares, 2023). The new fiscal rules, which were in line with the political preferences of those in the presidential office between 2016 and

2022 (Temer and Bolsonaro administrations), produced not only political and economic changes but also institutional shifts. The social assistance policy was directly affected.

Given this context of government turnover and restricted budget for social spending at the federal level, we ask: How have these events affected the provision of socio-assistance services through SUAS? We examine how certain events might have affected socio-assistance services. These events include the economic crisis that began in Rousseff's government, in 2015, the fiscal austerity policy imposed by Temer's government through EC95, Bolsonaro's election to the presidential office, and the Covid-19 pandemic. Has the trajectory of socio-assistance services changed? If so, when did it occur and what are the relevant factors? Is it possible to say that there has been a dismantling of SUAS and, consequently, of socio-assistance provision? To answer these questions, we examined the funding and indicators of the socio-assistance services that were effectively offered.

The remainder of this chapter is divided into three sections and the conclusion. In the first section, we briefly present the core concepts and the theoretical perspectives that guide our analysis. The second section analyzes the trajectory of SUAS from its creation, in 2005, until 2022. The goal is to show that socio-assistance services were consolidating and expanding across the Brazilian territory and that this trajectory was changed. In the third section, we analyze how funding for these services has evolved between 2014 and 2022. This analysis will allow us to present a series of arguments associated with the four landmark events: the economic crisis, the Temer government (with EC-95), the Bolsonaro government, and the Covid-19 pandemic. We hypothesize that these events might have changed the direction of SUAS' trajectory. We examine how these events have affected the provision of socio-assistance services between 2014 and 2022 and conclude that services have been affected. A progressive dismantling has been taking place, mainly due to federal defunding.

9.2   Change of direction: Dismantling by default and by defunding

Public policies change due to several factors and in different directions and intensities. However, when policy change implies a retrenchment, decrease, or diminution (commonly through deregulation, reregulation, budget cuts) that alters the structure or orientation of a particular policy, it is referred to as dismantling (Bauer and Knill, 2014; Jordan, Green-Pedersen and Turnpenny, 2012). Dismantling involves a variety of phenomena and different kinds of strategies shaped by the type and number of instruments used in a specific policy (Jordan, Green-Pedersen and Turnpenny, 2012). Therefore, dismantling is "a policy change that reduces the number of policy items as well as the number of policy instruments applied in a particular area and/or lowers their intensity" (Bauer and Knill, 2014, p. 34). Dismantling changes both the policy and the actors' ability to implement it. To realize their preferences, governments use strategies, understood as a "certain mode, method or plan chosen to bring about the desired dismantling effect" (Idem, p.37). The choice of dismantling strategy is affected by the type of policy (environmental or social, for example).

We believe that the social assistance policy represents a unique case of dismantling, which differs somewhat from the Bauer and Knill (2014)'s typology: strategic actions were carried out with low visibility (resembling a form of dismantling by default), yet they were implemented with intentionality (akin to active dismantling). Therefore, there was an active decision, but with low visibility, to dismantle the internal structures of this policy, disregarding the bodies tasked with reaching federative agreements and enabling social participation as mandated by law. Unlike the case of symbolic action seen in policies such as income transfer, family policy, and the environmental sector, the socio-assistance services were ignored (in symbolic terms) by Temer and Bolsonaro. Both presidents only publicly referred to the Happy Child Program (later called the Early Childhood Program in SUAS).

In this study, we examine four hypotheses: Hypothesis 1: The economic crisis that emerged during Rousseff's government marked the initial shift in the trajectory of the provision of socio-assistance services. This occurred because such services are classified as discretionary expenses, and during a crisis, they are typically the first to experience the effects of the cutback. Hypothesis 2: The rise of the mainstream right to national power has implications for social policies. In this case, the implementation of President Temer's new fiscal framework in 2017 further solidified this shift in trajectory. Given that EC95 has established a 20-year spending ceiling, this represents a long-term effect. Hypothesis 3: The rise of a far-right populist leader in the presidency (Bolsonaro's government) reinforces this changing trajectory in the provision of socio-assistance services, particularly because the target population is a great representation of those deemed unworthy of protection. Hypothesis 4: The Covid-19 pandemic led to social distancing measures that persisted for several months throughout 2020 and 2021, with variations across states and municipalities.[1] Considering that socio-assistance services are primarily delivered in person and are the responsibility of local governments, it was anticipated that in 2020 and 2021, services requiring follow-up care and face-to-face meetings would be reduced. The exception to this is sheltering services and other services that involve vulnerable individuals requiring shelter, institutionalization, and separation from their families because they might harm themselves. In this context, the provision of socio-assistance services is expected to reduce.

9.3 The consolidation of the social assistance policy and the provision of socio-assistance services

Social assistance was regulated in 1993, following its provision as a right in the Federal Constitution of 1988. It aims to provide shelter, protection, social interaction, income, and autonomy to individuals and families in vulnerable and socially risky situations. These situations include insufficient income, violations of rights (e.g., violence within families), and fragile social bonds (e.g., living on the streets). This is a redistributive policy, funded by the three levels of government but heavily dependent on federal funds, which are passed on to states and municipalities according to the rules agreed upon by the Tripartite Intermanagerial Committee (CIT). The CIT, composed of representatives of the Union, states, and municipalities, serves as an institutional space for establishing federative coordination. In other words, it is the arena where politically autonomous federative entities commit to each other to follow specific principles and guidelines. In addition, the social assistance policy design includes participatory institutions at the three levels of government – e.g., councils and conferences – so citizens can take part in decision-making processes. The National Social Assistance Council (CNAS) is the main deliberative body linked to this policy. It is established at the federal level and allows the joint participation of civil society representatives (workers, users, social assistance organizations) and government representatives (Sátyro and Cunha, 2014; 2018; Machado, 2023).

Although the right to social assistance is enshrined in the 1988 Constitution and was regulated in 1993, the National Social Assistance Policy (PNAS) was only formulated in 2004, during the governments of the Workers' Party (2003–2016). The federal government took on the role of coordinating this policy, while the three levels of government (Union, states, and municipalities) assumed different responsibilities in its implementation. This version of the PNAS was thoroughly discussed in the CNAS and agreed upon within the CIT, and it was an expression of the paradigm shift the policy community aspired to achieve. This policy encompasses services, money transfers, continuous or intermittent, in-kind or financial benefits, programs, and projects. To ensure nationwide coordinated implementation of the policy, SUAS was instituted with a decentralized and participatory management approach. Socio-assistance initiatives for the entire nation were regulated by the National Typification of Socio-Assistance Services (2009). Within the SUAS framework, socio-assistance initiatives are organized into two levels of protection: Basic Social Protection (PSB) and Special Social Protection (PSE). These two types of protection are provided in specific public facilities and through a network of civil society organizations that complement state actions.

The PSB aims to "prevent situations of risk by developing potentialities and acquisitions and by strengthening family and community bonds." It targets people who are socially vulnerable due to poverty and/or weak emotional bonds and social links (BRASIL, 2005, p.33). The Social Assistance Reference Center (CRAS) is a public facility where PSB services are provided within municipalities. These services seek to allow the coexistence, socialization, and reception of families whose family and community bonds have not been broken. CRAS is the main gateway to SUAS. The Service for Integrated Family Care and Protection (Serviço de Proteção e Atendimento Integral à Família – PAIF) is exclusively provided by CRAS facilities and "consists of social work with families, continuous in nature, to strengthen the protective role of families, prevent their bonds from breaking, promote their access and enjoyment of rights, and contribute to improving their quality of life" (BRASIL, 2009, p. 12). Another PSB service is the Social Interaction and Bond Strengthening Service (Serviço de Convivência e Fortalecimento de Vínculos – SCFV), a complement to the social work developed by PAIF. The SCFV is offered for groups and guarantees follow-up care consistent with users' age (children, adolescents, and the elderly). This service is also provided by social organizations. Finally, the Basic Social Protection Service at Home for People with Disabilities and the Elderly (Serviço de Proteção Social Básica no Domicílio para Pessoas com Deficiência e Idosas), which is also provided by CRAS facilities and social organizations, aims to prevent grievances that might disrupt users' family and social bonds. The goal is to promote autonomy for people with disabilities and the elderly (BRASIL, 2009). CRAS facilities are also tasked with including individuals and families in the Single Registry (Cadastro Único). They must keep registry information updated, an effort that includes home visits. In 2022, 8,557 CRAS facilities were identified across the country, most of which are in the Northeast (31.8%) and Southeast (35.1%) regions. Moreover, 47% of all facilities are in municipalities with less than 20,000 inhabitants, gathering 115,149 workers, 32.8% of which have security of tenure – 41% of them in the Northeast region (Censo SUAS, 2022).

The PSE, on the other hand, focuses on individuals and families facing both personal and social risks. Apart from dealing with the vulnerabilities and risks associated with their insufficient income, these individuals experience rights violations. This form of protection is subdivided into two levels of complexity: medium and high, with family and/or community bonds serving as the central distinction. If these bonds, albeit fragile, are still present, follow-up care falls into the medium complexity category. When these bonds have already been broken, sheltering and follow-up care are provided by high-complexity institutions (BRASIL, 2005). The Specialized Social Assistance Reference Center (CREAS)[2] is responsible for offering medium complexity socio-assistance services. It is primarily focused on providing the Specialized

Protection and Assistance Service for Families and Individuals (Serviço de Proteção e Atendimento Especializado a Famílias e Indivíduos – PAEFI). PAEFI provides support, guidance, and follow-up care to families where one or more members are at risk or facing rights violations. CREAS facilities also offer the Specialized Social Outreach Service (Serviço Especializado em Abordagem Social), which actively seeks to identify cases of child labor, sexual exploitation of children and adolescents, and homelessness, among others. The Social Protection Service for Adolescents Serving Socio-Educational Measures (Serviço de Proteção Social a Adolescentes em Cumprimento de Medida SocioEducativa) of Supervised Freedom (Liberdade Assistida – LA) and Community Services (Prestação de Serviços à Comunidade – PSC) aims to follow up on adolescents and young people who are required by a court of law to comply with socio-educational measures in an open regime. Another service offered by CREAS facilities is the Special Social Protection Service for People with Disabilities, the Elderly, and their Families (Serviço de Proteção Social Especial para Pessoas com Deficiência, Idosas e suas Famílias). This service focuses on families with individuals who have disabilities or elderly members who are to some extent dependent and whose limitations have been aggravated by instances of rights violation. Finally, the Specialized Service for People Experiencing Homelessness (Serviço Especializado para Pessoas em Situação de Rua) aims to provide people who use the streets as their place of residence and/or survival with an opportunity to build new life projects. This last service is offered at the Specialized Reference Center for People Experiencing Homelessness[3] (BRASIL, 2009). In 2022, there were 2,812 municipal and 33 regional CREAS facilities, predominantly in the Northeast (37.8%), followed by the Southeast (28.1%). Moreover, 69.5% of CREAS facilities are situated in municipalities with populations of up to 50,000 inhabitants, gathering 26,833 workers, most of which are in the Northeast (33.5%) and Southeast (33.1%) regions (Censo SUAS, 2022).

High-complexity social protection guarantees full protection by providing institutional sheltering to families and individuals facing severe social risks and threats (BRASIL, 2005) due to rights violations and broken family bonds. These services might be provided by the government or social organizations. The Institutional Shelter Service (Serviço de Acolhimento Institutional) provides temporary housing in extraordinary situations for children and adolescents, adults and families, women facing violence, young people and adults with disabilities, and the elderly. The Shared Housing Service (Serviço de Acolhimento em República) offers collectively managed subsidized housing to young people, adults in the process of leaving the streets, and the elderly. The Foster Family Placement Service (Serviço de Acolhimento em Família Acolhedora) places children and adolescents in homes of registered foster families. This is a protective and provisional measure applied until minors can return to their original family. In extreme cases, as a last-resort measure, minors may be permanently placed with substitute families. Finally, the Emergency and Public Disaster Protection Service (Serviço de Proteção em Situações de Calamidades Públicas e de Emergências) provides support and protection to people affected by these circumstances. It includes temporary accommodation, assistance, and material goods (BRASIL, 2009). In 2022, there were 5,536 institutional sheltering facilities in the country. Non-governmental institutions operate 63.4% of these facilities, which are mainly tasked with fostering children and adolescents (44.6%) and the elderly (31.5%). In total, there are 150,325 people in sheltering facilities, including refugees. There were 116,852 people working in these places – 46.5% of them were working under a formal contract in the private sector (Censo SUAS, 2022).

In addition to the services described above, the social assistance policy provides socio-assistance benefits to ensure income and autonomy to beneficiaries. These include the Continuous Cash Benefit Program (Benefício de Prestação Continuada), designed for people with disabilities and the elderly whose family income is insufficient to meet their basic needs, and sporadic benefits designed to address unforeseen events that exacerbate vulnerabilities, such as death and unemployment. It also includes a conditional cash transfer (Family Grant Program – Programa Bolsa Família) directly provided to the population, which will be discussed in Chapter 10 of this book.

During the PT governments, federal-level programs were only implemented after being discussed in the CIT and CNAS, where they were agreed upon and approved. The Michel Temer government, on the initiative of the social development minister, Osmar Terra, created the Happy Child Program (Programa Criança Feliz). This program was directly linked to the Presidency of the Republic and targeted children up to 72 months old. The goal was to ensure that children in this age group could fully develop through initiatives across different policy areas (education, health, culture, social assistance, human rights) involving the children and their families. It is important to note this was a top-down program formulated by the presidency to the detriment of participatory bodies and interfederative agreements – moreover, the president's wife was the program's godmother and sponsor. The program faced significant resistance within SUAS entities. The perception was that this program represented a movement back to the voluntarism and personalism attached to the role of the "first lady" and away from the institutionalization of the right to social protection and the policy itself. Since the program was not widely embraced by the municipalities, it was overhauled to fit into SUAS. It was discussed and later approved in the CIT and CNAS.[4] This new SUAS program, the Early Childhood Program (Programa Primeira Infância), was implemented through CRAS facilities with concurrent financing within the policy framework. This program relied heavily on home visits – which should be recorded for monitoring purposes – by municipal public agents. The program continued during the government of Jair Bolsonaro.

Temer's decision to establish his flagship program in this area without engaging in national-level negotiations, agreements, and deliberation within the social assistance system (specifically through the CIT and CNAS) set the tone for the policy's dynamics. First, these entities were clearly disregarded in many administrative decisions, diminishing the negotiating and deliberative role that was previously assigned to the CIT and CNAS. Second, there was a deliberate effort to abolish all national councils[5] during the first month of Bolsonaro's presidency. This attempt was blocked by the Supreme Court since the CNAS – as well as many other entities – had been established by federal law. Consequently, these spaces were hollowed out. Not only were government representatives deliberately absent or indifferent at the meetings but policy matters were not being deliberated at the CNAS. Therefore, in both the Temer and Bolsonaro administrations, the negotiation and deliberation bodies were deliberately ignored by the federal government. Bolsonaro's government explicitly tried to dissolve them.

As for the social assistance conferences, which had been held regularly every two years since 1995, the Bolsonaro government and the CNAS, which was at the time chaired by a government representative, decided to cancel the conference scheduled for 2019. In response, civil society and the Municipal Social Assistance Managers' Board (CONGEMAS) organized the "Democratic Conference," which took place without the participation of the federal government. While it may not have influenced the operational aspects of SUAS, the conference served to reaffirm the spirit of resistance against the changes imposed by the federal government – a trend that had been unfolding since the Temer administration. Therefore, the main decisions related to the social assistance policy (including those made during the pandemic) were not submitted to the participation, negotiation, and deliberation bodies within SUAS.

9.4 Changes in social assistance: gradual and silent defunding

We hypothesize that four landmark events have shifted the trajectory of the social assistance policy, affecting its funding from the federal government and consequently influencing the provision of socio-assistance services. These events are the economic crisis initiated during Dilma Rousseff's administration, the fiscal austerity policies in the form of Constitutional Amendment No. 95 during Michel Temer's administration, the political preferences of Jair Bolsonaro's government, and the country's response to the Covid-19 pandemic. We begin by examining the impact on federal funding.

Between 2005 and 2014, budget execution for the co-funding of services provided by states and municipalities was on the rise. Graph 9.1 shows that federal co-funding for the provision of socio-assistance services peaked in 2013, both in basic social protection and specialized services. The federal government contributed R$2.58 billion (in 2021 values), considering the expenses actually executed (IPEA, 2020; 2022). However, starting in the last quarter of 2014, the economic crisis began to negatively affect budget execution, with a small reversal between 2017 and 2019 (Graph 9.1). It was not until 2019 that it reached the 2013 level. However, when extraordinary expenses are excluded (Graph 9.2), it becomes clear that a full recovery did not occur. Annual government transfers reduced significantly, and funding in the following years became intermittent (IPEA, 2021) (Graphs 9.1 and 9.2). There were declines in co-funding for services in 2014, 2015, and 2018. Additionally, with the Covid-19 pandemic, the budget execution for socio-assistance services decreased even more (Graph 9.2). In 2020, the pandemic changed this situation as more resources were allocated to social assistance.

The analysis shows that, in 2017, mandatory expenditures increased by 1.9% while discretionary expenditures dropped by 12% compared to 2016. These fluctuations may be attributed to the austerity measures implemented by President Temer regarding social assistance, or they could reflect the cost of the economic crisis. Since EC95 was approved on December 15, 2016, its impact has reflected the government's need to hit the fiscal primary balance target, but it is not yet an effect of the spending ceiling (IPEA, 2019, p.vii). Two aspects help us make sense of this trajectory. First, the inconsistency in government transfers throughout the months over the years (Graph 9.2). Second, since EC95 determines that primary expenditures should not exceed inflation, austerity measures initially affect discretionary expenditures.

It is particularly important to examine the year 2019 and the first months of 2020 because this period characterizes the pre-pandemic Bolsonaro government. To fully understand the situation, the timing of the financial transfers in Graph 9.2 should be analyzed. This graph shows the cumulative monthly allocation of financial resources for socio-assistance services, offering a more comprehensive view of the scale of the problem. Although federal transfers increased in 2019 compared to the year before, they were highly irregular – almost half of the transfers were made only in the last month of the year. It is worth noting that by November of that year, only 53% of the budget had been executed, and the remaining 47% was spent in December (Graph 9.2). One could argue that these services were compromised because municipalities did not have access to funds throughout the year. Even though the funds were quickly spent in December, the regularity in the provision of services for that year had already been compromised (IPEA, 2021).

Furthermore, there was Ministerial Directive No. 2,362, issued in 2019 by the Ministry of Citizenship, with the goal of "promoting the equalization of federal co-funding of SUAS with the Budgetary Guidelines Act and the Annual

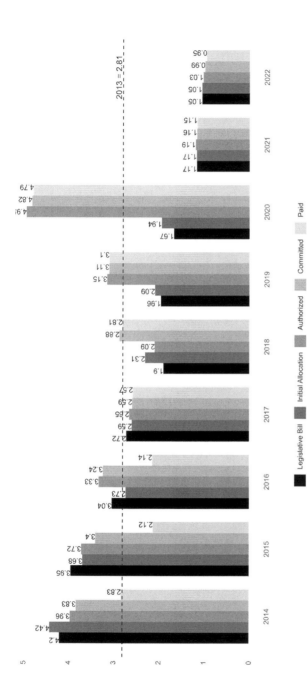

GRAPH 9.1 Evolution of budget execution for SUAS basic social protection and specialized services (2014–2022) (2014–2022), in billions (2022 values).Legend: Legislative Bill, Initial Allocation, Authorized, Committed, Paid.

Source: Siga Brasil (www12.senado.leg.br/orcamento/sigabrasil).

Note: The following budgetary actions were considered: i) in 2013 and 2017 , actions 2A60, 2A65, and 2A69; ii) in 2018, actions 2A60, 2A65, 2A69, and 00QR; iii) in 2019 and 2021, actions 219E and 219F; and iv) in 2020, action 219E, 219F, and 21C0 (only in reference to program 5031 – Social Protection in SUAS).

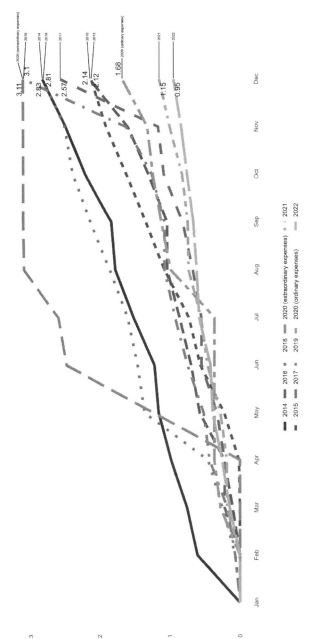

GRAPH 9.2 Progression of cumulative monthly federal transfers for basic and special social protection services (2014–2022), in billions (2022 values).Legend: (2020 – extraordinary expenses); (2020 – ordinary expenses).

Note: The following budgetary actions were considered: i) em 2013 and 2017, actions 2A60, 2A65 and 2A69; ii) in 2018, actions 2A60, 2A65, 2A69 and 00QR; iii) during the 2019–2022 period, actions 219E and 219F.

Source: Siga Brasil (www12.senado.leg.br/orcamento/sigabrasil).

Budget Law." This directive established that government transfers could only be made in the current year if there were available funds (IPEA, 2021, 2022). Therefore, if the federal government did not transfer funds to a federative entity in a specific month due to financial restrictions, these financial resources could not be transferred in the following year (IPEA, 2021, p.14). This affected municipalities since unpaid commitments from previous years were being paid with resources from the current year's budget. This change in the rules means more budgetary constraints.[6] The monthly transfers that used to be fixed became unstable, contingent on the available funds, which were distributed among the federative entities (IPEA, 2021, p.14).

For the year 2020, Graph 9.2 makes a distinction between extraordinary expenses directed toward pandemic response measures and ordinary financial resources. Ordinary resources refer to discretionary expenses allocated to basic and special social protection. This distinction enables a longitudinal analysis of funds regardless of what was spent on pandemic response – the extraordinary credit. When we exclude the large injection of resources at the end of that year, there was a significant reduction in ordinary resources compared to 2019: These resources decreased from R$2.50 billion to R$1.35 billion. A substantial share of these resources was allocated to programs that are a priority for the government, such as the Early Childhood Program in SUAS, which saw a 10% increase in its budget compared to the previous year. Indeed, only this program and the initiative to restructure public SUAS facilities – such as CRAS and CREAS facilities, the Centers for Homeless Population Assistance (Centro Pop), and other socio-assistance entities – received additional resources. However, it is important to highlight that only 58% of the authorized amount of financial resources was effectively disbursed.

This occurred because these initiatives started to receive funding through parliamentary amendments, leading to increased instability in resource allocation, an innovation introduced by the Bolsonaro government. Members of Congress have the authority to change the allocation of budgetary resources through budget amendments, which may deviate from the originally established allocation at the time of budget approval, known as the initial allocation. Additionally, the executive branch may choose not to release allocated appropriations. In 2021, the CNAS recommended a budget of R$2.52 billion for social assistance. However, the proposal sent by the federal executive to Congress allocated only R$975 million for socio-assistance services. By the end of 2021, additional resources were allocated, resulting in a total of R$1.1 billion for that year. Therefore, a significant portion of the resources used in 2020 came from budget amendments, included in the budget as extraordinary resources. It is worth noting that this was the government's smallest budget proposal presented in a decade (IPEA, 2021, 2022).

Finally, it is essential to understand the role played by the Early Childhood Program in SUAS regarding this budget, which decreased gradually but did not prevent the program from growing. In 2016, before the program was created, transfers to socio-assistance services represented about 85% of discretionary expenditures.[7] With the creation of the program in 2017, transfers to socio-assistance services decreased to 81%, while the funds allocated specifically for the program accounted for 5% of the total. In 2018 and 2019, the composition of discretionary expenses shifted, with 75% allocated to the program and 10% to all other services. In other words, the social assistance network has had to operate with a decreased amount of financial resources, which is evident in Graph 9.2, representing a reduction to only 10% (IPEA, 2019, 2020, 2021).

9.4.1 What is the federal government's contribution to funding social assistance?

Federal funds carry substantial weight in co-funding compared to the total amount of resources allocated to social assistance by the three levels of government. Until 2003, the federal government funded 66% of social assistance initiatives. The federal government's participation in co-funding increased significantly starting in 2003, when the PT assumed the presidency. In the following years, this percentage ranged between 78% and 85%, covering both basic social protection services and special social protection offered by states and municipalities. Starting in 2012, with the revision of the Basic Technical Guideline (Normas Operacionais Básicas – NOB-SUAS), the federal government's participation fluctuated slightly above 80% in the next decade (IPEA, 2022). In addition to funding services, these resources supported the Bolsa Família Program, created in 2004, and the Continuous Cash Benefit Program. With the enactment of NOB-SUAS and the Basic Technical Guideline about Human Resources (NOB-RH) in 2005 and 2006, respectively, these resources were also used to fund expenses with human resources at the municipal level. The actions taken by the federal government have contributed to the strengthening of the street-level bureaucracy responsible for socio-assistance services (Sátyro and Cunha, 2018).

9.4.2 How significant was this reduction in federal transfers for socio-assistance services?

As mentioned earlier, the emphasis given by the Temer administration to the Happy Child Program (later renamed First Childhood in SUAS) brought about substantial changes in the budget structure and had an impact on socio-assistance services. This represented a change by displacement (Araújo and Cunha, 2019). It introduced an institutional alternative to the previous approach and absorbed a substantial share of the resources that were previously allocated to services. Bolsonaro's government continued with this program. Therefore, the political choices made by these governments changed the funding pattern, affecting the provision of socio-assistance services.

It is important to know how the provision of these services evolved during this period. As mentioned earlier, PAIF, linked to the PSB, has the highest reach, as it must be provided by all CRAS facilities in 95% of Brazilian municipalities (Censo SUAS, 2022). PAIF encompasses two main types of initiatives: referrals, where users receive guidance and are directed to other services or institutions according to their needs, and follow-up care, which involves continuous actions conducted with families and individuals. Follow-up care entails a variety of collective and individual activities conducted over time. The instability in federal transfers and the reduction in funds allocated to municipalities have significantly affected the follow-up care carried out by PAIF. This has also had an impact on the inclusion of new families in the program, as demonstrated by the following graphs – A1, A2, B5, B6, D1 – from Panel 9.1. The reduction in federal funding has affected follow-up care with vulnerable, at-risk families, especially those with children or adolescents facing child labor or using shelter services, whose rights have been violated. In 2018, for example, the monthly average number of vulnerable families being monitored reduced by 17% compared to 2012. Likewise, the average number of new follow-ups dropped 57% compared to 2012 (IPEA, 2020).

Individual assistance and referrals, in turn, increased during the analyzed period, including in the pre-pandemic period, as shown in Panel 9.1 – Graphics C1, C2, C3, C4. We highlight the referrals for families to be included in the Single Registry or for their information to be updated. The Single Registry is a database used as a means for individuals and families to access several benefits, social programs, and the Continuous Cash Benefit Program. Notably, the number of referrals to CREAS facilities has increased, which suggests that instances of rights violations have become more frequent. Home visits, which were already in progress before 2016, experienced a substantial surge in activity during that year, as indicated in Panel 9.1 (C6). These visits were the primary strategy of the Early Childhood Program, even though SUAS had a similiar program in place prior to this. This increase serves as an example of how policy implementation can be affected by presidential decisions, in this case, the decisions made by two right-wing administrations.

The Social Interaction and Bond Strengthening Service experienced the least impact due to budget cuts and instabilities. This service is provided by CRAS facilities and by Social Interaction Centers (Centros de Convivência) maintained by civil society organizations (see graphs in Panel 9.2 –D2, D3, D4, D5, D6, D7). One possible explanation for the continued provision of services, especially for children and the elderly, is that municipalities have been independently

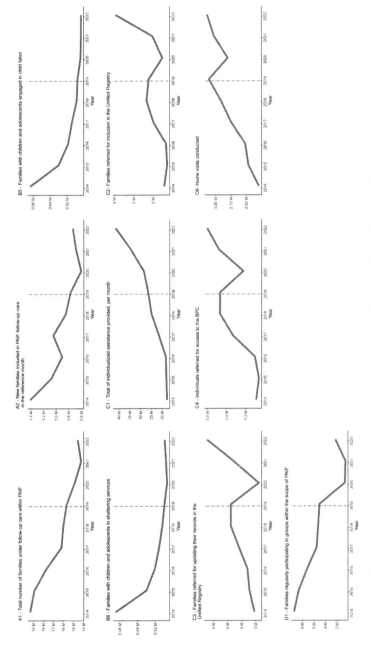

PANEL 9.1 Provision of socio-assistance services – PAIF – in CRAS facilities (2014–2022).

Source: Monthly Attendance Register (RMA) of CRAS and CREAS.

covering these expenses. Still, group activities involving families through PAIF have declined, as well as activities for adolescents aged 15 to 17.

From 2019 to 2020, the provision of socio-assistance services within the PSB reduced significantly, reaching levels lower than those of 2014. Some services were close to shutting down. We attribute this to social distancing due to the pandemic in most municipalities.

When examining the services provided within the PSE, it is important to make an initial distinction regarding their nature, characteristics, and the institutional environment in which they are offered, as this directly influences the continuity of these services. One of its specific characteristics refers to the profile of its users. These are individuals or families whose rights have been violated; in some cases, they are being sheltered in shelter centers or similar forms of accommodation. Another typical feature is that much of the follow-up care and placement in shelters is determined by judicial authorities (Justice System and Rights Guarantee System), such as cases of maltreated or abandoned children. To address some of these situations, vulnerable individuals must be placed in institutions. Therefore, when adolescents are serving court-ordered socio-educational measures or children are under institutional care, the services provided cannot be discontinued, as interruptions may even result in judicial sanctions.

These particularities of users may potentially account for the comparatively smaller variations in the delivery of medium-complexity services by the PSE from 2014 to 2019, in contrast to the fluctuations observed in the PSB. CREAS facilities offer a range of services, with the PAEFI being of medium complexity and considered the most critical. During the period under analysis, there was a slight reduction in follow-up cases for PAEFI, but there was an uptick in new cases, as illustrated in Panel 9.3 (A1, A2, B3, B6, C1, C2, C4). Research has indicated that domestic violence has increased during the implementation of social distancing measures during the pandemic (Vieira, Garcia and Maciel, 2020; Okabayashi, Tassara and Casaca, 2020). Our data seems to align with these findings, suggesting a similar increase in domestic violence, especially in Graphs A2, B6, C1, C2, and C4. To illustrate the significance of this situation, bills were introduced in the National Congress in 2020 to protect women who were victims of domestic violence during the Covid-19 pandemic. The first of these bills, PL 1.796/2020, proposed expediting judicial proceedings and maintaining legal proceedings in cases of domestic and family violence. The second one, PL 1.798/2020, allowed reports of domestic and family violence against women to be made online or through an emergency telephone number (Okabayashi, Tassara and Casaca, 2020).

The reduction in cases of sexual exploitation of children (C3) and adolescents, as well as child labor (C5) during the period, as shown in Panel 9.3, can be attributed to the result of vigorous awareness campaigns, enforcement actions

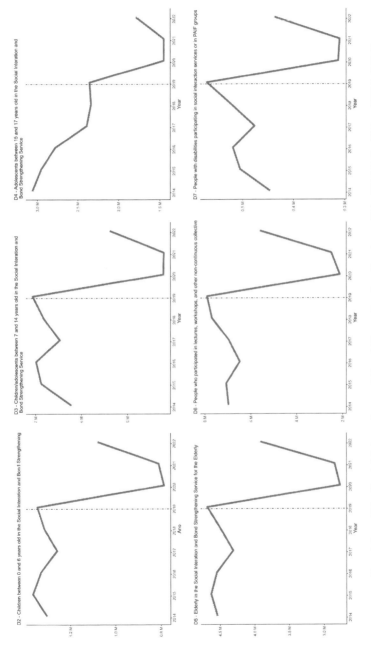

PANEL 9.2 Provision of the Social Interaction and Bond Strengthening Service within CRAS Facilities (2014–2022).

Source: Monthly Attendance Register (RMA) of CRAS and CREAS.

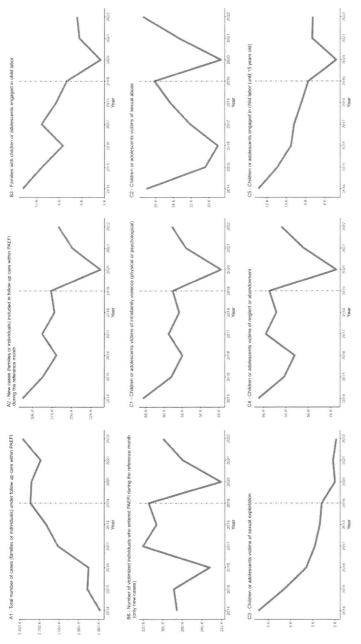

PANEL 9.3 Specialized Protection and Assistance Service for Families and Individuals – PAEFI in CREAS facilities (2014–2022) – Part 1.

Source: Monthly Attendance Register (RMA) of CRAS and CREAS.

carried out by relevant authorities, and concentrated efforts to combat these practices nationwide. This, in turn, might have led to a reduction in incidents and, naturally, a decreased need for follow-up care. However, the observed increase in service offerings from 2020 to 2021 suggests that the pandemic and social distancing measures had an impact on families. Finally, in the context of the PSE, it is equally notable that assistance to individuals experiencing homelessness has declined – these services represented 16.7% of the homeless population approached in 2014 but decreased to 7.1% in 2018 (IPEA, 2020).

9.4.3 Clarifying the Factors Influencing Service Variability during the pandemic

With respect to the resources allocated to social assistance during the pandemic, we have demonstrated that the budget allocated to this area in 2020 was considerably lower compared to previous years, excluding extraordinary expenses. Due to the increased demand for social protection caused by the pandemic, extra-budgetary allocations were directed to social assistance, resulting in a significant increase in budget execution (see Graph 9.1, years 2019 and 2020). Previously, budget execution had been declining. However, most of the extraordinary resources (as indicated in Graph 9.2) were directed towards funding the Emergency Aid, a cash benefit for the most vulnerable population. A smaller proportion of these funds was allocated to shelter units, such as shelter centers and shared housing, in order to maintain the regular operation of these facilities during the pandemic. In 2021, a year marked by the worsening of the pandemic in Brazil, there was a significant reduction in the transfer of federal funds for the co-funding of services conducted by states and municipalities (see Graphs 9.1 and 9.2). This indicates that most extraordinary resources were directed for the exclusive use of the federal government, particularly for the Emergency Aid program.

In what concerns the PSB services, particularly PAIF, the pandemic had a clear impact. Despite the federal government's regulation of social assistance as an essential policy in addressing the pandemic, the social distancing measures implemented by virtually all municipalities in Brazil had significant impacts on the provision of socio-assistance services. The data presented in the graphs indicate that group activities (SCFV) and follow-up care were virtually halted, while referrals were maintained to some extent. This is because some municipalities adopted remote work to provide some continuity to services. This measure was important to register or update users in the Single Registry, which, initially, was the means to access the Emergency Aid and the Continuous Cash Benefit Program. These resources were in high demand by citizens who became dependent on these benefits due to unemployment and hunger.

As for the PSE services, there was a decrease in follow-up activities carried out by CREAS facilities in 2020, with the most significant reduction observed in the case of socio-educational measures. However, this decline is substantially smaller when compared to what was observed in CRAS facilities. The restrictions imposed by social distancing measures certainly contributed to this reduction, although it is less significant when compared to the decrease in follow-up care within the PSB. The smaller variation observed in the case of the PSE could be attributed to the specific nature of the situations involved, which often concern rights violations and the fact that they involve court orders. The resumption of follow-up care in 2021 at practically pre-pandemic levels could be attributed to the institutional learning acquired in the previous year and the rapid progress of Covid-19 vaccination, which allowed a safer return to activities. However, a similar recovery was not observed in activities carried out in CRAS facilities.

9.5   Conclusion

Where there is no money there can be no policy. The global economic crisis and recession that began in 2008, along with the measures adopted by governments in response to these events, have shifted the dynamics of social policies and led to significant changes in existing policies. While Brazil's economy experienced a relatively stable period in the late 2000s, in 2015, during Dilma Rousseff's government, a significant economic crisis erupted, resulting in an immediate budget reduction, which had a widespread impact on social policies. At that time, the impact of budget constraints on the social assistance policy was already evident, especially in socio-assistance services, which are classified as discretionary expenses (Hypothesis 1). This situation marked the interruption of a trend of continuous growth in the funds allocated for social assistance, which had been contributing to the consolidation of this policy across the country. Since we did not find any other signs of a deliberate action to reduce the policy, we attribute the budget cut to difficult times.

Following the departure of Rousseff amidst a controversial impeachment process, her successor, a mainstream right-wing politician, implemented a strict fiscal austerity policy that would influence the actions of the next five administrations unless significant changes occurred. The impacts of these measures were evident in the federal government's transfers to municipalities, which are responsible for executing services, and, consequently, they affected the continuity of service provision (Hypothesis 2). Hence, EC-95 and its influence on funding have exacerbated the shift in trajectory. Additionally, former President Michel Temer introduced a program that competed with the institutional structure of SUAS, disregarding its mechanisms of social participation and agreement. This suggests what Pierson calls programmatic retrenchment. In other words, a reduction in short-term spending, therefore a classic dismantling: "where there is no Money there can be no policy" (Pierson, 1994, p.15). The analytical concept of "dismantling by default," introduced by Bauer and Knill, further explains this phenomenon. Former President Michel Temer did not publicly announce that the social assistance policy or its budget would be reduced or eliminated, nor did he respond to protests against the Happy Child Program. He simply did not emphasize the lack of action and instead focused his efforts on promoting and implementing the Happy Child Program, which was later integrated into SUAS as the Early Childhood Program. He promoted this program with a strong emphasis on child happiness. How could anyone resist? Indeed, the funds allocated to this program directly competed with the resources allocated to socio-assistance services, compromising the transfers to municipalities for the execution of these services. Therefore, the intention to defund services was associated with the low visibility given to it.

Bolsonaro's administration pursued a similar strategy of dismantling by default with low visibility. His intentions, however, were clear. There were no significant changes in the regulation of the social assistance policy, nor in the structure of SUAS. However, this administration disregarded the forums for social participation and the bodies where administrators could come to agreements. Consequently, decision-making processes overlooked these spaces. The policy was allowed to wither away due to systematic reductions in federal funds allocated to municipalities, which account for approximately 80% of the policy's funding. The increasing underfunding of this policy amplifies the transformation process. The avenues for consensus and participation are neglected within the system, thereby undermining the coordination that had previously existed among the different levels of government. Therefore, the significant decrease in resources allocated to services, which now represents less than 10% of what it was in 2014, represents a gradual, almost imperceptible weakening that threatens the continuity of the social assistance policy without attracting due attention. A death by starvation, without visibility. Although the literature on PRRP sees these parties as different from traditional right-wing parties, in the realm of social assistance services the approaches, both adopted similar neoliberal approaches. There were no significant differences between them, as neoliberal policies focus on the poorest individuals, who often share characteristics with "undeserving groups" and lack the ability to exert pressure.

The Covid-19 pandemic emerged in Brazil in the context of political and institutional changes, coupled with a rise in poverty levels, and we could see that it had an impact on the services offered (Hypothesis 4). The poverty rate, which was 4.5% in 2014, grew to 6.6% in 2019. Furthermore, food insecurity also increased, affecting 55.2% of the Brazilian population, with 0.5% facing severe or moderate food insufficiency, according to IPEA (2022). According to the Pessan Network, this situation further deteriorated in 2022, with 58.1% of Brazilian households experiencing varying degrees of food insecurity. Out of this total, 33 million households were grappling with severe food insecurity, according to National Survey on Food Insecurity 2023. In this context, the government's choice in 2020 was to concentrate social assistance investments on the Emergency Aid program, intended for individuals and families experiencing poverty and extreme poverty. However, as discussed in Chapter 10, this was determined by the National Congress. This measure not only would increase the government's visibility but also meet the expectations of public opinion, which was deeply concerned about the growing issues related to food insecurity faced by most of the population. Consequently, the federal funds allocated to social assistance services decreased even further, as observed. The government decided to prioritize the continuity of medium- and high-complexity socio-assistance services, particularly those that involve sheltering and are subject to legal oversight.

Therefore, consecutive changes have taken place within the social assistance policy, brought about by a confluence of factors that have profoundly influenced the policy's outcomes. Each of the four landmark events added a layer to the reduction in service offerings. These factors include the economic crisis, which prompted a reevaluation of discretionary expenditures, regulations imposing constraints on social spending (Constitutional Amendment No. 95), government decisions that reshaped the funding structure and policy priorities, and the context of the pandemic, which led to a shift towards allocating resources primarily to benefits rather than regular services. This process resulted in ongoing changes that altered the logic and institutional commitments that had been in effect up to that point. Consequently, the socio-assistance services were gradually and quietly dismantled, putting at risk the standards of socio-assistance protection that had been established over the past two decades.

Notes

1 The federal structure of Brazil grants states and municipalities autonomy to establish certain regulations. When Covid-19 transmission rates surged, state and municipal governments took the initiative to enact social distancing measures since the federal government failed to act.
2 This is a state-run public unit with a municipal or regional reach, serving as a focal point for delivering social services to families and individuals facing personal and social risks due to rights violations. It provides specialized interventions as part of the SUAS (Brasília, 2011).
3 This is the reference unit responsible for implementing the Special Social Protection of Medium Complexity. It is a publicly operated institution tasked with the important mission of achieving the goals outlined in the National Policy for the Homeless Population (Brasília, 2011).
4 CNAS Resolutions, No. 19 and No. 20, dated November 24, 2016.
5 Decree No. 9.759, of April 11, 2019.
6 CONGEMAS publicly denounced the measures adopted and warned that these changes could lead to the closure of CRAS facilities in small municipalities. Consequently, the provision of services and follow-up care would be reduced (see www.congemas.org.br/posicionamento-do-congemas---portaria-n%C2%BA-2362-noticias).

7 In 2017, for example, approximately 5% of the budgetary resources allocated to social assistance were executed as discretionary expenditures, which were used to fund programs, projects, and services. Most of the resources were allocated to the Continuous Cash Benefit Program (60%) and the Bolsa Família Program (35%) (IPEA, 2018).

References

ARAÚJO, C. E. L., E. S. M. CUNHA. (2019). "Análise de mudanças em políticas públicas: a perspectiva neoinstitucionalista." *Conhecer: Debate entre o público e o privado, 9*(22), 170–187.

BAUER, M. W., C. KNILL. (2014). "A conceptual framework for the comparative analysis of policy change: Measurement, explanation and strategies of policy dismantling." *Journal of Comparative Policy Analysis: Research and Practice, 16*(1), 28–44.

BRASIL. (2005). "Política Nacional de Assistência Social. Ministério do Desenvolvimento Social e Combate à Fome." *Ministério do Desenvolvimento Social e Combate à Fome.* Brasília: MDS. www.mds.gov.br/webarquivos/publicacao/assistencia_social/Normati vas/PNAS2004.pdf

BRASIL. (2006). "Norma Operacional Básica de Recursos Humanos do SUAS- NOB-RH/SUAS." *Ministério do Desenvolvimento Social e Combate à Fome.* Brasília: MDS. www.social.go.gov.br/files/arquivos-migrados/54ea65997b6c44c14aa59c27bc 4946a1.pdf

BRASIL. (2009). "Tipificação Nacional de Serviços Socioassistenciais." *Ministério do Desenvolvimento Social e Combate à Fome. 1 ed.* Brasília: MDS. www.mds.gov.br/ webarquivos/publicacao/assistencia_social/Normativas/tipificacao.pdf

BRASIL. (2011). "Orientações Técnicas: Centro de Referência Especializado para População em Situação de Rua–Centro Pop SUAS e População em Situação de Rua". Vol 3. *Ministério do Desenvolvimento Social e Combate à Fome.* Brasília.

CENSO SUAS. (2022). Secretaria Nacional de Assistência Social. *Vigilância Socioassistencial.* Accessed August 16, 2023. https://aplicacoes.mds.gov.br/snas/vig ilancia/index2.php

CHUERI, J. (2022). "An emerging populist welfare paradigm? How populist radical right-wing parties are reshaping the welfare state." *Scandinavian Political Studies*, *45*(4), 383–409.

IPEA – Instituto de Pesquisa Econômica Aplicada. (2018). Boletim de Acompanhamento de Políticas Sociais. No 25. Assistência Social. Brasília.

IPEA – Instituto de Pesquisa Econômica Aplicada. (2019). Boletim de Acompanhamento de Políticas Sociais. No 26. Assistência Social. Brasília.

IPEA – Instituto de Pesquisa Econômica Aplicada. (2020). Boletim de Acompanhamento de Políticas Sociais. No 27. Assistência Social. Brasília.

IPEA – Instituto de Pesquisa Econômica Aplicada. (2021). Boletim de Acompanhamento de Políticas Sociais. No 28. Assistência Social. Brasília.

IPEA – Instituto de Pesquisa Econômica Aplicada. (2022). Boletim de Acompanhamento de Políticas Sociais. No 29. Assistência Social. Brasília.

JORDAN, A., C. GREEN-PEDERSEN., J. TURNPENNY. (2012). "Policy dismantling: An introduction." In Bauer, M. W., Green-Pedersen, C., Héritier, A.,

& Jordan, A. (Eds.) *Dismantling public policy: Preferences, strategies, and effects.* Oxford University Press, Oxford, 230p 3–29.

MACHADO, J. A. (2023). "Federalismo e relações intergovernamentais nas políticas sociais – mais autonomia ou mais coordenação?" In: Sátyro, Natália and Cunha Eleonora, S. M. eds, *Descomplicando as políticas sociais no Brasil: A Constituição Federal de 1988 e a estrutura de proteção social brasileira* (*Vol.2*). Editora Fino Traço and Editora UFMG Belo Horizonte 178 pp; 39–58.

OKABAYASHI, N. Y. T., I. G. TASSARA, M. C. G. CASACA, et al. (2020). "Violência contra a mulher e feminicídio no Brasil – impacto do isolamento social pela COVID-19." *Brazilian Journal of Health Review*, *3*(3), 4511–4531.

OTJES, S. (2019). "What is left of the radical right." *Politics Low Countries*, *1*, 81.

PIERSON, P. (1994). *Dismantling the welfare state? Reagan, Thatcher, and the politics of retrenchment*. Cambridge University, Cambridge.

RATHGEB, P. (2020). "Makers against takers: the socio-economic ideology and policy of the Austrian Freedom Party." *West European Politics*, *44*(3), 635–660.

SÁTYRO, N. (2021). "The paradigmatic radical reform in Brazil's social policies: The impact of the Temer Administration." In: Natália Sátyro; Eloisa Del Pino; Carmen Midaglia (Org.)., *Latin American social policy developments in the twenty-first century*. 1ed. Springer International Publishing, Cham, pp. 317–340.

SÁTYRO, N., E. Cunha. (2014). "The path of Brazilian social assistance policy post-1988: the significance of institutions and ideas." *Brazilian Political Science Review*, *8*, 80–108.

SÁTYRO, N. G. D., E. S. M. CUNHA. (2018). "The transformative capacity of the Brazilian federal government in building a social welfare bureaucracy in the municipalities." *Revista de Administração Pública*, *52*, 363–385.

SOARES, M. M. (2023). "Por que o orçamento público é fundamental para as políticas sociais?" In: Sátyro, Natália and Cunha Eleonora, S. M. eds, *Descomplicando as políticas sociais no Brasil: O que, por que, como, de quem e para quem? (Vol.1).* Editora Fino Traço and Editora UFMG Belo Horizonte 205p; 97–118.

VIEIRA, P. R., L. P. GARCIA, E. L. N. MACIEL. (2020). "Isolamento Social e o Aumento da Violência Doméstica: o que isso nos revela?" *Revista Brasileira de Epidemiologia*, *23*, 1–5.

10

NON-CONTRIBUTIVE CASH TRANSFERS

Borderline social protection

Joana Mostafa[1]

10.1 Introduction

The aim of this chapter is to register and analyze the changes occurred in the two most important national social assistance cash transfers, *Bolsa Família* (family allowance program, PBF) and *Benefício de Prestação Continuada* (continuous cash transfer, BPC). Following the welfare state dismantling and public policy change literature, I am interested in observing the history of change within state regulations and outputs, but also to understand the *meaning* of these changes through actual practices and narratives around such non-contributory benefits, in the context of a radical neoliberal and conservative turn in Brazilian national politics. I start this tale in late 2015, when labor party president Dilma Rousseff impeachment was being rehearsed, up to the very tight election of Lula against Bolsonaro in late 2022. The last seven years were a political rollercoaster for Brazil, which imposed great uncertainty for PBF and BPC, albeit in very different ways.

The national social assistance system (SUAS) typifies benefits and services, offices, sub-systems, federative attributions and encompasses other definitions, all product of intense political debates and agreements, reached inter-federatively and in a quadripartite fashion, between local and national governments, social assistance workers, civil society service providers and social assistance clients. Within SUAS, two cash benefits stand out. *Bolsa Família* aims to alleviate poverty by benefiting *families*, mostly with children. The second social assistance benefit is the *Benefício de Prestação Continuada* to poor *individuals*, either old-age or with disability. As of August 2023, together these transfers covered 30% of Brazil's population, 54.8 million people are covered by PBF, and 5.3 million

DOI: 10.4324/9781003487777-12

by BPC. Although both benefits are embedded in definitions of poverty, the difference between them is huge.[2]

BPC was inherited from a limited benefit installed in 1974, as part of many new and underrated schemes created within the contributory pensions system by the authoritarian regime. The 1988 constitution has substantially expanded BPC by turning it into a constitutional right of all poor old-age individuals of 65 years of age or more (70 before the constitution, 68 just after, and 65 with the regulation social assistance in 1993) and established its benefit value in the constitution, of one minimum wage (half before) (Camarano and Fernandes, 2016, pp. 267–268). Specific legislation defines its poverty line as a proportion of the minimum wage, which makes it a relative poverty benefit, established at a quarter of the minimum wage per capita. BPC is also an individual benefit, not a familial one. That is, all old age and persons with disability living under the same roof can access their own benefit, as it follows the logic of work income substitution, like the benefits of the contributory schemes.

In many ways BPC is tangent to the public contributory scheme, given most of the latter render a basic protection. Unlike BPC, contributory protections are rendered during the whole life cycle and are extensible to dependents. But in terms of benefit value, 63% of the active contributory benefits pay no more than one minimum wage,[3] just like BPC, which is non-contributory. This is because the formal labor market in Brazil is still immensely unequal and renders extremely low incomes to the great majority.

Bolsa Família was established in 2003 as a unification and expansion of five different and scattered national cash transfer programs, all inaugurated in the 1990s across different line ministries (Soares and Sátyro, 2009). PBF is an income complementation benefit (not substitution), aimed to top up household incomes so that every family is at least above the per capita extreme poverty line (this feature is strengthened after 2012), varying its value over the line according to family composition, to account for families with more children, youth, and pregnant/breast-feeding women.[4] Unlike BPC, *Bolsa Família* is not a constitutional right, its parameters are discretionarily set by government, and its legislation explicitly considers fiscal availability. Its poverty line is set in nominal values which, in turn, determines its coverage goal. Although the program's eligibility line has revolved around the World Bank international poverty line, adjustment for inflation or any other national relative value, such as the minimum wage, is arbitrary. Furthermore, benefit values are also discretionary; the benefit is a familial one and it's conditioned to constant data updates, school attendance rates and a health check-up schedule, increasing the already enormous unpaid care burden of poor women. For feminist- and rights-based policy advocates, the program rationality and institutional design would most definitely signal a neoliberal and conservative stance from the very start. Is there a retrenchment story to tell? Yes, there is.

During this period, instead of a mere "reduction of policy commitment" (Bauer and Knill, 2014, p. 30), through the decrease of policy outputs, such as reduced benefit concessions, or a policy "drift" (Tomazini, 2023) towards "obfuscated dismantling" (Green-Pedersen, 2007, p. 11), my claim is that, in the case of *Bolsa Família*, it has been through a period of great instability and visibility, even though it has proved resilient with regard to poverty coverage. And this is because of its nuanced rights-based *dispositifs*, embedded in its publicized objective of ending hunger. The instability lived by PBF was a result of its well-known ambiguous institutional and political rationality, determined by its problematic role as the epiphenomena of competing imaginations of the nation.

Both entitlement cutbacks as well as institutional changes were attempted (Green-Pedersen, 2007) with the aim of dismantling PBF's original stance, to conform it to a marginal, deserving poor, conservative gender roles, meritocratic rationale. But the first gained the center stage, whilst institutional change was attempted only too late to be implemented. As we shall see, contingencies were as important for PBF dynamics as dismantling/expansion programmatic political rationales. In particular, the Covid-19 pandemic, congressional reactions to the executive branch's obsessive fiscalism, and the comeback of Lula after being imprisoned by the same neoliberal and conservative turn that impeached Rousseff, made quite a dramatic entry.

BPC, on the other hand, has had some thrills along the way, but given its pension-like institutionality, proposed changes were tied to the two processes of constitutional reform regarding the pensions system (failed attempt in 2017 and actual reform in 2019). These processes of change are much more predictable, regulated, and participatory than those affecting PBF. All in all, BPC came out of the pension reform unharmed, felt some fiscal steam from 2016 until the beginning of the pandemic, then experienced some upswings to come out of these years somewhat strengthened, both in terms of benefit entitlements as well as institutional density.

Besides this introduction, a second section will analyze the trajectory of *Bolsa Família* from 2005 to 2022. Then the third section will take BPC's trajectory into account. Lastly, I offer some concluding remarks.

10.2 Bolsa Família as an ambiguous showcase policy of the Brazilian left

The trajectory detailed here can be grouped into three main periods. Starting in 2015 until 2018, *Bolsa Família* goes through a *discrediting* campaign, voiced and practiced by a neoliberal, right wing, and auditing bodies' coalition, the same that impeached Roussef. This campaign dismissed and put into doubt the scientifically attested impacts and exemplary operation of the program.

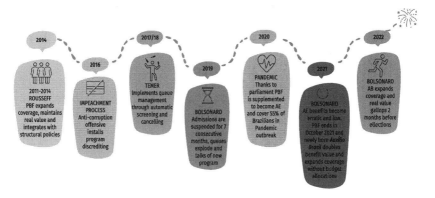

FIGURE 10.1 Ups and downs of Bolsa Família lifestile. By the author.

The second period was short but dramatic. During the year 2019 until the very beginning of the pandemic, open dismantling was practiced as new concessions were halted and talks of a new program design were leaked. Lastly, a third period was inaugurated by the pandemic, when *Bolsa Família* was revalued as part of the income crisis solution. By being conflated with another sociological category, the informal worker, PBF was expanded and used by the predatory electoral practices of the far right. The Bolsa Família instability can be seen in Figure 10.1.

10.2.1 Discredit

The year 2015 was marked by the gradual erosion of Rousseff's power and popular support, just after stepping into presidency for her second shift. The appointment of a neoliberal economist to lead the Ministry of Finance and his disagreement with Rousseff over the budget surplus goal were exploited by Congress, pressuring Rousseff to go against her minister's budget proposal, which lead to his resignation. Which policy was the epicenter of such political pressure? *Bolsa Família*.

Already during 2015 institutional pressure was felt by PBF national officers,[5] as they were being recurrently questioned by the economic and auditing sectors of government regarding rules and procedures that became central to the arguments of Congress. The proposed cut from Congress meant nothing less than cancelling out 35% of beneficiary families, based on an unpublished internal auditing report, according to which such beneficiaries *were not poor* and should not get the benefit.

The arguments to cut benefits had to do with the dispute over poverty definitions, inbuilt in program rules and procedures. *Bolsa Família* has four procedures to account for: (i) intertemporal poverty; (ii) the lack of updated government knowledge of formal employment status, as well as informal incomes, resulting in the use of self-declared incomes; (iii) the need to complement family incomes, even when someone is formally employed; and (iv) not giving incentives for informality, by, for instance ruling out the possibility of formal job workers to be PBF beneficiaries.

The procedures to account for these situations were deeply questioned during 2015 and 2016 by the now neoliberal economic sector and the internal auditing body, *Controladoria Geral da União* (CGU), forming an alliance group that actively scrutinized the program (CGU, 2017).[6] Coverage stagnated (see Graph 10.1). The impact of lifting such procedures was leaked to Dilma's opponents, pivotal for Congress attacks on her budget bill (Câmara dos Deputados, 2015) and, in fact, giving even more density to the narrative of labor party corruption, alleged PBF fraud, supposedly a labor vote buying machine. Despite the biased way in which CGU findings were being instrumentalized by the opposition, this was not refuted directly and *transparently* by the auditing authority, even though they published a confusing short note (CGU, 2015). The stage was set. The anti-corruption agenda could now try to affirm itself as independent, possibly scrounging more budgets and career guarantees (Arantes and Moreira, 2019).[7]

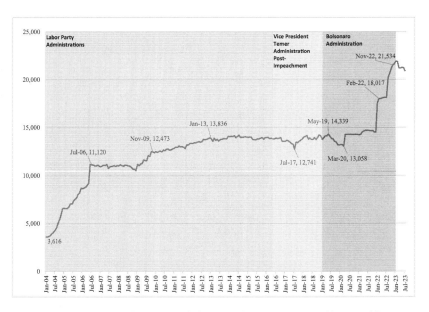

GRAPH 10.1 Number of PBF Beneficiary Families 2004–2023 (thousands).

Source: MDS, VisData, https://aplicacoes.cidadania.gov.br/vis/data3/data-explorer.php. From January 2004 to October 2021, Bolsa Família data, from November 2021 until February 2023, Auxílio Brasil data, then from March 2023 until July 2023 new Bolsa Família data.

According to informal conversations with PBF officers, until that moment the program had been *running ahead* of auditing sectors' interpretations and impositions. PBF high-level bureaucracy was always one step ahead. But now, program rules and the usual practices and proposed solutions did not suffice as arguments to deter more punitive and stringent recommendations. There was now little political power to back PBF officers' decisions in the space of policy discretion.

After Rousseff removal, PBF went through a scrutinizing phase coined by the new minister as a phase of fine-tooth combing (G1, 2016). This strategy was very successful to promote a higher turnover of families in and out of the program by more frequently suspending then cancelling families (Graph 10.2). This was achieved on the basis of data matching exercises.

Such database matchings had already been in place since 2005 and had been progressively refined, automatized, and integrated into *Cadastro Único* and social assistance routines (Bartholo, Mostafa and Osório, 2018, p. 24). These were done carefully to properly interact with localities and families, so that inconsistencies could be thoroughly solved and actual demands met. These centralized mechanisms were intensified in 2017 and PBF recipients would be now seen as always already a strategic subject that should be treated with distrust.

It was in this context of injury, public defamation of the Cadastro Único by the president that, instead of relying on the *Cadastro Único* data, that was

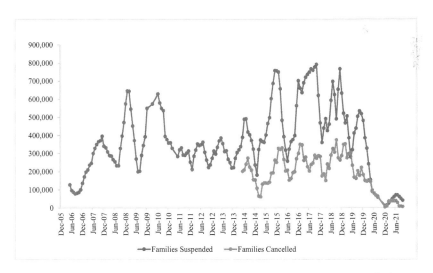

GRAPH 10.2 Number of PBF beneficiary families suspended and cancelled 2006–2021 (6 months moving average).

Source: MDS, VisData https://aplicacoes.cidadania.gov.br/vis/data3/data-explorer.php.

already being matched with other databases, which was then checked by the families and updated through self-declaration, PBF concession rules changed. Matchings with outdated formal employment status and incomes were done before every monthly concession decision (Silva et al., 2018, pp. 198–199). With this, the computation of the digital, administrative queue changed and was not traceable anymore, as it now went through a screening process beyond that of the eligibility criteria stated in *Cadastro Único*. A screening process that no one could reproduce, that was black-boxed. Conveniently, the queue was thinned and only government could calculate it.

In July 2017, Minister of Social Development Osmar Terra believed he could escape the queue pressure. He did not admit some 500 thousand families in line. But poverty rates were high, and media, scholar, and PBF advocates roared. He quickly changed his mind and started efficiently manipulating the queue to zero it for the next year and a half (Bartholo, 2022).

The registry's queue is a rights-based *dispositif* that has put expansionary pressure on *Bolsa Família*'s coverage since 2009. Through this *dispositif*, ending hunger translates to zeroing the queue. The greatest achievement of this first phase of dismantling was to annul, to render inconsequent, to outsmart the queue mechanism of PBF social control, possible through *Cadastro Único*. With these intensified screening practices, the right alliance was able to reinforce the image of an austere era for PBF, but balanced it with a legacy of generosity by having, seemingly, zero-queued PBF for the longest period in its history (MDS, 2018, pp. 3–4 and Graph 10.3).

This was done at the expense of great insecurity for PBF beneficiaries. Machado (2020) shows how, in this period of 2016 and 2017, beneficiaries were absolutely haunted by the fear of losing the benefit, given the experience of getting surprise household visits from social assistance workers that resulted in benefit reduction without notice or explanation. At the same time, beneficiaries experienced waning information on motives for benefit suspension and cancelling and felt the intensified fraud and corruption narratives circulating in local and national media (2020, p. 137).

10.2.2 Open dismantling

After Bolsonaro's election, the priority was set to take people out of the program, firstly by renewing the narrative of exit-doors, through work education for PBF youth (Pereira, 2019). Soon enough, attention was driven to passing the pension reform, and government concentrated efforts on retaining new PBF concessions for 7 months, whilst still cutting benefits through crosschecks. This resulted in a sustained fall in program coverage, which went against Bolsonaro's election program that promised a universal basic income (see Chapter 2). The program queue grew systematically from March 2019 to just before March 2020, when

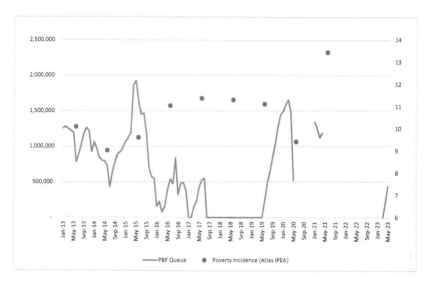

GRAPH 10.3 Number of families in the PBF queue and poverty incidence (Atlas-IPEA).

Note: This graph must be read with caution given the calculation of the queue changed drastically from 2017 onwards.

Source: MDS, VisData https://aplicacoes.cidadania.gov.br/vis/data3/data-explorer.php for queue data and IPEADATA Atlas do Desenvolvimento Humano based on IBGE/PNADC considering poverty line of R$140 of 2010 adjusted for inflation, same as PBF at the time.

the Covid-19 pandemic started in Brazil. During this pre-pandemic period, even though the ministry simply stopped publishing the data and responding to mandatory information access law (LAI) requests (Rossi, 2020), many high circulation articles came out to denounce the growing queue again.

Government frequently talked about changing PBF, until the very beginning of the Pandemic in Brazil (Resende, 2020). But the homicide attempts to PBF halted with the pandemic outbreak. Reluctantly, the executive branch mentioned an emergency benefit for the informal workers, with the same value of average PBF benefits, but were sluggish to act. Bolsonaro and his finance minister were finally run over by parliament, which surprisingly acted as a progressive player in relation to the exacerbated fiscalism, conservatism, anti-science and religious fundamentalism of the executive branch. Brazilian parliament passed a bill to establish the *Auxílio Emergencial* (emergency benefit, AE) three times the value wanted by the executive branch (Pozzebom, 2020). The benefit covered PBF beneficiaries, plus families already registered in *Cadastro Único* that earned up to ½ the minimum wage per capita or 3 minimum wages total, and additional informal workers and unemployed in general, also earning up to this limit, that registered through an application exclusively developed for them in record time.

10.2.3 Revaluation and electoral use

The AE had a great countercyclical, poverty, and inequality reduction impact for all (Menezes-Filho, Komatsu and Rosa, 2021; see Graph 10.3). It was also considered a great achievement, as it was implemented in no more than 20 days. Over half of the population got this benefit in the first months, including PBF beneficiaries. Nevertheless, the AE roll-out was erratic as pandemic events unfolded, which caused great uncertainty for beneficiaries. The generosity of benefits and coverage also became smaller as the phases rolled out and there was little possibility to demand inclusion after the first window to register was over, in the first three pandemic months of 2020. This meant a great deal of judicial trouble for PBF public officers to analyze and respond.

In the first 5 months, the AE benefit was set at a fixed amount of R$600 per adult, with a maximum of two benefits per family. Single-mother families with children were allowed to get double the benefit, plus one more adult, that is, a maximum of three benefit values. In the second round, the benefit only lasted 3 months, paid half the value of the first one, and did not let single-mother families accumulate more than two benefit values. After a period of 3 months with no AE from January to March 2021, just the usual PBF families getting the same old R$200 average per family, AE enters the last phase of 7 months with even smaller payments.[8]

Coverage of the AE was quite high at the beginning. It rendered 38.2 million benefits to so-called *informal workers* through the simplified and more individualized registration made via the CAIXA application and paid through a simplified digital bank account. Another 19.5 million benefits were paid to *Bolsa Família* participants, and new concessions were created to compensate for the enormous, accumulated queue. Finally, 10.5 million benefits were rendered to those already registered in *Cadastro Único* and found to be eligible. Therefore, there was an important use of *Cadastro Único* as a source of reliable administrative information for timely responses to crisis situations. But, also, given the circumstances, there was an important effort made to know and open state channels for a new public. These initially 38.2 million *informal workers* were relevant throughout the AE roll-out, representing over 50% of the benefit coverage through the whole period.

It is interesting to note a certain dissonance that the advent of the pandemic brought to the surface. On the one hand there were contributive, categorical protections for formal workers, and on the other, poverty, categorical BPC and familial PBF transfers. But because of the pandemic, a new sociological category took the stage to justify the growth of coverage and of benefit values of poverty transfers: the informal worker. On the basis of this category the *Auxílio Emergencial* was launched.

But PBF beneficiaries, the Poor, are also informal workers. And AE new recipients were now poor, without informal work incomes. Indeed, Bolsonaro's first proposal was to simply render the same PBF average benefit to people affected by the pandemic, because now they became poor, they became hungry. But because of parliament, the opposite occurred. PBF beneficiaries ended up getting the benefit considered to be *dignifying for those that were workers* but could not access the protections of formal employment. To get half a minimum wage per person, maximum two per family, adding up a minimum wage per family, is half of the amount rendered by the unemployment benefit. This was quite a significant step for Brazil. Even though temporary, it would have lasting effects for PBF. It was in this way that the PBF average benefit per family, the most undermining of its characteristics in terms of poverty and inequality impacts (Souza et al., 2018, pp. 169–170), suddenly increased (Graph 10.4).

Congress insisted on the distinction of *informal workers*. The AE legislation came out in a funny way, stating, naming, who were those workers to get AE (Cardoso, 2020). Congress also felt further pressure to enlarge the definition by recognizing all the working categories, naming the occupations under informality (Pozzebom, 2020). It soon became obvious that, as with PBF and *Cadastro Único* registered poor, there is no way of knowing in advance the working activities and incomes of the informal economy, and the only way

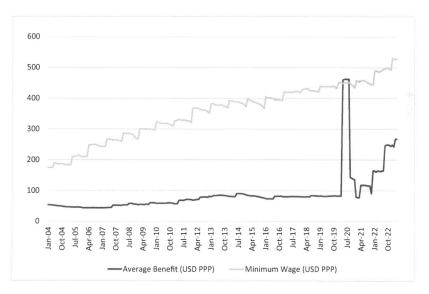

GRAPH 10.4   Average PBF benefit per family and the minimum wage 2004–2023 (USD PPP).

Source: own calculations based on Ministry of Social Development, https://aplicacoes.cidadania. gov.br/vis/data3/data-explorer.php for average benefits and IPEADATA for the current minimum wage and PPP deflator (family consumption), www.ipeadata.gov.br/Default.aspx.

to know them is through self-declaration. The bulk of the informal sector was invisible to the state, just as the poor once were before PBF.

Luckily for the new poor, state capacity was already in place for the old poor. The ministry of social development was able to lead the process, and because of its accumulated capacity, CAIXA was able to develop the application for registration and new simplified payment accounts because of its *Cadastro Único* and PBF capabilities, and finally, Dataprev was able to screen all payments and generate the payrolls because of its previous works in integrating data with *Cadastro Único* (Cardoso, 2020).

Bolsonaro and his supporters, including a highly contested IPEA study (Figueiredo, 2022), were time and time again anxious to dispel the image of promoting "laziness" by giving out non-contributive cash transfers. The same argument that justified *Auxílio Emergencial*, to rescue the informal worker,[9] was now extended to justify the decision to launch his own *Auxílio Brasil* in August 2021, the successor of *Bolsa Família*. Now PBF original clients, the Poor, were conflated with the *informal worker*.

Auxílio Brasil represented a significant change to the original ideas and practices surrounding *Bolsa Família*. It was not based, as was PBF, in practices that ensured structural rights such as social assistance services, public education and public health to beneficiaries. Rather, it enforced ideas and practices of merit and excellence achievement, religious and private care and education. It also abandons the idea of program simplicity coupled with integration with other sector policies, to inaugurate a myriad of new incentives and programs, that had no social assistance competencies involved, would hardly be implemented and could only be accessed by a few. It also deepened the possibility of family debt by giving more prerogatives to the financial partners that pay the benefits (Sordi, 2021; Bronzo and Oliveira, 2021; Brandão and Campello, 2021; Tomazini, 2023). Finally, *Auxílio Brasil* did not involve social assistance policies in any way, and even threatened to exclude social workers from the process of *Cadastro Único* active search and registering, by promising to automatize the whole process. From the past experience of automatized AE applications for the informal workers, which was quite messy, this would jeopardize the excellent targeting of the former PBF (World Bank, 2021).

Notwithstanding its neoliberal and conservatory design (see Chapter 12), the most immediate change was the payment of a minimum benefit per family of R\$400 starting in January 2022, which meant doubling the average PBF historical benefit. Coverage also expanded dramatically. Up to the election's second ballot, government Bolsonaro irresponsibly promoted a rush to the social assistance offices, whilst at the same time cutting social assistance services' national budgets. Stress over registering activities, benefit high values, and disregard of family composition deteriorated the quality of the *Cadastro Único* database, once a familial registry, to became more and more an individual adult's database (Bartholo et al., 2022). In June 2022 Bolsonaro was quick to announce another extraordinary elevation of the minimum benefit to R$600 per family, which would only come into effect in August 2022, after a budget maneuver to open fiscal space in that year, having no budget provision whatsoever after the elections.

Media reported endless lines in social assistance as well as banking correspondents. Pregnant women fainted while waiting in the sun, and one woman died in line (Brasil de Fato, 2022). Most people registered were admitted into the program, growing from 14.5 million families to 21.6 million in one year! No wonder Bolsonaro was convinced there was no more hunger in Brazil. Many people were. No wonder Bolsonaro was convinced he would win the election. Many people were. The election jingle came out only a few days after the R$600 payments started.[10]

Albeit disturbing, we should not be paralyzed by such a turn of events. Nor should we discredit them as sheer state irresponsibility, minimalism, or inability to plan and execute public policies. In hindsight, Bolsonaro's government was astute in mastering hunger-talk and steering it in its favor, not only electorally, but in the direction of claiming to tackle hunger whilst changing the nitty-gritty of the policy, in what regards its most structural elements. If *Auxílio Brasil* were to find its way through public policy instruments, it would have turned *Bolsa Família* into a deserving poor, financialized, and religious subjectivation machine, just like the neoliberal and neoconservatory turn did to social assistance transfers in the United States (Cooper, 2017). And this is not minimal.

> Hunger in Brazil, hunger for real…no…it doesn't exist as is said… whoever is, by any chance, in the hunger map can register for *Auxílio Brasil* (Bolsonaro's successor of PBF), there are no waiting lines (which means the registry queue)…This discourse saying that there are 30 million experiencing hunger is a lie…it is people that sell lies after an easy vote. If you go to any bakery, there is nobody there asking for you to buy bread for him, this does not exist. By saying this I'm losing votes, but the truth has to be said.
>
> *(Bolsonaro, 2022, our comments in brackets)*

Indeed, maybe hunger-talk has lost its effectiveness. It has been appropriated by the extreme right. More than just guaranteeing that coverage, poverty, and benefit parameters be set in more stable regulations, it might be the time to talk about and tackle the determinants of poverty more openly and decisively. Or else find another "boundary object"[11] that could create new alliances, no matter how unstable, strong enough to put the far right to sleep again.

As it turns out, *Bolsa Família* is not "transgovernamental," as some former officials of the program claimed before Bolsonaro (Paiva, Pereira and Cotta,

2018). After Bolsonaro, I would claim that nothing is "transgovernamental" and surely for the best. Unfortunately, *Bolsa Família* went into a coma for more than a year with the birth of *Auxílio Brasil*. If it was not for the half million votes that gave Lula a very tight victory in 2022, *Bolsa Família* would probably be dead by now. Fortunately, the period did create the political and social support for *Bolsa Família* to gain and maintain more coverage and greater benefit values, opening the possibility to give effective support to income volatility, thus having a greater impact on poverty and inequality, the historical claims of its advocates. Notwithstanding, I suggest this expansion will be historically claimed to be the deed of the far right.

10.3   BPC: Administrative dismantling halted by Pandemic regulatory overshooting

BPC also had its share of neoliberal steam after Dilma's impeachment, and more harshly in the first year of Bolsonaro's government, even though it has a much more stable institutionality as it is a constitutional guarantee. In both discussions of pension reform, BPC was fundamentally contested. There was pressure for its benefits to be set in values under the minimum wage guarantee and for its age of eligibility to be elevated from the constitutional 65 years of age, up to 70 years of age.

No constitutional change for BPC was passed in the 2019 reform. But administrative obstacles to concede the benefit as well as powerful mechanisms to revise benefit eligibility criteria have been taking form since 2016 and were fully implemented in 2019. Indeed, if it were not for the justification rendered by the pandemic, BPC might have slowly crumbled under such extensive "administrative reform" (Paiva and Pinheiro, 2021). These changes could have been characterized as a more invisible and stealth dismantling.

But the pandemic brought to the political arena, especially within Congress, the possibility to finally complexify eligibility criteria beyond that of monetary poverty. This was already being pushed by larger society via jurisprudence generalized by the Supreme Court since 2013. In 2015, the Brazilian inclusion law inserted a paragraph in the social assistance organic laws (LOA) stating that it would regulate how to encompass other criteria, such as different levels of dependency, of disability, and expenses with medication, care, and assistive technologies.

This is an expansionary pressure that comes through the judiciary branch and is only possible because of BPC's inscription in the constitution. Nevertheless, these changes were being postponed by the other branches, but came into play during the pandemic. This is now having expansionary effects on BPC's coverage (Graph 10.5 below), even though waiting lists are still long (Paiva and Pinheiro, 2021).

10.3.1 Invisible dismantling

BPC had always had a revision rule by which eligibility criteria should be checked biannually, but systematic and thorough revisions had never been implemented until 2019. This is because the operating agent of BPC, INSS, had very little information on the beneficiary family, in terms of composition as well as incomes, to undertake a benefit revision based on verifications of the per capita income. The pension institutionality, unlike the social assistance one, does not follow-up on its clients. Since BPC's population is closer to the competencies and attributions of social assistance, and since *Cadastro Único* became the informational backbone of the social assistance sector, especially post-2011, efforts were made in the direction of including BPC beneficiaries in its database. But none of the prior inclusion efforts were successful enough, and by the end of 2016 there were only 43% of BPC beneficiaries registered (Paiva and Pinheiro, 2021, p. 19).

Just like PBF, before Roussef's impeachment, pressure from auditing bodies and the economic sectors of government for BPC benefit revision was enormous. To fiscal adjustment delight, 2015 saw one of the longest strikes of INSS workers and medical experts that undertake the disability evaluation, which greatly impacted BPC concessions that year. With the impeachment, an inter-ministry group was forged to explore methodologies and adequacy of verification routines. Datachecks through datamatching with other government databases were recommended (MDS, 2017), but were only to be effective in 2019, when BPC beneficiaries were widely included in *Cadastro Único*'s database.

The process was upstarted by 2016 BPC regulation that stated *Cadastro Único* as a mandatory step for BPC beneficiaries, as both a concession and revision mechanism. Nevertheless, given the difficulty to access and bring to the guichet old-age and persons with disabilities, there was a transition period for implementation from 2016 until 2018. Local social assistance administrations were given time-limits to include BPC beneficiaries in *Cadastro Único*. From August 2018 onwards, BPC regulation made it indisputable that *Cadastro Único* registration and CPF number (Cadastro de Pessoa Física – CPF is an individual registration, it means one of the many Brazilian document numbers given out by the fiscal authority) were now mandatory, and that revisions of eligibility criteria, maintenance, and concession of benefits would only happen for registries that had their data updated at least once in the previous two years.

In 2018 and 2019 there was a great effort from local social assistance offices to locate and include BPC beneficiaries in *Cadastro Único*. Bonus payments were set to give incentives to INSS personnel to prioritize BPC benefit revisions. Concessions had also been consistently falling since 2016, mainly because of new registration burdens: *Cadastro Único*, CPF as well as the implementation of the digital *guichet* for benefit requirement (INSS digital). These became

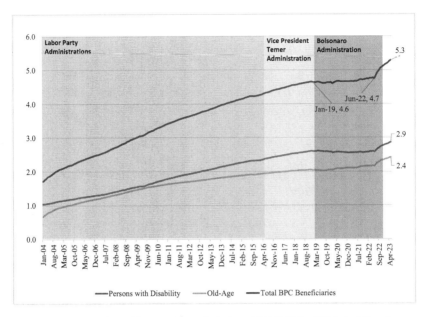

GRAPH 10.5   Number of Persons Beneficiaries of BPC 2004–2023 (millions).

Source: SAGICAD https://aplicacoes.cidadania.gov.br/vis/data3/data-explorer.php.

important access barriers for extremely poor persons with disability or old age (Paiva and Pinheiro, 2021). As a result, the number of persons receiving the benefit stagnated for the first time in BPC's history (Graph 10.5). By the pandemic outbreak 10% of beneficiaries were under time-limits to present themselves to *Cadastro Único* or else lose BPC.

10.3.2   Revaluation and regulatory overshooting

Together with *Auxílio Emergencial*, initiatives to expand BPC were taken during the pandemic. The most effective one was the anticipation of R$600, the same value as the *Auxílio Emergencial*, for those who were in line waiting to have their applications seen by INSS personnel. Thus, they would automatically get equivalent to half their rightful BPC, until their solicitation could be analyzed and approved, or disapproved, by INSS. If approved, the applicant would get a lump sum of their accumulated right less the value paid in advance. Advances were rendered from April to November 2020, and were paramount to counterbalance the slump in normal concessions (Graph 10.6 below) due to social isolation measures (MDS, 2021). Other measures during the pandemic were to suspend the deadline for *Cadastro Único* registry of BPC beneficiaries (MDS, 2021), cease benefit revisions, and reverse benefit suspensions (IPEA, 2022a).

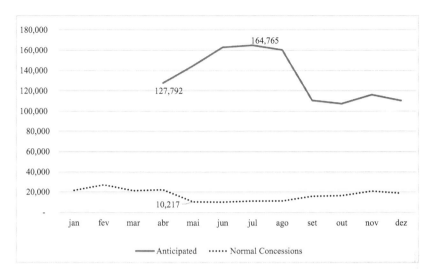

GRAPH 10.6   Number of BPC benefits anticipated and normally conceded through traditional approval process (2020).

Source: Ministry of Social Development (MDS, 2021).

BPC has a historical issue with delays in the INSS solicitation process, which results in long waiting times that can take up to 2 years. This worsened in the late 2000s, as INSS faced bigger demands with less and less qualified officers, particularly for disability evaluation and classification, a methodology that has changed recently. Therefore, the anticipation had an important coverage expansion effect, even though at lower values and not once and for all, given the normal rite would still be processed. But it created additional pressure for INSS to solve the queue problem, as medical exams and in-person services were suspended because of the pandemic. In 2021 and 2022 BPC was prioritized in a taskforce to diminish the queue (IPEA, 2022b, p. 24). As a result, concessions grew exponentially (Graph 10.7) and coverage levels went back to the trend of pre-Bolsonaro years (Graph 10.5).

Two major advancements for BPC happened during the pandemic in terms of policy density that in turn resulted in an expansion of people's entitlements. Firstly, after some shoving and pushing from Congress to the executive, BPC regulation finally stated the conditions in which the benefit could be rendered for families that earn more than its poverty line of a quarter minimum wage per capita. As previously stated, this change was required by the Supreme Court, but never regulated. But things changed. Even though the regulation is still waning of operationality for some of its parameters, and it was not in effect for most of the Pandemic, it became an expansionary frontier.

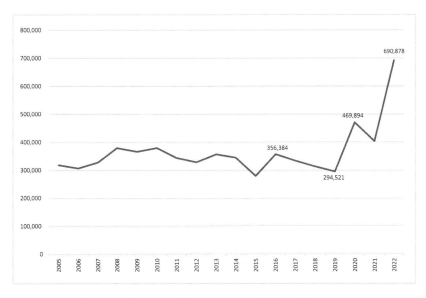

GRAPH 10.7   Number of yearly BPC concessions 2005–2022.

Source: Boletim de Estatísticas da Previdência Social Junho 2023. Available at www.gov.br/prev
idencia/pt-br/assuntos/previdencia-social/arquivos/beps062023_final-1.pdf.

The new regulation states that the BPC poverty line can go up to half a
minimum wage per capita (something of a limiting character), as long as the
quarter wage per capita is met after incomes have been discounted for average
costs of medicines and daycare. These have been effective since the second
semester of 2020. Still to be regulated are the levels of dependency and disability
that would entail further discounts in income, enabling to comply with the
quarter minimum wage threshold (IPEA, 2022b).

Another welcomed change was the setting up of a new benefit for BPC persons
with disability that are in the labor market, and moderate to severe disability.
Also a benefit that was pushed by the 2015 Brazilian inclusion law, it was only
effective by the end of 2022. It renders a benefit of half a minimum wage for ex-
BPC beneficiaries to cope with the additional costs of being occupied in formal
employment. Although celebrated, it is still to be evaluated if the very limited
income threshold and other access barriers will be significantly surmounted by
this inclusion benefit.

10.4   Concluding remarks: The limits of hunger-talk

The social assistance sector in Brazil, particularly *Bolsa Família* and BPC, has
conveniently navigated an ambivalent combination of what Nancy Fraser (2013)

has coined "rights-talk" and "needs-talk." Needs-talk is supposedly settled over an undisputed, basic, absolute requirement. But it is far from that. Needs-talk is a very lively public field of political *struggle*.

The first is the struggle to establish or deny the political status of a given need, the struggle to validate the need as a matter of legitimate political concern, or to enclave it as a nonpolitical matter. The second is the struggle over the interpretation of the need, the struggle for the power to define it and, thus, to determine what would satisfy it. The third moment is the struggle over the satisfaction of the need, the struggle to secure or withhold provision (Nancy Fraser, 2013, p. 57).

Different from a situation where needs have been politically recognized as rights, and the struggle would be around reduced or expanded entitlements, I argue that, for PBF, there is a lot of activity on the first and second struggles: (i) competition with other realms of protection that are supposedly non-political such as the family and the work/economy and; (ii) dispute over the meanings, the readings, the interpretations of the need that PBF is supposed to confront, its causes, and thus, what would satisfy it. Because BPC is nested in rights-talk, it has mostly battled with entitlement cutbacks, although the two pension reform discussions did try to shake the nest.

I follow Fraser's lead to unravel the "concrete vocabularies available for making claims" (2013, p. 57) in social assistance needs-talk by questioning, denaturalizing discourses of need. This is crucial to enable us to *politically* establish, not the true, but better, more just meanings of need than others.

In Brazil, I suggest that the major needs-talk that was adopted and promoted by the labor party was hunger-talk. This fits Veronica Gago's concept of "*neoliberalismo desde abajo*" (2015), that is, when situated, historic and territorially specific experiences, practices and narratives enter into productive assemblages with global capitalism axioms. Hunger-talk was able to promote and establish a very basic benefit for PBF, so that individuals would still be able to take risks. That is, to go look for employment, to be able to choose responsibly, to have at least some agency as opposed to be enslaved by necessity. Almost every liberal and neoliberal is in favor of that (Brown, 2019; Giddens, 1999). However, as I have argued, things are not that simple.

To end hunger. This is the needs-talk axiom[12] conveyed by left wing politicians, experts, and supporters. Indeed, by recognizing hunger as a national issue, we departed from an imagination of the nation (Kehl, 2018) as that which already fit the mold of normative liberal work and family patriarchal relations, that historically left behind those racialized and feminized subjects as an inbuilt mechanism of liberal biopolitics of the welfare-state (Foucault, 2010; Fraser, 2013). Nevertheless, hunger-talk is also problematic as it legitimizes state support by invoking our colonial habits of Christian morality, guilt, and charity, which erases differences and reiterates inequalities (Ahmed, 2004). This was the *concrete vocabulary* available to constitute the *need* to include vast populations: the religious language of help. And it was and is a powerful one.

Indeed, studies on the public perceptions of PBF show that "help" is ok, if it is minimal to avoid laziness and corruption, supposedly inherent human tendencies, usually articulated by the popular proverb of not giving the fish but teaching how to fish. It seems *Bolsa Família* was able to balance itself on the thin blade of this false opposition, proposing *to give just one fish, whilst teaching how to fish some more*. This is why, as per perceptions, it is of utmost importance that the benefit be conditioned to assure that the *immoral* (black) mothers work to at least guarantee that the *innocent* children go to school properly and are healthy.[13] Only then, as an unpaid caring mother, will she be a deserving poor. Not once were "rights" mentioned by the public as the justification for PBF benefits, only "help" (Natalino, 2020).

BPC changes have gone through a completely different track, from that taken by PBF. Because of its long history and categorical eligibility, it has greater support from interest groups that vocalize through the judiciary branch as well as Congress. Its expansion is also of great importance for Brazilian social protection, and tends to grow, as labor market deregulation becomes the norm. BPC already represents 20% of the old-age and disability protections in Brazil, the other being 80% contributory.

Notwithstanding, the period inaugurated by Rousseff's fall was one of perils for BPC too. Neoliberals were not successful in taming BPC's expansionary pressures constitutionally, but administrative and operative obstacles were put in place that were silently undermining its coverage, especially in 2018 and 2019. This was halted by the usefulness of such a transfer during the pandemic. By the end of 2022, long-lasting demands were incorporated to BPC. Still, revisions and administrative access barriers are currently up and running, and can be arbitrarily used by the ruling pen.

Both BPC and PBF have gone through roughly three moments since 2005. A time of benefit revision, screening, and discrediting through fine-combing and auditing discourses and practices. A second moment in 2019 and just before the pandemic when both benefits suffered severe entitlement cuts and concession stagnation, being PBF's a more open and visible dismantling and BPC's a more stealth and invisible one. Finally, this trajectory was halted by the Pandemic, which inaugurated the possibility of both benefits to be part of the solution for the income crisis. This imposed path-dependence, making it hard for the newly elected government to withdraw the expansion of entitlements.

The period analyzed took to the limit the "boundary object" (Star and Griesemer, 1989) hunger-talk. During this period, neoliberals and conservatives domesticated this object. From now on, the neoliberal government that took over after Rousseff can claim that it reached the longest period with no PBF queues, and even the most far-right extremist can claim he has ended hunger.

As Wendy Brown has shown for the case of the United States, even rights-talk can be appropriated by conservatives to crystalize moral rules through politics, beyond Hayek's dream of the omnipotent rule of law (2019, pp. 119–141).

If the *needs* of the poor, mainly black women and black men, are not (re) interpreted in such a way that they can raise sufficient support to maintain what hunger-talk has made possible up to now, they run the risk of being enclaved by the neoliberal and conservative claim that such *needs* are the responsibility of the individual and their families. Rest assured. Unlike the electoral *Auxílio Brasil*, these claims will be budgeted.

Notes

1 I am a feminist researcher and economist with a master's degree in economics and a PhD candidate in sociology, all by Unicamp (State University of Campinas, Brazil). As is required by the feminist positional and contingent epistemological stance (Donna Haraway, 2009), to take responsibility for the knowledge that might spur from my theoretical as well as experiential perspective, it is important to clearly identify my personal and institutional implication with the object. I worked for *Bolsa Família* for around 7 years, within its registry department, the *Cadastro Único*. I have occupied diverse positions within this bureaucracy, to finally be the director of Cadastro Único between 2014 and 2016, when I stepped down with Rousseff's removal. Since then, I have followed up on these policies through informal conversations with public officers, media, and specialized research, as a researcher myself of a federal government think tank, IPEA (Institute for Applied Economic Research).

2 It is relevant to state that both protections reach mostly racialized and feminized subjects. As of December 2022, 66% of BPC beneficiaries were black (https://apl icacoes.cidadania.gov.br/vis/data3/data-explorer.php). Old-age in poverty protected by BPC are 60% women. Persons with disability protected by BPC are mostly men and boys (54%), but 65% of their caretakers are women (Anuário Estatístico da Previdência Social position December 2021, table B4). As of May 2023, 75% of PBF beneficiaries, including family members, were black, 65% women and girls, and 48% black women and girls (Ministry of Social Development at https://cecad.cidadania. gov.br/tab_cad.php).

3 Boletim Estatístico da Previdência Social June/2023, Table 16, accounts for private sector pension and retirement schemes (RGPS), and includes all benefits emitted except BPC (www.gov.br/previdencia/pt-br/assuntos/previdencia-social/arquivos/ beps062023_final.xls).

4 PBF design and impacts is well documented. Refer to Neves (2022), Soares (2011), and Campello and Neri (2013).

5 Observed through context and meetings with PBF public officers, economic and internal audit officers, as well as other social protection officers during 2015 and 2016, whilst I occupied the chair of director of *Cadastro Único*.

6 "The committee was established by the inter-ministry regulation n°102, of April 7 2016, and is composed by representatives of the ministry of planning, budget and management (MP), Finance (MF), of the General Secretary of the Presidency, and of the ministry of Transparency and General Controlling of the Union (CGU); that can count on the participation of members of invited institutions, public or private" (CGU, 2017, p.11).

7 Significantly, the claim for Dilma's impeachment was decisively supported by the interpretation of *Tribunal de Contas da União* (TCU), the external auditing body under the legislative branch, of Dilma's budget management.

8 For a complete account of the *Auxilio Emergencial* benefits, coverage, institutional arrangements, and database treatments see World Bank (2021).
9 Bolsonaro on the radio program *Voz do Brasil*, https://agenciabrasil.ebc.com.br/polit ica/noticia/2022-02/presidente-bolsonaro-fala-sobre-auxilio-brasil#.
10 https://youtu.be/4whv45RRFUc
11 "Boundary objects are objects which are both plastic enough to adapt to local needs and constraints of the several parties employing them, yet robust enough to maintain a common identity across sites. They are weakly structured in common use, and become strongly structured in individual-site use. They may be abstract or concrete. They have different meanings in different social worlds but their structure is common enough to more than one world to make them recognizable, a means of translation. The creation and management of boundary objects is key in developing and maintaining coherence across intersecting social worlds" (Star and Griesemer, 1989).
12 As defined and used by Rodrigo Guerón (2017).
13 For the role of mothers as state disciplinary powers' representatives in the household and the immorality stigma casted over black women in Brazil see Jurandir Freire Costa (1989) and Silvana Santiago (2006).

References

Ahmed, S. (2004) *The cultural politics of emotion*. London: Routledge.

Arantes, R. and Moreira T. (2019) 'Democracia, instituições de controle e justiça sob a ótica do pluralismo estatal', *Opinião Pública,* 25 (1), 97–135. Available at: www.sci elo.br/j/op/a/y9dCbmHBdT8QJTDZh563fFx/?lang=pt

Bartholo, L. (2022) 'Direitos Improvisados: de como o Congresso e o governo perderam a oportunidade de corrigir as vulnerabilidades do *Bolsa Família* ao criar o *Auxílio Brasil*', *Folha de São Paulo*, 1 March. Available at: www.quatrocincoum.com.br/br/ artigos/desigualdades/direitos-improvisados

Bartholo, L. et al. (2022) 'Bolsonaro deturpa base de dados do *Bolsa Família* e *Auxílio Brasil*', *Folha de São Paulo*, 9 June. Available at: bit.ly/497XE9J

Bartholo, L., Mostafa J. and Osório R. (2018) 'Integration of administrative records for social protection policies: Contributions from the Brazilian experience', *IPC Working Paper*, 169. Available at: https://ipcig.org/sites/default/files/pub/en/WP169_ Integration_of_administrative_records_for_social_protection_policies.pdf

Bauer, M. W. and Knill C. (2014) 'A conceptual framework for the comparative analysis of policy change: Measurement, explanation and strategies of policy dismantling', *Journal of Comparative Policy Analysis: Research and Practice*, 16 (1), 28–44. Available at: https://doi.org/10.1080/13876988.2014.885186

Bolsonaro, Jair. (2022) 'Não existe 'fome pra valer' no Brasil, afirma Bolsonaro em podcast', Jornal o Globo, 28 August. Available at: www.youtube.com/watch?v= OWFfoLja51Q

Brandão, S. and Campello T. (2021) 'O Auxílio Brasil não é um novo *Bolsa Família*. É um pastel de vento...', *Carta Capital*, 10 October. Available at: www.cartacapital. com.br/politica/o-auxilio-brasil-nao-e-um-novo-bolsa-familia-e-um-pastel-de-vento/

Brasil de Fato. (2022) 'Fila do CRAS: Mulher morre enquanto aguardava atendimento no Paranoá', *Brasil de Fato*, 17 August. Available at: www.brasildefatodf.com.br/2022/ 08/17/filas-do-cras-mulher-morre-enquanto-aguardava-atendimento-no-paranoa

Bronzo, C. and Oliveira B. R. (2021) 'Auxílio Brasil não é o Bolsa Família melhorado: Um salto no abismo e o desmonte da proteção social no Brasil', *O Estado de São Paulo*, 3 November. Available at: bit.ly/3UAAeoS

Brown, W. (2019) *Nas ruínas do neoliberalismo: Ascensão da política antidemocrática no Ocidente*. São Paulo: Editora Filosófica Politéia.

Câmara dos Deputados. (2015) 'Relator do orçamento confirma corte de R$ 10 bilhões no *Bolsa Família*', *Agência Câmara de Notícias*, 11 December. Available at: www.camara.leg.br/noticias/477989-relator-do-orcamento-confirma-corte-de-r-10-bilhoes-no-bolsa-familia/

Camarano, A. A. and Fernandes D. (2016) 'A previdência social brasileira', in A. Alcântara, A. A. Camarano and K. C. Giacomin (eds.) *Política nacional do idoso: velhas e novas questões*. Rio de Janeiro: IPEA, pp. 265–294.

Campello, T. and Neri M. C. (2013) *Bolsa Família Program: A decade of social inclusion in Brazil*. Brasília: IPEA.

Cardoso, B. B. (2020) 'A implementação do Auxílio Emergencial como medida excepcional de proteção social', *Revista de Administração Pública da FGV*, 54 (4), 1052–1063. Available at: https://doi.org/10.1590/0034-761220200267

CGU. (2015) 'Nota de esclarecimento: CGU esclarece informações sobre o *Bolsa Família*', *Governo Federal*, 13 November. Available at: www.gov.br/cgu/pt-br/assuntos/noticias/2015/11/cgu-esclarece-informacoes-sobre-o-bolsa-familia

CGU. (2017) *Relatório de Avaliação da Execução de Programa de Governo n° 75:Bolsa Família.* Brasília: CGU.

Cooper, M. (2017) *Family values: Between neoliberalism and the new social conservatism*. New York: Zone Books.

Costa, J. F. (1989) *Ordem médica e norma familiar*. Rio de Janeiro: Graal, 3. edition.

Figueiredo, E. A. (2022) 'Expansão do Programa *Auxílio Brasil*: Uma reflexão preliminar', *IPEA Nota da Presidência,* 12 August. Available at: https://portalantigo.ipea.gov.br/portal/images/stories/PDFs/220810_219307_np_gabin_n12_web_novo.pdf

Foucault, M. (2010) 'Aula 17 de março de 1976', in M. Foucault (ed.) *Em defesa da sociedade*. São Paulo: Martins Fontes, pp. 211–222.

Fraser, N. (2013) 'Struggle over needs: Outline of a socialist-feminist critical theory of late-capitalist political culture', in *Fortunes of Feminism: From state-managed capitalism to neoliberal crisis and beyond*. London: Editora Verso, pp. 53–82.

G1. (2016) 'Ministro do Desenvolvimento Social prevê pente-fino no Bolsa Família', *G1*, 17 May. Available at: https://g1.globo.com/rs/rio-grande-do-sul/noticia/2016/05/ministro-do-desenvolvimento-social-preve-pente-fino-no-bolsa-familia.html

Gago, V. (2015) *La razón neoliberal: Economías barrocas y pragmática popular*. Madrid: Traficantes de Sueños.

Giddens, A. (1999) 'Risk and responsibility', *Modern Law Review*, 62 (1), 1–10.

Green-Pedersen, C. (2007) 'The dependent variable problem within the study of welfare state retrenchment: Defining the problem and looking for solutions', *Journal of Comparative Policy Analysis: Research and Practice*, 6 (1), 3–14. Available at: 10.1080/1387698042000222763

Guerón, R. (2017) 'A axiomática capitalista segundo Deleuze e Guattari. De Marx a Nietzsche, de Nietzsche a Marx', *Revista de Filosofia Aurora*, 29 (46), 257–282. Available at: https://drive.google.com/file/d/1k-xBTNZBwCbiOkt3zNzvaLNrdf1wnPmf/view?usp=sharing

Haraway, D. J. (2009) 'Saberes localizados: a questão da ciência para o feminismo e o privilégio da perspectiva parcial', *Cadernos Pagu*, 5, 7–41.

IPEA. (2022a) 'Previdência social', *Boletim de Políticas Sociais*, 29, Available at: https://portalantigo.ipea.gov.br/portal/images/stories/PDFs/politicas_sociais/220726_bol etim_bps_29_previdencia.pdf

IPEA. (2022b) 'Assistência social', *Boletim de Políticas Sociais*, 29, Available at: https://portalantigo.ipea.gov.br/portal/images/stories/PDFs/politicas_sociais/220719_21815 4_bps_29_assistencia_social.pdf

Kehl, M. R. (2018) *Bovarismo brasileiro*. São Paulo: Boitempo.

Machado, N. F. (2020) A construção de uma vida digna e a batalha por legitimidade moral: Fronteiras Simbólicas no Bolsa Família [phd. thesis]. João Pessoa (PB): Universidade Federal da Paraíba.

MDS. (2017) *Relatório Final do Grupo de Trabalho Interinstitucional (GTI) para Propor o Aperfeiçoamento das Rotinas de Verificação Cadastral e da Revisão do Benefício de Prestação Continuada BPC*. Brasília: MDS. Available at: https://aplicacoes.mds. gov.br/sagirmps/ferramentas/docs/Relatorio_grupo_trabalho_beneficio_prestacao_ continuada.pdf

MDS. (2018) *Caderno de Resultados 2016–2018*. Brasília: MDS. Available at: www. mds.gov.br/webarquivos/publicacao/caderno_resultados_2016_2018.pdf

MDS. (2021) 'Benefício de Prestação Continuada: Medidas adotadas no contexto da Pandemia para a proteção de idosos e pessoas com deficiência', *Série De Olho na Cidadania*, 5. Available at: https://aplicacoes.mds.gov.br/sagi/pesquisas/documentos/ relatorio/relatorio_216.pdf

Menezes-Filho, N., Komatsu B. K. and Rosa J. P. (2021) 'Reducing poverty and inequality during the Coronavirus outbreak: The emergency aid transfers in Brazil', *Insper Policy Paper*, 54. Available at: www.insper.edu.br/wp-content/uploads/2021/ 02/Policy_Paper_54.pdf

Natalino, M. (2020) 'Pobreza, Redistribuição e o *Bolsa Família* na Percepção dos Brasileiros', *Boletim de Análise de Político-Institucional IPEA*, 23. Available at: https://repositorio.ipea.gov.br/bitstream/11058/10164/8/bapi_23_pobreza.pdf

Neves, J. A. et al. (2022) 'The Brazilian cash transfer program (*Bolsa Família*): A tool for reducing inequalities and achieving social rights in Brazil', *Global Public Health*, 17 (1), 26–42. Available at: https://doi.org/10.1080/17441692.2020.1850828

Paiva, A. and Pinheiro, M. (2021) 'BPC em disputa: Como alterações operacionais e regulatórias recentes se refletem no acesso ao benefício', *Texto para Discussão IPEA*, 2703. Available at: https://repositorio.ipea.gov.br/handle/11058/10890

Paiva, L. H., Pereira E. S. and Cotta T. (2018) 'Uma agenda para o Programa Bolsa Família', in T. F. Silva (org.) *Bolsa Família 15 Anos (2003–2018)*. Brasília: Enap, pp. 445–468.

Pereira, F. (2019) 'Governo vai continuar pente fino e quer *Bolsa Família* com porta de saída', *UOL*, 3 January. Available at: https://noticias.uol.com.br/politica/ultimas-notic ias/2019/01/03/governo-vai-continuar-pente-fino-e-quer-bolsa-familia-com-porta-de-saida.htm

Pozzebom, E. R. (2020) 'Aprovado pelo congresso, Auxílio Emergencial deu dignidade a cidadãos durante a pandemia', *Senado Notícias*, 30 December. Available at: bit.ly/3wf1IXd

Resende, T. (2020) 'Bolsonaro trava *Bolsa Família* em cidades pobres e fila chega a 1 milhão', *Folha de São Paulo*, 10 February. Available at: www1.folha.uol.com.br/mercado/2020/02/bolsonaro-trava-bolsa-familia-em-cidades-pobres-e-fila-chega-a-1-milhao.shtml

Rossi, M. (2020) 'Governo Bolsonaro não explica tamanho real da fila do Bolsa Família', *El País*, 31 January. Available at: https://brasil.elpais.com/brasil/2020-01-31/governo-bolsonaro-nao-explica-tamanho-real-da-fila-do-bolsa-familia.html

Santiago, S. (2006) *Tal Conceição, Conceição de tal: Classe, gênero e cotidiano de mulheres pobres no Rio de Janeiro das primeiras décadas republicanas.* Campinas: [n.n.].

Silva, T. F. et al. (2018) 'Programa Bolsa Família: Uma estratégia de focalização bem-sucedida' in T. F. Silva (org.) *Bolsa Família 15 Anos (2003–2018)*. Brasília: Enap, pp. 191–224.

Soares, F. V. (2011) 'Brazil's Bolsa Família: A review', *Economic and Political Weekly*, 46 (21), 55–60.

Soares, S. and Sátyro N. (2009) 'O Programa Bolsa Família: Desenho institucional, impactos e possibilidades futuras', *Texto para Discussão IPEA*, 1424. Available at: www.ipea.gov.br/portal/images/stories/PDFs/TDs/td_1424.pdf

Sordi, D. (2021) 'Auxílio Brasil é um retrocesso que corrói rede de proteção social', *Folha de São Paulo*, 23 October. Available at: www1.folha.uol.com.br/ilustrissima/2021/10/auxilio-brasil-e-um-retrocesso-que-corroi-rede-de-protecao-social.shtml

Souza, P. H. G. et al. (2018) 'Os efeitos do *Bolsa Família* sobre a pobreza e a desigualdade: Um balanço dos primeiros 15 anos' in T. F. Silva (org.) *Bolsa Família 15 Anos (2003–2018)*. Brasília: Enap, pp. 155–190.

Star, S. and Griesemer, J. (1989) 'Institutional ecology, 'translations' and boundary objects: Amateurs and professionals in Berkeley's Museum of Vertebrate Zoology 1907–39', *Social Studies of Science*, 19 (3), 387–420. Available at:10.1177/030631289019003001

Tomazini, C. (2023) 'Adeus Bolsa Família? Ambiguidades e (Des)continuidades de uma Política à Deriva' in A. Gomide (org.) *Desmonte e Reconfiguração de Políticas Públicas (2016–2022)*. Brasília: IPEA, pp. 75–98.

World Bank. (2021) *Auxílio Emergencial: Lessons from the Brazilian experience responding to COVID-19*. Washington DC: World Bank.

PART III

Social investment policies

11

CREDIT-CLAIMING AND NONDECISION-MAKING AS AN IDEOLOGICAL AGENDA

Did Bolsonaro succeed in changing education policies in Brazil?[1]

Sandra Gomes and Catarina Ianni Segatto

11.1 Introduction

The rise of far-right populists in power has reintroduced the debate on policy dismantling on a new basis, imposing challenges to the existing literature. Seeking to debate this question, recent studies have sought to grasp the main characteristics and patterns of public policies, including policymaking, their changes, and effects on citizens' rights within radical right-wing populist contexts (Gomide, Silva and Leopoldi, 2023).

In October 2018, Jair Bolsonaro, a retired Armed Forces captain, was elected President of Brazil, winning by a significant majority of 55.1% of the votes against the PT (the workers party) candidate. Bolsonaro's campaign was built upon a platform that merged an ultra-conservative ideology concerning moral values with a neoliberal agenda in economics, in a "Chicago's boys" style from the 1970s, in which privatization and cutting public spending (or the size of the State) were foremost aims. Bolsonaro had a populist right-wing discourse, similar to what has been seen in other countries, producing a political division between proud and deserving Brazilian nationals against the "corrupt elite," "traditional politicians," and minority groups (Segatto, Alves and Pineda, 2023).

In this chapter, we aim to contribute to the debate about what types of changes far right populists do once they get to power by looking at the case of education policies during Bolsonaro's government (2019–2022). As Milhorance (2022) highlights, Bolsonaro's strategies did not pursue blame-avoidance in all its attempts at policy dismantling. On the contrary, he was elected with a promise of radical political change, and education had a significant role in it (Abrucio, 2021). For far right populist parties, social policies, particularly education,

DOI: 10.4324/9781003487777-14

are the targets for changes as they are key for national identity formation and territorial integration. Through social policies, governments build solidarity and determine who is included as "citizens" and "the people," i.e., who belongs and who has rights (Banting and Myles, 2013; Lall, 2008).

Education for far-right parties is the locus in which left-wing or progressive ideas can be identified as enemies, and, in the case of Bolsonaro idealogues, understood as a cultural war against Marxism, Paulo Freire's pedagogy, and gender ideology (Alves, Segatto and Pineda, 2023). Many of these conservative ideologues will be nominated to office positions in the Ministry of Education during Bolsonaro's government. As the first Ministry of Education stated in the swearing-in ceremony in January 2019: "Jair Bolsonaro has paid attention to the voice of fathers and mothers repressed by the Marxist rhetoric that has taken over national education" and states the objectives of ending "cultural Marxism" by combating "(…) the globalist ideology [that has] began to destroy one by one the cultural values that rule the country, family, church, state, homeland and schools" (Tajra and Andrade, 2019). The composition of the Ministry of Education will also count on military personnel that influenced policy proposals and shared a nationalist and conservative view of social order, praising and even proposing a historical review of the military authoritarian regime that took place in Brazil from 1964 to 1985 (Brito et al., 2022). In this sense, the promise of radical political change was part of a credit-claiming strategy to respond and mobilize supporters.

At the same time, during the pandemic, Bolsonaro adopted the opposite position: a blame-avoidance strategy attempting to transfer the blame to state governors and mayors concerning the negative outcomes of both the increase in the number of COVID-19 deaths and infections and the economic downturn. Bolsonaro publicly denied international guidelines and scientific evidence and opposed measures taken by state governments concerning physical distancing and the closure of schools, churches, businesses, and other activities. There were no attempts to promote a coordinated national health response to the crisis. In a similar fashion, the federal government also did not coordinate subnational governments' responses in education during the pandemic and weakened the federal role in setting national guidelines and assisting financially subnational governments in all areas of education (Béland et al., 2021; Segatto et al., 2022).

Given the radical transformations that the extreme conservative Bolsonaro´s electoral manifesto promised for the whole polity structure, we are interested in analyzing what was achieved and not achieved in education. Analyzing the characteristics and patterns of policy changes is important to unpack the dependent variable and allow further studies on the factors that explain these changes, which is supported by the scholarship (Green-Pedersen, 2004). The analysis looks at changes in education policies at the national or federal level during Bolsonaro government (2019–2022) through a historical and qualitative study based on data obtained from documents, legislation, governmental reports, and academic literature.

The next section discusses the analytical tools and concepts of policy and institutional changes that we find useful to understand our empirical case and the limitations we find in the current literature on policy dismantling. Subsequently, we describe the historical path inaugurated by the democratic 1988 constitution concerning social rights and policy-building to argue that the overall attempt of Bolsonaro's government in education was to break with this social and political consensus inaugurated since the redemocratization of the country. Some of this consensus was already weakened in the previous Temer´s government (2016–2028) which came to power after the impeachment of President Dilma Rousseff (2011–2016), from the traditional left-wing party in Brazil, the Workers Party. The context of political, economic, and social crises – intensified by the 2016 impeachment process – gave the initial conditions for a policy agenda change, especially concerning cuts of public spending on education and an option for solemnly market-based supply for higher education. We then analyze policy initiatives adopted by Bolsonaro that can be considered a novelty in terms of change, organized into three topics: 1) institutional weakening of national coordination of education; 2) credit-claiming dismantling as an ideological war; and 3) new-path breaking policies. Although the promise to break with the status quo was intense, and the government did succeed in eliminating some policies and cutting public spending, the rate of success in effectively approving proposals was very low. As an "outsider," Bolsonaro´s Cabinet was formed by Ministries isolated from traditional policy communities and with a limited political coalition to support his proposals to change education in parliament.

11.2 Policy change under far right governments

In Brazil, there has been a growing body of literature that attempts to understand whether policy changes in far right populist governments could be understood as a process of policy dismantling (Gomide, Silva and Leopoldi, 2023). Mello (2023, p. 416) characterized policy dismantling as "(…) processes marked by [deliberate] intention to disrupt or to change the direction of the ways policies are formulated and implemented." The scholarship highlights that understanding policy dismantling processes, including who gets less, when, and how (Jordan et al., 2012), is key to unpacking the dependent variable (i.e., defining the object of the change). This can involve dramatic changes or numerous minor cutbacks in program entitlements and eligibility, benefit levels, and other changes in policy instruments. Although these changes may seem minor, they can alter the level of generosity and universalism of welfare policies.

The most engaging attempt to define policy dismantling was done by Bauer and colleagues. Bauer and Kill (2012; 2014) argue that policy dismantling can be related to the elimination or abolishment of policies and their instruments and loosening regulation; in their words, "we can now define policy dismantling as a policy change that reduces the number of policy items as well as the number of policy instruments applied in a particular area and/or lowers their intensity" (Bauer and Knill, 2014, p. 34). Policy changes can involve the density and intensity of policy instruments. Policy density refers to "[...] the extent to which a certain policy area is addressed by governmental activities," being related to the penetration and the internal differentiation of policies, and it can be assessed by the number of policies and the number of policy instruments that suffered changes. Policy intensity describes "the relative strictness and generosity of policies" that can be divided in substantial intensity (instrument settings of regulatory stringency or service generosity) and formal intensity (including instrument scope and enforcement, administrative, and procedural capacities) (Bauer and Knill, 2014).

Bauer and Knill (2014) suggest capturing the phenomenon of policy dismantling in this particular way as they argue that the conventional ways of measuring outcomes – such as budget or spending or results – do not necessarily mean that a policy has been dismantled. In attempting to classify different forms of dismantling, they include a taxonomy that combines active or no active dismantling with high or low visibility. Green-Pedersen (2004) argues that we should consider policy retrenchment "as cutbacks in people's entitlements and retrenchment as institutional change."

However, as the opening chapter of this book puts it, these analytical models are not able to fully capture policy change in populist right-wing contexts as the "ultra-right does not fit into a taxonomy that only considers mainstream parties; they have created a different modus operandi," which includes different approaches to credit-claiming and blame-avoidance strategies concerning policy dismantling or retrenchment. Other authors have argued that democratic backsliding is also a new factor to consider when analyzing populist or extreme right-wing leaders as their core objective is to reform or to destroy core elements of the policy system or regime (Gomide, Silva and Leopoldi, 2023; Milhorance, 2022). These understandings, nonetheless, are still an open question in academic studies.

As some authors have already highlighted (Milhorance, 2022), Bolsonaro's strategies, in a similar fashion as other far right populist leaders, did not pursue blame-avoidance to policy dismantling. On the contrary, he was elected with a promise of radical political change, and education had a significant role in it (Abrucio, 2021). Cuts in public education spending, especially in higher education for example, achieved an unprecedented level. Could this mean a deliberate policy-dismantling strategy? The literature on the development of welfare state regimes cautions that spending is an insufficient factor to understand both welfare state expansion and retrenchment (Esping-Andersen, 1995; Pierson, 2001). The argument is that understanding welfare state regimes involves analyzing policy features related to decommodification and egalitarianism (Esping-Andersen, 1995) or access, generosity and quality, and equity, besides spending (Arza et al., 2022). In the case of Bolsonaro's education policies, however, there were no changes in terms of social rights' entitlements, but the government did succeed in changing some institutional patterns that would compromise those rights. Contrary to some authors analytical framework (Green-Pedersen, 2004; Bauer and Knill, 2014), in Bolsonaro's case, changes in budget allocations were a strategy to dismantle specific areas of education as will be detailed further on.

Other scholars present different categories to comprehend these dismantling processes. Campbell (2023) proposes an interpretation of President Trump that we find useful to discuss Bolsonaro's case. For the author, some of the changes made by Trump cannot be considered incremental as there were radical institutional ruptures with the traditions of formal rules and informal norms in comparison to previous governments. In fact, Campbell's description of Trump's decisions shows a lot of similarity with Bolsonaro, including questioning elections results, an attack on professional administrative personnel and ignoring their advice, a narrative on the need to fight a cultural war against a "deep state," the nomination of incompetent people in offices, among other aspects. The main difference is that Bolsonaro did not control a political party as Trump did (and apparently still does). In this sense, Bolsonaro narratives seem much closer to Trump's than other illiberal leaders such as Orban in Hungary or Erdogan in Turkey (Times Higher Education, 2016). In fact, the latter two governments have done a comprehensive dismantling of the educational system. In the case of Hungary, effectively replacing the education system by nationalizing schools, transferring local-run schools to the central government, and the various actions taken in higher education that produced a substantial reduction in higher education access in Hungary (Freedom House, 2014). Nothing on this level of rupture or transformation was achieved either by Bolsonaro's or Trump's governments in education.

When one observes the actions (and inactions) regarding education in Bolsonaro's government, there were deliberately narratives used to disrupt a path-dependency route that existed since redemocratization in Brazil at the end of the 1980s and to promote a conservative turn in different public policies, including education.

11.3 Changes from what? The path inaugurated by the 1988 democratic Constitution

The 1988 Brazilian Constitution is understood as a moment of policy change paradigm in social rights. Written during the process of transition from the authoritarian military regime to democracy, the new Constitution was a critical juncture that inaugurated a new path concerning universal social rights and citizenship and the role of the State as one of the main providers of public services. For the first time in Brazil, education becomes a right to all citizens with a view to break with the historical pattern of social exclusion and unequal access to education in the country. The Constitution also established the need for a complex intergovernmental collaboration between the three levels of governments in order to achieve the universalization of education. Social, regional, racial, and urban vs. rural inequalities in education were immense at the time with no universal access even considering only the first four years of primary education and, consequently, a high level of illiteracy even compared to other Latin American neighboring countries.

In the aftermath of the 1988 Constitution, one of the crucial aspects to expand access to basic education was related to the autonomous character of the Brazilian federation. The new Constitution maintained and reinforced the decentralized path of Brazil's basic education, featured by a "dual" model in which states and municipalities were responsible for service provision with limited national coordination among the three levels of governments (Cury, 2008). In the case of higher education, the path was different as the federal government historically occupied a central role in managing and financing higher education institutions.

Given the overall evaluation this decentralized provision of education would not render universal or equal access – given the levels of inequalities regarding fiscal and state capacities among more than five thousand municipalities and the 27 States and the Federal District in the country[2] -- initiatives to produce equalization by national coordination in education started to take place from the mid-1990s. A landmark for this is the approval of a constitutional amendment in 1996, during Cardoso's presidency (1995–2001), which established a national fund determining the redistribution of education revenues based now on a per pupil rule, compulsory priority spending in primary education, and in teacher's wages. The fiscal incentives contained in this institutional design made subnational governments increase student enrollments and at the same time produced constraints of losing revenues if enrollments did not expand. Extra federal revenue to subnational governments that did not achieve a certain level of minimal spending level inaugurated the role of redistribution and equalization from the federal government. This policy is considered to be the main explanatory factor for the universalization of elementary education for the first time in the country around the year 2000. This model of national coordination will be adopted by all subsequent federal governments and expanded to other levels of education and other areas, such as free school meals to all public schools in the country, national curriculum guidelines, and other initiatives financed by the federal government to support state and municipal schools. Bolsonaro's government will be the first government to break with this path of national coordination and equalization in education.

Within this context, other changes were important to strengthen national coordination, particularly the approval of national guidelines to guarantee similar standards in education results across the country. Among them, there were the national curriculum guidelines, approved in 1997 and 1998; a national norm defining service provision and responsibilities for all education systems in the country, approved in 1996; or a mandatory national 10-year plan for education with targets to be achieved by all levels of governments.

Throughout the 2000s, new initiatives with the aim of expanding education access and equality were further adopted with intense mobilization of members of education policy communities – trade unions, student and education institutions, specialists, including university researchers, and social movements, among many other organized civil society actors – and representatives in Congress. During the PT governments, a new fund (Fundeb) was approved in 2006 expanding revenue redistribution to all basic education (including childcare and secondary education, besides elementary education). New guidelines were approved, such as the ones related to teachers' training, professional development, and a minimum national wage policy for teachers in all public schools in the country (Diretrizes para formação inicial de continuada de professores approved in 2005 and Piso Salarial approved in 2008). Compulsory education was elevated to 4 to 17 year olds (Constitutional Amendment n. 59 approved in 2009). Aligned with the strategy of including historically excluded social groups to education, in 2003 teaching African history and Afro-Brazilian culture was established as part of school curriculum, influencing subsequent legislation on the topic, such as indigenous history or Law number 12,711/2012 for Affirmative Action in higher education that established quotas for the black population, low-income youth and students from public schools to access federal-run universities. A national education plan for 2014–2024 established many targets to be achieved nationally in terms of universal access and learning achievements. Given the central role of the State in the public provision of education within this context, the Education Plan determined the goal of spending 10% of its GDP in public education. There was also the adoption of policies and institutional changes to promote identity recognition and to address inequalities in access to and quality of education, with a particular focus on minority groups, such as the black population, the Indigenous peoples, or Quilombola (descendants of Afro-Brazilian slaves) communities.

In sum, social inclusion and equality regarding education were progressively and incrementally adopted in the policy-making process throughout different governments in Brazil (Gomes, Silva and Costa, 2019; Arretche, 2018). While during the 1990s, changes were more focused on expanding access to all, guided by the idea of universalization, during the 2000s, specific guidelines and project grants were developed to promote equality (i.e., to address inequalities in access to and quality of education, with a particular focus on marginalized groups, such as illiterate youth and adults, rural residents, Indigenous peoples, ethnic groups, and Quilombola communities or LGBTQIA+ communities that will become one of the targets of Bolsonaro's cultural war (Alves, Segatto and Pineda, 2023). As a result of these changes, intergovernmental relations remained primarily vertical centered with federal-local revenue redistribution, guideline setting, and project grants being key to encourage subnational governments to implement targeted policies, establish minimum national standards, and redistribute revenue aiming to reduce fiscal inequalities among regions (Arretche, 2012).

There are many social and political implications of these transformations in education. The first one is the size of the Brazilian population that directly or indirectly benefits from public education. By the end of the 2010s, Brazilian education had been rapidly expanded, in all levels of education, including higher education, and transformed the profile of future workers, citizens, and also voters. With more than 80% of students in basic education attending public schools, the stakes of being against spending or improving public education for politicians are extremely high if they are to face voters' rewards. Another consequence is the change in education payoffs in terms of future income. Given that access to basic, even primary education, had historically been the most accurate predictor of future wages for decades in Brazil – thus, vulnerability to poverty – the universalization of basic education has transferred the political dispute of education as a redistributive policy (Ansell, 2009; Busemeyer, 2017) to higher education. As we will see, this level of education was the main target of Bolsonaro's cultural war to demoralize public Universities.

The next three sections detail the types of changes in education adopted in Bolsonaro's government and their rate of success and failure.

11.4 Traditional right-wing politics: cutting public spending and fostering private education

From a neoliberal economic point of view, Bolsonaro's government saw education spending in Brazil as inefficient, especially higher education, and officials from the Ministry of Education proclaimed time and again that the private sector would be treated as a partner and not a rival, referring to previous left-wing administrations. In this sense, the actions of Bolsonaro government are closely related to what right-wing governments tend to pursue once in power with diminished public spending and fostering private options for higher education and limiting redistributive access to Universities (Ansell, 2009; Busemeyer, 2017). Berg, Jungblut and Jupskås (2023) propose that parties with an authoritarian root will use fiscal constraints to control education institutions.

As Couto and Reche (2023) estimate, the cuts in the four-year budget plan show the deliberate intention to underfinance education. Comparing the proposal of Bolsonaro (2020–2023) with previous governments (2016–2020), there is approximately a 65% cut in technical or vocational education funds and a 37% reduction for higher education. In terms of comparison, basic education (including transfers to support subnational governments) had a smaller 1.6% decrease between these two 4-year budgets plans. If, on the one hand, constitutional mandatory devices and also Congress resistance to cut funds for basic education protected further cuts in Bolsonaro's budget proposal for this level of education, the higher education and vocational training schools were the object of significant downsize, even though they also counted on some mandatory protected spending (such as personnel wages). There were also significant cuts and low levels of spending capacity in science & technology (Luz, 2022) affecting again federal research units within public universities. By the end of the government, in 2022, the continuous cuts forced federal institutions to stop the payment of utility bills and also scholarships to students as there was no fund provision. Defunding public higher education was part of a cultural war agenda raged against federal universities.

From the first announcement of cuts, the government faced demonstrations in the streets from highly organized and traditional education associations, such as unions and students' organizations, showing resistance and resilience. In May 2019, it was reported in all national media. Funds were sometimes released by the government and at other times "frozen," but the overall result was a significant amount of losses.[3]

Another initiative, which, in reality began in the previous government, but was expanded in Bolsonaro's government included the flexibilization of regulations for distance-learning in higher education, responding to the interests of private institutions to expand provision at a lower cost. Bolsonaro's government also adopted other measures to support private enrollments in education institutions such as allowing students from private schools to apply for a federal-funded scholarship to attend private higher education (previously, only students that had studied in public schools were entitled) in 2021. This was again a demand from the private sector given that the number of applicants had been decreasing since the COVID-19 and the economic crisis. There was also pandemic relief for students' debts on federal loans (although initiated more than 22 months after the beginning of the pandemic but with effects on the electoral year of 2022). These initiatives did not suffer any resistance from Congress and were indeed approved as the majority of its members were from traditional right-wing parties (Limongi et al., 2022) and open to private interests. On this topic, the government had no unsurpassable veto points; on the contrary, in these conventional or traditional politics Bolsonaro succeeded.

Aligned with traditional right-wing choices, Bolsonaro's government produced limited access or expansion of higher education, but the narratives and actions went to the extreme of maintaining Universities for an elite. For the first time, since the return to democracy in Brazil, a Minister of Education publicly stated his intention of limiting higher education access: "the idea of a university for all does not exist (…). Universities must be reserved for an intellectual elite, which is not the same as the economic elite" said the first Minister of Education in January 2019. He also declared his inspiration for the German model of universities, known for being one of the most elitist in Europe (Busemeyer, 2015), and its vocational schools.

The government succeeded partially on this front. Access to undergraduate courses reduced a little between 2021 and 2022 among 18-24 year olds. However, the main policy change was to stop plans of federal universities expansion. This retrenchment was the result of a combination of policy choices: eliminating projects to finance the expansion of enrollments in federal universities and federal technical/vocational institutions, not increasing subsidies to students in private institutions, and the deregulation of distant learning which became the majority of new enrolments in higher education for the first time in 2020. Distant learning in Brazil is a quite controversial topic as some argue that quality control has been inadequate since the deregulation of norms and standards approved by Temer's government in 2017/2018. For the first time since the return to democracy at the end of the 1980s, new enrollments in undergraduate courses in federal institutions decreased (Gomes, 2022).

On the other hand, Bolsonaro's government lost in the case of the approval of a new mechanism of revenue redistribution (known as Fundeb) in 2020 in which Congress raised the compulsory financing of basic education from federal funds. This new legislation maintained the mechanisms of revenue redistribution with a more equitable formula, adding subnational governments' fiscal capacity and students' vulnerability as criteria. Civil society organizations and policy communities linked to education in Brazil were key in convincing members of the National Congress and the public opinion about the importance of this mechanism for increasing coverage and decreasing inequalities. Bolsonaro's government was against raising federal revenues for the new fund as his Minister of Education stated, but Congress approved the measure despite the government position.

Table 11.1 sums up the policies described above, showing that the main policy choice of Bolsonaro's government was to stop the expansion of federal institutions and to stimulate private provision.

In sum, concerning funding and spending, there was no increase of public spending (nor taxation) for higher education. Defunding public higher education can be seen as a form of dismantling in Bolsonaro's government as it was a

TABLE 11.1 Initiatives related to cutting public spending and support for private provision in Bolsonaro's government (2019–2022)

Successful policy measures	Cutting public spending (defunding)	Support for the Expansion of Private Provision
Basic Education	- 1.6% reduction in the four-year budget plan. - low capacity of spending: 43.4% of the budget spent for basic education	- none[a]
Higher Education	- 65% cut in budget provisions for technical/vocational education funds and a 37% reduction for universities - low capacity of spending: 38.6% of the budget spent for vocational schools and 48.4% for universities	- Support for the expansion of private distant learning enrollments[b] - Negotiation of students' loans/debts in private higher education[c] - Allows students from private schools to apply to federal scholarship funds (Prouni)[c] - no policies for expansion of enrollments in federal higher education from 2019

Source: own compilation. Budget and spending estimates for 2019 and 2021 by Couto and Rech (2023).

Notes

[a] a voucher program for private childcare was approved in 2021 but never implemented. It was part of a social assistance program focused on families and children in social vulnerability, known as Auxílio Brasil.

[b] Executive administrative ordinance with no need for Congress referral.

[c] Bill approved by Congress.

deliberate strategy to take federal institutions to the brink of administrative collapse and eventually forcing a radical reform. These federal institutions in Brazil are free of fees and also contain affirmative action for the social inclusion of traditionally excluded social groups, which hampered more democratic access to them. On the other hand, basic education was not the object of the same level of cuts as higher education. This is explained by a set of factors, such as including decentralized provision by subnational governments, minimal constitutional spending mandate for basic education, and a wide public opinion support for public education as the vast majority of the electorate depends on public school provision in Brazil (over 80% of students). Targeting federal public institutions of higher education was the main locus of promoting a cultural war as we will explore further on.

11.5 Institutional weakening of national coordination as a blame-avoidance strategy

Bolsonaro's platform was based on the slogan "More Brazil, Less Brasilia," Brasília being the city and political capital of the country. The phrase sought to decrease the federal government's role in national coordination and leaving states and municipalities to adopt their own policies, changing the intergovernmental pattern towards a dualistic model. This was grounded in the assumption that subnational governments were more efficient in making decisions about resource allocation at the subnational level. At the same time, subnational governments had limited space for dialogue and negotiation of national decisions. In some policy fields, such as environment, subnational governments were excluded from the national council of the Amazon region (Abrucio et al., 2020).

Bolsonaro's government also established a pattern of intergovernmental confrontation against perceived opponents, including states and municipalities. According to Abrucio et al. (2020), the adversaries included the institutions and their leaders, as the Bolsonarist approach to presidentialism rejected institutional negotiations and the checks and balances of the Brazilian State, including federalism.

A series of decisions (nondecisions in reality) deeply affected inter-governmental relations in Brazil and produced negative consequences for public schools and students. The absence of national coordination left states and municipalities to take actions on their own. This was not restricted to education, as it was observed in all policy areas that involved intergovernmental relations in what Mello (2023, p. 419) interprets as a dismantling by default.

Table 11.2 summarizes these initiatives to weaken institutional rules and informal norms for intergovernmental collaboration and a preference not to use authority devices that were available both to the President and its Ministry of Education to produce national coordination in education.

In the first days of the administration, Bolsonaro's government made organizational changes, eliminating the Secretariat of Articulation of the Education Systems (SASE in Portuguese) within the Ministry of Education, which was responsible for strengthening intergovernmental coordination mechanisms. Moreover, there was a weakening of the federal government's role in setting national guidelines and inducing the implementation of specific strategies by subnational governments with the reduction or discontinuation of several project grants. In the case of the national program for expanding school hours at secondary schools, a key strategy to support technically and financially the implementation of secondary education reform approved in 2017, the program was not discontinued, but the total planned budget was not transferred to states (Todos Pela Educação, 2020), and, between 2017 and 2021, only 7% of schools were funded by this program (Carvalho, 2023).

TABLE 11.2 List of initiatives to weaken the institutional role of federal education coordination in Bolsonaro's government

Institutional Weakening of the Federal government (blame-avoidance)	Successful Institutional Change
Basic Education and Higher Education	Abstained from national coordination with subnational education systems:
	1. office for national coordination (SASE) closed
	2. no national guidelines or support to schools and education systems during the pandemic
	3. opposed raising equalizing funds subnational schools (FUNDEB)
	4. no support for secondary education reform
	5. abandoned the redistributive role of transfers to diminish education inequalities in public schools

Source: Own compilation.

During the acute period of the pandemic, the lack of national coordination that had prevailed in the responses to the healthcare crisis (Abrucio et al., 2020; Jaccoud et al., 2021) also featured education policies, but it followed blame-avoidance strategies by passing the buck for governors (Béland et al., 2021). There was an absence of national guidelines for the subnational government's responses related to social distancing measures and their effects. Given the high level of social inequalities in Brazil, the long suspension of classes during the pandemic disproportionately affected learning losses of the most vulnerable students. The federal government did not issue guidelines to support subnational governments in the case of school closures, the distribution of school meals, and the adoption of online teaching strategies. Also, it did not allocate funding for subnational governments to facilitate distance learning or enhance access to and quality of education.

This lack of national coordination guidelines forced municipal and state governments to make local decisions, resulting in fragmented and uncoordinated responses. Only a few months after the pandemic had started, the federal government issued a resolution providing guidelines for states and municipalities to distribute food products (funded by the federal government) directly to students' homes or guardians to collect them at schools. However, states and municipalities rejected this resolution due to logistic issues and advocated for more coordination with other policies, as food products could be distributed with other social benefits. The federal government did not change the resolution, resulting in great heterogeneity in subnational governments' responses (Segatto et al., 2022).

These changes made by Bolsonaro's government were not related to policy but to institutional change in the sense proposed by Campbell (2023) concerning the abandonment of the national role of the Ministry of Education as a coordinator of subnational government policies. In a similar manner as observed by Wong (2020) for Trump's case, Bolsonaro's government also deliberately diminished the traditional role of the federal government to use federal transfers to induce equality among public schools with the use of redistributive policy tools.

In sum, the lack of national coordination left subnational governments on their own to act in education policies which has had negative impacts on the implementation of policies and increased even more the historical inequalities among Brazilian students with effects that will remain for years or generations. This blame-avoidance strategy, by transferring responsibilities to decentralized subnational schools' systems, combined with an absence of dialogue and negotiation of national decisions with subnational governments, broke with a system in place since the mid-1990s which was adopted by different governments in Brazil.

11.6   Policy dismantling through ideological war as a credit-claiming retrenchment

Similar to other far right parties around the world (Berg, Jungblut, and Jupskås, 2023), Bolsonaro mobilized his supporters, which includes neo-Pentecostal evangelical leaders, members of the Armed Forces as well as other police forces in Brazil, around a conservative cultural war involving moral values, extreme nationalism, discipline and no left-wing indoctrination in education, and in the State apparatus. All in all, the enemy was the traditional policy agenda of the left in Brazil, including parties, unions, social movements, associations, and the like. The cultural war of Bolsonaro had many reasonings, such as the need to fight against Marxist ideology (sometimes Gramscian or Communists) as militants (or ideologues) were supposed to be impregnated in Brazilian institutions since Cardoso's government (from 1995) in all education teaching and the State (or bureaucracy) apparatus. This war was also against what Bolsonaro supporters labelled as an indoctrination of "gender ideology" and minorities.

Since the beginning of the government, Bolsonaro framed minority groups as enemies. In his inauguration speech, Bolsonaro stated: "We are going to unite the people, rescue the family, respect religions and our Judeo-Christian tradition, combat gender ideology, [and] conserve our values" (Phillips, 2019).

Regarding gender and sexual and reproductive rights policies, shifts started to occur in previous governments, particularly Dilma's and Temer's, due to the pressure of two groups: the "No Partisan School" (Escola sem Partido) movement and politicians linked to Pentecostal groups. The first was created in 2004 by a conservative Catholic lawyer that advocated for the elimination of any political, ideological, and religious censorship in education, i.e., "de-ideologizing" teaching, criticizing the influences of Marxism and Paulo Freire, a famous Brazilian pedagogue who advocated a learning method based on political awareness of reality. Days before the second round of the presidential election, this movement launched a manifesto called "Brazil for the Brazilians," stating that education policy should "free public education from the authoritarianism of the gender ideology, of the ideology of pornography, and to give families the right to sexual education of their children and adolescents. To defend the child's right to innocence as a universal human right" (Câmara dos Deputados, 2018). The second group emerged as vocal opponents of gender equality and LGBTQ+ recognition, organized through a coalition called the "Evangelical Parliamentary Front" with representatives in Congress. This front was successful at vetoing specific policies and bills, particularly the distribution of an informational booklet addressing homophobia in primary schools in 2011. Also, these groups influenced the debate of the national curriculum guidelines, eliminating the discussion of gender (Segatto, Alves and Pineda, 2023). Many attempts to review the contents of schoolbooks were made by eliminating gender issues as well as a revisionism of the military regime seen not as a coup d'état but as a "sovereign decision of the Brazilian society" as Bolsonaro's first Minister of Education stated in March 2019. The federal government has a traditional program of distribution of free schoolbooks to all public schools in Brazil on a massive scale.

Affirmative action was also a target. In the case of ethnic and racial relations, since the 2000s, different changes were adopted seeking to overcome the elitist and unequal Brazil's education policy legacy. Among these changes, there were the inclusion of Afro-Brazilian and African history and culture content in the curriculum (Law 10,639/2003) and the creation of the Secretariat of Continuing Education, Literacy, Diversity, and Inclusion (SECADI) within the Ministry of Education, responsible for monitoring Quilombola schools and developing various project grants, such as the production of pedagogical material. The first Minister of Education stated in an interview that he did not agree with the solution of affirmative action for public schools, low income, and black or indigenous students, adopted since 2012. The second Minister of Education, in line with his "demoralizing" strategy to please a minority of extreme right-wing supporters in Brazil, revoked one norm of affirmative action in graduate courses just before leaving office and fleeing to the USA. The uproar was intense in the public debate and even the Supreme Court was called to analyze the case, but it was not necessary. A couple of days later, the substitute Minister of Education revoked the norm.

Higher education, however, was targeted in a very particular way. From the beginning, public universities were seen as enemies to be fought against. The nomination of the first two Ministers of Education reveals a close alignment to

Bolsonaro's principles of a cultural war, and the third, closer to conservative-evangelical values. The first minister of Education, a university professor with no links to traditional policy communities, stated that public universities were a target: "I never got a scholarship [in his academic career] because of the rigging of the Ministry of Education by PT [militants] (…) who have taken over the Ministry since the 1990s" said the Minister in his first month in office.[4] Rectors of federal universities, he continues, have become hostages of the Labor Unified Central (CUT) – a large trade union historically connected to PT – and he proposes a more coherent method to select them, which he will enforce. Attempts to change the law were carried out by the second Minister.

In Brazil, the President has the authority to choose and nominate the Rectors of all federal-run education institutions. Traditionally, the President chooses the candidate who has received the most votes by the academic community, thus, accepted as a legitimate head to lead the university. Bolsonaro did not follow this informal tradition and at least 22 nominations were barred and replaced by other names by the government, even ones outside the nomination lists. Two legislative initiatives – Presidential decrees which have immediate force of law – were attempted as Table 11.3 shows and both were repealed by Congress.

TABLE 11.3 Initiatives related to the cultural war agenda in Bolsonaro's government (2019–2022) and the rate of success and failure

Cultural War (credit-claiming)	Successful Changes	Failure to Change
Basic Education	- Office for diversity issues closed (SECADI) - Revision of gender and military regime in national exams and schoolbooks	- "No Partisan School" bill[b]
Higher Education	none	- Eliminates affirmative action in graduate courses[a] - Change rules to choose Rectors of Federal Universities and Institutes[b] - New attempt to change nomination of Rectors during the pandemic[b]
Both	none	- Defunding students' organizations[b]

Source: Own compilation.

Notes

[a] The Executive administrative ordinance was repealed by the substitute Ministry of Education.

[b] Bill not approved by Congress.

In the second attempt, days after the first decree was repealed, the Speaker of the Senate himself returned the new decree to the President. It is difficult to believe that both the President and the Minister of Education had any expectation of approval. It seems more likely to be part of a cultural war to attack the enemy or to demoralize opponents in the public arena. Along with this type of strategy, it is the attempt to remove the rights of students' unions to issue students' cards identification which financed part of their activities. Again, the Presidential decree caused enormous uproar in the public scene, Congress did not even consider it, and the decree lost legal validity. It seems that the main objective was to respond to Bolsonaro's supporters with some public action against public universities as enemies.

As Table 11.3 summarizes, although the cultural war was an important agenda for Bolsonaro (and a very noisy too) the rate of success on this front was minimal. Although higher education was the main target of this war, it is also noticeable that there were no successful attempts. The vast majority of the attempts failed and all of them were dismissed by Congress. The only two successful initiatives did not involve Congress consideration as they required only administrative acts issued by the Minister of Education. These types of issues, connected to political polarization, did not receive the support of the majority of members in Congress at that time.

11.7 New path-breaking policies in education with no support from policy communities

Although Bolsonaro's government was unsuccessful at approving policies related to the ideological war at the National Congress, the government promoted policy changes that did not require parliamentary approval.

Two policies for basic education were implemented during Bolsonaro's government that have in common the fact that they did not receive the support of the traditional policy communities involved in education in Brazil as they deviated from the previous path of education beliefs fostered by the 1988 Constitution (Table 11.4).

The first policy was a new national literacy program that differed from the ones implemented in previous governments. It required the adoption of phonics-based approaches, breaking with the standard. The program was created by the new Secretariat of Literacy and the National Literacy policy in 2019. The head of this office was a critic of constructivist methods and of the pedagogue Paulo Freire and was also connected to the far right ideologue Olavo de Carvalho. The policy, which contained federal transfers to subnational governments, was later rewritten allowing teachers to choose the preferred methods. The ideas of the literacy program came from international experiences and evidence, and due

TABLE 11.4 List of path-breaking policies with no support from traditional policy communities in Bolsonaro's government (2019–2022)

Level	Policy Changes	Outcome
Basic Education	- New Literacy policy[a] - Military-Civic schools program[a] - Homeschooling bill	Both policies were approved and implemented, but the homeschooling bill was repealed by the Supreme Court.
Higher Education	- Bill for a new management, hiring contracts, and to raise private funds for universities (public defunding) - Bill to introduce fees in public universities	Both bills not approved by Congress.

Note
[a] Executive administrative ordinance with no need for Congress referral.

Source: Own compilation.

to conflicts in its implementation, a commission with subnational governments was created to make adjustments to its design. In a similar but different policy, the Minister of Women, Family and Human Rights together with the Ministry of Education sponsored the Homeschooling bill, a demand from a small group of parents, many of them from neo-Pentecostal groups, that sought to have the legal authorization to remove their kids from conventional schools.

The second policy was the program known as "Civic-Military Schools" (PECIM) with the participation of military or police personnel in the running of schools. This policy was the extreme opposite of all beliefs around the traditional policy communities in Brazil as it assumed that the problem of education was a lack of discipline and order, and it received strong opposition from many traditional political actors. This option was supposed to produce better performance than regular public schools, even though there was no evidence supporting such claims. State or municipal governments that joined this federal program would receive federal funds. The pedagogical management of the school would remain with teachers, but the administration of them would be carried out by retired police or military people. This policy was created by the many military personnel that worked in the Bolsonaro transition team and it was first outlined in December of 2018. One of the initial actions of the first Minister of Education, in 2019, was to create an office to exclusively manage these civic-military schools. The program had many critics and some governors or mayors refused to adopt such types of military school and cases of abuse of authority towards students have been reported in the media.

Concerning public higher education, although it was one of the main targets of Bolsonaro's government officials in the cultural war, effective policy initiatives that would break with previous patterns did not succeed as Table 11.4 shows. A first attempt to reform universities (a project called "Future-se") was presented by the second Minister of Education of Bolsonaro. The bill sent to Congress in 2020 aimed to radically transform the Brazilian higher education system. A complex transformation in the nature of higher education institutions, ways of raising private funds, flexibility norms to hire and dismiss personnel, and other tools applying a private-market organizational setting to public universities and private sector managerial tools was announced to stimulate applied innovation (Chiarini et al., 2020).

The whole project was constructed by economists with a neoliberal view of economics and the role of the State in society and ideologues of the cultural war with the main objective of diminishing public spending with federal universities and with a view of the superiority of applied knowledge instead of abstract, philosophical, or basic research. The minister of Education frequently diminished the worth of human and especially the social sciences. As Berg, Jungblut, and Jupskås (2023) characterize, populists prefer practical applications of education in what they call an instrumental approach in which education must be "useful." Not one of the many associations or organizations of universities were consulted during the formulation process. In fact, one of the main associations of federal Rectors (ANDIFES) stated that they had a meeting with the Minister the day before the launching of the proposal and were not told about it. There was widespread skepticism of the real intentions behind the proposal, and it did not gather support from the main political actors. The legislative bill had no support and Congress did not even start to consider it to date.

Finally, it is worth mentioning the attempt of one congressman, supporter of Bolsonaro, and also a retired military officer, to introduce fees in public universities. The bill presented in Congress was an extremely weak piece of legislation in terms of poor or nonexistent technical reasoning or even estimates of the effects it would produce. However, this case mobilized a lot of attention and the mobilization of groups connected to public universities communities. The bill was dismissed but it was the first time that a consideration of charging fees in public universities was brought to public attention. This idea is, for now, in the garbage can, waiting, as Kingdon (1995) would put it, for its time to come.

In sum, the government had little success concerning the adoption of new policies that would radically deviate from the path in place in the case of higher education, although it did succeed in two policies for basic education. Again, the government only succeeded in policies that did not need to be considered by Congress.

Conclusions

Bolsonaro got to power with a promise to completely overhaul the education system, engaging in a cultural war that framed previous education policies and communities as enemies. However, Bolsonaro's government was not successful in promoting a conservative turn, instead it dismantled or changed some policies. Some of these changes brought negative consequences in terms of equality and fairness to education that will resonate for years or generations of students, such as the effects of the absence of national coordination during the pandemic's school closures or the failed secondary school reform implementation.

The government succeeded in cutting public spending and supporting the expansion of private provision, particularly in the case of higher education. However, these changes were not a novelty of Bolsonaro's government as cuts and private provision were policies initiated in 2016 in the previous traditional right-wing Temer government. In this sense, the government agenda was of a traditional right-wing government that had support of the majority of members of Congress. The same level of public cuts was not, however, observed in the case of basic education in which even Congress opposed. Given the fact that the vast majority of Brazilian students attend a public school in this level of schooling, representatives did not support cuts and voted against the interests of the President and his Minister of Education.

The other changes identified, including the weakening of the institutional role of federal education coordination, eliminating specific policies based on a cultural war agenda, and promoting path-breaking policies with no support from traditional policy communities, varied greatly in its success of effectively producing changes and in their levels of intensity and density. These findings reinforce the scholarship, which argue that policy changes promoted by far-right or ultra-conservative governments are not necessarily equivalent to traditional policy retrenchment. The analysis of Brazil's education policy shows that Bolsonaro's government promoted few policy changes, although it succeeded in various minor changes regarding policy instruments.

Strategies adopted by Bolsonaro's government did not necessarily avoid claiming, on the contrary, some included credit-claiming in very loudly deliberately narratives even it meant little success in practice, which deviates from traditional descriptions of policy dismantling. Other strategies included nondecision-making that produced institutional disruption with the traditional formal rules and informal norms over the political authority of producing national coordination in the Brazilian federation.

Nevertheless, the overall evaluation of the effective changes shows the resilience of the path inaugurated by the democratic 1988 Constitution as no structural or radical reform succeeded before now. This resilience is explained by a series of factors combined, but as this analysis shows, Bolsonaro's government was unable to build an alternative coalition to form a majority that would go beyond the most extreme and minority radical supporters. Bolsonaro's government had no alternative coalition large enough to array majority support to produce a radical change that could be path-breaking with the 1988 democratic Constitution with regard to public education. Not in society nor in Congress.

Notes

1 We thank Professor Michael Bauer for the insightful comments for this chapter.
2 The 1988 Constitution established political autonomy to all three levels of governments, which means that municipalities in Brazil are not politically subjected to (or a creation of) State governments. The number of municipalities grew fast in the aftermath of the Constitution, mainly as a result of incentives given by fiscal (constitutional) automatic transfers to this level of government, and in 2023 the Brazilian federation is formed by the federal government, 26 State governments plus the Federal District, and 5,568 municipalities all over the country.
3 Street demonstrations were mounting throughout 2019 until the COVID-19 pandemic removed them from the streets.
4 Interview published by Veja Magazine on the 1st of February 2019 - https://veja.abril.com.br/revista-veja/faxina-ideologica/.

References

Abrucio, F. L. (2021). "Bolsonarismo e Educação: Quando a meta é desconstruir uma política pública." In L. Avritzer, F. Kerche, & M. Marona (eds.). *Governo Bolsonaro: Retrocesso democrático e degradação política* (pp. 255–270). Autêntica.

Abrucio, F. L., Grin, E. J., Franzese, C., Segatto, C. I., & Couto, C. G. (2020). Combate à COVID-19 sob o federalismo bolsonarista: Um caso de descoordenação intergovernamental. *Revista de Administração Pública*, 54(4), 663–677.

Alves, M. A., Segatto, C. I., & Pineda, A. (2021). Changes in Brazilian education policy and the rise of right-wing populism. *British Educational Research Journal*, 47(2), 332–354.

Ansell, B. W. (2009). *From the ballot to the blackboard: The redistributive political economy of education.* Cambridge University Press.

Arretche, M. (2012). *Democracia, federalismo e centralização no Brasil.* FGV.

Arretche, M. (2018). Democracia e redução da desigualdade econômica no brasil: A inclusão dos outsiders. *Revista Brasileira De Ciências Sociais*, 33(96), e339613. https://doi.org/10.17666/339613/2018

Arza, C., Castiglioni, R., Franzoni, J. M., Niedzwiecki, S., Pribble, J., & Sánchez-Ancochea, D. (2022). *The political economy of segmented expansion: Latin American social policy in the 2000s.* Cambridge University Press.

Banting, K. G. & Myles, J. (2013) Introduction: Inequality and the fading of redistributive politics. In K. G. Banting & J. Myles (eds.). *Inequality and the fading of redistributive politics* (pp. 165–186). UBC Press.

Bauer, M. W. & Knill, C. (2012). Understanding policy dismantling: An analytical framework. In M. W. Bauer, C. Green-Pedersen, A. Héritier, & A. Jordan, (eds.).

(2012). *Dismantling public policy: Preferences, strategies, and effects* (pp. 30–56). OUP Oxford.

Bauer, M. W. & Knill, C. (2014). A conceptual framework for the comparative analysis of policy change: Measurement, explanation and strategies of policy dismantling. *Journal of Comparative Policy Analysis: Research and Practice*, 16(1), 28–44.

Béland, D., Rocco, P., Segatto, C. I., & Waddan, A. (2021). Trump, Bolsonaro, and the framing of the COVID-19 crisis: How political institutions shaped presidential strategies. *World Affairs*, 184(4), 413–440.

Berg, A. E., Jungblut, J., & Jupskås, A. R. (2023). We don't need no education? Education policies of Western European populist radical right parties. *West European Politics*, 467, 1312–1342.

Brito A. S., Mendes C. H., Sales F. R., Amaral M. C. S., & Barreto M. S. (2022). *São Paulo. O caminho da autocracia – Estratégias atuais de erosão democrática.* Centro de Análise da Liberdade e do Autoritarismo (LAUT).

Busemeyer, M. R. (2015). *Skills and inequality: Partisan politics and the political economy of Education Reforms in Welfare States.* Cambridge University Press.

Busemeyer, M. R. (2017). Education and the welfare state: A Short comment on a complex relationship. *Political Science & Politics*, 50(2), 426–427.

Câmara dos Deputados (2018, October 24). Frente Evangélica lança manifesto com propostas para gestão do Brasil. www.camara.leg.br/noticias/546684-frente-evangel ica-lanca-manifesto-com-propostas-para-gestao-do-brasil/

Campbell, J. L. (2023). *Institutions under siege: Donald Trump's attack on the deep state.* Cambridge University Press.

Carvalho, J. M. A. (2023). Uma política, várias camadas: os desafios da implementação do Novo Ensino Médio no Brasil. (Doctoral dissertation).

Chiarini, T., Cimini, F., Rapini, M. S., & Silva, L. A. (2020). The political economy of innovation: Why is Brazil stuck in the technology ladder? *Brazilian Political Science Review*, 14(2), 1–39.

Couto, L. F. & Rech, L. T. (2023). Desmonte Ativo No Governo Bolsonaro: Uma Aproximação Pela Perspectiva Orçamentária. In A. Á. Gomide, M. M. S. Silva, & M. A. Leopoldi (eds.). *Desmonte e reconfiguração de políticas públicas* (2016–2022) (pp. 443–474). Ipea.

Cury, C. R. J. (2008). Sistema nacional de educação: Desafio para uma educação igualitária e federativa. *Educação & Sociedade*, 29, 1187–1209.

Dias, M. L., Segatto, C. I., & Ximenes, S. (2023). Duas políticas nacionais, dois municípios: A mobilidade de políticas de educação de tempo integral em diferentes contextos. In K. Frey & L. N. Bittencourt (eds.). *Poder local, políticas públicas e relações federativas: O caso do ABC paulista* (pp. 111–138). CRV.

Esping-Andersen, G. (1995). O futuro do Welfare State na nova ordem mundial. *Lua Nova: Revista de Cultura e Política*, 35, 73–111.

Gomes, S. (2022). Padrões partidários das mudanças e continuidades na educação superior no Brasil: elitização versus massificação do acesso. Paper presented at the 46º Encontro Anual da Anpocs.

Gomes, S., Silva, A., & Costa, F. (2019). Governos partidários e políticas educacionais no Brasil do século XXI: A eficácia da democracia. In M. Arretche, E. Marques & C.A.P. Faria (eds.). *As políticas da política: desigualdades e inclusão nos governos do PSDB e do PT.* 1 ed (pp. 217–242). Editora UNESP.

Gomide, A. de A., Silva, M. M. de S., & Leopoldi, M. A. (eds.). (2023). *Desmonte e reconfiguração de políticas públicas* (2016–2022). Ipea.

Green-Pedersen, C. (2004). The dependent variable problem within the study of welfare state retrenchment: Defining the problem and looking for solutions. *Journal of Comparative Policy Analysis: Research and Practice,* 6(1), 3–14.

House, F. (2014). *Freedom in the world 2014: The annual survey of political rights and civil liberties.* Rowman & Littlefield.

Jaccoud, L., Sátyro, N., Gomes, S., Vieira, F., Servo, L., & Fernandez, M. (2021). Por que a coordenação nacional de políticas públicas importa para os direitos dos cidadãos, especialmente na pandemia? Rede Brasileira de Mulheres Cientistas, Nota Técnica n. 11. https://mulherescientistas.org/wp-content/uploads/2021/07/NT-11.pdf

Jordan, A., Benson, D., Wurzel, R., Zito, A. R., & Richardson, J. J. (2012). Environmental policy: Governing by multiple policy instruments? In J. Richardson (ed.). *Constructing a Policy-Making State? Policy Dynamics in the EU* (pp. 104–124). Oxford University Press.

Kingdon, J. (1995). *Agendas, alternatives, and public policies.* Harper Collins.

Lall, M. (2008). Educate to hate: The use of education in the creation of antagonistic national identities in India and Pakistan. *Compare: A Journal of Comparative and International Education,* 38(1), 103–119.

Limongi, F., Freitas, A., Medeiros, D., & Luz, J. (2022). Government and Congress. In P. Birle & B. Speck (ed.). *Brazil under Bolsonaro. How endangered is democracy?* (pp. 30–43). Ibero-Amerikanisches Institut Preußischer Kulturbesitz.

Luz, J. (2022). *Os cortes na Educação no atual Governo. Observatório do Legislativo Brasileiro.* IESP-UERJ. https://olb.org.br/os-cortes-na-educacao-no-atual-governo/

Mello, J. (2023). Condicionantes Institucionais do Desmonte e da Resiliência de Políticas Públicas no Brasil. In A. Á. Gomide, M. M. S. Silva, & M. A. Leopoldi (eds.). *Desmonte e reconfiguração de políticas públicas* (2016–2022) (pp. 411–442). Ipea.

Milhorance, C. (2022). Policy dismantling and democratic regression in Brazil under Bolsonaro: Coalition politics, ideas, and underlying discourses. *Review of Policy Research,* 39, 752–770.

Phillips, D. (2019, January 2). Jair Bolsonaro launches assault on Amazon rainforest protections. *The Guardian.* www.theguardian.com/world/2019/jan/02/brazil-jair-bolsonaro-amazon-rainforest-protections

Pierson, P. (2001). Coping with permanent austerity welfare state restructuring in affluent democracies. In P. Pierson (ed.). *The new politics of the welfare state* (pp. 410–456). Oxford University Press.

Segatto, C. I., Alves, M. A., & Pineda, A. (2022). Populism and religion in Brazil: The view from education policy. *Social Policy and Society,* 21(4), 560–574.

Segatto, C. I., Alves, M. A., & Pineda, A. (2023). Uncivil society and social policies in Brazil: The backlash in the gender, sexual, and reproductive rights and ethnic and racial relations fields. *Public Administration and Development,* 43(1), 60–69.

Segatto, C. I., Santos, F. B. P. D., Bichir, R. M., & Morandi, E. L. (2022). Inequalities and the COVID-19 pandemic in Brazil: Analyzing un-coordinated responses in social assistance and education. *Policy and Society,* 41(2), 306–320.

Tajra, A. & Andrade, H. de. (2019, January 2). Novo ministro critica "marxismo cultural" nas escolas: "faz mal à saúde." Uol. https://noticias.uol.com.br/politica/ultimas-noticias/2019/01/02/ministro-da-educacao-cita-deus-e-critica-marxismo-cultural-nas-escolas.htm?cmpid=copiaecola

Times Higher Education. (2016). Turkey: powers for president on rector jobs "eradicate autonomy." www.timeshighereducation.com/news/turkey-powers-president-rector-jobseradicate-autonomy

Todos Pela Educação. (2020). *6° Relatório Bimestral: Execução Orçamentária do Ministério da Educação (MEC)*. https://todospelaeducacao.org.br/wordpress/wp-content/uploads/2021/02/6%C2%B0-Relatorio-Bimestral-da-Execucao-Orcamentaria-do-MEC.pdf

Wong, K. K. (2020). Education policy Trump Style: The administrative presidency and deference to states in ESSA implementation. *Publius: The Journal of Federalism*, 50(3), 423–445.

12

BRAZILIAN FAMILY POLICIES UNDER THE NEO-CONSERVATISM RHETORIC OF BOLSONARO

Gabriel Penna[1] and Natália Sátyro

Introduction

The family is an important matter within the far-right ideology, which portrays the institution as a natural cell that should be protected from attacks coming from the political left, who, in these agents' view, try to undermine its traditional patriarchal structure (Biroli, Quintela, 2021). In that sense, right-wing political agents defend explicit action from the State in defense of the patriarchal arrangement, as well as for dismantling policies that would threaten the traditional family, especially those targeted at women and the LGBT population, which have gained space in federal public policies of the so-called 'pink tide' governments (2003–2016) (Lacerda, 2019; Biroli, Machado, Vaggione, 2020). The Brazilian far-right defends the end of public policies directly targeted at affirming the rights of gender and sexual-orientation minorities (Biroli, Machado, Vaggione, 2020).

The election of Jair Messias Bolsonaro in 2018 marks a change in the political scenario. Bolsonaro was a backbencher professional politician, a term used to describe Congress members of low relevance in the political game of the National Congress. Countering all predictions, his campaign was victorious and the country elected a populist far-right politician as the President of the Republic (Moura, Corbellini, 2019). The election of a politician that spoke openly of being on the far-right reflects the consolidation, in the public sphere, of a 'new right', different from the Brazilian 'ashamed right' (Quadros, Madeira, 2018) that is characteristic of the post-Dictatorship period, when right-wing politicians refrained from speaking openly about being on the right. This new right has been conceived during Lula's second administration; at first through social media,

DOI: 10.4324/9781003487777-15

then through a network that gathered social movements, intellectuals, and politicians in a decentralized manner, and lastly, through institutional politics (Rocha, 2021). Ideologically, this movement is driven by the conjunction of neoliberal and neoconservative ideologies (Brown, 2006; 2015; 2019; Cooper, 2015) defending agendas that include privatization and dismantling of public services, less State participation in the economy, the ending of gender equality policies, as well as those against the discrimination of LGBT people, and public safety policies based on the upsurge of penal legislation and inclusion of militarization into sectorial such as education (Lacerda, 2019; Biroli, Machado, Vaggione, 2020; Rocha, 2021).

The research question that guides us is how does a populist radical right party (PRRP) affect family policies? The objective of this chapter is to identify and reflect on the changes carried out by Bolsonaro's government regarding the existing family policies of the Brazilian federal government, analyzing the direction of such changes and the strategies used; specifically, the chapter will focus on care policies.

The analytic lense of the work is based on an approach that analyzes the advance of the new right in the world and its affiliation to neoliberalism and neoconservatism (Brown, 2006; 2015; 2019; Cooper, 2015). Neoconservatism is the political ideology that appears in opposition to the advances of feminism and the LGBT community (countermovement) and that, through mobilization in contexts of democracy or erosion of democracy, mobilizes public opinion with the objective of reinforcing traditional gender roles and heteronormative sexuality, reinforcing the patriarchal family, and adopting punitive and militaristic policies (Brown, 2006; 2015; 2019; Cooper, 2015; Lacerda, 2019). Lacerda (2019) defines neoconservatism as the combination of five main axes: (I) defense of the patriarchal family; (II) Zionism; (III) militarism; (IV) punitiveness; and (V) neoliberalism. That is, the author includes neoliberalism as a part of neoconservatism. For us, these are different phenomena that are brought together when it comes to Populists Radical Right Parties (PRRPs). A neoliberal State is one in which social provision duties lay fundamentally with the market and the family, the State having the overriding duty of facilitating Capital accumulation and the free circulation of goods and services. Broadly speaking, this is a political rationality that places all human relations under economic terms while redefining the role of the State not as an entity that aims for the common good and the creation of public policies for its citizens, but rather a mere facilitator of commercial activities (Brown, 2019). According to Cooper (2017) and Brown (2019), the goals of neoliberals and neoconservatives for the social protection agenda are distinct – the first intend to reduce the provision of resources by the State to a maximum, while the second hold the purpose of controlling sexuality through family policies – and the PRRP agendas converge on the need to reinstall the family as the main institution responsible for citizens' well-being (Cooper, 2017). The alliance between neoliberalism and neoconservatism is therefore one of thematic convergence in the field of family relations, reinforcing the need to reinstall the family as a relevant element for the provision of subsistence for individuals (Cooper, 2017; Brown, 2019).

Choosing care policies allows for analyzing precisely how the privileged place of the traditional, patriarchal family in far-right discourse is reflected in governmental decisions on the maintenance or dismantling of policies that modify the dynamics and power relations within the family nucleus. Care policies are essential to ensure values such as gender equality, given that they free women from the socially established caregiver position and enable them to have a gainful occupation and get into the workforce. Paradigmatic examples of care policies include daycare facilities and measures for the care of elders and persons with disability.

According to our theoretical point of view, we come from the generic hypothesis that PRRPs are associated with the mercantilization of family policies, as well as with reinforcing women's roles within a specific type of family. This work contemplates the hypothesis that Bolsonaro's government dismantles existing policies while also redefining, symbolically and in practice, the State's actions as those of a structure that is supposed to promote traditional morality and carries out social provision through the private sector.

This chapter is composed of four sections, as well as this introduction and the final considerations, which will systematize the findings. First, a brief discussion on the concept of family policies will take place. Then, there will be a brief analysis of daycare and early childhood development policies starting with the 1988 Constitution (CF88) until the most recent administrations, as well as of the evolution of daycare enrollments in the 20th century. The third section will approach the paradigm change in daycare social-assistance programs aimed at vulnerable populations, from the public financing of public daycare to the public financing of the private sector. The fourth section shows the strategies used to formulate the ideas of traditional family and mercantilization.

What are family policies?

The term family policies does not determine the provision or the right that is the object of a policy, as it is the case, for instance, with social-assistance, health, or educational policies. Rather, when talking of family policies, we talk about the target demographic for the policies, that is, families. But such demographic is not a given. As Daly (2020) points out, 'family' is both a social structure and a collective of individuals. Thus, family policies are guided by a normative frontier of what the family is or should be, indeed participating in the construction of such an ensemble, even though actual practices can escape the state norm.

Therefore, the first question guiding an analysis of family policies is, which types of families are supported by such policies and which are left behind?

Even within the traditional structure, the definition of what a 'family' is for the delimitation of family policies is complex. There are authors who propose restrictive concepts, who define family policies as those aimed at families with children, which help regulate the institution of the family (Daly, 2020; Eydal, Rostgard, 2018). However, restrictive definitions are not consensual, and a series of authors have been working on care policies for elders and people with disabilities as part of the concept of family policies (Dykstra, Djundeva, 2020). Robilla (2014, p. 3) brings forth a wider definition, considering family policies 'government activities that are intentionally designed to support families, enhance family members' well-being, and strengthen family relationships'. However, the author's own definition of family policies as 'intentionally designed' weakens in face of her affirmation that family policies can be implicit, that is, that they can affect families only laterally (Robilla, 2014). There are non-restrictive definitions such as those from Abrão and Mioto, who define family policies as a 'set of public administration interventions that aim at benefiting people with family responsibilities so that they can satisfactorily perform that work both privately and publicly, mostly regarding the care for the dependent' (Abrão, Mioto, 2017, p. 421).

However, Sátyro and Midaglia (2021) characterize Latin American family policies from a typology that sorts them into five groups: (I) sequential policies: maternity, paternity, and parental leave, as well as workload flexibility measures that enable the conciliation of care work and employment; (II) care services that can relieve the family from the duty of directly providing care work; (III) income safety policies, with income transfers of many natures (contributive or non-contributive) and tax incentives that reduce the cost of social reproduction, that is, maternity or paternity; (IV) regulation that interferes in the dynamics of family formation, ranging from family planning policies to civil regulations regarding marriage, divorce, and heritage, as well as policies against domestic violence; and, lastly, (V) the State's inaction, which ends up reinforcing traditional sociability patterns and creating what the authors call actual or default familism (Sátyro, Midaglia, 2021). This inaction can also be seen as blindness about several dimensions; for example, gender blindness reinforces traditional takes and practices on gender roles within public policies. The typology has three practical advantages: (I) it does not restrain the concept to explicit family policies, which allows to understand the phenomenon of the relation between State and family with more width and depth; (II) it does not restrain the target demographic for the policies, allowing for the analysis of the interactions between public policies and a series of vulnerable subjects – such as elders, women, children, teenagers, and people with disabilities; and (III) it brings up inaction as a type of public policy, linked to the theoretical milestone of welfare regimes, which assume the distribution of social provision between many actors, not exclusive to the State, especially in Latin America (e.g., Barrientos, 2008; Gough, 2008; Franzoni, Voorend, 2009).

This work aims to analyze the dismantling through structural changes as a way of understanding if Bolsonaro's government is qualitatively different from the defunding of social policies that had been happening in Brazil since the mid-2010s. This does not mean that the budget reductions occurred in Bolsonaro's government will not be considered, but that they will be looked at as one of the possible strategies in a context of dismantling. Thus, the intention is to observe whether it is possible to affirm that the ideology of the far-right follows a direction that mixes neoliberalism and neoconservatism to defend a traditional social order in which care work should be provided by a very specific family unit, as by the case of policies for care support.

To answer those questions, this work presents a qualitative approach. The trajectory of the policies studied was assessed by consulting websites, newspapers, publications on the Brazilian Federal Official Jounal (Diário Oficial da União), as well as internal documents from the federal government, requested through the Information Access Law. Such documents contain technical notes, reports, and preliminary versions of those changes, and allow for the in-depth understanding of the formulation process and the reasons given by the political agents for each of the enacted changes. Adding to the analytic lenses brought about in the introduction, we go on to the distinction between familializing and de-familializing policies (Sátyro, Midaglia, 2021; Lohmann, Zagel, 2016; Saraceno, Keck, 2010; Leitner, 2003), arguing that PRRPs have different implications for these two types (Ennser-Jedenastik, 2022), but that for this chapter we will focus on analyzing one single policy.

Daycare and early childhood development between the CF88 and Temer

Daycare in Brazil is a constitutional right of the working mother as well as of the child being cared for but this is a recent construction. Its provision fell under the responsibility of local powers, with financial and technical aid from the states and the federal government (*Constitution of the Federative Republic of Brazil of 1988*). Until 2009, daycare centers were the responsibility of Social Assistance, designed to serve poor working mothers, and had never been an arena of much dispute or importance. Schooling in daycare accommodates children from zero to three years of age and the guardians of these children are not obliged to enroll them in daycare (*Statute 9.394 of December 20th, 1996*). For its non-mandatory character, municipal powers have had historically low incentives to provide daycare, choosing to focus on Elementary School, a mandatory stage (Cruz, 2017).

The induction mechanism for municipalities to expand daycare openings using the budget for education only occurred in 2009, with the reformulation of the Fund for Maintenance and Development of Elementary School and Valorization of Teaching (FUNDEF), which had been created in 1996 (during Fernando Henrique Cardoso's government), and its transformation into the Fund for Maintenance and Development of Basic Education (FUNDEB) (Cruz, Farah, Sugiyama, 2014). One of the political arguments for the transition from Social Assistance to Education was exactly the indisputable superior availability of resources the latter has. FUNDEF was focused on elementary school and on children from 7 to 14 years of age, fulfilling its constitutional stipulation. During Lula's administration, FUNDEF was transformed into FUNDEB through Constitutional Amendment n. 53/2006 (*Constitutional Amendment 53 of December 19th, 2006*), making schooling mandatory for children from 6 to 14 years old. Another Constitutional Amendment, n. 59 of 2009, extended the financing from Preschool to High School, making the mandatory schooling age 4 to 17 years old. This allowed for an increase in the number and quality of the services provided in both spheres, as well as an equalization in the provision of services (Cruz, Farah, Sugiyama, 2014). Therefore, daycare policies, specifically in Brazil, are allocated under Education and are under municipalities' responsibility, while most of its financing comes from the federal government.

Therefore, it is important to understand that the prerogative of daycare centers became that of education; however, what we will see here are the social-assistance care programs for early childhood that aim at complementing daycare policies, but are implemented by social assistance. Thus, in Dilma Rousseff's government (2010–2016) an important policy was implemented for the financing of daycare in Brazil, the Affectionate Brazil (Brasil Carinhoso) program,[2] instituted by Provisional Measure[3] n. 570, from 14 May, 2012, turned into Federal Law n. 12,722, from 3 October, 2012 (*Provisional Measure 570 of 14th May, 2012, Statute 12.722 of October 3rd, 2012*). This occurs in parallel and without competition with the programs and financing of the educational policy aimed at early childhood within the Ministry of Education. Affectionate Brazil was a multi-sectoral policy with the goal of integrating social-assistance actions in the scope of Brazil without Privation (Brasil sem Miséria), part of the Family Grant Program (Programa Bolsa Família), with health actions and daycare for the assisted children (Cruz, 2017). In order to do that, resource transfers to municipalities were set according to the population of children from 0 to 48 months assisted by PBF and, after that, also by the Continuous Cash Benefit (*Statute 12.722 of October 3rd, 2012*).

Affectionate Brazil was an important social assistance policy for expanding daycare access in many Brazilian municipalities. There was great adhesion to the program by municipalities, making the number of municipalities covered jump from 2,246 in 2012 (40% of municipalities) to 5,419 (97% of municipalities)

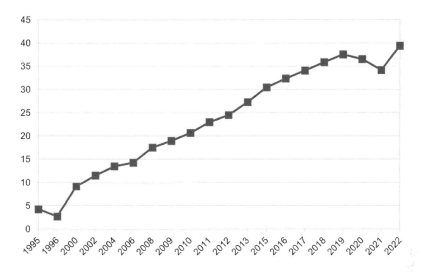

GRAPH 12.1 Enrollments in daycare between 1995 and 2022 (in hundreds of thousands).

Source: Inep–School Census.

in 2022. In the same period, openings in public daycare facilities receiving resources from Affectionate Brazil increased 130%, and openings in associated private daycare facilities increased 212%. The number of children receiving Family Grant that were covered by Affectionate Brazil whether in the public or private associated networks grew from 261,890 in 2012 to 636,711 in 2015 (Cruz, 2017). Such adhesion happened due to a strategy of daycare financing (in Education) through the National Fund for Social Assistance.

As it can be seen in Graph 12.1, enrollments in daycare facilities increased steadily over time with those joint efforts. In 2012, 25.7% of children from 0 to 3 years old were in daycare, in 2019 it was 35.6%, and in 2022 the rate was 36% (Instituto Nacional de Estudos e Pesquisas Educacionais Anísio Teixeira [Anísio Teixeira Institute for Research and Studies in Education], 2022[4]). However, among children of the upper classes, 54.3% were enrolled, while the rate was 27.8% for children coming from poor families (Todos Pela Educação Institute, 2021).

In Temer's government (2016–2018) no programs were created regarding daycare specifically within social assistance, beyond the Education's office. Its flagship for early childhood was the Happy Child Program (Criança Feliz), aimed at integrated early childhood development with actions in health, education, justice, and culture, but with different targets from its predecessor. The Program was operated by the Ministry of Social Development and Fight Against Hunger, but it was formulated and implemented without the approval of the Unified System for Social Welfare (SUAS) and the instances for participation and agreement that are part of the institutional and legal structure of the policy. As can be seen in Chapter 9 on social assistance services, the Program was created under the sponsorship of the then president's wife, a format completely outside the already institutionalized models of Social Assistance. It disregarded all participatory, deliberative, and federative pact instances of SUAS. Subsequently, there was a prototype agreement for its incorporation into SUAS, and it was renamed the First Childhood Program. Fact is that, once created, it began to compete with the financing of other services. For that reason, Affectionate Brazil was immediately defunded.

Lastly, the graph shows a decrease in daycare enrollments in 2019, 2020, and 2021, precisely Bolsonaro's administration, when Affectionate Brazil was financially drained. It is important to note that the information given by schools to the School Census is compiled annually on the second half of August, therefore the data for 2020 and 2021 was most probably contaminated by the effects of social distancing due to the COVID-19 pandemic. The decrease in 2019, however, does not reflect that issue.

Defunding, voucher proposals, and the formulation of the Citizen Child Aid

The first major change when thinking of family policies is the change of arena. Despite the maintenance of the Ministry of Citizenship (former Ministry of Social Development and Fight Against Hunger), at the beginning of Bolsonaro's government the Ministry of Women, Family, and Human Rights (MMFDH) was created (*Statute 13.844 of June 18th, 2019*). There was also the creation of the National Strategy for the Strengthening of Family Bonds, by Decree 10,570, from December 9th, 2020 (*Executive Order 10.570 of 9th December, 2020*). With regard to the proposition of bond-strengthening policies, we see here not only the change of arena from Social Assistance to the newly created MMFDH, but a disregard of the existence of a program already structured since the creation of SUAS with the same name and objective.

The necessary actions for the fulfillment of the goals of the Brazil Aid programs ignored the National Policy for Social Assistance (PNAS), existing since 2004, and within it the Unified System for Social Welfare (SUAS), well-established in all municipalities and designed to strengthen the protective role of the family, avoiding the worsening of social risks (such as violence, child labor and human rights violations), and helping to overcome situations of social vulnerability (Conselho Nacional de Assistência Social [National Council for Social Assistance], 2009). Within SUAS, basic care is structured through social-assistance services in the Program for Integral Family Care (PAIF) and the Service for Coexistence and Bond Strengthening (SCFV). The new National Strategy for the Strengthening of Family Bonds is structured without the approval of PAIF/SCFV, ignoring the instances for participation and deliberation of SUAS by proposing changes to the social-assistance services while overlooking such instances. In one stroke, a whole apparatus that already worked was invalidated and concurrent programs were created despite those already existing under social assistance.

The second point concerns financing. Within the Education policy there is greater legal normatization which renders interference more difficult, given the rules established for the federal pact. Differently, additional daycare policies and early childhood development implemented through Social Assistance enjoy greater flexibility, but less institutional structure and legal predictibility. As well as with other social policies, Affectionate Brazil went through a defunding process over the last years. Financing reached a peak of R$ 764.5 million in 2014 and had a decrease in 2015, still under Rousseff. In 2016, now under Temer's government, changes in standardization included the creation of new conditions for municipalities to receive the complementation and alteration as value calculation. This decreased the number of beneficiary municipalities, with a 35% drop in the first year of the new rules (Cruz, 2017). In Temer's government all social-assistance services that were discretionary expenses were drained to give space to the Happy Child program, due to the Spending Cap ('Teto de Gastos'), as seen in Chapters 2 and 9 of this book. In Bolsonaro's government there was also a reduction in the program's total spendings, which hit only 7.3 million BRL in 2019, that is, 1% of what it was when it peaked in Rousseff's government (Secretaria Nacional de Atenção à Primeira Infância [National Secretary for Early Childhood Care], 2020). Taking into account that most of public daycare facilities are under municipal responsibility, the absence of federal financing overburdens these federate entities.

Therefore, we can affirm that Bolsonaro's government was characterized, regarding federal daycare financing (under social assistance), by active dismantling of public daycare financing (Affectionate Brazil), while Temer's government defunded Affectionate Brazil but invested in Happy Child, which is targeted at other dimensions of child development. However, Happy Child was already a huge change because there was maternal responsibility for the first childhood. In other words, Temer already exchanges public daycare for familism, when focusing on poor women, therefore burdening and making poor black women even more responsible for the well-being and growth of their children.

In Bolsonaro's government, as important as the defunding is the fact that he tried to promote a policy of vouchers, in which the federal government would transfer money to families that enrolled their children in private daycare, a paradigmatic change. In 2020, the Minister of Economy, Paulo Guedes, at the World Economic Forum in Davos, promised a vouchers program for early childhood that would be, in his words, 'gigantic' (Teixeira, Henriques, 2022). The proposal for vouchers in education was present since Bolsonaro's presidency campaign (Pires, 2018). Even if the government was not able to operationalize the proposal, the inferred symbolic aspect was rather strong. In 2019, the so-called Proposed Constitutional Amendment (PEC) of the Federal Pact, presented by the government, suggested to remove the projection of obligation of expansion of the teaching network in places with a deficit in openings from the constitutional text (on Education). At the time, experts from the Ministry of Economy defended the measure based on economicity and on the parents' right to choose, affirming that the granting of scholarships in private schools with public resources would be more feasible (Caram, 2019).

In 2021, during legislative discussions related to the legal regulation of FUNDEB, the government proposed that a part of the FUNDEB's money would be directed at a voucher program, but the proposal was rejected following the resistance of education lawmakers. In the same year, however, the Provisional Measure that created Brazil Aid (Auxílio Brasil), a conditional cash transfer policy that replaced Family Grant, revoked the federal transfer for daycare funding projected for Affectionate Brazil (*Provisional Measure 1.061 of August 9th, 2021*). The same Measure created the vouchers system for Brazil Aid[5] beneficiaries, called Citizen Child Aid (Auxílio Criança Cidadã). The Provisional Measure ended up being approved by the lawmakers, becoming a law. Thus, if in the FUNDEB discussion the decision by the legislative was not to use public money to finance private activity, with the Brazil Aid the decision was the opposite: a policy of financing public facilities was extinguished in order to finance private daycare facilities.

The Citizen Child Aid intended to be a social-assistance benefit given to preferably single parent families covered by Brazil Aid with children from zero to 48 months of age meant for them to enroll children in private daycare, with or without profit motives, whenever there are no openings in public daycare facilities or in private daycare facilities affiliated to the public sector. In addition to the unavailability of openings, the benefit is conditioned to proof of employment by the guardian, who must ascertain income through gainful occupation. This means it is aimed at single mothers who are formally employed or self-employed. For this benefit, there would be an additional condition to the general health and education conditions applicable to Brazil Aid beneficiaries, which is attendance at counseling meetings on parenthood and early childhood care.

It is important to highlight that the Citizen Child Aid (CCA) was built to target a much more restricted public than the one impacted by Affectionate Brazil. That is because, unlike Affectionate Brazil, which calculated the transference to municipalities based on the population of children from zero to 48 months old which were beneficiaries of the federal policies as Family Grant or Continuous

Cash Benefit or with disabilities, the Criança Cidadã requires that one of the guardians in the family is employed. Added to that, the conversion of the Provisional Measure into a law meant that the families working for companies that provided daycare assistance would not be eligible for the benefit (*Statute 14.284 of December 29th, 2021*).

Such redefinition points to an inversion in the trend of universal offer of daycare by the public power. Despite early childhood development being mentioned as one of the goals of Brazil Aid as a whole (art. 2, III), the determining of the condition of being employed suggests the understanding that daycare should be a space of care for children while their parents are working. This is, therefore, a familializing policy, given that it takes the duty to provide care services for children away from the State when the family has means to provide them. The policy mercantilizes children's education, turning it into a primary obligation of the market. Such transformation is seen by agents in the federal government as having an advantage over Affectionate Brazil's model, and their justification is carried out in terms very similar to those of Milton Friedman, as shown in a technical note by the National Secretary of Early Childhood (SNAPI) that justifies the extinction of the transfer to municipalities for its 'incentive to the opening of new daycare openings in the private sector' as well as with the argument that 'this modality will give the family the opportunity to choose the institution they deem best according to their reality' (Secretaria Nacional de Atenção à Primeira Infância [National Secretariat for Early Childhood Care], 2021, p. 3–4). That is, the federal Executive does not prioritize the public daycare network. The financing is, in the Brazilian dynamic of social policies, an important tool of the government for inducing the implementation of local social services (Arretche, 2004). When it extinguishes a financing source, the federal government causes a decrease in the incentive for local governments to expand the network.

The government's success in approving the Citizen Child Aid a few months after the rejection of the vouchers proposal for FUNDEB can be explained by a number of factors. First, the conversion of provisional measures into laws is a simpler procedure than that of the approval of constitutional amendments, which requires qualified quorum and two voting rounds (*Constitution of the Federative Republic of Brazil of 1988*). Second, provisional measures are considered a powerful tool of the Executive branch for setting the agenda for the Legislative Power, although the strength of such strategy seems to be diminishing over time (Limongi, Figueiredo, 2001; Bedritichuk, Araújo, 2019). Thus, different from FUNDEB proposed changes, when the executive branch refused to take the initial steps and tried to force its agenda upon alliances that were already formed, with Brazil Aid the initiator of the proceedings was the Executive, which gave it a privileged position to form winning alliances. Another factor that cannot be disregarded is the fact that Brazil Aid brought in-depth changes to a series of social-assistance rules, which complexified the lawmakers' and the public opinion comprehension on the matter. It is well-known, at least since Downs (1957), that collecting information on a given matter involves costs, and that the decision-making process often involves ignoring certain dimensions of a problem and using cognitive shortcuts to define the desirability of a given choice. The end of Affectionate Brazil and the creation of Citizen Child Aid may thus have been concealed during the voting of the measure, which led to its approval.

Such effect on the Brazil Aid can be illustrated with the media coverage on the subject. An automated analysis was carried out with 550 news articles published between August 10th, 2021 (date of publication of the PM) and December 9th, 2021 (date of its referral for approval) in the Folha de São Paulo, one of the biggest newspapers in the country, using the keyword 'Auxílio Brasil', with the goal of assessing whether the media coverage mentioned the changes in daycare funding policies. Only 31 of those used the word 'daycare', which corresponds to 5.6% of the *corpus*. The term 'Affectionate Brazil' was mentioned in only five articles, less than 1% of the *corpus*. This finding indicates the likelihood that the demand for the end of Affectionate Brazil and creation of a voucher system did not mobilize public opinion when compared to other subjects, such as the value of the benefits. Such 'concealment' may have diminished the opposing sectors' ability to resist the measure, enabling its approval.

Lastly, a fifth important factor is the change in topic for the discussion on daycare. Different from the educational discussion on the FUNDEB, the discussion on Brazil Aid has a social-assistance nature. This change may be responsible for mobilizing the parliamentary bench concerned with education, responsible for deterring the deviation of resources during the FUNDEB voting. That is, the proposal passed when it left the sphere of Education and went into the sphere of Social Assistance, specifically income transfer, which has greater popular appeal with the public opinion, mainly because of the pandemic period.

The Citizen Child Aid is linked to the far-right ideology on at least two fronts. First, the defunding of the public education system and the transferring of resources to the private sector through vouchers is a classically neoliberal proposal, presented for the first time by Milton Friedman in the 1950s (Friedman, 1955). But the Citizen Child Aid also represents a return of the responsibility of child care back to families, given that its target demographic is restricted to families with remunerative occupations, a requirement that did not exist in the calculation of the values that would be transferred through Affectionate Brazil. Thus, the design of the Citizen Child Aid treats daycare not as a right of the child, but as a service that should only be offered when it is impossible for parents to provide it. When the family is not able to provide care work, the new design of Brazil Aid privileges its provision by the private sector. When dismantling an essential program for the financing of public daycare, Affectionate Brazil, and securing resources for the private sector, the policy mercantilizes children's education, making it a primary obligation of the market. In addition to commodifying, it passes into the sphere of private and religious morals, without state control and supervision.

Throwing light at the real meaning and at the symbolic and real ACC strategies

In terms of care policies, a few highlights of the president's performance were the creation of the social-assistance benefit known as Citizen Child Aid (ACC), the end of the federal complementation sent to municipal governments as part of the Affectionate Brazil program, and the possibility of making withdrawals from FGTS for private daycare funding. Although Graph 12.1 shows a decrease in the number of enrollments, it is rash to make causal affirmations, due to the pandemic. However, the symbolic aspects entailed in the ACC are enough to support our hypothesis.

The first relevant factor for analyzing ACC is the inclusion of the conditioning to parenthood counseling, representing a demand of the Ministry of Women, Family, and Human Rights, which dates from the beginning of Bolsonaro's government. In 2020, minister Damares Alves declared in an interview that the conditions for what was then called Family Grant were being altered, and that 'these folks [the program's beneficiaries] will have to have at least three meetings a year with the Guardianship Council. *We will teach a mother to be a mother*' (Gugliano, 2020, s.p., emphasis added). We highlight the symbolic aspect: The ministers' speech shows a heavily gendered and normative view of care work. There is no mention of the father, instead only of the mother, even when the condition is supposed to be aimed at the whole family. Added to that, there is the premise that it is possible to 'teach' a mother to perform motherhood, which reveals an ideal of motherhood. It is important to highlight that Happy Child already had this assumption and this practice. In other words, there is an assumption that poor mothers are ignorant and that they are to blame for transmitting the bad habits of poverty to their children. Another relevant point is the fact that there was a change in arena with the creation of a new Ministry.

In the official articles collected for the research, mentions were more subtle and had a less gendered character. The technical note n. 147/2021 of the National Secretary for Family, issued during the projects' proceedings, suggests the inclusion of family education not as conditional, but as a service available to the families (Secretaria Nacional da Família [National Secretary for Family], 2021a, p. 4). The Secretary's declaration steers away from the minister's speech, therefore, when it suggests that such meetings are not a condition for the program. The proposal, however, was only partially successful, since the inclusion of programs for family education was conditional for one subprogram only – the Citizen Child Aid. However, we highlight the symbolic aspect of the

Minister's speech, especially considering that she was one of the ministers with most media presence, making striking declarations on gender and family: 'boys should wear blue and girls should wear pink'.

Such restriction to one program was not prohibitive for the approval of Brazil Aid by the National Secretary for Family (SNF). The SNF, in a statement aimed at opining on the sanction of Conversion Law Project 26/2021, which resulted in the legislative process of appreciation of the PM that created the Brazil Aid program, highlighted the importance of the condition of attendance to parenthood counseling, suggesting that the National Strategy for the Strengthening of Family Bonds would be used to guide the construction of such activities (Secretaria Nacional da Família [National Secretary for Family], 2021b, p. 4). The design of the Citizen Child Aid program created a disproportionate burden on women and reinforced traditional gender roles in several levels. First, because it can be said that the program is primarily targeted at single-parent families and, therefore, in the Brazilian context, most families made to attend parenthood education are going to be women. Second, because the literature has long been describing how the presence of conditions in income transfer programs can generate contradictory effects on gender equality: while many programs focus on women as heads of household and the ones responsible for receiving resources, thus ensuring these women economic autonomy, the presence of conditions related to child care ultimately reinforces gender stereotypes and awards women who perform tasks seen as typical of 'good mothers' (Concern Worldwide, Oxfam, 2011; Scheel, Scheel, Fretheim, 2020). The presence of extra conditions falling mostly onto women and with the main focus on care work can ultimately worsen the excessive burden women carry with parental care due to gender, reinforcing gendering.

The third key to understand how the condition of family education can reinforce gender roles lies in the argument of Ciccia and Lombardo (2019), who say discourse is an important factor when considering care policies scientifically. For the authors, the fact that social policies depend heavily on actors for the implementation of commands and that these actors act according to their own ideological notions makes it so that care policies remain heavily dependent on the ideology of the actors of their implementation. The presence of a previous notion that the program should 'teach a mother to be a mother' can ideologically influence the implementation by municipalities, even if there is formally no specific gender view.

Moving past the presence of conditions, it should be noted that resorting to a public financing policy to fund openings in private schools, many times with profit motives, is part of the agenda of the neoliberalism-neoconservatism alliance, first proposed by exponent of the School of Chicago Milton Friedman, and later implemented in places such as Pinochet's Chile and the United States (Teixeira, Henriques, 2022).

Friedman's classic proposal brought with it the notion that there were only three situations in which a government could act considering a society that 'takes freedom of the individual, *or more realistically the family*, as its ultimate objective, and seeks to further this objective by relying primarily on voluntary exchange among individuals for the organization of economic activity' (Friedman, 1955, p. 123, emphasis added): (I) cases in which there is a natural monopoly; (II) cases in which there is an overflow effect (neighborhood effect); (III)iii) cases involving persons that could not determine their own autonomy, such as with children (Friedman, 1955). Assuming that primary education would have a relevant neighborhood effect, Friedman (1955) concluded that it was desirable that it was financed by the government.

However, to Friedman, the obligation of financing does not mean the obligation of managing the schools. It would be possible for the government to finance private schools with payments so that the families could enroll their children at the school of their liking. To Friedman, this proposal had clear advantages, uniting two different notions: (I) that the parents or guardians of a child would have legitimate and ample right to define, with absolute priority, the kind of education given to their children, respecting a minimum common curriculum determined by the State; (II) and that the educational service could, through mercantilization and competition mediated by the State's financing, improve in variety and quality, given that it would be possible to choose the best private facility (Friedman, 1955: pp. 4–5).

One last relevant aspect of the change in the complementary social-assistance daycare policy is in the use of the presidential devolution powers. According to Abrucio and others (2020), devolution powers are decentralizations done by the central government to subnational entities without there being articulation and integration between the different entities of the federation. This technique, which can generate inequality, was applied by the president in the fight against the COVID-19 pandemic (Abrucio et al., 2020) and it also seems to be present in the federal decision to decrease funding for public daycare. Although the law places the Citizen Child Aid as complementary and declares that establishing it does not mean authorization for subnational governments to not expand the public daycare network, the critical defunding of municipalities, along with the lack of centrality of daycares in the investment agenda, suggests that the goal was private expansion mediated by public financing. However, due to the timing of the whole process, the Citizen Child Aid, although foreseen by the law, had no feasible time for implementation and was formally extinct with the relaunch of the Family Grant program, already under Lula's government. In our case, non-implementation makes no difference to the argument since, if Bolsonaro had emerged victorious at the polls in 2022, this project would probably have its implementation guaranteed.

In 2022, after the approval of Brazil Aid and the ending of the federal transfers of Affectionate Brazil, the government launched the program More Employments for Women and for the Youth (Emprega + Mulheres e Jovens), destined to expand employment for women and youth. With that Provisional Measure, guardians of children from zero to 3 years of age were authorized to withdraw funds from the individual Length-of-Service Guarantee Fund (FGTS[6]) with the goal of funding private daycare facilities (*Provisional Measure 1.116 of May 4th, 2022*). Thus, workers would be able to count on extra resources – created through the defunding of a system meant for protection at the moment of dismissal – to fund the private sector, reinforcing the mercantilizing character of the daycare policy. Reinforcing the dual character, the families would be in three groups: (I) families that receive Brazil Aid and are eligible for Citizen Child; (II) families with formally employed guardians that can withdraw money to pay for daycare; and (III) a mass of people who are not targeted by either benefit, and must seek public openings – which will probably become scarce due to defunding – pay for private daycare with their own resources, or use support network within the family for childcare. However, the proposal for the use of FGTS for funding private daycare was rejected in the Chamber of Deputies.

Summarizing, the federal government's complementary daycare policy creates an assistance-based, familistic, mercantilizing reversion for the matter. The input for social assistance has been essential over the last few years as a complement for education to move forward and reach the National Plan for Education, which envisages 50% of children from 0 to 3 years old in daycare and, as already seen, there have been only 3.9 million enrollments. The view created by the policy is one where the family must be the child's main caregiver, and that in their absence, the most efficient caregiver would be the Market, through contracting services in the private sector. The end of Affectionate Brazil and the beginning of Brazil Aid show how the ideas of academics belonging to the neoliberalism-neoconservatism alliance were strong in the federal government's agenda. Additionally, it shows how the Executive can use the weapons available such as provisional measures and resource contingency to push its agenda within the legislative power as well as use its power of inducing subnational entities toward specific behavior.

Final considerations

The research highlighted how the Bolsonaro government reinforced neoconservative and liberal values with the use of tools that go beyond dismantling by default. The change in arena caused by the appearance of the Ministry of Women, Family, and Human Rights, which began defining family policies through the traditionalist bias of its agents; the creation of a National Strategy for the Strengthening of Family Bonds, which removed part of the decisive power of the instances for participation and deliberation of SUAS by proposing changes to the social-assistance services, creating parallel structures that were non-participative and non-aligned, as well as concurrent to the existing ones; and the active dismantling of one of the social-assistance income transfer policies for public daycare facilities that are complementary to the actions of Education.

In this work, we argued that Bolsonaro's far-right ideology caused a redefinition in family policies that reinforced the State's subsidiarity and supported a traditionalist view of family. Jair Bolsonaro's government's actions in the daycare policies were characterized by at least three major factors: (I) mercantilization and (II) familialization of childcare policies; and (III) resorting to devolution powers and to decreasing the power of the federal government to induce the policy's expansion. To reach that goal, the government used the broad normative power the Presidency of the Republic holds to carry out active dismantling strategies, changes in arena, and the continuance of a process of dismantling by default.

However, we do not want to reduce the discussion here to this idea of commodification, as what happened here is much broader and goes beyond this concept. The early childhood education sector, with this type of state funding, would be reorganized in this direction. But the symbolic scope here is different, as it met a need to moralize early childhood education, which is the focus of religious criticism of secular public education. It is part of a symbolic set of strategies to spread disinformation through fake news, as can be seen in the chapter on disinformation and democracy. Like, for example, stating that the PT would distribute gay kits in schools and had manufactured dick bottles (see Chapter 5). It is more than commodification, it is conservatism and familism to reinforce traditional gender roles.

In the face of the observation that in the end the ACC was not implemented, it could be argued that the changes were not in depth. However, these changes are strongly symbolic of the reinforcement of the traditional family and of the transferring of certain responsibilities from the state to the market. In a context in which Bolsonarism is still an important force within the Legislative Power – Bolsonaro's party, Partido Liberal (Liberal Party), even in the new legislature has the largest bench at the Chamber of Deputies – and in which a growing number of Brazilians identify with the right-wing political spectrum, it is possible that there would still be constraints on policies targeted at sexual and gender minorities, as well as at non-traditional family arrangements, or policies boosting the profiting private sector at the expense of dismantling the public sector.

Notes

1 Penna was granted with scholarships by Fundação de Amparo à Pesquisa de Minas Gerais and Konrad Adenauer Stiftung, this study resulted from that.
2 The Affectionate Brazil program is part of the Brazil without Privation program, flagship of president Rousseff's Social Assistance.
3 A provisional measure is a type of temporary legal act enacted by the Executive branch that carries the status of an ordinary Statute. It must be approved by the National Congress within sixty days, or it loses its efficacy (*Constitution of the Federative Republic of Brazil of 1988*).
4 Available at www.gov.br/inep/pt-br/areas-de-atuacao/pesquisas-estatisticas-e-indi cadores/censo-escolar/resultados/2022 (Accessed 9 November 2023)
5 The Brazil Aid program is the conditional cash transfer program that replaced Family Grant between November 2021 and December 2022; see Chapter 10.
6 FGTS is a governmental fund that aims to compensate formally employed workers in case of severance.

References

Abrão, K. C. L. and Mioto, R. C. T. (2017) 'Políticas familiares: Uma introdução ao debate contemporâneo', *Revista Katálysis*, 20, pp. 420–429. doi: https://doi.org/10.1590/1982-02592017v20n3p420

Abrucio, F. L. et al. (2020) 'Combate à COVID-19 sob o federalismo bolsonarista: Um caso de descoordenação intergovernamental', *Revista de Administração Pública*, 54(4), pp. 663–677.

Arretche, M. (2004) 'Federalismo e políticas sociais no Brasil: Problemas de coordenação e autonomia', *São Paulo em Perspectiva*, 18(2), pp. 17–26.

Barrientos, A. (2008) 'Latin America: Towards a liberal-informal welfare regime' in Gough, I. and Wood, G. (eds.) *Insecurity and welfare regimes in Asia, Africa and Latin America: Social policy in development contexts*. Cambridge: Cambridge University Press, pp. 121–168.

Bedritichuk, R. and Araújo, S. (2012) 'Fortalecimento das comissões mistas: Poder de barganha e desgaste na coalizão a partir de 2012' in Perlin, G. and Santos, M. (eds.) *Presidencialismo de coalizão em movimento*. Brasília: Câmara dos Deputados, pp. 61–88.

Biroli, F., Machado, M. and Vaggione, J. (2020) 'Introdução: Matrizes do neoconservadorismo religioso na América Latina' in Biroli, F., Machado, M. and Vaggione, J. (eds.) *Gênero, neoconservadorismo e democracia*. São Paulo: Boitempo, pp. 13–40.

Biroli, F. and Quintela, D. (2021) 'Mulheres e direitos humanos sob a ideologia da defesa da família' in Avritzer, L., Kerche, F. and Marona, M. (eds.) *Governo Bolsonaro: Retrocesso Democrático e Degradação Política*. Belo Horizonte: Autêntica, pp. 343–358.

Brown, W. (2006) 'American nightmare: neoliberalism, neoconservatism and de democratization', *Political Theory*, 34(6), pp. 690–714.

Brown, W. (2015) *Undoing the demos: Neoliberalism's stealth revolution*. New York: Zone Books.

Brown, W. (2019) *In the ruins of neoliberalism: The rise of antidemocratic politics in the West*. New York: Columbia University Press.

Caram, B. (2019) 'PEC de Guedes desobriga poder público de construir escolas', *Folha de São Paulo*, 14 Nov. Available at: www1.folha.uol.com.br/mercado/2019/11/pec-de-bolsonaro-e-guedes-desobriga-poder-publico-de-construir-escolas.shtml (Accessed 21 July 2022).

Ciccia, R. and Lombardo, E. (2019) 'Care policies in practice: How discourse matters for policy implementation', *Policy and Society*, 38(4), pp. 537–553.

Concern Worldwide and Oxfam. (2011) *Walking the talk: Cash transfers and gender dynamics*. Dublin: Concern Worldwide and Oxfam.

Conselho Nacional de Assistência Social [National Council for Social Assistance] (2009). *Tipificação Nacional dos Serviços Socioassistenciais*. Brasília: Conselho Nacional de Assistência Social. Available at: www.mds.gov.br/webarquivos/publicacao/assistencia_social/Normativas/ tipificacao.pdf (Accessed 25 February 2023).

Constitution of the Federative Republic of Brazil of 1988 (1988). Available at: www.planalto.gov.br/ccivil_03/constituicao/constituicaocompilado.htm (Accessed 9 November 2023).

Constitutional Amendment 53 of December 19th, 2006 (2006). Available at: www.planalto.gov.br/ccivil_03/constituicao/emendas/emc/emc53.htm (Accessed 22 May 2023).

Cooper, M. (2017) *Family values: Between neoliberalism and the new social conservatism*. New York: Zone Books.

Cruz, M. (2017) *Implementação da política de creches nos municípios brasileiros após 1988: avanços e desafios nas relações intergovernamentais e intersetoriais*. PhD Thesis. Fundação Getúlio Vargas.

Cruz, M., Farah, M. and Sugiyama, N. (2014) 'Normatizações federais e a oferta de matrículas em creches no Brasil', *Estudos em Avaliação Educacional*, 25(59), pp. 202–241.

Daly, M. (2020) 'Conceptualizing and analyzing family policy and how it is changing' in Nieuwenhuis, R. and Van Lancker, W. (eds.) *The Palgrave handbook of family policy*. Cham: Palgrave Macmillan, pp. 25–41.

Downs, A. (1957) *An economic theory of democracy*. New York: Harper e Row.

Dykstra, P. and Djundeva, M. (2020) 'Policies for later-life families in a comparative european perspective' in Nieuwenhuis, R. and Van Lancker, W. (eds.) *The Palgrave handbook of family policy*. Cham: Palgrave Macmillan, pp. 331–367.

Ennser-Jedenastik, L. (2022) 'The impact of radical right parties on family benefits', *West European Politics*, 45(1), pp. 154–176.

Executive Order 10.570 of 9th December, 2020. Available at: www.planalto.gov.br/ccivil_03/_ato2019-2022/2020/decreto/D10570.htm (Accessed 15 June 2022).

Eydal, G. and Rostgaard, T. (2018) 'Introduction to the Handbook of family policy' in Eydal, G. and Rostgaard, T. (eds.) *Handbook of family policy*. Cheltenham: Edward Elgar, pp. 2–9.

Franzoni, J. and Voorend, K. (2009) *Sistemas de patriarcado y regímenes de bienestar en América Latina ¿Una cosa lleva a la otra? Documento de trabajo no 37*. Madrid: Fundación Carolina.

Friedman, M. (1955) 'The role of government in education' in Solo, R. (ed.), *Economics and the public interest*. New Brunswick: Rutgers University Press, pp. 123–144.

Gough, I. (2008) 'Welfare regimes in development contexts: A global and regional analysis' in Gough, I. and Wood, G. (eds.) *Insecurity and welfare regimes in Asia, Africa and Latin America: Social policy in development contexts.* Cambridge: Cambridge University Press, pp. 15–48.

Gugliano, M. (2020) ' "Vamos ensinar uma mãe a ser mãe," diz Damares Alves sobre mudança no Bolsa Família', *Valor Econômico*, 7 fev. Available at: https://valor.globo.com/eu-e/noticia/2020/02/07/vamos-ensinar-uma-mae-a-ser-mae-diz-damares-alves-sobre-mudanca-no-bolsa-familia.ghtml (Accessed 7 Mars 2023).

Instituto Nacional de Estudos e Pesquisas Educacionais Anísio Teixeira [Anísio Teixeira Institute for Research and Studies in Education (2022) *Microdata of the 2022 Educational Census.* Available at: www.gov.br/inep/pt-br/areas-de-atuacao/pesquisas-estatisticas-e-indicadores/censo-escolar/resultados/2022 (Accessed 9 November 2023).

Lacerda, M. (2019) *O novo conservadorismo brasileiro: de Reagan a Bolsonaro.* Porto Alegre: Zouk.

Leitner, S. (2003) 'Varieties of familialism: The caring function of the family in comparative perspective', *European Societies*, 5(4), pp. 353–375.

Limongi, F. and Figueiredo, A. (2001) *Executivo e legislativo na nova ordem constitucional.* 2nd edn. Rio de Janeiro: Editora FGV.

Lohmann, H. and Zagel, H. (2016) 'Family policy in comparative perspective: The concepts and measurement of familization and defamilization', *Journal of European Social Policy*, 26(1), pp. 48–65.

Moura, M. and Corbellini, J. (2019) *A eleição disruptiva: Por que Bolsonaro venceu.* São Paulo: Record.

Pires, B. (2018) ' "Vouchers," ensino à distância e universidade paga, os planos na mesa de Bolsonaro', El País, 5 nov. Available at: https://brasil.elpais.com/brasil/2018/11/01/politica/1541111385_565042.html. (Accessed 21 July 2022).

Provisional Measure 1.061 of August 9th, 2021 (2021). Available at: www.planalto.gov.br/ccivil_03/_ato2019-2022/2021/Mpv/mpv1061impressao.htm (Accessed 21 July 2022).

Provisional Measure 1.116 of May 4th, 2022 (2022). Available at www.planalto.gov.br/ccivil_03/_ato2019-2022/2022/mpv/mpv1116.htm (Accessed 10 Mars 2023).

Provisional Measure 570 of 14th May, 2012 (2012). Available at: www.planalto.gov.br/ccivil_03/_ato2011-2014/2012/Mpv/570.htmimpress %C3%A3o.htm (Accessed 21 July 2022).

Quadros, M. and Madeira, R. (2018) 'Fim da direita envergonhada? Atuação da bancada evangélica e da bancada da bala e os caminhos da representação do conservadorismo no Brasil', *Opinião Pública*, 24(3), pp. 486–522.

Robilla, M. (2014) 'Introduction' in Robilla, M. (ed.) *Handbook of family policies across the globe.* Nova York: Springer, pp. 3–11.

Rocha, C. (2021) *Menos Marx, mais Mises: o liberalismo e a nova direita no Brasil.* São Paulo: Todavia.

Saraceno, C. and Keck, W. (2010) 'Can we identify intergenerational policy regimes in Europe?', *European Societies*, 12(5), pp. 675–696.

Sátyro. N. and Midaglia, C. (2021) 'Family policies in Latin American countries: Re-enforcing familialism' in Sátyro, N., Del Pino, E. and Midaglia, C. (eds.) *Latin American social policy developments in the twenty-first century.* Cham: Palgrave Macmillan, pp. 287–314.

Scheel, I., Scheel, A. and Fretheim, A. (2020) 'The moral perils of conditional cash transfer programmes and their significance for policy: A meta-ethnography of the ethical debate', *Health Policy And Planning*, 35(6), pp. 718–734.

Secretaria Nacional da Família [National Secretary for Family] (2021a). *White Paper 147/2021/DEFDFF/SNF/MMFDH*. Brasília: Secretaria Nacional da Família.

Secretaria Nacional da Família [National Secretary for Family] (2021b). *White Paper 175/2021/DEFDFF/SNF/MMFDH*. Brasília: Secretaria Nacional da Família, 2021b.

Secretaria Nacional de Atenção à Primeira Infância [National Secretary for Early Childhood Care] (2020). *White Paper 75/2020*. Brasília: Secretária Nacional da Primeira Infância.

Secretaria Nacional de Atenção à Primeira Infância [National Secretary for Early Childhood Care] (2021). *White Paper 22/2021*. Brasília: Secretária Nacional da Primeira Infância.

Statute 9.394 of December 20th, 1996 (1996). Available at www.planalto.gov.br/ccivil_03/leis/l9394.htm (Accessed 21 July 2022).

Statute 12.722 of October 3rd, 2012 (2012). Available at: www.planalto.gov.br/ccivil_03/_ato2011-2014/2012/Lei/L12722.htm (Accessed 21 July 2022).

Statute 13.844 of June 18th, 2019 (2019). Available at: www.planalto.gov.br/ccivil_03/_Ato2019-2022/2019/Lei/L13844.htm (Accessed 09 November 2023).

Statute 14.284 of December 29th, 2021 (2021). Available at: www.planalto.gov.br/ccivil_03/_ato2019-2022/2021/Lei/L14284.htm (Accessed 21 July 2022).

Teixeira, P. and Henriques, A. (2022) 'O novo conservadorismo brasileiro e a educação: Mapeando suas linhas de força', *Arquivos Analíticos de Políticas Educativas*, 30(89), pp. 1–21.

Todos pela Educação Institute (2021) *Anuário Estatístico da Educação Básica 2021*. São Paulo: Todos pela Educação.

13

LABOR MARKET FROM 2015 TO 2022

Heightened risks and dismantling policies

Regina Coeli Moreira Camargos and
Pedro M. R. Barbosa

13.1 Introduction

Analyses of welfare states have traditionally stressed their role in ensuring protection against market-based risks, such as unemployment, as well as in amortizing market-generated allocative failures in terms of social inequality and poverty. Over the past three decades, however, structural transformations have presented new challenges in managing social risks. These transformations include the transition from the industrial economy to a knowledge-based service economy in affluent countries, demographic aging, gender and family changes, and instability of the labor market. Facing these new challenges, welfare states have adjusted social policies in order to address new goals: improving average worker earnings and creating new jobs (Kenworthy, 2010; Hemerijck, 2013).

In this sense, labor market policies have taken center stage in contemporary welfare state research. Nonetheless, the emphasis on a given labor market policy varies across different approaches. The "social investment perspective" assumes that labor market deregulation reforms are inexorable, given the greater pressure for economic competitiveness brought about by economic globalization (Crouch, 2017). Hence, it stresses the role of active policies – specifically training programs and other capacitating initiatives – focusing on enhancing labor force skills as a means of fostering higher levels of employability and better jobs (Hemerijck, 2013). Another approach advocates, in turn, direct public job creation as a manner of restoring more stable employment relations and expanding public services. This strategy aims to promote public consumption

DOI: 10.4324/9781003487777-16

over private consumption, enabling an economic structure more friendly to today's environmental demands (Gough, 2021; Kerstenetzky, 2021).

In the wake of this emerging agenda in welfare states research, this chapter describes labor market policy changes in Brazil between 2015 and 2022. Following the general hypothesis underlying this book regarding the retrenchment of the Brazilian welfare state, we discuss whether a dismantling process took place in this policy area.

First, we briefly trace past trends in the institutional development of labor market policy in Brazil. Doing so allows us to contrast the legacy of this policy with the changes enacted since 2015. The periodization adopted in this analysis follows the framework proposed by Arretche, Marques, and Faria (2019). They claim that, notwithstanding disagreements in economic management, institutional development of public policies throughout Brazilian Social Democratic Party (PSDB, per its Portuguese name) (1995–2002) and Worker's Party (PT, per its Portuguese name) (2003–2014) governments were characterized by an incremental rather than a disruptive process.

Secondly, this chapter focuses on the changes in four subfields of labor market policy between 2015 and 2022. These subfields include labor market regulation, minimum wage policy, passive policies, and active policies. We then examine the trajectory of labor market outcomes, encompassing occupational quality, unemployment levels, and income inequality.

Finally, we provide an assessment of changes in labor market policies regarding the issue of retrenchment. As previously discussed in this book, the debate on the extent to which policy changes imply retrenchment is not trivial. In this sense, Bauer and Knill (2014) offer a more comprehensive approach to the understanding of this phenomenon, distinguishing changes in density – regulatory penetration – and intensity – the scope of policies and the number of instruments applied. We also include the social demand dimension in this analysis, underlining the qualitative difference when labor market policies are dismantled under a context of high unemployment.

Overall, we contend that the main changes implemented between 2015 and 2022 pursued the dismantling of labor market policy in Brazil by means of the implementation of an austerity plan, deregulation reform, suspension of the minimum wage valorization policy, and the dismantling or neglect of both active and passive policies. Moreover, we consider that the government of Michel Temer (from May 2016 to December 2018) undertook the most extensive dismantling of the labor market policy, combining a decrease in density and intensity, under an environment of high demand for social protection. Rousseff (in her unfinished second term, from January 2015 until mid-2016) and Bolsonaro (from 2019 to 2022), in turn, promoted especially a decline in policy intensity.

13.2 The legacy of labor market policy in Brazil: a brief overview (1930–2014)

The first government of Getúlio Vargas (1930–1945) is commonly acknowledged in the literature as a critical juncture of the working-class political incorporation, marking the emergence of the Brazilian Welfare State (Collier and Collier, 1991; Draibe and Riesco, 2007). During this period, the regulatory institutions for capital-labor relations and social safety net were established, and to some extent they have persisted until the present day.

In the aftermath of urbanization and industrialization processes, Vargas established a corporatist model of labor relations. This model introduced a new political and social pact that arose following the so-called Revolution of 1930, which marked a departure from the intra-oligarchic competition era (1889–1930). In contrast to the European corporatist model, which emerged from bottom-up pressures, the Brazilian model – along with other Latin American countries, particularly Argentina, Chile, and Mexico – was enacted from top-down decision-making, wherein interest organizations of capital and labor were somewhat subordinate to the State, given the authoritarian environment (Diniz and Boschi, 1991; Cardoso and Gindin, 2008).

The key components of the Brazilian corporatist model included the creation of the Ministry of Labor; the Work Permit – a document verifying eligibility for labor rights; the Labor Court, a specialized body of the Judiciary to solve capital and labor disputes; the social security system; the formation of a state-controlled union structure; the meticulous regulation of general wage labor conditions; and the introduction of the first minimum wage law. Vargas launched the Consolidation of Labor Legislation (CLT, per its Portuguese name) in 1943, by bringing together a set of fragmented legislations enacted in the 1930s (and even before), thus integrating the Brazilian corporatist model of labor regulation.

Vargas' institutional legacy persisted, despite the political and economic turmoil throughout the twentieth century. Although undergoing significant changes over its 80-year history, the CLT remained a major real and symbolic benchmark for Brazilian workers. The resilience of the CLT in the face of varied historical, social, and political circumstances can be attributed to two quite ambiguous factors. From the employees' point of view, considering the unequal and heterogeneous nature of the Brazilian labor market, the CLT grants fundamental rights to a significant portion of the labor force. From the employers' point of view, it exerts a level of control over the working class by imposing certain restrictions on their right to organize and engage in collective action.

Even during the authoritarian regime (1964–1985), right-wing civil-military governments largely preserved Vargas' legacy. Furthermore, in this period, they launched key labor market policy instruments, such as the General Register of Employed and Unemployed (CAGED),[1] in 1965 – which is an important database on the formal labor market – and the National Employment System[2] (SINE), in 1975, which promotes labor intermediation (Silva, 2021).

Amid the transition to democracy, the new Federal Constitution of 1988 repealed many elements of the original CLT restrictions regarding restricted union organization freedom, as well as other prescriptions enacted during the authoritarian regime. In this way, the original corporatist arrangement, with a more authoritarian bias, was greatly modified, in line with the country's redemocratization process. The Constitution also broadened the scope of labor rights, categorizing them as fundamental and irreducible, while specifying the funding sources for unemployment insurance and social security. It enabled the foundation of the Workers' Support Fund[3] (FAT), in 1990, as a component of the social security budget, but which centralizes resources offunding for financing unemployment insurance, wage subsidy, other passive and active labor market policies. The FAT is funded by company contributions to the Social Integration Program (PIS) and Public Servants' Equity Formation Program (Pasep) (Silva, 2021).

Whereas Brazilian democratization prompted the expansion of social and labor rights on the domestic level, from 1985 on, neoliberalism ideology and agenda increased influence on a global scale, encouraging pro-market reforms including cuts in welfare provisions or even privatization of social security. In the 1990s, in several Latin American countries, the economic instability induced by the external debt crisis and the superinflation facilitated the election of many governments committed to austerity plans and pro-market reforms, reducing the role of the state.

In Brazil, the implementation of the neoliberal agenda began during the government of Fernando Collor de Mello (1990–1992), who was the first directly elected civil president following the authoritarian regime. However, surrounded by a political crisis, Collor lost parliamentary support and failed to achieve most of the neoliberal reforms proposed in his government program, such as the privatization of the Social Security and the replacement of Vargas' labor relations model by another, closer to the Anglo-Saxon contractualist tradition (Roberts, 2013; Huber and Stephens, 2012).

Collor de Mello was impeached in September 1992 and succeeded by Itamar Franco (the vice-president) who governed until December 1994. From the beginning of 1995, the new elected president, Fernando Henrique Cardoso (1995–2002), although member of the PSDB, embraced some aspects of the neoliberal economic agenda. However, he did not promote a drastic rollback in the realm of social and labor policies, despite being a staunch critic of Vargas' legacy. Cardoso enjoyed strong parliamentary support and then successfully implemented liberal reforms such as privatizations, lower taxes for corporations and the wealthy, and the flexibilization of some aspects of Vargas' labor legislation (Huber and Stephens, 2012; Roberts, 2013).

Cook (1998) draws a comparative typology of labor reforms implemented in Latin America in the 1990s, based on three categories: (a) *flexible changes*, which are reforms that deregulate the labor market and reduce labor costs for firms; (b) *liberal changes*, which remove the state from the regulation of capital-labor relations, encourage pluralism as opposed to the monopoly of representation found in corporatist systems, and promote the primacy of collective bargaining over state regulation of labor relations; and (c) *protective changes*, which expand public policies for the unemployed.

According to the author, Cardoso's reforms combined flexible, liberal, and protective elements. On the one hand, an attempt was made to turn important aspects of the labor relations more flexible, such as working hours regulation. In the liberal direction, wage adjustments became entirely reliant on collective bargaining, and companies could hire employees through work cooperatives without establishing formal employment relations, exempting companies from complying with the labor rights guaranteed by the CLT and regular employees' collective agreements.[4] In the protective direction; public spending and coverage of passive policies were enlarged, mainly unemployment insurance, amid a sharp rise in unemployment in the late 1990s. In addition, the government expanded active labor market policies by introducing the National Plan for Worker Qualification (PLANFOR), in 1995, which aimed at promoting training and qualification programs for workers (Cardoso, Façanha and Marinho, 2002; Cardoso Jr. and Gonzalez, 2007).

Between 2003 and 2014, governments of PT pursued policies that diverged not only from the PSDB agenda but also from the trend of labor market flexibility reforms witnessed in Europe in the 2000s. Instead, they moved towards greater labor market regulation that correlated with an increase in formal employment. While economic growth played a crucial role in expanding formal employment between 2004 and 2014, it was not the sole factor, as, during the 1990s, economic growth increased along with informality (Kerstenetzky, 2017; 2019).

Scholars note that the expansion of formal employment also resulted in several measures adopted by the PT governments to strengthen state regulation of the labor market. These measures included bolstering institutions for monitoring working conditions and enacting laws that extended labor and social security rights to self-employed and domestic workers (Neri and Fontes, 2010; Alejo and Parada, 2017). Within labor market policies, increasing the minimum wage stands out as a pivotal instrument in reducing social and wage inequalities from 2002 to 2014. Studies have also demonstrated a decrease in gender and racial wage disparities during this period (Brito, Foguel and Kerstenetzky, 2017; Arretche, 2018).

However, like in many Latin American countries during this period, the significant improvement in workers' social welfare was not accompanied by a significant change in the labor market's main features (Palma, 2011; Abramo, Cecchini and Morales, 2019). These features include the prevalence of low-skilled formal jobs across most economic sectors, a consistently low average labor income that closely mirrors the minimum wage, and elevated rates of turnover and informality (up to 40% of the occupied labor force, even after some reduction trend).

These enduring labor market features can be attributed to a variety of factors that took place over the last four decades: the early deindustrialization; the weak introduction of productive innovation of higher technological content; the expansion of the Service sector based on low productivity standards; and the increasing share of agribusiness and extractive industry in the Gross National Product (Palma, 2011).

13.2.1 Minimum wage policy

As previously stated, the PT governments pursued a policy of raising the real minimum wage. It is worth noting that regulatory changes occurred in this policy throughout this period. During the first Lula administration, between 2003 and 2006, minimum wage adjustments were determined without a pre-defined criterion. In 2007, in turn, the government and trade unions signed a Protocol of Intentions that agreed on a minimum wage increase in April 2007 based on the accumulated inflation since the previous adjustment (3.3%) and the economic growth rate occurred two years before, in 2005 (5.1%). The Protocol defined, as well, the anticipation of the date of new adjustments, one month each year, until it was fixed in January, from 2010 on.

Until January 2011, at the very beginning of Rousseff's first term, the minimum wage was adjusted through a series of Provisional Measures issued by the Presidency of the Republic, based on the Protocol's criteria. In February 2011, the National Congress approved the Project of Law on Minimum Wage Valorization, which was contained in Law 12.382/2011. The policy should be in effect until 2023, but depending on the approval of a new law, each four years. In January 2015, in Rousseff's second term, the National Congress renewed the Minimum Wage Policy for another four years, extending it until January 2019, enacting Law 13.152/2015.

As can be seen in Figure 13.1, after the rise of the Temer government in May 2016, the minimum wage experienced no real increase, in January 2017 and 2018, reflecting the economic recession in 2015–2016 and the deepening of austerity plan. Since the level of social security benefits is tied to the value of the minimum wage, the appreciation policy requires, consequently, the expansion of nominal public spending, which was constrained, in turn, by the austerity plan.

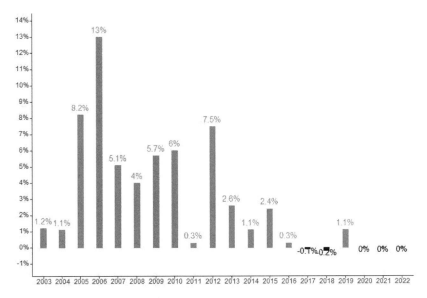

FIGURE 13.1   Minimum wage valuation across governments in Brazil, 2003–2022.

Source: Author's elaboration based on DIEESE

In January 2019, the minimum wage obtained the last adjustment in line with the criteria established in 2011 and 2015, with a real increase of just 1.1%, due to the slight economic recovery in 2017. President-elected Jair Bolsonaro was expected to submit a new bill to Congress to define the criteria for adjusting the minimum wage until January 2023. In a departure from the previous policy, he chose not to submit the renewal of the minimum wage law to Congress and discontinued the policy of real minimum wage appreciation. From January 2020 to January 2023, the minimum wage was adjusted only according to the inflation rate.

As shown in Figure 13.1, an evaluation of the whole period in which the minimum wage valorization policy was in effect, from April 2002 (the last adjustment in Cardoso's government) until January 2019 (the last adjustment based on its criteria), reveals that the minimum wage had a real increase (above inflation) of 78.51%.

13.3   The rise of the conservative coalition and the ultra-right (2016–2022)

In terms of labor market policies, we assert that a rupture with the PSDB (1995–2002) and PT (2003–2014) government policies began to take place in the ephemeral Dilma Rousseff's second term, from January 2015 to May 2016, and was deepened in Temer (May 2016 to December 2018) and Bolsonaro's (2019–2022) governments.

Rousseff had been reelected in November 2014 under seriously challenging circumstances: i) her victory over the opponent was the narrowest since re-democratization; ii) Rousseff clashed with the Chamber President whose party (Democratic Movement Party, PMDB) was part of the government coalition; iii) the PT's parliamentary representation suffered a sharp reduction in the number of votes cast; iv) the so-called Operation Car Wash, coordinated by the Federal Public Prosecutor's Office and organs of the Judiciary, unleashed an offensive against alleged cases of corruption involving the government; iv) above all, a severe economic crisis arose by mid-2014 on, as a late consequence of the international economic and financial crisis started in 2008 and the end of the global commodities valorization cycle that favored Brazilian economy in the previous years.

Facing political isolation, Rousseff endeavored to retain the support of economic agents and appointed Joaquim Levy as the Minister of Finance, an individual with ties to the financial market committed to a fiscal austerity agenda, in strong contradiction with the president's reelection platform. While leading to an intense fall in her popularity and severe criticism from her own party, the message to the business community and the financial market was insufficient to prevent her demise, and thus she was impeached in May 2016[5] amid an escalating economic crisis (Singer, 2018; Santos and Tanscheit, 2019).

With the rise of his vice-president Temer, the government was recomposed by the PMDB's alliance with the PSDB, throwing the left out of government and forming a conservative coalition. In contrast to the failed neoliberal reform attempts of the 1990s, especially by Fernando Collor, Temer effectively implemented the most comprehensive neoliberal reform since re-democratization. To this outcome contributed the establishment of a strong parliamentary base, as well as the absence of re-election aims. The latter neutralized the dynamics of blame avoidance, a common mechanism in democracies that constraints attempts at retrenchments (Pierson, 1994). The unpopularity of these reforms was evident, given that the government ended with only 7% popular approval (Datafolha, 2019), the lowest since re-democratization.

13.3.1 The regulation of employment: the 2017 Labor Reform

One of the pillars of the Temer government's neoliberal policy was the 2017 labor reform, which entailed a greater removal of the state from labor relations regulation and a partial break with the Vargas corporative model. This reform, approved in July 2017 to take effect from the following November, followed the guidelines of reforms carried out in several European countries. The law no longer serves as the minimum benchmark for rights, and the institutions responsible for regulating, mediating, and resolving conflicts have been either depleted or abolished (Boltanski and Chiapello, 2009; Freyssinet, 2010).

Among the main changes in labor regulation promoted by Law 13.467/ 2017 are: 1) prevalence of negotiation over the infraconstitucional law; 2) prevalence of collective agreements signed at the companies level over sector collective bargaining agreements, including to establish less favorable working conditions; 3) elimination of compulsory union contributions (so called Union Tax), making them conditional on the worker's prior and express permission; 4) strict limitations on the Labor Courts' normative and hermeneutic power; 5) prohibition of automatic extension (ultrativity) of agreements and conventions beyond their term of validity until the entry into effect of a new collective instrument; 6) encouragement of individual bargaining on critical areas of working conditions, such as working hours (length, compensation, and breaks) and remuneration; and 7) encouragement of individual negotiation for workers with higher education and higher salaries (equal to or greater than twice the highest benefit paid by the General Social Security System-RGPS).

The 2017 labor reform had a profound impact on trade union collective action, affecting its structural, institutional, and organizational aspects, as described by Lehndorff, Dribbush and Schulten (2017), significantly diminishing union power in collective bargaining. The prevalence of negotiating over the law, even to establish less favorable working conditions, compelled unions to accept less advantageous agreements.[6] Moreover, the prohibition of automatic extension of collective agreements after their expiration poses a risk of losing rights if negotiations are not promptly concluded. The encouragement of individual negotiation for working conditions further separates trade unions from the process of collective bargaining. The labor reform also impacted the institutional dimension of union power, which concerns the extent of state enforcement. Additionally, the reform changed the organizational dimension of trade union power, precisely involving financial sustainability and union density rates. Before the reform, the union structure relied on a compulsory contribution of one-day's wage deducted from all workers each year (so-called Union Tax). However, the reform made this funding voluntary, requiring the prior and explicit approval of workers for its deduction.

Costa (2018) contends that labor reforms and fiscal austerity policies diminish union strength and reshape the role of labor in the economy. Labor relations and their actors – primarily trade unions – are their preferred targets. The weakening of union power is one of the pillars of the labor reforms implemented in several countries around the world since the 2008 crisis. Union reaction against austerity policies and labor reforms, he said, depends on several aspects, including its representativeness and financial independence. Union representativeness, itself, is an outcome of various factors, especially the extent to which collective agreements cover the labor force and the density of the organization in the workplace.

Given the high degree of informality underlying the labor market structure in Brazil, collective bargaining coverage has traditionally been low, at about less than 50 percent of the labor force. In addition, significant turnover hampers improvement in working conditions, even for workers covered by collective agreements. The extension of the economic crisis exacerbates the deterioration of labor market conditions, leading to an increase in informality and underemployment and, as a result, a reduction in the collective bargaining coverage. At the same time, due to the proliferation of non-regular contracts induced by the 2017 labor reform, turnover in the labor market is likely to increase, leading to a decline in the union density rate in Brazil.

13.3.2 Passive labor market policies

Labor market policies are conventionally distinguished into two broad categories: passives and actives. While the former attempt to safeguard workers outside the labor market – unemployment insurance and other forms of cash transfers to jobless workers – the latter aim to promote their reintegration into the labor market (Kenworthy, 2010). In this section, we trace the trajectory of passive policies focusing on unemployment insurance.[7]

It is worth noting that another pillar of the Temer administration's agenda was the New Fiscal Regime (NFR), which set a 20-year constraint on the growth of federal primary expenditure, mainly encompassing social expenditures (including unemployment benefits), with only inflation adjustments allowed. As a consequence, NFR resulted in a reduction of social spending both in relation to GDP and in terms of population size adequacy (Rossi and Dweck, 2016). This has led scholars to argue that the NFR drove the Brazilian welfare state into a retrenchment process (Paiva et al., 2016; Sátyro, 2021).

Elected in 2018, Bolsonaro's government followed Temer's pro-market reform agenda, promoting a comprehensive reform of the Social Security system, in 2019. Nevertheless, Bolsonaro did not really pursue an austerity plan, as he transferred to the legislative branch part of the executive's budget execution prerogatives, through mainly the so-called rapporteur's amendments, in order to hold a majority of parliament and halt more than one hundred impeachment demands in the face of mounting allegations against him and his family (Tanscheit and Barbosa, 2023). Yet, while the NFR did not address the resources allocated to such amendments, it continued to constrain social spending (Vieira, 2021).

Empirical studies on Latin American countries consistently indicate a correlation between rises in the unemployment rate and growth in social spending, which is mostly explained by increases in spending on passive labor markets policies, such as social assistance and unemployment insurance

(Avelino, Brown and Hunter, 2005; Mayoral and Nabernegg, 2014). However, Brazil has not followed this pattern during the two recent major exogenous shocks.

During the peak of the economic crisis, amid the transition from the Rousseff to the Temer government, unemployment climbed from 6.8 million people in 2014 to 13.3 in 2018 (Figure 13.1). Even though unemployment insurance spending is mandatory, as established by the Constitution, and thus less subject to a fiscal restriction (Silva, 2021), overall public spending (2015 constant values) on this item declined from 44 billion BRL to 38 billion BRL during this period. Spending per unemployed person fell from 6,554 BRL in 2014 to 2,200 BRL (2015 constant values) in 2021.[8] This sharp drop in spending per unemployed person is related to the fall in unemployment insurance coverage amid the climb in unemployment (Figure 13.2).

Faced with the pandemic shock, the number of unemployed increased from 12.8 million to 13.8 million between 2019 and 2021 under the Bolsonaro government. Once again, total unemployment insurance spending declined from 34 billion BRL to 30 billion BRL, as did the number of unemployment benefits paid (Figure 13.2). This data demonstrates the state's negligence in supporting

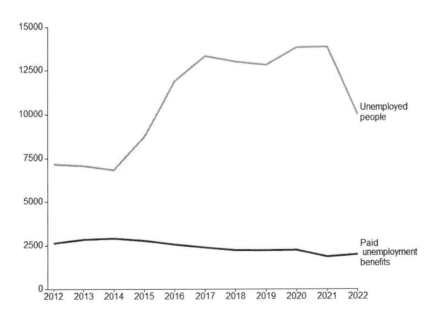

FIGURE 13.2   Number of unemployed people and number of paid unemployment benefits (in thousands) in Brazil, 2012–2022.

Source: Author's elaboration based on IBGE (unemployment) and Ministry of Labor (unemployment insurance).

workers when they needed it most, from Rousseff's second term to Bolsonaro's government.

This process is linked to the prolonged deterioration of the labor market amid the economic recession, which is marked by the rise of informal jobs – a trend that persists even after the 2017 labor reform. Hence, as formal employment declined since 2014, access to unemployment insurance has been reduced. Additionally, this process is linked to the enactment of Law No. 13,134/2015, during the Rousseff administration, which extended the minimum required working time for workers to claim the benefit by an additional six months.

13.3.3 Active labor market policies

As previously noted, active labor market policies (ALMP) are aimed at either reintegrating workers into the labor market or preparing them for the competitive labor market, seeking to maintain their employment and fostering better rewards (Kenworthy, 2010; Hemerijck, 2013). They comprise job-related vocational training, job search and job creation schemes in the public sector, and in work benefits, among other instruments (Bonoli, 2013).

Despite the effort of ALMPs expansion since the 1990s among many Latin American countries, these policies have historically played a less relevant role in the region compared to European Union countries (Barbosa, 2022). Considering the heterogeneous structure of the Latin American labor market, particularly considerable segmentation or dualism, the impact of ALMPs is not expected to be the same as in European countries. Even so, by analyzing 51 Latin American countries, including Brazil, Escudero et al. (2019) found that ALMPs have a significant impact on employability and access to formal employment. Training programs, in particular, have a significant impact on earnings growth.

In Brazil, ALMPs – particularly training and job search programs – are funded by the FAT, whose resources are managed by the Ministry of Labor and Employment. Unlike mandated spending on unemployment insurance and wage subsidies, expenditures on ALMPs are discretionary relying on specific resource allocation in the annual fiscal budget. For this reason, Silva (2021) shows that FAT spending on ALMPs was constrained to the extent that spending on unemployment insurance payments increased, during a period of formal employment expansion.

However, Figure 13.3 reveals reasonably distinct trajectories between ALMPs, indicating in a certain sense political choices: after a period of substantive increase between 2007 and 2009, in the second Lula government, public spending on training programs gradually reduced after 2010, the beginning of the Rousseff government, while job search showed a period of increase between 2010 and 2014. Yet, both policies were significantly impacted

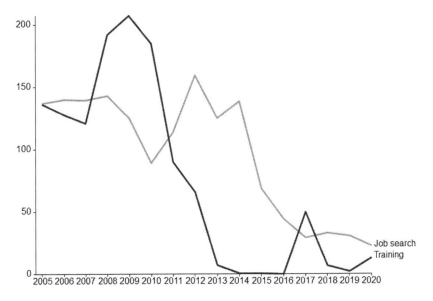

FIGURE 13.3   Total public spending (in national currency and in millions) on job search and training programs, in constant values of 2014.

Source: Author's elaboration based on observatório-política-fiscal.ibre.fgv.br and FAT reports.

by the austerity plan implemented from 2014 onwards. Spending on training programs was nearly eliminated, even during the peak of unemployment in 2015–2016, during the severe recession. As a result, it can be concluded that since 2010, governments have essentially abandoned ALMPs.

Furthermore, Figure 13.4 depicts the average spending on ALMPs, between 2010 and 2018, as a proportion of GDP and weighted by unemployment rate[9] among Organization for Economic and Development (OECD) and Latin American countries. As can be seen, Brazil had one of the least effort in ALMP policy, even in the face of a potential increase in demand for these policies due to rising unemployment. This finding indicates the loss of intensity of these policies on the public agenda in the period considered.

13.3.4   Labor market outcomes

The recession of the 2015–2016 period, caused by the adoption of a strong fiscal adjustment, had immediate impacts on the labor market. According to the Continuous National Household Sample Survey (PNAD) the total number of unemployed people climbed from 9.2 million in the 4th quarter of 2015 to 12.5 million in the 4th quarter of 2016. In percentage terms, the unemployment rate escalated from 8.5% to 11.5% in comparison between the two quarters.

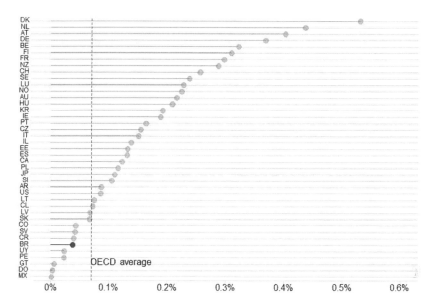

FIGURE 13.4 Public spending on ALMPs as share of GDP and weighted by unemployment rate (ILO modeled), average between 2010 and 2018, Latin American and OECD countries.

Source: Author's elaboration based on ECLAC stat and OECD stat.

The increase in unemployment, however, was only one aspect of the deterioration of the labor market in Brazil. According to DIEESE (Interunion Department of Statistics and Socioeconomic Studies), since 2015 there has been a continuous deterioration in the general conditions of the labor market, as measured by the evolution of the Labor Condition Index (LCI, or ICT, in Portuguese) calculated by the institution. The ICT-DIEESE is based on information from the Continuous PNAD-IBGE and is composed of three sub-indices, ICT-Occupational Insertion, ICT-Unemployment, and ICT-Income, each with the same weight (1/3) in the composition of the overall index. The closer the value of the index to 1, the better the overall situation of the labor market, and the closer to zero, the worse.[10] For the purposes of this section, we mainly analyze the evolution of the General LCI and the Occupational Insertion LCI.

The General LCI decreased steadily from 2015 until the beginning of 2018. During this time period, the index's behavior was influenced by two distinct movements. The indicator declined between 2015 and 2016, because of the severe recession, due to an increase in overall unemployment and the time spent looking for work by the unemployed. When the economy showed a slight recovery in 2017, the sub-index "Occupational Insertion" drove the fall in the ICT-General, which was mostly due to a reduction in formal employment.

Between 2017 and 2019, this indicator was stable at 0.4. However, the Occupational Insertion LCI continued to decline, reaching 0.3 in the fourth quarter of 2019. These findings indicate a deterioration in the Brazilian labor market conditions due to an increase in precarious job opportunities during the severe recession of 2015–2016, followed by a slow and uneven economic recovery. Consequently, the 2017 labor reform did not achieve its objective of promoting labor market recovery after the period of severe economic downturn.

Howell (2010) stresses that the behavior of the employment level is influenced by several factors, including macroeconomic policy management, the interrelationships between labor relations and social welfare systems, company expansion strategies, and public labor market policies. According to the author, the deregulation of labor market reforms, itself, yields a negative but weak impact on employment and economic growth.

Additionally, it is worth analyzing the behavior of the ICT-DIEESE in the context of the pandemic (2020–2021) and in 2022, when the Brazilian economy recovered a relative stability. In the context of the pandemic, there was a drop in occupation, especially among informal and self-employed workers, whose work depends heavily on direct contact with the public. Those who remained active in the occupied labor force were in a good measure formal employees, then the proportion of formal employment increased in comparison to the total employment. Indeed, there seemed to be an improvement in labor market conditions, as the LCI returned to the 0.5 level. However, this improvement was spurious and can be attributed to the significant reduction in informal and self-employed occupations caused by the pandemic's impact on the economy.

When the economy reopened in early 2022, the General LCI returned to its original level of 0.4, primarily due to a higher increase of informal and self-employed employment compared to formal employment. Consequently, the ICT-Occupational Insertion rate dropped to 0.3, the lowest recorded since 2015. By the last quarter of 2022, the Overall LCI stood at 0.52, the highest since the fourth quarter of 2016, but still below the 2014 level of 0.6. The Occupational Insertion LCI, though, ceased its decline, yet it remained at a very low level, approximately 0.3, indicating the decisive role of informal and self-employed occupations within the Brazilian labor market composition.

Finally, it is important to note that the deterioration of general labor market conditions had a greater impact on the most vulnerable social categories. Black women were disproportionately affected by the rise in unemployment, poverty, and hunger (Tanscheit and Barbosa, 2023). Moreover, between 2015 and 2018, the Gini Index of household income concentration climbed from 0.525 to 0.545 (IBGE, 2021). While the ongoing economic downturn undoubtedly influenced this process, it must be considered, on the other hand, that GDP growth is not a necessary condition for a fall in inequality. It reflects to some extent the type of state intervention in the response to the economic shock. For instance, during the pandemic shock, which led to a 4 percent contraction in GDP in 2020, there was a reduction in the Gini Index from 0.544 to 0.524. This reduction is largely explained by the granting of Emergency Aid (Barbosa and Prates, 2020) whose initiative was led by the national Congress in those circumstances (Campello, 2022).

13.4   Conclusion

This chapter analyzed the changes in the Brazilian labor market policies between 2015 and 2022. Table 13.1 presents a summary of these changes in light of the analytical framework proposed by Bauer and Knill (2012). In order to capture qualitative and quantitative changes in these policies, this framework is divided into two dimensions: a) public policy density, which refers to changes in the regulatory field and in the number of instruments used within each public policy area; and b) public policy intensity, which refers to the scope of the policy and includes variables such as the value and breadth of benefit coverage. In addition, we propose an extra dimension regarding the analysis of active and passive labor market policies: the demand for such policies. More specifically, the qualitative nature of policy changes concerns the proportion of unemployed people demanding state support.

Labor market reforms began during Rousseff's second term when she shifted to a more austerity agenda amid a political and economic crisis. During this period, the dismantling in terms of both the density and intensity of labor market policy was undertaken. However, since the emphasis during this period was on budgetary restraint, the primary mechanism of dismantling was in the realm of policy intensity. The austerity plan implied social spending cuts, resulting in a coverage decline for both passive and active policies.

While Rousseff's adjustments focused primarily on the intensity policy, Temer addressed both dimensions, including the density policy. Table 13.1 shows that the most significant changes in labor market policy density took place during the Temer administration (2016–2018). Temer implemented reforms that affected the density of labor market policies, such as the New Fiscal Regime and the 2017 labor reform. These regulatory changes led as well to a noticeable decrease in policy intensity, regarding the deepening of budget cuts for passive and active policies, the reduction in minimum wage appreciation, as well as the reduction of unemployment insurance beneficiaries despite a sharp rising unemployment rate.

The effectiveness of the Temer government in promoting the dismantling of labor market policies is supported by the literature on welfare state retrenchment. According to Pierson (1994), the main mechanism that constrains governments from promoting retraction is blame avoidance. That is, the political cost of imposing unpopular reforms, especially those that affect organized interest

TABLE 13.1 Summary of dismantling measures in labor market policies in Brazil, between 2015 and 2022

	Dilma Rousseff (2015-May 2016)	Michel Temer (May 2016–2018)	Jair Bolsonaro (2019–2022)
Density changes	- Training programs suspended (zero budget) - Extension of working time to apply for unemployment benefits	- 2017 Labor reform with stimulus to individual negotiation. - NFR affecting passive and active policies - Trade union reform	- Suspension of minimum wage appreciation.
Intensity changes	- Drop in the number of people receiving unemployment benefits (amid rising unemployment) - Depletion of job search programs - Budget cuts for active and passive policy	- Reduction in minimum wage appreciation process - Budget cuts deepening for passive and active policies. - The number of persons obtaining unemployment benefits continues to fall	- Budget cuts deepening for passive and active policies.
Demand	Unemployment rate rises from 6.8 to 11.6 (2014–2016)	Unemployment rate stabilized at a high level between 11 and 12 percent (2016–2018)	Pandemic Shock, the unemployment rate rises to 13.7 (2020–2021)

groups, is avoided when the incumbent government has some expectation of re-election. However, this expectation was absent during the Temer government, despite its strong parliamentary support base. The political costs of his reforms were largely reaped by the parties that made up his governing coalition, mainly the PSDB. In the 2018 general elections, the PSDB candidate received only 6% of the vote for the presidency, the worst result since 1994, when Fernando Henrique Cardoso was elected for his first term as president.

Finally, the analysis of Jair Bolsonaro's government is more complex due to a series of specificities. On the one hand, there was a reconfiguration of the forces within the political system, as the Executive decentralized part of its prerogatives to the Legislative to ensure Bolsonaro's political survival. The Bolsonaro government lacked a distinct agenda and continued the policies initiated by the Temer government, including reducing the intensity of labor market policies. Although it tried to approve regulatory changes in the labor field, aiming to deepen the 2017 reform, the Bolsonaro government was unable to go beyond the suspension of the minimum wage appreciation policy. On the other hand, passive and active labor market policies were not resumed, deepening the loss of intensity observed since 2015.

Notes

1 *"Cadastro Geral de Empregados e Desempregados."*
2 *"Sistema Nacional de Emprego."*
3 *"Fundo de Amparo ao Trabalhador."*
4 At the end of his second term, Cardoso attempted to enact a law establishing the prevalence of collective bargaining over labor legislation. This bill was approved in the Lower House and sent to the Senate. However, the PSDB's defeat in the presidential elections in November 2002 prevented it from being passed in the Senate. The bill was removed from the parliamentary agenda by Lula da Silva upon taking office in January 2003.
5 Rousseff was temporarily removed from office in May 2016, for 90 days, when the impeachment process was admitted by the Senate, while it was concluded on August 31.
6 A study by Boltansky and Chiapello (2009) depicts a similar trend in France, where the negotiated right has deteriorated alongside labor legislation flexibilization, even during favorable economic circumstances.
7 Strictly speaking, social assistance policies are also passive labor market policies, insofar as they are designed to support jobless individuals. Social assistance provides financial support to people who are not currently employed and have not had recent formal employment. Unemployment insurance provides financial support to people who have recently been in formal employment relationships and have become unemployed. Since social assistance is discussed in another chapter of this book, we will limit ourselves to discussing unemployment insurance here.
8 Author's calculation based on FAT (Workers Support Fund) website linked to the Ministry of Labor and Employment. Available at: https://portalfat.mte.gov.br/
9 Weighting public spending on ALMPs by the unemployment rate is a methodological recommendation for longitudinal or comparative analyses. This is due to the fact that the demand represented by unemployment levels is endogenous to the public effort in ALMPs (Hemerijck, 2013).
10 DIEESE. Índice da Condição do Trabalho. Nota Metodológica. www.dieese.org.br/analiseict/2019/notaSintetica042019.html

References

Abramo L, Cecchini S, Morales B. *Social programmes, poverty eradication and labour inclusion. Lessons from Latin America and the Caribbean.* Santiago: Economic Commission for Latin America and the Caribbean, 2019.

Alejo J, Parada C. Desigualdad e informalidad en América Latina: El caso de Brasil. *Desarro Soc* 2017;78:143–99.

Arretche M. Democracia e redução da desigualdade econômica no Brasil. *Rev Bras Ciênc Sociais* 2018;33: 1–23, DOI: 10.17666/339613/2018

Arretche M, Marques E, Faria CAP. *As Políticas Da Política: Desigualdades e Inclusão Nos Governos Do PSDB e Do PT.* São Paulo: Editora Unesp, 2019.

Avelino G, Brown DS, Hunter W. The effects of capital mobility, trade openness, and democracy on social spending in Latin America, 1980–1999. *Am J Polit Sci* 2005;49:625–41.

Barbosa PMR. *As Políticas Ativas de Mercado de Trabalho Na América Latina Em Perspectiva Comparada.* Rio de Janeiro: IESP-UERJ, 2022.

Barbosa R, Prates I. Efeitos do desemprego, do auxílio emergencial e do Programa Emergencial de Preservação do Emprego e da Renda (MP n 936/2020) sobre a renda, a pobreza ea desigualdade durante e depois da Pandemia. 2020.

Bauer MW, Knill C. A conceptual framework for the comparative analysis of policy change: Measurement, explanation and strategies of policy dismantling. *J Comp Policy Anal Res Pract* 2014;16:28–44.

Boltanski L, Chiapello È. *O Novo Espírito Do Capitalismo.* São Paulo: WMF Martins Fontes, 2009.

Bonoli G. *The origins of active social policy: Labour market and childcare polices in a comparative perspective.* 1st ed. Oxford: Oxford University Press, 2013.

Brito A, Foguel M, Kerstenetzky C. The contribution of minimum wage valorization policy to the decline in household income inequality in Brazil: A decomposition approach. *J Post Keynes Econ* 2017;40:540–75.

Campello D. When incompetence meets bad luck: Bolsonaro's third year in the Brazilian presidency. *Rev Cienc Política* 2022;42:203–223.

Cardoso A, Gindin J. *Relações de Trabalho, Sindicalismo e Coesão Social Na América Latina.* São Paulo: IFHC-Instituto Fernando Henrique Cardoso, 2008.

Cardoso LC, Façanha LO, Marinho A. Avaliação de programas sociais (PNAE, PLANFOR, PROGER): Eficiência relativa e esquemas de incentivo. *Inst Pesqui Econômica Apl IPEA.* Working Paper N859, 2002: 1–43.

Cardoso Jr JC, Gonzalez R. Dilemas e alternativas ao financiamento das políticas públicas de trabalho e renda no Brasil. *Rev Econômica* 2007;9:1–30.

Collier RB, Collier D. *Shaping the political arena: Critical junctures, the labor movement and regime dynamics in Latin America.* Princeton, N.J.: Princeton University Press, 1991.

Cook ML. Toward flexible industrial relations? Neo-liberalism, democracy, and labor reform in Latin America. *Ind Relat J Econ Soc* 1998;37:311–36.

Costa HA. O sindicalismo ainda conta? Poderes sindicais em debate no contexto europeu. *Lua Nova Rev Cult E Política* 2018;104:259–85.

Crouch C. Social investment, social democracy, neoliberalism, and xenophobia. In Hemerijck, A. (ed.). *The Uses of Social Investment.* Oxford: New York: Oxford University Press, 2017, pp. 368–77.

Datafolha. Mais impopular desde Collor, Temer fecha com reprovação em baixa. *Datafolha Instituto de pesquisas*, 2019. Available from: https://datafolha.folha.uol. com.br/opiniaopublica/2019/01/1985723-mais-impopular-desde-collor-temer-fecha-com-reprovacao-em-baixa.shtml

Diniz E, Boschi R. O corporativismo na construção do espaço público. In Boschi, R. (ed.). *Corporativismo E Desigualdade: a Construção do Espaço Público. Rio de Janeiro: IUPERJ/ Ed. Rio Fundo*, 1991, 11–29

Draibe S, Riesco M. Latin America: A new developmental welfare state model in the making? *Latin America: A new developmental welfare state model in the making?* New York: UNRISD, 2007, 1–17.

Escudero V, Kluve J, López Mourelo E et al. Active labour market programmes in Latin America and the Caribbean: Evidence from a meta-analysis. *J Dev Stud* 2019;55:2644–61.

Freyssinet J. As trajetórias nacionais rumo à flexibilidade da relação salarial: A experiência europeia. In Guimarães, N. A; Hirata, H; Sugita, K. (ed.) *Trabalho Flexível, Empregos Precários? Uma Comparação Brasil, França, Japão.* São `Paulo: EdUSP, 2010, 16–48.

Gough I. From welfare states to planetary well-being. In Béland, D.; Leibfried, S.; Morgan, K.; Obinger, H; Pierson, Christopher (ed.) *The Oxford handbook of the welfare state.* Second edition. Oxford: New York: Oxford University Press, 2021, 901–19.

Hemerijck A. *Changing welfare states.* First edition. Oxford: Oxford University Press, 2013.

Howell DR. *Institutions, aggregate demand and cross-country employment performance: Alternative theoretical perspectives and the evidence.* Bernard Schwartz Center for Economic Policy Analysis. Amherst: University of Massachusetts Amherst, 2010.

Huber E, Stephens JD. *Democracy and the Left: Social policy and inequality in Latin America.* Chicago, IL: University of Chicago Press, 2012.

IBGE. *Pesquisa Nacional Por Amostra de Domicílios Contínua.* Brasília: IBGE, 2021.

Kenworthy L. Labour market activation. In Castles, F; Leibfried, S; Lewis, J, *The Oxford handbook of the welfare state.* Oxford: New York: Oxford University First edition. 2010, 435–447.

Kerstenetzky CL. Foi Um Pássaro, Foi Um Avião? Redistribuição no Brasil no século XXI1. *Novos Estud CEBRAP* 2017;36:15–34.

Kerstenetzky CL. Redistribuição no Brasil no século XXI. In Arrecthe, M.; Marques, E.; Aurélio Pimenta de Faria, C (eds.). *As Políticas Da Política: Desigualdades e Inclusão Nos Governos Do PSDB e Do PT.* in São Paulo: Editora Unesp, 2019, 49–74.

Kerstenetzky CL. Why we need an allocative (and resourceful) welfare state. *Braz J Polit Econ* 2021;41:745–59.

Lehndorff S, Dribbusch H, Schulten T. *Rough waters: European trade unions in a time of crisis.* Brussels: Europe Trade Union Institue, 2017.

Mayoral FM, Nabernegg M. Determinants of social spending in Latin America. A dynamic panel data error-correction model analysis. *XXI Encuentro Economía Pública.* Girona: Universitat de Girona, 2014, 92–129. Available from: https://dialnet.unirioja.es/servlet/articulo?codigo=5191814

Neri M, Fontes A. *Informalidade e Trabalho No Brasil: Causas, Consequências e Caminhos de Políticas Públicas.* Rio de Janeiro: FGV Social, 2010.

Paiva AB de, Mesquita ACS, Jaccoud L de B, Passos L.. O novo regime fiscal e suas implicações para a política de assistência social no Brasil. Nota Técnica. Brasília: *Inst Pesqui Econômica Apl IPEA*, 2016; 27.

Palma JG. Why has productivity growth stagnated in most Latin American countries since the neo-liberal reforms? São Paulo: *FGV EESP* 2011. Available from: https://repositorio.fgv.br/items/f4e601f2-1f24-47a4-be87-7f80f089c3f9

Pierson P. *Dismantling the welfare state?: Reagan, Thatcher and the politics of retrenchment.* New York: Cambridge University Press, 1994.

Roberts KM. Market reform, programmatic (de) alignment, and party system stability in Latin America. *Comp Polit Stud* 2013;46:1422–52.

Rossi P, Dweck E. Impacts of the new fiscal regime on health and education. *Cad Saude Publica* 2016;32:e00194316.

Santos F, Tanscheit T. Quando velhos atores saem de cena: A ascensão da nova direita política no Brasil. *Colomb Int* 2019; 99 151–86.

Sátyro N. The paradigmatic radical reform in Brazil's social policies: The impact of the Temer administration. In Sátyro, N; Midaglia, Carmen (eds.). *Latin American social policy developments in the twenty-first century*. Springer, 2021, 317–40.

Silva SP. A economia política do Fundo de Amparo ao Trabalhador (FAT): uma análise de seu desempenho recente (2005–2018). *Braz J Polit Econ* 2021;41:588–610.

Singer A. *O Lulismo Em Crise: Um Quebra-Cabeça Do Período Dilma (2011–2016)*. São Paulo: Editora Companhia das Letras, 2018.

Tanscheit T, Barbosa PM. A battle of two presidents: Lula vs Bolsonaro in the Brazilian Elections of 2022. *Rev Cienc Política Santiago* 2023; 43; n 2; 167-191

Vieira FS. Gasto federal com políticas sociais e os determinantes sociais da saúde: Para onde caminhamos? *Saúde Em Debate* 2021;44:947–61.

PART IV

Policies outside of welfare state traditional scope

14

OPPORTUNITIES AND STRATEGIES OF THE DISMANTLING PROCESS OF BRAZILIAN ENVIRONMENTAL POLICY

Forests and indigenous populations under attack

*Maria Dolores Lima da Silva and
Ana Luiza Martins de Medeiros[1]*

14.1 Introduction

The article 225 of the Federal Constitution of 1988 consolidated the basis of the environmental policy subsystem in Brazil, imparting the status of fundamental rights to the determinations of the National Policy for the Environment (PNMA) and providing for the legal protection of these collective rights, specially the indigenous rights. In 1989, the Brazilian Institute for the Environment (Ibama[2]) was created as a subordinate board of the Ministry of the Environment, consolidating several environmental policy-enforcement agencies. The regulation and the bureaucratic-political apparatus created during the democratic period imparted coherence to the actions of public institutions regarding environmental protection.

The PNMA (Law No. 6938/1981) determined that public agencies encompassing several spheres of the Brazilian Union were to be coordinated by the National Environment System (Sisnama), with the National Environment Council (Conama) acting as the advisory and deliberative board. Ibama and the Chico Mendes Institute for Biodiversity Conservation (ICMBio) were to be responsible for implementing policies. By establishing standards and processes to govern activities and products, the legislation approved by the National Congress and infra-legal regulations issued by executive agents impose varying costs on economic agents. The existence of these costs is emphasized in political arenas by advocates of 'loosening' regulation.

DOI: 10.4324/9781003487777-18

In Dilma Rousseff and President Lula's administrations, indigenous communities faced rights violations for large projects in the Amazon, exemplified by the Belo Monte hydroelectric dam. Under Dilma Rousseff's leadership, the commitment to pave the deserted BR-319 highway initiated another wave of deforestation and encroachments on indigenous territories. Bolsonaro later embraced the promise of paving BR-319, leading to heightened deforestation and land seizures along the route from Porto Velho in the "arc of deforestation" to Manaus in the pristine central Amazon. During Michel Temer's presidency (2016–2018), indigenous policies regressed significantly. Measures were implemented to loosen the demarcation of indigenous lands, ease natural resource exploitation in these areas, and weaken the National Indian Foundation (FUNAI). This had far-reaching consequences, diminishing indigenous peoples' rights and the preservation of their lands.

Antônio Fernandes Toninho Costa, a dentist, parliamentary advisor, and evangelical pastor, was appointed to the presidency of Funai under the Temer government. Evangelical pastors in the Amazon have been linked to activities that contribute to the vulnerability of indigenous lands, such as promoting encroachment and resource exploitation. Their influence can worsen the already precarious situation of these territories and the communities relying on them. Additionally, the militarization for ideological puorposes of Funai, iniciated by Temer, continued on a larger scale under his successor (Soares and Baines, 2021). However, in Bolsonaro's government, the actions reached a different level, which is why it deserves specific attention.

In the 2018 election period, presidential candidate Jair Bolsonaro accused Ibama of being a 'ticket mill' and an 'obstacle' to be removed. The candidate also promised to not establish even one centimeter of land more for traditional peoples (Maisonnave and Valente, 2018; Resende, 2018). At various junctures in Bolsonaro's speeches just dehumanize specific groups. During one of his live-streams in January 2020, the president discussed indigenous populations openly racist and pseudo-"evolutionist": "The Indigenous have changed, they are evolving… Ever more so each day, the Indigenous is a human being like us" (Poder360, 2020). Since his election, attacks on environmental policies have taken on new proportions, having been the analytical focus of different studies (Abessa, Famá, and Buruaem, 2019; Araújo, 2020; Capelari et al., 2020; Menezes and Barbosa Jr., 2021; Barbosa, Alves, and Grelle, 2021). For Capelari et al. (2020), 'large-scale changes' were triggered in the environmental policy subsystem.

This chapter aims to analyze the actions intended to disrupt the environmental policy subsystem and identify the strategies that were enacted under the active power of the president. We consider that all policies related to the environment are directly linked to policies focused on indigenous people due to their connection with their native land. However, it is important to emphasize that indigenous policy complexities go beyond their connection to environmental issues. In other words, we recognize that the dismantling of indigenous policy involved various sectorial policies, but we have chosen to focus solely on those directly tied to environmental policy. What strategies were used to secure environmental policy changes and under what conditions and constraints these changes occurred? We hypothesized that, from 2019 onwards, under the advocacy of the federal government, an active dismantling process was initiated, aimed at undermining regulation and its institutional structures. Our analysis covers the period between 2019 and 2022, during the government of Jair Bolsonaro,[3] to understand the direction of the changes that have occurred.

We present a descriptive case study with a mixed approach, based on official documents obtained from institutional websites, and secondary data from Siga Brasil (2023), the Personnel Statistical Panel, and newspaper stories. Our document analysis used the Sigalei platform to automate the selection of regulatory actions, complementing it with manually selected documents, which resulted in a corpus comprising 1,051 documents, analyzed using the Content Analysis technique (Bardin, 2017). Quantitative data were analyzed using simple descriptive statistics. We also read publications of interest to our analysis on the Ibama and Conama websites and, finally, journalistic materials, in order to review discourses and fill in gaps.

Our analysis identified different strategies for the dismantling of environmental policy during the Bolsonaro administration. The advances of groups that historically advocate for deregulation to benefit the market economy, have taken on greater dimensions with the favorable advocacy of the central government. In this scenario, it should be considered that the main player of the dismantling policy counted on the advantage of support from the economic sectors. The main supporter would be the agribusiness economy as a political force that would support the devised changes and guarantee its future electoral dividends.

In addition to this introduction and the final considerations, we have separated our arguments into four sections. In the second section, we present literature that deals with deregulation and dismantling of public policies, establishing the analytical focus of our work through said literature. Next, we highlight the political context of the changes in the Brazilian environmental policy, showing that attempts at deregulation were already ongoing in Parliament, but were deepened in the Bolsonaro government; we also emphasize that the symbolic behavior of the president created resistance in national and international public opinion. In the fourth section, we deal with each dimension of the dismantling of environmental policies as active processes carried out by the president and the environmental executive staff. Finally, we conclude by identifying the dismantling strategies employed by the political actors, detailing the nature of our findings.

14.2 Deregulation and other factors of the dismantling of environmental policy in Brazil

Four types of strategies were employed by the Bolsonaro administration in its process of dismantling the environmental policies of Brazil that have direct impact on forests and indigenous peoples, concerning four different areas: financial, regulatory, bureaucratic, and accountability. We focus on a regulatory-type policy (Lowi, 1972), whose complexity requires the legislation to be complemented with norms that detail processes and standards for implementation. In the USA, several approaches to the deregulation of this type of public policy are consolidated. These approaches prioritize control by the Agencies, while disregarding other dimensions of policy (Majone, 1989). However, the term 'deregulation' is commonly used to address the dismantling of public policies where the regulatory aspect is dominant (Jordan, Bauer, and Green-Pedersen, 2012). In our analysis, we emphasize dimensions that, when combined, trigger changes in the direction of these policies.

Deregulation is the process in which traditional structures of regulation and control are dismantled or radically reshaped by pressure exerted by ideological, technological and economic forces (Majone, 1990). For Hancher and Moran (1989), this concept comprises both changes in the structures and content of rules and the breaking of mechanisms that maintain a system. Two types of processes are included: 'active deregulation', in which political actors take the initiative to change rules and instruments, and 'passive deregulation', where exogenous factors contribute to deregulating the system. In Bauer and Knill (2012), we identify several active and passive dismantling strategies, that is, 'direct, indirect, veiled or symbolic change that can decrease the number of policies in a given area, reduce the number of policy instruments used and/or decrease their severity', classified as high and low visibility strategies.

In budgetary terms, we define defunding as a strategy for dismantling or withdrawal of actions of the environmental policy sector. Financial limitation is considered 'a key strategy of systemic retrenchment' (Pierson, 1994, p.15). According to Araújo (2020), budgetary restrictions in the Bolsonaro government were a strategy to lead environmental sector institutions to 'inaction'.

In the regulatory dimension, we focus on legislation and infra-legal norms to understand the scope of actions in the Legislative and Executive branches aimed at undermining regulation. In environmental policy, characterized by socially diffuse benefits and concentrated costs (Bauer and Knill, 2012), deregulation and re-regulation are typically pursued by powerful economic groups aiming to remove regulations, perceived as obstacles.

While the defense of retrenchment in social policies has its political costs, deregulation can be seen as necessary when the legal framework is understood as 'excessive' (Jordan, Bauer, and Green-Pedersen, 2012), manifesting itself as a 'request for credit' by certain political groups. Capelari et al. (2020, p. 1695) identify this discursive construction where *the restrictions of environmental regulation* would limit *economic growth* and *access to natural resources,* imposing an *absorption of costs* by the economy.

The third dimension of our analysis deals with the administrative framework, called 'ideological cleansing of staff' by Bauer et al. (2021, p.14). It is the introduction of ideological allies into the public administration, accompanied by the repression of career bureaucrats, to allow for the execution of a dismantling project by the central government.

Finally, in the dimension of accountability, we analyze the occurrences of social participation and transparency, which are the basis of legitimacy in state actions (Avritzer, 2007). In Sisnama, Conama is the main accountability instrument where social participation produces cooperation and interaction between actors and agencies to improve environmental policy (Leme, 2016).

The dimensions of the dismantling of environmental policies in Brazil will be observed through the lens of Bauer and Knill (2012; 2014), who recommend that the density and intensity of policies, and their instruments, be measured in their substantial and formal dimensions, in order to grasp the direction of change. Density measures the extent of state coverage and regulatory capacity, and intensity measures the rigor of state intervention. Moreover, our analysis is also based on the analytical dimensions presented by Bauer et al. (2021), by analyzing the actions of authoritarian governments aimed at adapting public administration to their ideological projects, through changes in the structure, resources, personnel, norms and accountability of policies. We identified other strategies through Bauer and Knill (2012), such as 'dismantling by arena shifting' and by 'default', which are low-visibility actions, and 'active' and 'symbolic dismantling', which are high-visibility actions.

14.3 From Parliament to the Executive Branch: arenas of environmental policy change

When considering the institutional scenario where the dismantling policy takes part, it should be noted that in Brazilian coalition presidentialism, the president relies on fragmented support of parties in the National Congress. The president's power of agenda requires cooperation between the Executive and the parliamentary majority (Freitas, 2016; Figueiredo and Limongi, 1999); therefore, the opposing party forces and those supporting the environmental and indigenous agenda define the scope of the ruler's discretion.

It should also be considered that the so-called 'Centrão' (swinging parties) upholds governability for the president and brings together parties whose members aim to neutralize the actions of environmental institutions. They are also organized in the Parliamentary Front for Agriculture and Agribusiness

(FPA), known as ruralists (large landholders and their representatives), opposing the Environmentalist Parliamentary Front (FPAM) in an attempt to reformulate environmental legislation. Araújo (2020) notes that in the legislative arena, FPAM sought the support of public opinion to curb initiatives aimed at loosening environmental legislation with the support of the Bolsonaro government. Moreover, during the Bolsonaro government, the FPAM agenda gained support from the so-called "Bancada do Cocar" which, assembled in the Parliamentary Front in Defense of the Rights of Indigenous Peoples (FPMDDPI), brought together deputies and senators to block initiatives contrary to the rights of indigenous communities (Santana, 2019).

Throughout its democratic period, Brazil gained international respect by building an important legal and administrative framework for the environment (Barbosa, Alves, and Grelle, 2021; Abessa, Famá, and Buruaem, 2019). Prior to the political context of 2019, attempts to weaken the sector sought re-regulation to reach less rigor and the creation of uncontrolled and decentralized incentive mechanisms. The economic sectors that export commodities could be harmed by the anti-environmental discourse and their representatives in Parliament do not refer to dismantling but to a 'flexibilization' of legislation. Hancher and Moran (1989) stress that deregulation processes often create a new modality for the distribution of costs and benefits and that the transition from the implementation of command and control regulation to an implementation that occurs through market or negotiation mechanisms is characteristic of demands arising in liberalizing contexts.

With Bolsonaro, however, an ideological project for dismantling policy gained prominence, without concern for its political costs. News organizations spread the purpose of the government, unauthorizing control (Bragança, 2019), and the establishment of both environmentally protected areas and areas for traditional peoples (Resende, 2018). The extension of indigenous lands was cited by Bolsonaro as an impediment to economic expansion. The president's project was asserted daily to the political and economic sectors aligned with his vision, especially when speaking against Ibama's inspection efforts (Saraiva, 2023). Bolsonaro also began his government with the intention of merging the Ministry of the Environment with the Ministry of Agriculture, but was discouraged by the rural sector itself, which feared international sanctions (Ferrante and Fearnside, 2019). According to Bauer and Knill (2012), symbolic dismantling actions have high visibility but may not result in concrete changes if they are prevented by institutional constraints.

The president's statements, such as: 'people's interest in the Amazon is not focused on Indians or the [...] trees, it is in the minerals', (Carta Capital, 2019), caused shock in the domestic and international spheres. At the 2019 World Economic Forum, the president reaffirmed his commitment to expanding the domain of agribusiness and his strictly economic view of the environment.

However, the international repercussions of this project intensified the pressures of civil society and entities and financial actors (Araújo, 2020). The blocking of international resources from the Amazon Fund was a response to the extinction of the Advisory Committee and the Technical Committee of the Fund (Carvalho et al., 2022), an initiative of the Executive Power (Decree 9.759/2019) revoked by a Direct Action of Constitutionality with the STF.

Brazil refused to host the United Nations Climate Change Conference (COP25) and, for the first time, had no official booth. Furthermore, civil society organizations were not authorized to participate. The Minister of the Environment, Ricardo Sales, who represented the government, advocated for the use of technological efficiency in agribusiness and the monetization of environmental services as solutions to environmental problems. Attuned to the president's ideology, in 2020 the minister said that the Covid-19 pandemic would be an opportune moment to accelerate environmental deregulation measures, using the Brazilian Portuguese expression 'passar a boiada' (to force or enable the passage of a proposal, in this case specifically a legislative bill), taking advantage of the public's inattention to environmental issues.[4] This statement shows the disposition towards the environment and the indigenous people. It is not fallacious to say that this has resulted in a drastic surge in deforestation, wildfires, land grabbing, illicit mining, and encroachments on indigenous territories. In reaction, international investment funds warned, for the third time since 2019, about the damage that the direction of its environmental policy could cause to Brazil's business, demonstrating concern about the deforestation and irregular occupation of the Amazon (Jornal Nacional, 2020). The statements delivered by the president and the ministers exhibit the strong symbolic dimension of the dismantling policy in the Bolsonaro government that, together with other high-visibility actions (Bauer and Knill, 2012; 2014), extended their project beyond changes in legislation.

14.4 Strategies for the dismantling of Brazilian environmental policy

We interpret the events that have occurred in recent years in Brazilian politics as an active dismantling process aimed at undermining the environmental policy established by the PNMA and the Federal Constitution of 1988, without any concern for the protection of indigenous peoples. Using different sources and techniques, we analyzed the strategies employed to change the *status quo* of Brazilian environmental policy and found that high-visibility actions predominated, although low-visibility initiatives also existed. Figure 14.1 illustrates the variables and indicators of each variable articulated in this chapter.

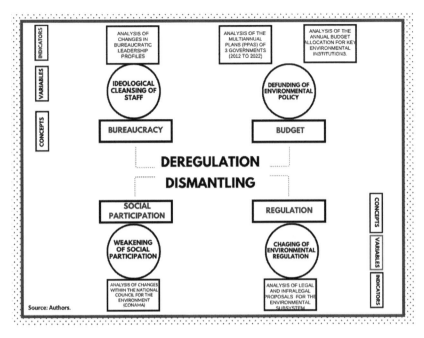

FIGURE 14.1   Theory.

Source: Authors.

14.4.1   Changes in the allocation of budgetary resources

In Brazil, the instrument for planning public policies provided for in the Constitution is the Pluriannual Plan (PPA), devised in the first year of each government to be executed in the next four years. The PPA is complemented by the Budget Guidelines Law (LDO) and the Annual Budget Law (LOA), both allocating resources for each policy sector to carry out its actions and programs. The Executive Branch draws up the proposals and sends them to the National Congress to evaluate, amend, and approve.

The 2012–2015 (Law No. 12.593/2012) and 2016–2019 PPAs (Law No. 13.249/2016) were developed during the terms of Dilma Rousseff (2011–2016), but the latter was completed during the Temer period, due to the impeachment of Dilma Rousseff. Planned goals included management actions for the Ministry, such as conservation of biodiversity, measures to handle the effects of climate change, combating deforestation, forest fires, environmental licensing, and water resources management. Other Ministries, such as the Ministry of Agriculture, with the 2016–2019 PPA, specified more goals regarding the creation of more environmentally sustainable agricultural practices. The PPA allocated about

20% of the Budget for Thematic Programs for productive and environmental development.

In the 2020–2023 PPA (Law No. 13.971/2019), created by the Bolsonaro government, the planning for environmental policies was simplified, under the argument of making it compatible with the national macroeconomic context. The scope of this PPA was limited to seven programs and did not include new

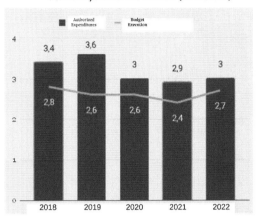

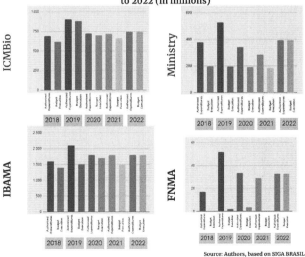

FIGURE 14.2   Budget.

Sources: Authors.

initiatives or thematic programs. According to Araújo and Feldmann (2019), 98.4% of the amount set apart for environmental action was allocated to the Ministry of Agriculture to execute the sustainable agricultural program.

Observing the amounts allocated to the MMA by the annual budget (LOA), we have to consider that the environmental sector involves significantly lower resources than the amounts handled by other areas, due to its being a regulatory policy. However, the impact of decreasing the budget to about a third of its previous available amount starting in 2015 remains significant, as demonstrated by Pinheiro and Araújo (2022). In Figure 14.2 we present the distribution of resources both for direct administration and for main institutions available for the implementation of environmental policy, starting at the end of the Temer government until the Bolsonaro government. The Budget Execution for each year was actually lower than the authorized values. In the direct administration of the MMA, we observed that the financial execution was well below the authorized values and remained in decline since 2018, except for the election year of 2022.

This decrease in the use of resources is clearly not to be seen in isolation since the period in question is one of global economic austerity. However, our analysis of the PPAs and the annual budgets shows that environmental protection lost prestige over time. The crucial activities of Ibama, such as environmental control, counteracting and preventing forest fires, suffered substantial impacts, according to Araújo (2022). And this is focusing solely on the budget allocated exclusively for the environmental category, without including those intended for indigenous peoples. Bauer et al. (2021) note that the dismantling policy carried out by authoritarian governments manipulates budgets and other administrative mechanisms as part of a strategy to restrict the implementation of public policies. Since the seminal literature on dismantling public policies, budget allocations stand out as an important indicator of this process (Pierson, 1994).

14.4.2 Changes in the profile of the Federal bureaucracy

Bauer et al. (2021) define the changes in public policy staff desired by the government as an 'ideological cleansing of staff'. In order to understand the effect said cleansing can impart on environmental policy, it is important to analyze the profile of the main veto-players in environmental policy, that is, the profile of the head management of key political institutions. In this case, we will limit ourselves to the Ministry of the Environment, Ibama, and ICMBio, as shown in Figure 14.3.

During the Bolsonaro administration, the presence of military personnel in command positions is notorious, especially in ICMBIO, with Simanovic, Lorencini, and Cerqueira, but also in the Executive Secretariat, with Biagioni.

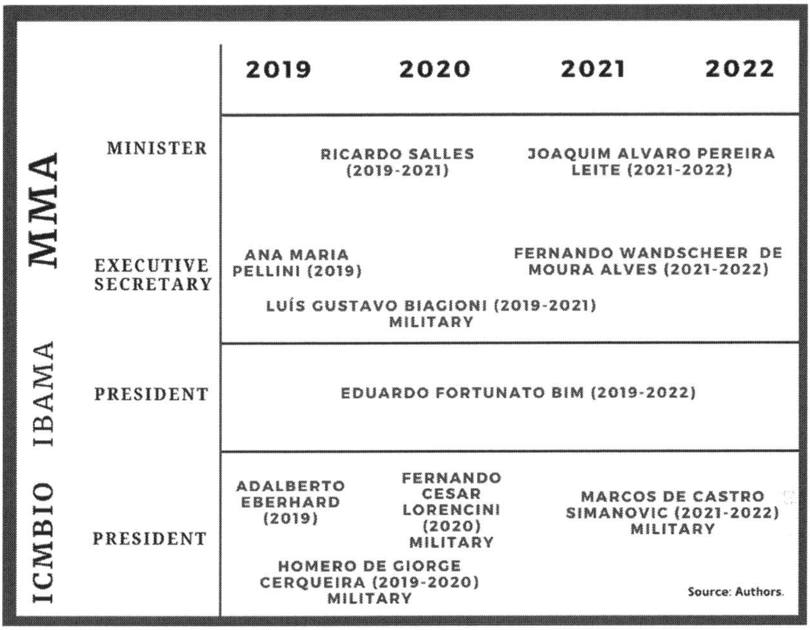

		2019	2020	2021	2022
MMA	MINISTER		RICARDO SALLES (2019-2021)	JOAQUIM ALVARO PEREIRA LEITE (2021-2022)	
	EXECUTIVE SECRETARY	ANA MARIA PELLINI (2019)		FERNANDO WANDSCHEER DE MOURA ALVES (2021-2022)	
		LUÍS GUSTAVO BIAGIONI (2019-2021) MILITARY			
IBAMA	PRESIDENT		EDUARDO FORTUNATO BIM (2019-2022)		
ICMBIO	PRESIDENT	ADALBERTO EBERHARD (2019)	FERNANDO CESAR LORENCINI (2020) MILITARY	MARCOS DE CASTRO SIMANOVIC (2021-2022) MILITARY	
		HOMERO DE GIORGE CERQUEIRA (2019-2020) MILITARY		Source: Authors.	

FIGURE 14.3   Bureaucracy.

Sources: Authors.

The militarization of leadership positions is one of the aspects of the government's strategy of oppression aimed at silencing bureaucrats (Lotta, Silveira, and Fernandez, 2022). This process intensifies both politicization, creating a counterpoint between the appointment of leadership positions and the legal precepts of the policy field, and also exacerbating an air of oppression and control derived from the demand of discipline and loyalty in the military forces (Andrade, Nogueira, and Lotta, 2021). Moreover, 21 Ibama superintendents were replaced (Ferrante and Fearnside, 2019).

Militarization was a notable feature of the Bolsonaro government that permeated various institutions within the administrative apparatus, with a particularly significant impact on those areas where the government sought to alter policy directions. Soares and Baines (2021) highlight a process of "remilitarization" within Funai, emphasizing the historical involvement of the military in shaping and regulating indigenous policies in Brazil. The substitution of military personnel within the agency aimed to guarantee the cessation of the indigenous land demarcation process. While there was a significant decline in demarcation efforts during Dilma's administration, they came to a complete halt during the terms of both Temer and Bolsonaro (Soares and Baines, 2021), impacting the vital role these lands play in preserving indigenous culture and livelihoods. During that period, 25 out of 39 Regional Coordination Headquarters underwent changes, with 21 being led by military personnel, including retired Army captains, subtenant, sergeant, Marine rifleman, and military police officer (Costa, 2023). Additionally, Franklimberg Ribeiro de Freitas, a military officer, served as the president of Funai from the Temer administration through the Bolsonaro administration (Fellet, 2022). In 2019, he was succeeded by Marcelo Xavier, a representative from the agribusiness sector (Valente, 2019).

During processes of ideological cleansing of staff, intimidation of low bureaucrats by leaders is a common practice. For instance, when public employees were threatened with retaliation by means of internal investigation when they did not take part in an event attended by Minister Salles (Wenzel, 2019). The employees' servants were also disqualified, called 'a bunch of crazy people' by the president of Ibama, Eduardo Bim (Prizibisczki, 2022). Additionally, both Ministers Salles and Leite, as well as the Executive Secretary Pellini and the president of Ibama, Bim, are known to be in favor of deregulation and are closely linked to the industries affected by the regulations, such as mining and agribusiness.

By contrast, for instance, the well-succeeded Plan to Prevent and Combat Deforestation in the Amazon (PPCDAm), implemented during Marina Silva tenure as Minister of the Environment in the Lula government, prioritized technical knowledge and the participation of diverse actors and sectors of society (Oliveira, 2021). Oliveira (2021) points out that the political system was open to the influence of social movements, the opposite of what we observe during the Bolsonaro administration. As Cavalcante, Lotta, and Oliveira (2018, p.78) observe, in democratic governance 'the chances of bureaucratic insulation are greatly reduced, given the presence of important mechanisms for controlling bureaucracy and its being influenced by politics [...]'.

14.4.3 Restrictions on participation and accountability in Brazilian environmental policy

We also note among the strategies used the undermining of the Conama, the institutional arena for environmental governance established in 1981 by the PNMA, as a deliberative and advisory body of the SISNAMA. Its structure with representatives from the three powers of government and civil society strives for participation and social control towards greater accountability. According to Silva, Ribeiro, and Medeiros (2020), Conama government councilors, who alternately represent both civil society and the government, are the crucial link promoting the integration of the public policy arenas.

As of 2019, several initiatives have affected the participatory principles that have governed Brazilian public policies since the Federal Constitution of 1988. The Decree 9.759/2019 (Brasil, 2019c) extinguished and impaired a wide list of collegial bodies established through presidential decrees and normative acts. In turn, Decree No. 9.806/2019 (Brasil, 2019e) altered Conama's participatory decision-making power by modifying its structure and composition,[5] as shown in Figure 14.4.

The Special Appeal Chamber, the last instance of administrative appeal in notices of infraction drawn up by Ibama, was extinguished. Additionally, the terms of council members were also decreased, from biannual to annual terms, without the possibility of re-election.

The most important change was a decrease in the number of members of the Council, from 96 to 23, which added a new layer of difficulty to the participation of entities in the processes (as shown in Figure 14.5). The seats for civil society, social movements, and environmentalists decreased from 22 to four advisors. There was also the addition of the requirement of registration of the would-be entities in a National Register of Environmental Entities for at least a year before participation. The states were no longer represented by 26 seats, plus the Federal District, instead being represented by five chairs, one for each of the country's subregions. City halls, which already shared a small space with eight seats, were to be represented by two capitals only and the terms went from being determined by direct election to a drawing of lots.

In addition, the Environment Committee of the Chamber of Deputies, ICMBio, and the Water and Sanitation Agency no longer have seats in Conama. Rural workers, traditional populations, indigenous communities, the scientific community, and market entities also lost representation, a 75% decrease in participation. The weakening of representation of regional diversity, in a socio-environmentally diverse country like Brazil, is part of the changes in the relations between the State and society that affect, especially, the environmental area, whose complexity imposes debate, disclosure of information and transparency in decisions (Carvalho et al., 2022; Moura, 2016).

Restrictions on social participation in Conama impaired accountability in a context in which the federal government tried to restrict access to information of public interest. Examples of great public repercussion were the dismissal of Ricardo Galvão, Director of INPE, after the disclosure of deforestation rates (Barrucho, 2019) and the requirement of prior authorization from the Director of Biodiversity Research, Evaluation, and Monitoring (Brasil, 2021a), former lieutenant colonel Marcos Aurélio Venâncio, to publish the scientific papers produced by ICMBio (Camargo, 2021).

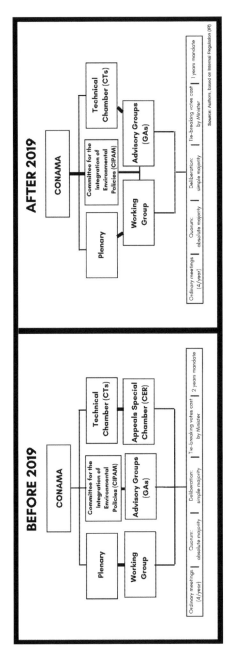

FIGURE 14.4 Conama's structure.

Sources: Authors.

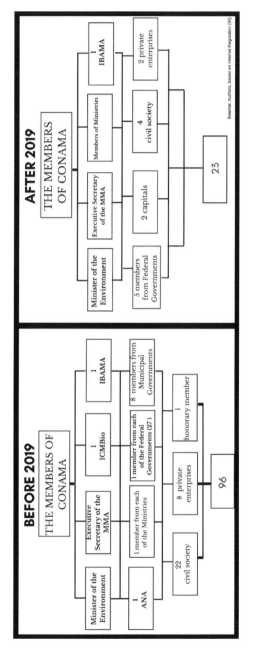

FIGURE 14.5   Conama representation.

Sources: Authors.

14.4.4 From deregulation to the use of regulation to dismantle environmental policy

We note two strategies aimed at changing the regulatory system structuring environmental governance: proposals for changes in legislation within the scope of the Legislative Branch and infra-legal measures issued by the Executive Branch and by the institutions that implement environmental policy. Such actions meet the old aspirations of extractivist economic forces that aim to advance over the Amazon forest (Ferreira et al., 2014) and that were re-invigorated by Bolsonaro's positions in defense of mining and agribusiness (Resende, 2018). The suggested actions to expand agriculture and infrastructure in the Amazon, particularly the initiative to finalize Highway BR-319, pose a significant risk of widespread deforestation, further jeopardizing the region's ecosystems and the well-being of indigenous and local communities. Exploiting the oxygen crisis in Manaus during the COVID-19 pandemic, the Bolsonaro government seized the opportunity to advocate for the paving of the BR-319 highway, neglecting consultations with indigenous peoples. They were notably excluded from public hearings during the pandemic. A longer-lasting process of re-regulation advances in Parliament with the aim of loosening mechanisms of legislation to make it less stringent, while creating mechanisms to encourage the adherence of private economic actors, creating a liberal perspective on environmental protection (Hancher and Moran, 1989).

One should consider the convenience flexible regulatory mechanisms can create for offenders in a federative country of continental dimensions such as Brazil, where the supervision and visibility of decisions is costly and complex. The Brazilian institutional arrangement is complex, involving federative relations, intersectionality, and a significant and heterogeneous number of social actors (Lotta and Vaz, 2015). In the National Congress, proposals aimed at 'loosening' environmental legislation have a long trajectory and have advanced in recent decades. The Bill No. 1875/1999, which gave rise to the Native Vegetation Protection Law (Law No. 12.651/2012), was approved under many controversies (Brancalion et al., 2016) during the Dilma government. On one hand, the Law innovated in creating control mechanisms and incentives for rural producers to adhere to legal determinations, such as the Rural Environmental Registry (CAR) and the Environmental Regularization Program (Silva, 2023); it also pardoned offenders who would be punished by the Environmental Crimes Law (Law No. 9.605/1998).

Other proposals aimed at regulating and re-regulating (Hancher and Moran, 1989) environmental matters are the Bills approved by the Chamber of Deputies, which continue to be processed by the Federal Senate: Bill No. 3729/2004, approved in 2021, regulating environmental licensing based on the determination of the Federal Constitution of 1988, which determined that subsequent legislation should discipline this activity. The proposal, known as the Bill for the General Environmental Licensing Law, aims to ease the establishment of construction sites with potential environmental impacts, as well as decentralizing permit authorizations to the local entities. Environmentalists fear that the removal of control exerted by national environmental institutions will weaken this instrument established by PNMA in 1981 (Milanez, Magno, and Wanderley, 2021; Pinheiro and Araújo, 2023).

In another example, we have Bill No. 6.299/2002, which amends the General Pesticide Law of 1989, approved in 2022 by Congress. Known as the 'Poison Bill', its defenders aim to eliminate veto power, by limiting the authorizations for the use of these products only to the Ministry of Agriculture, eliminating the evaluation of the Ministry of Environment and ANVISA (Brazilian Health Regulatory Agency). In addition, it proposes a cut to the approval time and a cleanse from the negative connotation of the term 'agrotóxico' (literally 'agrotoxic products') to 'phytosanitary products' (Cruz, 2021). The Bolsonaro government strengthened the purposes of parliamentarians who wished to modify environmental legislation, as well as gave rise to new legislation weakening the instruments created by the PNMA (Abessa, Famá, and Buruaem, 2019).

New proposals for laws stirred public opinion at the beginning of the Covid-19 pandemic. Bill No. 191/2020, authored by the Executive Branch, aiming to regulate the exploitation of mineral resources in indigenous lands, and Bill No. 2633/2020, originating in the Legislative Branch, which provides for regularization of the lands of the Union, are symbolic of the president's position and that of his allies. The first Bill did not pass the Chamber of Deputies and the second, known as the 'Land grabbing Bill', was approved under protests from environmental representatives. Created to facilitate the access of intensive economic activities to indigenous lands, as mining and large-scale farming activities, where the forest is better preserved, as well as for the access of the private initiative to public lands (Araújo, 2020; Soares and Baines, 2021; Capelari et. al, 2023), such initiatives faced the scrutiny of society.

In the Legislative field, battles between the political forces that draft the regulation are publicized and the process of change can become slow, as we observed in previous bills. Such difficulties were felt by government staff and expressed by the Environment Minister during a ministerial meeting. As an alternative to the difficulties of effecting changes through the Parliament, Salles proposed '[...] changing all the rules and simplifying norms [...] of the Ministry of the Environment, the ministry of this, the ministry of that [...]'[6]. To identify other deregulation strategies, we used the Decrees, Ordinances, and other normative acts of the President, the Minister of the Environment, and other government authorities, aimed at changing the functioning of the environmental protection system, in the period between 2019 and 2020. The complexity of the

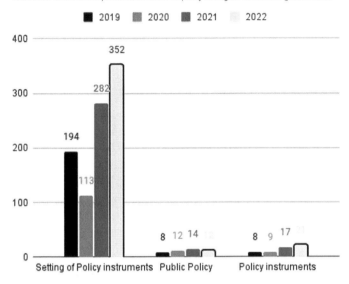

FIGURE 14.6   Policy instruments.

Sources: Authors.

environmental policy lends special importance to the infralegal normative acts interfering in the action of the institutions that implement, control, and inspect legislation.

Guided by the recommendations of Bauer and Knill (2012), in Figures 14.6 and 14.7 we identify government measures separated in the following categories: 'public policies, policy instruments, and rigor of instruments'. We found that the strategies for setting policy instruments aimed at decreasing the severity of environmental policy increased exponentially in number, with the exception of 2020, the beginning of the Covid-19 pandemic.

Through Bauer et al. (2021), we classified the setting of policy instruments by the dimensions of change in norms, structure, personnel, resources, and accountability. We identified that staff-related actions (personnel) such as dismissals, appointments, retirement, etc, were the main measures. Next were normative acts focusing on 'resources, structures, norms, and accountability'. Included in the 'resources' category of Bauer and Knill (2021) are changes that seek to modify bureaucratic activities by manipulating budget allocation, the administrative, and informational mechanisms of policy. 'Structure' contains the rules of the game, changes in scope, policy design, veto players, and institutional mechanisms of environmental policy. Combined, these changes shape the policy in the direction of the ruler's purposes.

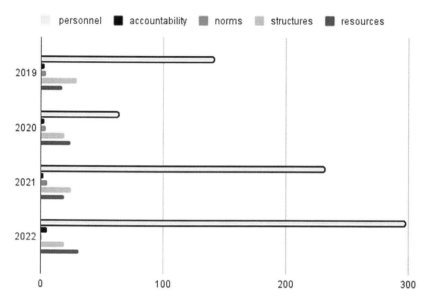

FIGURE 14.7   Policy instruments.

Sources: Authors.

However, it is still necessary to determine whether the molding of policy through government normative acts of the 'setting of policy instruments' type follows the direction of dismantling the public policy, as recommended by Bauer and Knill (2012; 2014). Firstly, concerning the established deadlines for Ibama's State Superintendencies to submit their Programs for converting fines into environmental services to the institution's presidency (Brasil, 2019b; Brasil, 2019f), it appears to promote centralization and encourages federated entities to embrace an innovation created by the New Forest Code. This innovation encourages offenders to engage in activities that benefit the environment, in line with the preferences of liberals who reject punitive action in environmental policy.

In another direction, through a 2019 normative instruction, Ibama was authorized to delegate environmental licensing to subnational environmental agencies (Brasil, 2019a), a measure that alters the design of the policy. Through decentralization, the national implementation agent moves away from direct accountability and local political forces that reject the controls of environmental legislation are strengthened (Xu, 2022). Environmental policy is a shared competence in a federation with several veto points, which, therefore, increase the importance of delegating measures. The federative dimension of Brazilian environmental policy is unusually explored in the literature and the issue of licensing is a central theme in this regulation (Pinheiro and Araújo, 2023).

Another relevant change in policy design is seen in Decree No. 9.760/ 2019 (Brasil, 2019d) and its regulations on the application of administrative sanctions to violators. The offenses began to be judged in Conciliation Chambers, weakening an instrument policy (Bauer and Knill, 2012) once central to environmental policy. The infractions uncovered by field agents, even when directly witnessed, would be validated by 'higher authorities' before any sanctioning process (Brasil 2020a; Brasil, 2021b), limiting the discretion of environmental inspectors, which is a crucial aspect of their role as street-level bureaucrats (Lipsky, 2019). In addition, the government extinguished six of ICMBio's 11 regional coordinations, through the Decree No.[7] 10.234/ 2020 (Brasil, 2020b). In addition, Provisional Measure No. 900/2019, which lost its validity without being voted (Brasil, 2019g; Brasil, 2020f), directed the attribution to the Ministry of the Environment before Ibama and ICMBio, of hiring a financial institution to manage the private fund consisting of resources coming from the conversion of environmental fines.

Such measures, seen as a factor that paralyzes the sanctioning process (Werneck, 2021), materialized the purpose of Bolsonaro and Salles who threatened to punish, through administrative measures, acts of destruction of equipment used in the practice of environmental crimes (Bragança, 2019). Other changes in policy implementation structures can be seen through the Ordinance No. 524/ 2020 that merged Ibama and ICMBio in a single institution (Brasil, 2020e), and in the transfer of the National Council of the Legal Amazon, through Decree No. 10.239/2020, from the Ministry of Environment to the Vice-Presidency of the Republic (Brasil, 2020c). Note that this Council, comprising 19 military personnel and four Federal Police deputies, did not include representatives from Ibama, ICMBio, or Funai (ASCEMA, 2020). Changes in Committee members and space for agreement between federative entities are strategies that affect environmental governance. Decree No. 10.347/2020 transferred the concession of public forests, an important policy instrument, to the competence of the Ministry of Agriculture (Brasil, 2020d) and a privatization program included the Conservation Units (Brasil, 2019h), contrary to the determinations of the PNMA and the purposes of the National System of Conservation Units.

The favorable scenario, during the Bolsonaro administration, led to changes in legislation and alterations in policy instruments, through normative acts of the Executive and its agents. The regulation of the period promoted changes in the institutional arena, changes in the policy implementation structure, and modeled the bureaucracy to achieve the objectives of the dismantling policy (Bauer and Knill, 2012; 2014; Bauer et. al, 2021).

14.5 Final Considerations: strategies, scope, and direction of change

We analyzed the changes observed in environmental policies during the Bolsonaro administration and identified different dismantling strategies used by political actors to weaken or dismantle the environmental policy subsystem. The analyzed data allows us to evaluate the scope of changes in the environmental policy subsystem. We found that in the context analyzed, the dismantling policy was implemented through high-visibility strategies, combining active dismantling with dismantling by symbolic actions (Bauer and Knill, 2012; 2014).

Starting with policy density, we did not identify a decrease in the number of environmental policies in the period, since the structuring legislation, the PNMA, and the broad legal coverage created during the democratic period were maintained. Therefore, we deduce that, due to the path dependence of the policy instituted since the 1980s, the costs of its suppression increase (Pierson, 2000). Bauer and Knill (2014) compared changes in OECD social and environmental policies and found that dismantling is less pronounced in environmental policies.

On the other hand, the presence of groups in Parliament that work to decrease the rigor of legislation is not new. Re-regulation, in some cases, moves towards more liberal, decentralized legislation filled with economic incentives for the adherence of private agents, as in some provisions of the Native Vegetation Protection Law, known as the New Forest Code (Brancalion et al., 2016), and in the proposal of the General Environmental Licensing Law (Milanez, Magno, and Wanderley, 2021). However, in the process of building and rebuilding environmental legislation, there are not only proposals for milder legislation, which in itself is already a dismantling of sorts, but also political actors who reject any environmental protection control. Moreover, while the re-regulation processes were being carried out, new legislation proposals began to be processed, such as the president's bill to legalize mining on indigenous lands, an activity that would exert a high environmental impact (Bill No. 191/2020). The project to dismantle environmental protection policies has nonetheless been met with resistance by the Parliament and public opinion. Several attempts at infra-legal norms were judicialized, suspended by the Supreme Court, or lost their validity. There is still an ongoing project asserting itself according to a more or less favorable political context.

Furthermore, in the instrument density dimension, when there is a loosening of regulation or the displacement of policy instruments to other institutional arenas, the dismantling policy was an active process (Bauer and Knill, 2012; 2014). As identified by the loss of discretion of environmental inspectors was removed through infra-legal measures. The private sector was gifted a leading role within licensing and privatization of Conservation Units. These initiatives weaken the determinations of the PNMA that assigns these attributions to the government. The transfer of responsibility of the National Council of the Legal Amazon to the Vice-Presidency of the Republic was excused by a need to solve the environmental crimes that shocked the world, but the military de facto take over of this council weakens environmental governance. Additionality, there is the decentralization of environmental licensing, which is being regulated by Parliament (Bill No. 3729/2004) and was also the subject of the Normative Instruction of MMA/Ibama (No. 8, 20/02/2019), delegating environmental licensing to each state.

Moreover, in terms of formal intensity, as measured by changes in the setting of policy instruments (Bauer and Knill, 2012; 2014), combined with the strategies adopted to transform the public administration (Bauer et al., 2021) we have been able to identify a co-optation of bureaucratic capacity. This is evident through the politicization of technical positions, characterized by ideological appointments as well as an increase in an oppressive and controlling atmosphere, and the militarization of leadership positions. The modeling of bureaucracy was endeavored through changes in the power structure for implementing regulation, administrative, and informational resources, the ideological cleansing of staff, the norms created to foster a new administrative culture, and a decrease in accountability. Regarding resources, there have been constant changes in the composition of committees, councils, and other bodies, with a particular emphasis on the National Tripartite Commission (CTN). Financially, there has been a reduction in planning within the PPA, and authorized resources from the LOAs have not been fully utilized. In terms of information, there has been a compulsory requirement for the Director of ICMBio, at the time a military officer, to review scientific publications.

Finally, regarding substantial intensity, we observed that the regulatory system, considered rigorous, undergoes changes in the scope of its instruments, especially where the application of rules and procedures is made more flexible and where control is delegated to subnational entities, which are strongly constrained by local interests.

In sum, active dismantling was observed in the loss of intensity, formal, and substantial, of the instrument setting that weakened the government capacity needed for the implementation of the regulatory policy. Moreover, the symbolic strategy was evident in Salles' statements, where he perceived the pandemic as an 'opportunity,' as well as in President Bolsonaro's speeches advocating a singular focus on the minerals in the Amazon. Low visibility strategies, such as moving the policy or its instruments to another arena, also happened. However, it is relevant to emphasize that the focus is on the highly visible actions, due to the aim of gaining political credit with strong economic sectors. Bolsonaro and his aligned politicians were 'ideologically convinced that dismantling is the most appropriate solution' (Bauer and Knill, 2014, p. 40) to boost the country's economy. At the base of the dismantling policy, we find deregulation and re-regulation actions all moving towards the goal of undermining environmental policy. The impact of all this on indigenous peoples, specifically in the forest, the environment, and the climate, is difficult to quantify. However, we can assert that the reversibility of the damages done will be slow and costly.

Notes

1 As a scholar who was awarded a master's scholarship by the Coordenação de Aperfeiçoamento de Pessoal de Nível Superior (CAPES) – Brazil, this study received partial funding from CAPES, for which I am grateful.
2 Established through Law No. 7,735 dated 02/22/1989 and subsequently modified by Law No. 11,516 dated 08/28/2007, which established ICMBio.
3 Bolsonaro was elected under the PSL (Social Liberal Party) but disaffiliated during his mandate and joined the PL (Liberal Party), in order to compete in the 2022 elections.
4 The video was made public by determination of the Supreme Federal Court (STF). Available at: www.youtube.com/watch?v=TjndWfgiRQQ.
5 Determination revoked through Decree 11.417/2023
6 The video was made public by determination of the Supreme Federal Court (STF). Available at: www.youtube.com/watch?v=TjndWfgiRQQ
7 Repealed through Decree 11.193/2022.

Bibliography

Abessa, D., Famá, A., and Buruaem, L. (2019) 'The systematic dismantling of Brazilian environmental laws risks losses on all fronts', *Nature Ecology & Evolution*, 3, pp. 510–511.

Andrade, D., Nogueira, F., and Lotta, G. (2021) 'Missão dada é missão cumprida: Management militar no governo Bolsonaro', *Estadão, Blog Gestão, Política e Sociedade*. 16 March. Available at: www.estadao.com.br/politica/gestao-politica-e-sociedade/missao-dada-e-missao-cumprida-management-militar-no-gove rno-bolsonaro/ (Accessed: 20 June 2023).

Araújo, S. (2020) 'Environmental policy in the Bolsonaro Government: The response of environmentalists in the legislative arena', *Brazilian Political Science Review*, 14(2), pp. 1–20.

Araújo, S. (2022) 'Proteção ambiental baseada em evidências? Evolução institucional, planejamento e execução orçamentária no IBAMA', in Koga, N. et al. (eds.) *Políticas públicas e usos de evidências no Brasil: Conceitos, métodos, contextos e práticas*. Brasília: IPEA, pp.725–746.

Araújo, S. and Feldmann, F. (2019) 'Onde está o meio ambiente no Plano Plurianual?', *Valor Econômico*. 3 October. Available at: https://valor.globo.com/opiniao/coluna/onde-esta-o-meio-ambiente-no-plano-plurianual.ghtml (Accessed: 18 June 2023).

ASCEMA (2020) 'Dossiê Cronologia de um desastre anunciado: Ações do Governo Bolsonaro para desmontar as políticas de Meio Ambiente no Brasil', *Associação Nacional dos Servidores do Meio Ambiente*, 9 September. Available at: https://asc emanacional.org.br/2020/09/09/dossie-sobre-desmonte-ambiental-brasileiro-chega-ao-papa-francisco/ (Accessed: 13 May 2023).

Avritzer, L. (2007) 'Sociedade civil, instituições participativas e representação: Da autorização à legitimidade da ação', *Dados*, 50, pp. 443–464.

Barbosa, L., Alves, M., and Grelle, C. (2021) 'Actions against sustainability: Dismantling of the environmental policies in Brazil', *Land Use Policy*, 104.

Bardin, L. (2017) *Análise de Conteúdo*. São Paulo: Edição 70, pp.1-4.

Barrucho, L. (2019) 'Demissão de chefe do Inpe é 'alarmante', diz diretor de centro da Nasa', *BBC News Brasil in London,* 7 August. Available at: www.bbc.com/portugu ese/brasil-49256294 (Accessed: 4 June 2023).

Bauer, M. and Knill, C. (2012) 'Understanding policy dismantling: An analytical framework', in Bauer, M., Jordan, A., Green-Pedersen, C., and Heritier, A. (eds.) *Dismantling public policy: Preferences, strategies, and effects*. Oxford: Oxford University Press, pp. 331–348.

Bauer, M. and Knill, C. (2014) 'A conceptual framework for the comparative analysis of policy change: Measurement, explanation and strategies of policy dismantling', *Journal of Comparative Policy Analysis: Research and Practice*, 16(1), pp. 28–44.

Bauer, M. et al. (2021) 'Introduction: Populists, democratic backsliding, and public administration', in Bauer, M. et al. (eds.). *Democratic backsliding and public administration: How populists in government transform state bureaucracies*. Cambridge: Cambridge University Press, pp. 1–21.

Bragança, D. (2019) 'Bolsonaro desautoriza operação do Ibama em UC desmatada', *((o)) eco*, 14 April. Available at: https://oeco.org.br/noticias/bolsonaro-desautoriza-opera cao-do-ibama-em-uc-desmatada/ (Accessed on: 18 June 2023).

Brancalion, P. et al. (2016) 'Análise crítica da Lei de Proteção da Vegetação Nativa (2012), que substituiu o antigo Código Florestal: atualizações e ações em curso', *Natureza & Conservação*, pp. 1–16. Available at: http://dx.doi.org/10.1016/j.ncon.2016.03.004

Brasil (2019a). Instrução Normativa nº 8, de 20 de fevereiro de 2019.

Brasil (2019b). Instrução Normativa nº 7, de 15 de fevereiro de 2019.

Brasil (2019c). Decreto nº 9.759, de 11 de abril de 2019.

Brasil (2019d). Decreto nº 9.760, de 11 de abril de 2019.

Brasil (2019e). Decreto nº 9.806, de 28 de maio de 2019.

Brasil (2019f). Instrução Normativa nº 22, de 30 de julho de 2019.

Brasil (2019g). Medida Provisória nº 900 de 17 de outubro de 2019.

Brasil (2019h). Decreto nº 10.147, de 2 dezembro de 2019.

Brasil (2020a). Instrução Normativa Conjunta nº 2, de 29 de janeiro de 2020.

Brasil (2020b). Decreto nº 10.234, de 11 de fevereiro de 2020.

Brasil (2020c). Decreto nº 10.239, 11 de fevereiro de 2020.

Brasil (2020d). Decreto nº 10.347 de 13 de maio de 2020.

Brasil (2020e). Portaria nº 524, de 1 de outubro de 2020

Brasil (2020f). Ato Declaratório do Presidente da Mesa do CN nº 22/2020.

Brasil (2021a). Portaria nº 151, de 10 de março de 2021.

Brasil (2021b). Instrução Normativa Conjunta MMA/IBAMA/ICMBio nº 1 de 12 de abril de 2021.

Camargo, S. (2021) 'ICMBio proíbe servidores de publicarem textos e artigos científicos sem autorização prévia', *Conexão Planeta*, 16 March. Available at: https://conexao planeta.com.br/blog/icmbio-proibe-servidores-de-publicarem-textos-e-artigos-cien tificos-sem-autorizacao-previa/ (Accessed: 18 June 2023).

Capelari, M. et al. (2020) 'Mudança de larga escala na política ambiental: Análise da realidade brasileira', *Revista de Administração Pública*, 54(6), pp. 1691–1710.

Capelari, M., Pereira, A. K., Rivera, N. M., and Araújo, S. M. V. G. (2023) 'Radical reorganization of environmental policy contemporaneous evidence from Brazil', *Latin American Perspectives*, 50(1), January, pp. 115–132.

Carta Capital (2019) 'Interesse na Amazônia não é no índio nem na [...] árvore, é no minério', diz Bolsonaro', *Carta Capital*, 1 October. Available at: bit.ly/48dNH9v (Accessed: 14 July 2023).

Carvalho, R. et al. (2022) 'Lack of transparency and social participation undermine the fight against deforestation in Brazil', *Die Erde*, 153(1), pp. 65–69.

Cavalcante, P., Lotta, G., and Oliveira, V. (2018) 'Do insulamento burocrático à governança democrática: as transformações institucionais e a burocracia no Brasil', in Pires, R., Lotta, G., and Oliveira, V. (eds.) *Burocracia e políticas públicas no Brasil: interseções analíticas*. Brasília: IPEA, ENAP, pp. 59–83.

Costa, E. (2023) 'Funai inicia 'desmilitarização' após quatro anos de governo Bolsonaro', *Infoamazonia*. 19 January. Avaiable at: https://infoamazonia.org/2023/01/19/funai-inicia-desmilitarizacao-do-quadro-apos-quatro-anos-de-governo-bolsonaro/ (Accessed: 7 December 2023).

Cruz, M. (2021) *Ideias, atores e instituições: A formulação da política regulatória para agrotóxicos no Poder Legislativo brasileiro*, Dissertation of UFPA-Programa de Pós-Graduação em Ciência Política.

Fellet, J. (2022) 'Agenda do presidente da Funai registra só 2 encontros com indígenas em 2022', *BBC News Brasil*. 16 June 2022. Avaiable at: www.bbc.com/portuguese/brasil-61818932 (Accessed: 7 December 2023).

Ferrante, L. and Fearnside, P. (2019) 'Brazil's new president and 'ruralists' threaten Amazonia's environment, traditional peoples and the global climate', *Environmental Conservation*, 46(4), pp. 261–263.

Ferreira, J. et al. (2014) 'Brazil's environmental leadership at risk – Mining and dams threaten protected áreas', *Science*, 346, pp. 706–707.

Figueiredo, A. and Limongi, F. (1999) *Executivo e Legislativo na nova ordem constitucional*. Rio de Janeiro: editora FGV.

Freitas, A. (2016) *O presidencialismo de coalizão*. Rio de Janeiro: Fundação Konrad Adenauer.

Hancher, L. and Moran, M. (1989) 'Introduction: Regulation and deregulation', *European Journal of Political Research*, 17, pp. 129–136.

Jordan, A., Bauer, M., and Green-Pedersen, C. (2012) 'Policy dismantling: An introduction', in Bauer, M., Jordan, A., Green-Pedersen, C., and Heritier, A. (eds.) *Dismantling public policy: Preferences, strategies, and effects*. Oxford: Oxford, pp. 2–29.

Jornal Nacional (2020) 'Investidores internacionais manifestam a embaixadas do Brasil preocupação com desmatamento', *Jornal Nacional*, 23 June. Available at: https://g1.globo.com/jornal-nacional/noticia/2020/06/23/investidores-internacionais-manifestam-a-embaixadas-do-brasil-preocupacao-com-desmatamento.ghtml (Accessed: 18 June 2023).

Leme, T. (2016) 'Governança ambiental no nível municipal', in Moura, A. (ed.). *Governança ambiental no Brasil: Instituições, atores e políticas públicas,* Brasília: Ipea, pp. 147–174.

Lipsky, M. (2019) *Burocracia de nível de rua. Dilemas do indivíduo nos serviços públicos* , Brasília: ENAP.

Lotta, G., Silveira, M., and Fernandez, M. (2022) 'Ações e reações: mecanismos de opressão à burocracia e suas diferentes estratégias de reação', in Gomide, A.,Sá e Silva, M. and, Leopoldi, M. (eds.). *Desmonte e reconfiguração das políticas públicas (2016-2022)*, Brasília: Ipea, pp. 501–527.

Lotta, Gabriela S. and Vaz, José C. (2015) 'Arranjos institucionais de políticas públicas: Aprendizados a partir de casos de arranjos institucionais complexos no Brasil', *Revista do Serviço Público. Brasília*, 2, p. 66.

Lowi, T. (1972) 'Four systems of policy, politics, and choice', *Public Administration Review*, 32(4), pp. 298–310.

Maisonnave, F. and Valente, R. (2018) 'Bolsonaro retaliou fiscais do Ibama após ser multado por pesca irregular', *Folha de São Paulo*, 15 November. Available at: www1. folha.uol.com.br/poder/2018/10/bolsonaro-retaliou-fiscais-do-ibama-apos-ser-mult ado-por-pesca-irregular.shtml (Accessed: 25 May 2023).

Majone, G. (1989) *Regulating Europe*. London: Routledge.

Majone, G. (1990) *Deregulation or Re-regulation?* London: Pinter.

Menezes, R. and Barbosa Jr., R. (2021) 'Environmental governance under Bolsonaro: Dismantling institutions, curtailing participation, delegitimising opposition', *Zeitschrift für vergleichende Politikwissenschaft,* 15, pp. 229–247.

Milanez, B., Magno, L., and Wanderley, L. (2021) 'O Projeto de Lei Geral do Licenciamento (PL 3.729/2004) e seus efeitos para o setor mineral', *Versos – Textos para Discussão PoEMAS*, 5(1), pp. 1–32.

Moura, A. (2016) 'Trajetória da política ambiental federal no Brasil', in Moura, A. (ed.) *Governança ambiental no Brasil: Instituições, atores e políticas públicas,* Brasília: Ipea, pp. 13-44.

Oliveira, M. (2021) 'Movimentos sociais, ocupação de cargos públicos e políticas públicas: Uma relação de sucesso. O caso da produção do Plano de Prevenção e Combate ao Desmatamento na Amazônia – PPCDAM', in Abers, R.(ed.) *Ativismo institucional: Criatividade e luta na burocracia brasileira*, Brasília: Editora UnB, pp. 123–153.

Pierson, P. (1994) *Dismantling the welfare state?: Reagan, Thatcher, and the politics of retrenchment*. Cambridge: Cambridge University Press.

Pierson, P. (2000) 'Increasing returns, path dependence, and the study of Politics', *American Political Science Review*, 94(2), pp. 251–267.

Pinheiro, A. and Araújo, A. (2023) 'O papel dos estados nos debates e nos produtos do processo sobre a Lei Geral do Licenciamento Ambiental', in Palotti, P. et al. (eds.) *E os Estados? Federalismo, relações intergovernamentais e políticas públicas no Brasil contemporâneo*. Rio de Janeiro: IPEA, pp. 645–673.

Poder360 (2020) 'Cada vez mais o índio é 1 ser humano igual a nós', diz Bolsonaro', YouTube, 23 January 2020. Available at: www.youtube.com/watch?v=WX7Xrs2Y 3QY&t=5s (Accessed: 6 December 2023).

Prizibisczki, C. (2022) 'Servidores do Ibama repudiam fala de Eduardo Bim sobre seus funcionários: "muita gente louca", *((o))eco*, 11 May. Available at: https://oeco.org.br/ noticias/servidores-do-ibama-repudiam-fala-de-eduardo-bim-sobre-seus-funcionar ios-muita-gente-louca/ (Accessed: 18 June 2023).

Resende, S. (2018) 'No que depender de mim, não tem mais demarcação de terra indígena', diz Bolsonaro a TV', *Folha de São Paulo,* 5 November. Available at: www1.folha.uol. com.br/poder/2018/11/no-que-depender-de-mim-nao-tem-mais-demarcacao-de-terra-indigena-diz-bolsonaro-a-tv.shtml (Accessed: 26 May 2023).

Santana, R. (2019) 'Frente em Defesa dos Direitos dos Povos Indígenas é lançada no Congresso Nacional com 248 parlamentares', *CIMI*, 4 April. Available at: https://cimi.org.br/2019/04/frente-em-defesa-dos-direitos-dos-povos-indigenas-e-lancada-no-congresso-nacional-com-248-parlamentares (Accessed: 6 December 2023).

Saraiva, A. (2023) *Selva: Madeireiros, garimpeiros e corruptos na Amazônia sem lei*. Rio de Janeiro: Intrínseca.

Siga Brasil (2023) *Siga Brasil Painel Cidadão*. Available at: bit.ly/49yhScj (Accessed: 24 July 2023).

Silva, D. (2023) 'Quem tem medo do Cadastro Ambiental Rural (CAR)?', *Estadão*. 13 June. Available at: www.estadao.com.br/politica/legis-ativo/quem-tem-medo-do-cadastro-ambiental-rural-car/ (Accessed: 27 June 2023).

Silva, E., Ribeiro, A., and Medeiros, A. (2020) 'Repertórios de interação e instituições participativas: o subsistema estadual e federal de direitos humanos', in *Anais Eletrônico do 12º Encontro da Associação Brasileira de Ciência Política*, Available at: www. abcp2020.sinteseeventos.com.br/simposio/view?ID_SIMPOSIO=8 (Accessed: 26 Februar 2023)

Soares, L. and Baines, S. (2021) "They are almost humans like us". Indigenous politics and policy dismantling under Bolsonaro's government, *Videre*, 13(28), pp.124–149.

Valente, R. (2019) 'General cai da presidência da Funai após pressão de ruralistas', *Folha de São Paulo*, 11 June. Available at: www1.folha.uol.com.br/poder/2019/06/general-cai-da-presidencia-da-funai-apos-pressao-de-ruralistas.shtml (Accessed: 07 December 2023).

Wenzel, F. (2019) 'Após ministro ameaçar servidores, presidente do ICMBio pede demissão', *((o))eco*, 15 April. Available at: https://oeco.org.br/reportagens/apos-ministro-ameacar-servidores-presidente-do-icmbio-pede-demissao/ (Accessed: 18 June 2023).

Werneck, F. (2021) 'Norma imposta por Salles "paralisa Ibama", afirmam servidores', *Observatório do Clima*, 20 April. Available at: www.oc.eco.br/norma-imposta-por-salles-paralisa-ibama-afirmam-servidores/ (Accessed: 18 June 2023).

Xu, A. (2020) 'The political origins of deforestation in the Brazilian Amazon, 2000-2012', *SSRN*, pp. 1–62. doi: http://dx.doi.org/10.2139/ssrn.3707331

15

DISARMAMENT IN PERIL

The Right Wing and the Unraveling of Gun Control

Ludmila Ribeiro, Valéria Oliveira, Rafael Rocha and Alexandre Diniz

Introduction

On July 21, 2023, the Brazilian government issued Decree 11,615/2023, suggesting the reimplementation of more stringent parameters for weapons control. This represents a pivotal moment in the ongoing discourse within one of the world's most violent nations. In 2022, the homicide rate reached 20 per 100,000 inhabitants, historically one of the lowest, yet Brazil remains among the most lethal countries globally. Notably, over 70% of these deaths are attributable to firearms, both legal and illicit, proliferating daily across the national landscape (FBSP, 2023).

Two decades ago, Brazil was a role model for responsible firearms and ammunition regulation under Law 10,826/2003, known locally as the Disarmament Statute. The initial anticipation was that restricting access to firearms and ammunition would lead to a decline in homicides committed with these instruments, significantly reducing rates of intentional and lethal violence (Cerqueira et al., 2020). However, as history often deviates from econometric model predictions, firearm control policies also respond to shifts in economic, social, and political dynamics (Rupert, 2015). The erosion of the Disarmament Statute aligns with the political ascendancy of Jair Bolsonaro, the Brazilian president from 2019 to 2022, sharing characteristics with other far-right administrations in the United States and Hungary during the same period (Solano et al., 2018).

To comprehend these changes, it is crucial to underscore how the pervasive sense of insecurity constitutes a cornerstone for populist far-right campaigns globally. This was evident in Brazil during Jair Bolsonaro's 2018 electoral

DOI: 10.4324/9781003487777-19

campaign (Holt et al., 2020). Apart from being one of the most violent nations globally, Brazil boasts the second-largest small firearms industry. These companies actively sought to revoke the Disarmament Statute and, to accomplish this, financially backed right-wing congressional candidates, including the longstanding deputy Jair Bolsonaro, for decades (Macaulay, 2020). This strategic support has contributed to the formation of a legislative bloc crucial to shaping firearm control policies in the country, known as the "bullet caucus" (Macaulay, 2017).

Comprising primarily current and former Armed Forces and Public Security professionals, this group, expanding with each election post-Disarmament Statute, has adopted the rhetoric of freedom of defense and insecurity to advocate for arming the civilian population (Miranda, 2019). The primary argument is that firearms save lives by enabling individuals to defend themselves against perceived threats, an argument resonating with pro-arms values in the United States (Carlson, 2019). Since the early 2000s, subsequent to the approval of the Disarmament Statute and a referendum on even stricter rules for firearm acquisition and possession, there have been numerous changes in the normative framework. These changes progressively extended access to firearms and ammunition to more actors, culminating in the Bolsonaro government's peak deregulation, significantly expanding both the quantity of accessible firearms for Brazilian citizens and altering provisions regarding eligibility and permitted ammunition (Ribeiro & Oliveira, 2021).

To reconstruct this narrative conceptually, we draw on the insights of Bauer & Knill (2014) concerning the role of laws in shaping and reforming the Welfare State. Building on the work of Jordan and Bauer (2013), we aim to comprehend the dismantling of firearm control policies by exploring factors such as the origins of political preferences (the role of the "bullet caucus"), dismantling strategies (through the approval of new laws and presidential decrees), and the ensuing effects, particularly the surge in firearms, especially those with higher lethal potential, and their impact on homicide rates. In analyzing the patterns of dismantling firearm control policy in Brazil, we conducted a thorough review of legislative changes over the past two decades, highlighting key legal milestones created or amended. Our approach seeks to elucidate the factors influencing the quantity and diversity of weapons registered by the Army – our response variable – while considering fluctuations in the regulation of firearms and ammunition in the country.

To accomplish our aim, we utilize a database supplied by the Non-Governmental Organization "Fiquem Sabendo,"[1] which organizes a range of public data obtained through government requests under the Access to Information Law (LAI). Specifically, this database mirrors the Military Weapons Management System (SIGMA),[2] and contains records of weapons held by Hunters, Shooters, and Collectors (CACs). These records were obtained through an information access request filed under LAI, assigned number 601430020692022-99, and subsequently made public through the newsletter "Don't LAI to me." The publication's name cleverly plays on the law's acronym (LAI) and the phonetic resemblance of "lie" in English.[3] The database encompasses 1,671,763 registered weapons, covering nearly a century of history (1900–2023) based on acquisition dates. The weapons included are typically designated for restricted use due to their high lethality, traditionally reserved for state agencies. However, legislative allowances extend authorization to hunters, shooters, and collectors, provided they are duly registered with the Army. For the purpose of our study, we concentrate on the years leading up to the approval of the Disarmament Statute and up to the present day, emphasizing the recent surge in the number of armed civilians.

In this chapter, we reconstruct the framework of firearms regulation in Brazil from 1997 to 2023. This involves scrutinizing the political dynamics (with a focus on the right wing), the opportunity structures shaped by new laws, and the effects and outcomes associated with policy changes. Before delving into the reconstruction of this narrative, it is imperative to make two disclaimers. Our analysis focuses on records of firearms in the possession of CACs, irrespective of whether they are currently in circulation. This is due to the unavailability of seizure databases from the Federal Police, despite repeated requests based on the Access to Information Law (LAI). Additionally, we operate under the assumption that the purchase and registration of a firearm with the Army indicate the intent to use it actively, implying a higher level of commitment from the citizen to its safekeeping and potential loss. Furthermore, our scope is limited to legal firearms, excluding those entering the country illegally, a factor with significant implications for the quantity of violent deaths recorded in Brazil (Sanjurjo, 2022).[4]

Three Steps Back: the context before the Disarmament Statute

To comprehend the significance of Law No. 10,826/2003, commonly referred to as the Disarmament Statute, it is imperative to delve into historical context. According to Benetti (2022), the regulatory framework concerning the production, commercialization, possession, and carrying of firearms in Brazil originated with Presidential Decree No. 24,602/1934. Initially, this decree only governed the manufacture of war weapons and ammunition, expressly prohibiting access by individuals.

During the early years of the civil-military dictatorship established in 1964, Decree 55,649/1965 was introduced, regulating the production, trade, and circulation of "weapons, ammunition, powders, explosives, and their elements and accessories." This was under the exclusive control of the Military Government and its Ministry of War (Pekny et al., 2015). This decree played a pivotal role in the creation of SIGMA and marked a milestone when the Army assumed a key role in the oversight of firearms and ammunition. However, it is also responsible for Brazil ranking second globally in the production of small arms, as one of its objectives was to promote the development of the national arms industry, including firearms and ammunition, in the Brazilian export agenda (Pekny et al., 2015, p. 5).

In 1980, Ministerial Order 1,261 mandated that state Secretariats of Public Security register firearms acquired by citizens. This move was a clear attempt to exert greater control over armed violence, particularly in the context of the return to democracy (Benetti, 2022). Citizens seeking to acquire a firearm were required to meet certain criteria, including being over 21 years old, having a defined profession, possessing a clean criminal record, and exhibiting impeccable conduct. In socio-political terms (Pekny et al., 2015), this often meant having no affiliation with leftist movements, given that the civil-military dictatorship persisted until 1985, and various tensions prevailed during that period. This decree aimed, on one hand, to secure a market for the burgeoning arms industry and, on the other hand, to regulate the expanding market for firearms and ammunition. At the time, homicide rates were still relatively low but had already reached double digits, hovering around 12 deaths per 100,000 inhabitants (IPEA/FBSP, 2021).

However, the 1990s marked a stark contrast in terms of armed violence. The influx of cocaine into illegal markets in major cities coincided with the use of highly lethal weapons (Leeds, 1998). This triggered more violent conflicts related to the "war on drugs," involving both the police and organized crime (Manso & Dias, 2018). Police lethality became evident in infamous incidents like Carandiru (1992), Candelária (1993), Vigário Geral (1993), and Favela Naval (1997), highlighting the unpreparedness of law enforcement to handle available weapons in Brazil (Sanjurjo, 2020; 2022). In response to this situation, in 1997, students from the Law School of the University of São Paulo (USP) initiated the Sou da Paz (I Am for Peace) campaign, advocating for civilian disarmament. This marked the first civil society initiative to raise awareness about the rapid surge in urban violence and the necessity for gun control (Lucas, 2008, p. 27). Similar campaigns had proven successful in Albania, Cambodia, and Liberia, leading to the formation of the Sou da Paz Institute in Brazil, drawing support from other non-governmental organizations (NGOs) addressing public safety concerns (Sanjurjo, 2020).

Pressured by these events, the National Congress approved Law 9,437 in 1997, establishing the National Firearms System (SINARM) as the initial step to curb the circulation of firearms (Benetti, 2022). The concept was that an information system would contribute to a better understanding of how firearms legally circulated within Brazilian society, a circulation that had multiplied substantially in the 1990s. Focusing specifically on CACs, the data revealed a conspicuous increase in the number of available weapons – Brazil witnessed a more than sixfold rise in the number of weapons acquired by this group within a decade, going from four weapons for every 100,000 inhabitants in 1990 to 25 per 100,000 inhabitants in 2000. This surge essentially flooded the market with artifacts capable of significantly contributing to the rise in violent deaths.

Pekny et al. (2015) underscore two additional innovations introduced by Law No. 9,437/1997. First, firearms would be granted based on the criterion of "effective necessity." Second, the law prohibited carrying firearms, meaning individuals could possess a firearm but were not permitted to carry it, as doing so could escalate ordinary conflicts into lethal encounters. This prohibition was particularly relevant given that 70% of homicides recorded at that time resulted from close-proximity conflicts, such as tensions between friends, neighbors, and partners, that, due to the availability of firearms, often ended tragically. These concerns were not trivial, especially considering that by 1997, the homicide rate had already reached almost 25 per 100,000 inhabitants, more than double that observed in the early 1980s (see Graph 15.1).

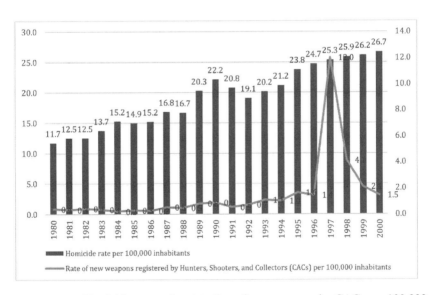

GRAPH 15.1 Homicide rate and registration of new weapons by CACs per 100,000 inhabitants (1980–2000).

Notes

a *Death due to external or non-natural causes, meaning injuries caused by violence (accidents, homicides, suicides, or suspicious deaths). Information comes from SIM-DATASUS and is made available by IPEAdata*

b *Military Weapons Management System, provided by Fiquem Sabendo.*

The introduction of new legislation, coupled with movements advocating increased control over weapons and ammunition, resulted in a significant upswing in new weapon registrations by CACs, reaching unprecedented levels (12 per 100,000 inhabitants). Despite a decline in the acquisition of new weapons by this segment in 1998, homicide rates remained alarmingly high. Consequently, SINARM (the SIGMA already existed but only recorded CACs and was under the jurisdiction of the Armed Forces) presented an opportunity for the police to register confiscated weapons. Subsequently, this information could be cross-referenced to discern the methods by which violent, lethal, and intentional deaths occurred in Brazil (Benetti, 2022). This marked a pivotal advancement in crime prevention and the confiscation of illegal weapons by police forces (Pekny et al., 2015).

Two steps back: the approval of the Disarmament Statute and the subsequent years

The onset of the new century in Brazil was marked by bloodshed, with approximately 29 deaths per 100,000 inhabitants in 2001, representing a growth of over 40% compared to 1980 when the rate stood at 12 homicides per 100,000 inhabitants (FBSP, 2023). When isolating deaths from firearms, these rates surged from 5 to 19 deaths per 100,000 inhabitants over two decades (IPEA; FBSP, 2020), underscoring the critical role of weaponry in the issue. Despite ample evidence linking the proliferation of firearms to increased homicide rates, persuading a vast majority to support more restrictive gun control legislation was no easy feat (Pekny et al., 2015; Benetti, 2022). Adding to the challenge was Brazil's standing as one of the world's largest producers of small arms by the early 2000s (Lucas, 2008, p. 28). Several congressmen, including Jair Bolsonaro, were financially supported by these industries and vehemently opposed any tighter legislation (Macaulay, 2017, 2020).

During this period, the term "bullet caucus" emerged in the media, designating lawmakers, primarily from the police (such as Alberto Fraga and later Flávio Bolsonaro) or the Armed Forces (like former President Bolsonaro himself), funded by lobbyists from the firearms industry and supported by advocates of tough policies (Macaulay, 2017, 2020; Miranda, 2019). Despite significant financial support for pro-gun initiatives, a shift in public opinion in favor of gun and ammunition control managed to sway deputies and senators (Miranda, 2019; Sanjurjo, 2022). Surprisingly, by the end of 2003, the Disarmament Statute was approved. Key changes introduced by Law No. 10,826 included: (1) raising the minimum age for firearm purchases from 21 to 25 years; (2) requiring a demonstration of effective need to acquire a firearm, along with psychological and technical proficiency tests for handling it; (3) prohibiting carrying (being armed), except under special conditions like hunting; and (4) implementing new measures for ammunition control, including identification to facilitate tracking (Lucas, 2008; Pekny et al., 2015; Sanjurjo, 2020).

Article 35 of the Disarmament Statute also mandated a referendum in 2005 to decide on prohibiting the sale of firearms to civilians nationwide (Miranda, 2019). According to Sanjurjo (2022), the choice of a referendum was unusual as no country in Latin America had approved firearms control legislation, and this option delegated decision-making powers to voters. Despite initial support for ending the arms trade reaching 82% during the campaign announcement (Lucas, 2008, p. 32), the nascent "bullet caucus" mobilized, leveraging the influence of print media, advertising, and public propaganda to secure an unexpected outcome (Sanjurjo, 2023). Against all expectations, 63.9% rejected the prohibition, maintaining the sale of firearms within the limits imposed by Law No. 10,826 of 2003, which can still be deemed "the most comprehensive firearms control policy in national history" (Sanjurjo, 2020, p. 136).

The contentious approval of the Disarmament Statute and the subsequent referendum did not equate to substantial losses for the arms industry (Macaulay, 2020). As depicted in Graph 15.2, in the year of the legislative debate (2003), there was an upswing in weapon acquisitions by CACs (5.3). Over the following two years, new registrations increased even more, reaching a rate of 22.1 per 100,000 inhabitants. Only in 2006, the year following the referendum, did the first significant drop in the rate of new weapon registrations by CACs occur. In other words, despite the heightened difficulty of acquisition, the curve of new weapon purchases trended upward, resulting in the country concluding 2010 with a rate of new weapons registered by CACs exceeding 20 per 100,000 inhabitants (Graph 15.2).

Examining Graphs 15.1 and 15.2 allows for insights into studies linking the approval of the Disarmament Statute with intentional lethal violence. Pekny et al. (2015) highlight that, in addition to the decline observed in 2004, the growth rate of the homicide rate somewhat diminished in the subsequent years. According to Benetti (2022), whereas the homicide rate was increasing by 6.9% per year before the Disarmament Statute, from 2004 onwards, the growth remained around 0.3% per year, on average. Souza et al. (2007, p. 581) found that a significant part of the reduction in deaths and hospitalizations resulting from firearm incidents could be attributed to government measures stemming from Law No. 10,826, enacted in 2003. According to the authors, the legislation prevented up to 5,563 deaths in 2004 alone. Cerqueira and Mello (2013) noted that, if it weren't for the Disarmament Statute, between 2004 and 2007, the homicide rate would have been 12% higher than observed.

Despite the positive outcomes, in 2008, efforts to relax the Disarmament Statute gained momentum, spearheaded by what later became known as the "new right," prominently featuring Jair Bolsonaro, then a deputy for Rio de Janeiro (Solano et al., 2018). The approval of Law No. 11,706 allowed residents

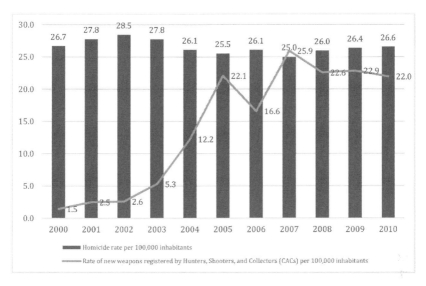

GRAPH 15.2   Homicide[a] Rate and Rate of New Weapon Registrations by CACs[b] per 100,000 Inhabitants (2000–2010).

Notes

a *Death due to external or non-natural causes, meaning injuries caused by violence (accidents, homicides, suicides, or suspicious deaths). Information comes from SIM-DATASUS and is made available by IPEAdata.*

b *Military Weapons Management System, provided by Fiquem Sabendo.*

in rural areas, aged 25 or older, who relied on firearms for family sustenance, to carry weapons under the "subsistence hunter" category. Members of municipal guards in metropolitan areas were granted the right to carry firearms while on duty. Additionally, specific accreditation rules from the Federal Police were imposed on other occupations, such as private security personnel, responsible for evaluating psychological fitness and technical proficiency in firearm handling (Sanjurjo, 2022, 2023). Notably, Brazil was governed by the Workers' Party with Lula as president during this time, marking the period when the "new right" began to gain more traction against the left (Solano et al., 2018; Sanjurjo, 2023). Interestingly, despite these changes, in 2008, there was a reduction in the rate of new weapons registered by CACs, returning to levels similar to those observed during the implementation of the Disarmament Statute (22.6).

Howerver, between 2007 and 2010, the increase in homicide rates (following a decline in previous years) coincided with a decrease in the rate of new weapons registered by CACs (though still significantly higher than in the previous decade) (Sanjurjo, 2022). Pro-gun associations interpreted these trends as indicating that the), but it overlooks what research in the United States has demonstrated for decades: new weapons do not immediately produce effects, and there is a certain delay between the purchase and the occurrence of violent and intentional deaths (Braga et al., 2021).

A step backward: the intensification of armament between 2010 and 2018

The 2010s began with an unprecedented quantity of weapons, considering only those already registered by CACs in the SIGMA. If, in the year 2000, there were 25 weapons for every 100,000 inhabitants, by 2010 this ratio had already risen to 151 weapons for every group of 100,000 inhabitants. It was also one of the most violent decades in the history of Brazil. There was not only a rise in intentional violent deaths in states previously considered peaceful but also the consolidation of criminal factions, which often, at this point, used the prerogatives of CACs for the legal acquisition of highly lethal weapons (Sanjurjo, 2022, 2023).[5] It also marks the direct involvement of the National Association of the Arms and Ammunition Industry (ANIAM) in openly financing the electoral campaigns of right-wing deputies and senators, both in 2010 and later in 2014 (Pekny et al., 2015).

Previously, companies like Taurus and CBC individually financed some candidates, but now they were collectively supporting the already consolidated "bullet caucus" (Benetti, 2022). This pivotal moment solidified the distinction between the "law-abiding citizen" and the "criminal" (and those who defend them) in the Brazilian congress and society at large (Miranda, 2019). It is crucial to mention that this moment played a significant role in shaping the agendas of what we now recognize as the extreme right, an ideological and political movement that propelled Jair Bolsonaro to the presidency (Rupert, 2015). The "law-abiding citizen," represented by lawmakers of the "bullet caucus," advocated for the relaxation of the Disarmament Statute to protect themselves and their families from "unjust aggressions" (Benetti, 2022). The "criminals" encompassed lawbreakers, criminals, robbers, rapists, and drug dealers, living outside the norms that regulate life in society (Benetti, 2022).

The opposition between these two groups facilitated several legislative changes regarding civilian arms, including the expansion of gun ownership for different categories (Miranda, 2019). Up to that point, this progressive relaxation, allowing the carrying of firearms on duty, extended to municipal guards in cities with more than 50,000 inhabitants during Lula's presidency (2003 to 2010) (Law No. 10,867/2004), auditors from the Federal Revenue and Labor Auditors (Law No. 11,501/2007), and, during Dilma's term, it extended to security personnel from the Courts and Public Prosecutor's Office (Law No. 12,694/2012) and prison officers (Law No. 12,993/2014) (Macaulay, 2017). The year 2016 marked the impeachment of the popularly elected president, Dilma

Rousseff of the Workers' Party (PT), and the rise to the presidency of her vice president, Michel Temer of the Brazilian Democratic Movement (MDB), an old Brazilian right-wing party more aligned with the pro-gun discourse (Solano et al., 2018).

The Michel Temer government began on May 12, 2016, following the acceptance of the impeachment process against Rousseff by the Federal Senate, and it was marked by the deregulation of gun control with the approval of various proposals from the "bullet caucus" in the Chamber of Deputies (Miranda, 2019). Decree No. 8,938/2016 introduced several changes, including (i) extending the validity of firearm registration from three to five years, allowing civilians to possess them; (ii) requiring a technical capacity certificate every three years, making it mandatory only every ten years or every two renewals; (iii) expanding the psychological test and criminal record certificate to a period of five years. Ordinance No. 356/2017 regulated the possibility for public security agencies and the armed forces to use confiscated weapons. And Ordinance No. 28/2017 allowed members of shooting clubs to carry their loaded weapons to the training site, whereas before, ammunition had to be transported separately. Due to these changes, in 2018, when the Statute of Disarmament turned 15 years old, the rate of new weapons acquired by CACs reached the highest point in its history so far, with 44 new artifacts for every 100,000 inhabitants (Graph 15.3).

Lethal violence continued to surge in the country, reaching its zenith in 2017 with a rate of 31.3 homicides per 100,000 inhabitants (Graph 15.3). The majority (72%) was committed with firearms, propelling the country to the top of the global ranking for firearm-related deaths. This position was attributed to the vast number of circulating firearms and their immense lethality (Szabó & Risso, 2018, p. 100). Another pertinent aspect of the SIGMA database is its ability to uncover changes in the types of weapons acquired by CACs over time, considering the lethality potential of these weapons (Graph 15.4). To comprehend these changes, we categorized them into four groups: (i) revolvers, small arms characterized by a rotating cylinder with a limited amount of ammunition, often used for personal defense; (ii) pistols, medium-sized and semi-automatic weapons with a single projectile per shot, having the capacity for more ammunition and greater firepower than revolvers; (iii) shotguns, featuring a long barrel, generally with a larger caliber than revolvers, employed in activities such as hunting and personal defense due to their greater impact at short distances; (iv) rifles, weapons that should be restricted to security forces, as they have the ability for selective or automatic firing, reaching targets at a greater distance. The remaining weapons were categorized as "Others" and represent a very small percentage throughout the entire period. Observing the percentage of each of these four types of weapons acquired from 1997 to 2018, the year of Jair Bolsonaro's election, it is noticeable that there is a reduction in the percentage of revolvers vis-à-vis a

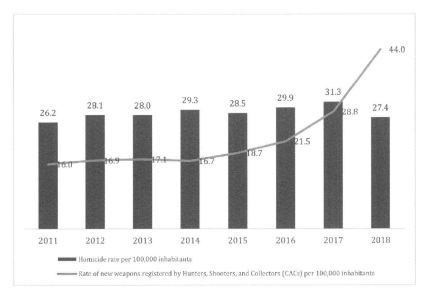

GRAPH 15.3 Homicide[a] rate and registration of new weapons by CACs[b] per 100,000 inhabitants (2011–2018).

Notes

a *Death due to external or non-natural causes, meaning injuries caused by violence (accidents, homicides, suicides, or suspicious deaths). Information comes from SIM-DATASUS and is made available by IPEAdata.*

b *Military Weapons Management System, provided by Fiquem Sabendo.*

substantive increase in rifles. The latter went from 10% of the total new weapons in 1997 to 18% of the new CAC registrations in 2018, even though they should be the exclusive property of the Armed Forces in wartime contexts (Szabó & Risso, 2018).

In 2018, the year of the presidential elections that would bring victory to Bolsonaro, Brazil not only faced significantly high rates of intentional violent deaths but also became one of the countries with the highest number of weapons in circulation, including those with high offensive potential, such as rifles (Szabó & Risso, 2018). Jair Bolsonaro's presidential campaign heightened these two dimensions. With the hand gesture symbolizing a gun, a campaign symbol, the candidate clearly indicated his main agenda: to increase the number of weapons owned civillians (Ribeiro & Oliveira, 2021). To address the issue of homicides, the presidential candidate echoed a characteristic discourse of the "bullet caucus," stating that "by making self-defense difficult for citizens, the State facilitated the life of the criminal," as the criminal could commit crimes without fearing the victim's reaction (Oliveira & Ribeiro, 2021).

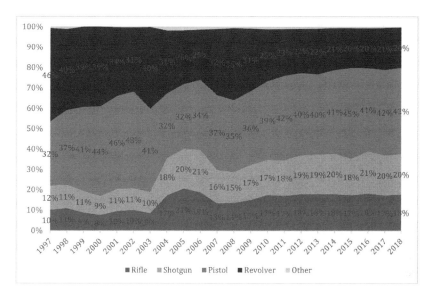

GRAPH 15.4 Registration of new weapons recorded by CACs in the SIGMA by type of equipment (1997–2018).

Source: Military Weapons Management System, provided by Fiquem Sabendo.

For Bolsonaro, the issue of public security should be "addressed" with more weapons in the hands of civilians, an argument supported by the military and police forces (Solano et al., 2018). The backing from defense and public security agents seems somewhat contradictory because more weapons represent increased risks for this category, a fact documented in research primarily conducted in the United States (Carlson, 2021). In that country, despite the strength of the argument for the freedom to own guns, security professionals are already resistant to the lack of regulation in the firearms and ammunition market (Carlson, 2021). This is a curious fact, considering that from the perspective of pro-gun groups, the United States has always been an example to be emulated by Brazil, given that the country "has more guns than people and a low homicide rate" (Pekny et al., 2015). This statement ignores efforts by the Clinton and Obama administrations to tighten rules for civilian access to firearms (Rostron, 2016). It also ignores that states with more flexible rules have homicide rates similar to those in Brazil (Braga et al., 2021, 2022). However, with this discourse, the "bullet caucus" saw in Bolsonaro's election a way to maintain and increase the profits of the arms industry, which, despite being high, were constrained by the rules established by the Disarmament Statute (Miranda, 2019). The plan was to gradually, slowly, and safely weaken the Statute, using the grammar of the dictatorship that the former president appreciates so much (Macaulay, 2020).

Bolsonaro Government: 2019 a 2022

During the early days of Jair Bolsonaro's administration in 2019, a significant move occurred in the chaotic realm of regulations concerning firearms and ammunition with the signing of Decree 9,685 by the new president of Brazil. Among the most impactful changes, the document eliminated the requirement to demonstrate effective necessity as a criterion for acquiring firearms. Furthermore, it further expanded the group of public agents authorized to own and carry firearms, extending this permission to residents in rural and urban areas located in states with more than ten homicides per one hundred thousand inhabitants in the year 2016 (which, in practice, included any state in the federation), to those responsible for commercial or industrial establishments, and, of course, to CACs registered with the Army.

The January regulation was revoked in May 2019 by Decree 9,785/2019, which took further steps towards the relaxation of access to firearms in the country. By the end of 2020, "eleven decrees, one law, and fifteen army ordinances that decharacterized the Statute, generated incentives for the spread of firearms and ammunition, and imposed obstacles to the ability to trace ammunition used in crimes" had been issued (Cerqueira et al., 2020, p. 11). In 2021, the federal government issued four more decrees regarding the relaxation of arms and ammunition.

With the changes, each individual could acquire triple the number of firearms, increasing from two to six. Ammunition was no longer restricted to 50 units, and it could range up to 2,000 per month, depending on the caliber. The validity period of firearm registration was doubled, going from 5 to 10 years. The justification for purchasing a firearm no longer needed to be proven and became presumed, as the sense of insecurity became a sufficient argument for granting possession. CACs were significantly favored, especially by Decree 10,629/ 2021, which relaxed the rules for obtaining the technical capacity certificate for firearm handling (which could be replaced by a declaration of participation in training and competitions). Another important change concerns transit carry, which was originally prohibited, modified during the Temer government, and in 2021, it became allowed for all CACs, allowing them to carry ready-to-use weapons during travels. Additionally, the limits of this category were substantially expanded, reaching a maximum of 60 firearms and 180,000 rounds of ammunition per year.

In terms of control, another setback for the Armed Forces and the Statute of Disarmament occurred with the revocation of three ordinances from the Logistics Command of the Army (Colog), which regulated the marking and tracking of firearms, ammunition, and other products controlled by the institution. These instruments aimed to modernize the systems for controlling firearms and ammunition, which were previously concentrated in SINARM. However, as they were perceived by the government as too progressive, they were revoked to ensure greater freedom in the circulation of these products (Cerqueira et al., 2020, p. 75). The exclusivity of SIGMA, restricted to use by the Armed Forces, for registering CACs, a group especially favored by the then-president, was also maintained.

Several of these decrees and ordinances did not endure. Some of them were revoked by the president himself after their announcement when they began to be questioned for their legality by civil associations. Others were subject to scrutiny by the Legislative or Judicial branches, ultimately undermining their viability. For example, in March 2021, the Supreme Federal Court began to examine the constitutionality of the decrees published discreetly on the eve of Carnival through Direct Actions of Unconstitutionality (ADI) 6675, 6676, 6677, and 6680. These judgments did not take place during the Bolsonaro administration, although some ministers voted in favor of a full reinstatement of the Statute of Disarmament.

In the midst of all the dispute regarding what could endure in the next president's term, in 2022, the "bullet caucus" went into action again, approving in the Chamber of Deputies the Bill 3723/2019 (Sanjurjo, 2023). Ultimately, this bill sought to turn into law the 40 normative acts published by Bolsonaro during his presidency, given the legal disputes surrounding urgent legislation. According to the Sou da Paz/Igarapé Institute (2023), the justification for the approval of the bill was to provide "legal certainty" to CACs, allowing them easier access to rifles. In response to the bill, Minister Edson Fachin determined in a provisional decision that the use of this type of weaponry should be authorized only in cases of public security interest or national defense (Instituto Sou da Paz/Igarapé, 2023, p. 3). Observing the SIGMA data, we find that the changes undertaken during the Bolsonaro government contributed to an explosion in the rate of new weapons registered by CACs.

This is a contentious hypothesis because, if proven true, it would suggest that the impact of the relaxation policy manifested almost immediately in the first year of the Bolsonaro administration, indicating an abrupt effect of the legislative change. It is crucial to acknowledge that a purely descriptive analysis of this data doesn't provide concrete evidence for this hypothesis. However, by examining other research findings, we came across the work of Braga et al. (2022), who assert that the average time between the acquisition of a firearm and a fatality caused by it is approximately three years, with only 18% of guns acquired in a given year leading to deaths in that same year. In a similar vein, Donohue, Aneja, and Weber (2019) explored that the eleven U.S. states that embraced more lenient firearm access laws in the last two decades witnessed their rates of violent deaths increasing between 3% and 4% in the subsequent years (Graph 15.5). The effect doesn't materialize in the same year because newly acquired guns take time to circulate.

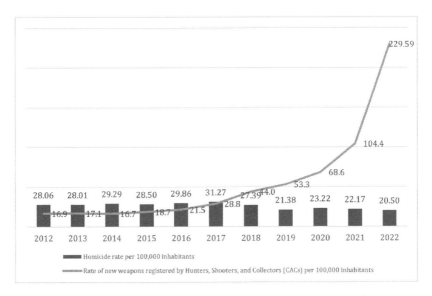

GRAPH 15.5   Homicide[a] rate and registration of new weapons by CACs[b] per 100,000 inhabitants and the percentage share of rifles and revolvers in the total new registrations by CACs (2008–2022).

Notes

a Death due to external or non-natural causes, meaning injuries caused by violence (accidents, homicides, suicides, or suspicious deaths). Information comes from SIM-DATASUS and is made available by IPEAdata.

b Military Weapons Management System, provided by Fiquem Sabendo.

In the Brazilian context, as elucidated in this chapter, the impact of gun control was a reduction in the rate of growth in homicide rates from 2004 onwards. Therefore, it is perplexing to observe a decline in intentional and lethal violent deaths at a time when the rate of new firearms registered by CACs (Collectors, Hunters, and Sports Shooters) experienced a substantial increase. To delve deeper into this matter, we initially followed the methodology of Donohue, Aneja, and Weber (2019) in investigating the relationship between firearms and violent deaths across different U.S. states. To test this hypothesis, we used the number of firearms registered in 2003 by CACs as a baseline. For each subsequent year, we calculated the growth rate of registrations for each of the 27 Brazilian states annually (from 2003 to 2022). Next, we computed the growth averages for the entire analysis period (Map 15.1). Subsequently, we conducted a parallel analysis for the homicide rate, determining the growth (or reduction) speed for all states in the federation between 2003 and 2022 (Map 15.2). Upon comparing Map 15.1 with Map 15.2, it becomes apparent that the states that underwent the highest growth in terms of firearms registered by CACs

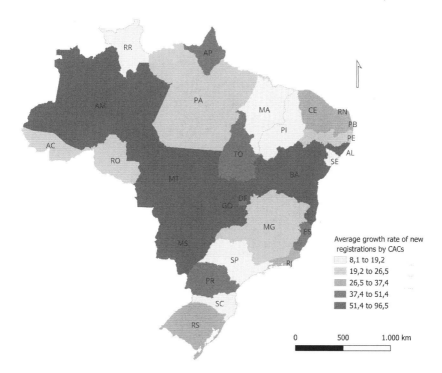

MAP 15.1 Average growth rate of new weapon registrations by CACs[a] (2003–2022).

Note

a Military Weapons Management System, provided by Fiquem Sabendo.

are also the ones that exhibited the highest average growth rate in homicides during the same period.

In some states, such as Bahia, Ceará, Piauí, Rio Grande do Norte, Pará, and Tocantins, there appears to be a positive correlation between the growth rate of firearms owned by CACs and the growth rate of homicides. This suggests that an increase in the number of firearms may be associated with an increase in homicide rates. Conversely, in other states, such as Rio de Janeiro, Minas Gerais, Distrito Federal, Espírito Santo, Santa Catarina, and São Paulo, the relationship seems to be inverse, indicating that there has been an increase in the number of firearms but a slight decrease in homicide rates. In Roraima and Sergipe, the growth rates of firearms and homicides are relatively low, suggesting a relative stability in these indicators. States like Goiás have a high growth rate of firearms but maintain a similar level in homicide rates. On the other hand, Rio de Janeiro experienced a significant increase in homicide rates despite a relatively moderate growth rate of firearms. In essence, there is no single pattern in Brazil, but rather 27 distinct realities.

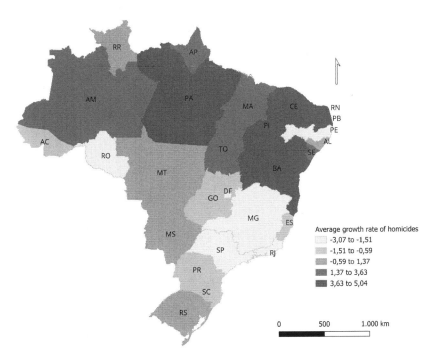

MAP 15.2 Average growth rate of homicides[a] (2003–2022).

Note

a Death due to external or non-natural causes, meaning injuries caused by violence (accidents, homicides, suicides, or suspicious deaths). Information comes from SIM-DATASUS and is made available by IPEAdata.

Another noteworthy aspect, as highlighted by Carlson (2021), is the relationship between the increased availability of firearms in the hands of civilians and the violence committed by the police. According to her, a significant portion of the literature overlooks the fact that police violence is a consequence of the prevalence of firearms, a point also emphasized in the literature review conducted by Braga et al. (2021). This argument is crucial in the Brazilian context, not only because the police constituted a significant support base for Bolsonarism but also because they strongly advocated for the (lack of) gun control policy (Bueno et al., 2021). Furthermore, they consistently advocated for the "shoot first, ask questions later" rule due to the fear that the opponent could be heavily armed, potentially with equipment such as rifles, which are supposed to be restricted to security forces (Ribeiro et al., 2022).

Our analysis aimed to compare the rates of deaths resulting from police interventions (on-duty and off-duty) with the rates of new firearms registered in the hands of CACs from 2008 to 2022. Unlike the homicide rates, in this

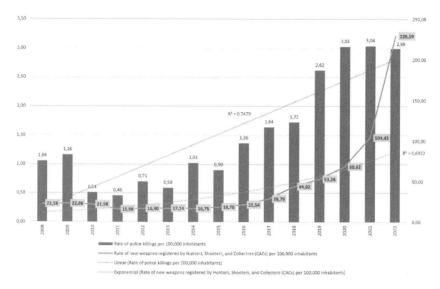

GRAPH 15.6   Rate of deaths resulting from police interventions (on duty and off duty)[a] and registration of new weapons by CACs[b] per 100,000 inhabitants (2008–2022).

Notes

a Fórum Brasileiro de Segurança Pública.

b Military Weapons Management System, provided by Fiquem Sabendo.

case, there is a convergence of two trend curves that start from the same point of origin in 2008. However, the curve of new firearms registered in the hands of CACs grows exponentially, while the curve of death rates caused by the police grows linearly. Graph 15.6 indicates that an increase in firearms in the hands of civilians leads to an acceleration of death rates caused by the police. In other words, it appears that Brazil effectively mirrored the United States during the Bolsonaro government, not only concerning the armament policy but also in terms of police violence. Thus, we affirm the findings of Carlson (2021) and Braga et al. (2021).

Therefore, when considering the policies related to access and control of firearms during the Bolsonaro government, we observe an unprecedented growth in the quantity and variety of weapons in the hands of civilians who self-classify as CACs, with direct effects on mortality rates in certain states, an increase in police violence, and extending to other scenarios such as violence against women (Instituto Sou da Paz, 2022) and attacks in schools, which have become increasingly frequent in the Brazilian reality (Instituto Sou da Paz/ Igarapé, 2023). Regaining some control over this policy has been the challenge proposed by Luiz Inácio Lula da Silva since his victorious campaign in 2022.

Our Present: Harm Reduction Policy?

President Luiz Inácio Lula da Silva's inaugural speech was characterized by the national press as a direct critique of the policies adopted by the previous government of Jair Bolsonaro. In the context of our article, Lula announced the immediate revocation of decrees that expanded the carrying of firearms, labeling them as "criminal." Decree 11,615/2023 on gun control was only published in July, as mentioned in the introduction of this text. This delay occurred because, as anticipated by Bauer et al. (2022), President Lula's alternative was to step back because simply repealing the decrees issued by Bolsonaro would be a worse alternative, especially for CACs who would be directly affected by the measures. Thus, the alternative found was, in some aspects, to restore elements of the 2003 Disarmament Statute and, in others, to create options understood as a middle ground, which still require further regulation for implementation but allow, in some way, the exploration of scenarios. Table 15.1 summarizes the main changes observed in these policies over 20 years of discussion about gun control in Brazil.

For civilians in general, the minimum age for purchasing firearms remains at 25 years. However, Decree 11,615/2023 requires a declaration that the applicant has a secure location for storage, with guaranteed measures to prevent access by minors or incapable individuals. Furthermore, the approval criteria have been adjusted, reintroducing the need to demonstrate a genuine necessity to acquire firearms, and the psychological examination is now required, similar to the licensing for driving vehicles. Finally, the maximum quantity of firearms for personal defense is once again limited to two, revoking the increase to six during the Bolsonaro government. Similarly, the allowed quantity of ammunition returns to 50 units per year, per registered firearm.

For CACs, the changes include the requirement for proof of psychological fitness and technical proficiency in handling firearms, issued by the Federal Police. Additionally, the transit permit has been terminated, requiring movement with unloaded firearms and a digital traffic guide. Possession for shooters, hunters, and collectors has been adjusted, limiting the quantity of firearms and ammunition allowed per year for each category. These changes reflect a more rigorous approach to the possession and purchase of firearms, reintroducing requirements and restrictions that had been relaxed during the Bolsonaro government.

However, the allowance for owners to retain firearms considered restricted and acquired before the decree's entry into force stands out as a significant challenge in combating armed violence (Instituto Sou da Paz/ Igarapé, 2023). The retention of such firearms, especially semi-automatic rifles, poses a risk, given that there are over 50,000 firearms considered restricted acquired before the Bolsonaro government's decree came into effect. Among these,

TABLE 15.1 Changes made in access to firearms and ammunition in Brazil (2003 to 2023)

Public	Criteria	Disarmament Statute (Law 10.826/2003)	During the Bolsonaro administration (amended by various Decrees and Ordinances between 2019 and 2022)	Decree 11.615/2023
Civilians in general	Minimum age for the purchase of firearms	25 years of age	It remains the same	It remains the same, but adds that the person applying must declare that 'their residence has a safe or secure place, with a lock, for the storage of unloaded firearms that they own, and that they will take necessary measures to prevent individuals under eighteen years of age or legally incapacitated individuals from seizing firearms under their possession or ownership.
	Approval criteria	Demonstration of effective need, integrity, lawful occupation, physical and mental fitness	There is no need to prove effective need	The effective need to purchase firearms is required again for each purchase, and the psychological examination is now required similarly to obtaining a driver's license
	Quantity of firearms	Maximum of 2 firearms for personal defense	A maximum of 6 firearms for personal defense is allowed	Maximum of 2 firearms for personal defense
	Firearm potency	Only allowed are handguns, repeating or semi-automatic firearms whose ammunition has energy up to 407 Joules. Firearms with calibers such as .357 Magnum, 9mm, .40, .44, .45 can only be used by security forces	Handguns, repeating or semi-automatic firearms are permitted, with ammunition energy up to 1620 Joules. Firearms with calibers such as .357 Magnum, 9mm, .40, .44, .45 are now allowed, as well as rifles of calibers .223, 5.56mm, and 7.62mm	Only handguns, repeating, or semi-automatic firearms with ammunition energy up to 407 Joules are allowed. Firearms with calibers such as .357 Magnum, 9mm, .40, .44, .45 become restricted again to security forces, along with rifles

(Continued)

TABLE 15.1 (Continued)

Public	Criteria	Disarmament Statute (Law 10.826/2003)	During the Bolsonaro administration (amended by various Decrees and Ordinances between 2019 and 2022)	Decree 11.615/2023
	Quantity of ammunition	50 units per year, per registered firearm	2,000 units per month, per registered firearm	50 units per year, per registered firearm
	Validity of the registration	5 years	10 years	5 years, and renewal is conditioned on the demonstration of effective need, integrity, lawful occupation, physical and mental fitness
CACs	Attestation of technical competence	Technical competence report, issued by the Federal Police	Certificate of regular practice, issued by shooting clubs	Evidence of psychological aptitude and technical ability to handle firearms, issued by the Federal Police
	Carry permit	Ban on transit carry	Transit carries of loaded firearms – allowed CACs to carry handguns ready for use during travel	End of transit carry: travel for the practice of activities must be done with the firearm unloaded and secured in a way that immediate use is not possible, after the issuance of a digital traffic permit, within specified route and period
	Ownership	For shooters: 16 firearms, 60,000 rounds of ammunition, and 12 kg of gunpowder. For hunters: 12 firearms, 6,000 rounds of ammunition, and 2 kg of gunpowder. For collectors: one firearm of each type and one ammunition per model	For shooters: 60 firearms, 180,000 rounds of ammunition per year, and 20 kg of gunpowder. For hunters: 30 firearms, 90,000 rounds of ammunition, and 20 kg of gunpowder. For collectors: 5 firearms of each type, a thousand rounds for each restricted-use firearm, and 5 thousand rounds for each permitted-use firearm	For shooters: 16 firearms, with up to 4 being restricted; 20,000 rounds of ammunition per year. For hunters: up to 6 firearms, with two being restricted; 500 rounds per firearm, per year. For collectors: one firearm of each type, model, and caliber

approximately 30,000 semi-automatic rifles remain in circulation, with the potential to be diverted to the illegal market, organized crime, or used against police forces in their daily operations in the coming years. Despite the alert about the retention of firearms considered restricted and acquired before the decree's entry into force, the overall assessment of Decree 11,615/2023 was positive, particularly due to the inclusion of two essential changes for monitoring and controlling the inventory of firearms among civilians (Instituto Sou da Paz/Igarapé, 2023). Firstly, the establishment of procedures for punishing individuals who do not renew firearm registrations was introduced. According to FBSP (2023), there are 1,542,168 firearms registered in SINARM whose registrations have expired and have not been renewed. One of the innovations of Decree 11,615/2023 was the inclusion of the provision for the revocation of firearm registration (CRAF) and the seizure of the weapons if the person fails to regularize the registration.

Secondly, there was an improvement in firearm controls with the concentration of civilian firearm registrations in a single database (SINARM) under the supervision of the Federal Police. The significant expansion of firearm registrations during Jair Bolsonaro's government highlighted the difficulties and mistakes made by the armed forces in overseeing the part of the firearms market under their control (Instituto Sou da Paz/Igarapé, 2023). The inspection of the CACs' inventories in recent years was marked by management difficulties, organizational issues, and a lack of integration with other agencies, as well as a lack of transparency (Instituto Sou da Paz/Igarapé, 2023). With Decree 11,615/ 2023, only firearms belonging to the Armed Forces, Auxiliary Forces, and the Institutional Security Cabinet will remain in the Military Arms Management System (SIGMA), which was used as a source for this analysis. All other firearms, including those of CACs, will be registered in SINARM. In other words, all civilian weaponry will be controlled and supervised by the Federal Police, addressing the issue of a lack of integration and difficulty of access to these records by other security forces. This strengthens not only control over this arsenal but also the investigation of crimes in which registered firearms have been used.

The effects of the significant increase in the purchase and registration of firearms in Brazil between the years 2019 and 2022, especially by CACs, particularly of high offensive potential weapons such as semi-automatic rifles, may have medium- and long-term impacts on the dynamics of violent crime in Brazilian states. Therefore, it is not enough to simply revert to the measures outlined in Law 10,826/2003 of the Disarmament Statute with incremental improvements. It is the responsibility of the federal and state governments to develop specific strategies and measures to address this large volume of firearms introduced into Brazilian society during the Bolsonaro administration.

Notes

1 In this regard, see: https://fiquemsabendo.com.br/, accessed on November 6, 2023.
2 The Military Weapons Management System (SIGMA) is a system created exclusively for the registration of data on firearms and Certificates of Registration granted by the Army
3 In this regard, see: https://fiquemsabendo.com.br/transparencia/newsletter-dont-lai-to-me, accessed on November 6, 2023.
4 Information about these artifacts is hard to access, and until 2018, it was compiled by the Small Arms Survey. Since the most substantial changes in Brazil took place from 2019 onwards, it was not possible to include these data in the analysis due to a lack of temporal series correspondence
5 Research carried out by the Instituto Sou da Paz Institute and the Igarapé Institute, both specialized in the field of firearms, reveals a growing trend of individuals authorized to carry (CACs) acquiring weaponry for criminal organizations during the Bolsonaro administration. This surge is particularly notable with the availability of higher-caliber weapons to CACs, and in larger quantities. Previously, criminal factions primarily obtained weapons through importation or the diversion of firearms from armed forces and private security, though it is important to note that records of these transactions are in SINARM and could not be analyzed in this text.

References

Bauer, M. W., & Knill, C. (2014). A conceptual framework for the comparative analysis of policy change: Measurement, explanation and strategies of policy dismantling. *Journal of Comparative Policy Analysis: Research and Practice*, 16(1), 28–44.

Bauer, M. D., Lakdawala, A., Mueller, P. (2022). Market-based monetary policy uncertainty. *The Economic Journal*, 132 (644), 1290–1308.

Benetti, P. R. (2022). Na Antessala da Bancada da Bala: Argumentos Contra o Estatuto do Desarmamento (2003). *Dilemas: Revista de Estudos de Conflito e Controle Social*, 15, 859–882.

Braga, A. A., et al. (2021). Firearm instrumentality: Do guns make violent situations more lethal? *Annual Review of Criminology*, 4, 147–164.

Braga, A. A., et al. (2022). Privately manufactured firearms, newly purchased firearms, and the rise of urban gun violence. *Preventive Medicine,* 165, 107231.

Buenoo, S., Lima, R. S. de, Costa, A. T. M. Quando o Estado mata: desafios para medir os crimes contra a vida de autoria de policiais. *Sociologias*, 23, 154–183, 2021.

Carlson, J. (2019). Revisiting the Weberian presumption: Gun militarism, gun populism, and the racial politics of legitimate violence in policing. *American Journal of Sociology*, 125(3), 633–682.

Carlson, J. (2021). Beyond law and order in the gun debate: Black Lives Matter, abolitionism, and anti-racist gun policy. In Foley, Conor (Ed). *In spite of you: Bolsonaro and the new Brazilian resistance*, 56–70. New York: OR Books.

Cerqueira, D., & Mello, J. M. (2013). Evaluating a national anti-firearm law and estimating the causal effect of guns on crime. In *Texto para Discussão*, n. 607, 1-48. Brasília: IPEA.

Cerqueira, D., et al. (2020). *Atlas da violência 2020*. IPEA: Brasília.

Donohue, J. J., Aneja, A., & Weber, K. D. (2019). Right-to-carry laws and violent crime: A comprehensive assessment using panel data and a state-level synthetic control analysis. *Journal of Empirical Legal Studies*, 16(2), 198–247.

FBSP. (2023). *Anuário Brasileiro de Segurança Pública – 2023*. São Paulo: Fórum Brasileiro se Segurança Pública.

Holt, T. J., Freilich, J. D., & Chermak, S. M. (2020). Examining the online expression of ideology among far-right extremist forum users. *Terrorism and Political Violence,* 34(2), 1–21.

Instituto Sou da Paz. (2022). *O papel da arma de fogo na violência contra a mulher*. São Paulo: Instituto Sou da Paz.

Instituto Sou da Paz/Igarapé. (2023). *Balanço preliminar das principais mudanças na política de controle de armas e munições no Brasil em 2023*. Rio de Janeiro: Instituto Sou da Paz/Igarapé.

IPEA/FBSP. (2020). *Atlas da violência no Brasil: Dados estatísticos*. Brasília: IPEA/ FBSP.

IPEA/FBSP. (2021). *Atlas da violência no Brasil: Dados estatísticos*. Brasília: IPEA/ FBSP.

Jordan, A., & Bauer, M., & Green-Pedersen, C. (2013). Policy Dismantling. *Journal of European Public Policy*, 20(5), 795–805.

Lucas, P. (2008). Disarming Brazil: Lessons and challenges. *NACLA Report on the Americas*, 41(2), 27–31.

Macaulay, F. (2017). Presidents, producers and politics: Law-and-order policy in Brazil from Cardoso to Dilma. *Policy Studies*, 38(3), 248–261.

Macaulay, F. (2020). Bancada da Bala: The growing influence of the security sector in Brazilian politics. In: Foley, Conor (Ed). *In spite of you: Bolsonaro and the new Brazilian resistance*, 56–70. New York: OR Books.

Manso, B. P., & Dias, C. N. (2018). *A guerra: a ascensão do PCC e o mundo do crime no Brasil*. São Paulo: Editora Todavia SA.

Miranda, J. V. S., et al. (2019). Composição e atuação da "Bancada da Bala" *na* Câmara dos Deputados. *Dissertação de Mestrado. Programa de Pós-Graduação em Ciência Política*. Belo Horizonte: UFMG.

Oliveira, V. C., & Ribeiro, L. (2021). Bolsonaro e a peculiar agenda de segurança pública. In: Sá, T. A. O., (Ed), Extremo: O mandato Bolsonaro, 129–150. Curitiba: Kotter Editorial.

Pekny, A. C., et al. (2015). *Controle de armas no Brasil: O caminho a seguir*. Sao Paulo: Friedrich Ebert Stiftung (FES).

Ribeiro, L., & Oliveira, V. (2021). "Eu quero que o povo se arme": A política de segurança pública de Bolsonaro. In: Avritzer, Leonardo; Kerche, Fábio; Marona, Marjorie (Eds). *Governo Bolsonaro: Retrocesso e degradação política*, 327–342. Belo Horizonte: Autêntica.

Ribeiro L., Oliveira V. C., Diniz A. M. (2022). Are the Brazilian police forces lethal weapons? *In: Policing & firearms: New perspectives and insights*. Switzerland. Springer International Publishing, 33–56.

Rostron A. (2016) A new state ice age for gun policy. *Harvard Law & Policy Review*. 10(2), 327–59.

Rupert, M. (2015). *From Neoliberalism to Far-Right conspiracism: The case of the American 'Gun rights' culture*. Uploaded at Academia.edu.

Sanjurjo, D. (2020). The Brazilian Disarmament Statute. In: Sanjurjo, D.,(Ed) *Gun control policies in Latin America*, 129–150. Curitiba: Kotter Editorial.

Sanjurjo, D. (2022). Why are Brazilians so interested in gun control? Putting the Multiple Streams Framework to the test. *Opinião pública,* 27, 730–756.

Sanjurjo, D. (2023). More guns, less violence? Putting the Multiple Streams Framework to the test against Bolsonaro's gun liberalization agenda. In*:* Zahariadis, N. et al. (Ed) *A Modern guide to the multiple streams framework* [s.l.] Edward Elgar Publishing, 160–189.

Solano, E. (2018). *O ódio como política: A reinvenção das direitas no Brasil.* São Paulo: Boitempo Editorial.

Souza, M., et al. (2007). Reductions in firearm-related mortality and hospitalizations in Brazil after gun control. *Health Affairs*, 26(2), 575–584.

Szabó, I., & Risso, M. (2018). *Segurança pública para virar o jogo.* São Paulo: Editora Companhia das Letras.

16

CONCLUSION

Policies dismantling and system retrenchment

Natália Sátyro

Between 2015 and 2022, Brazil's democracy faced significant challenges in multiple domains, during a period marked by considerable instability. The social domain was particularly affected, allowing us to assess how the welfare state has evolved and adapted over the three administrations in this period: Dilma Rousseff (2011–2014; 2014–2016); Michel Temer (2016–2018), and Jair Messias Bolsonaro (2019–2022), in addition to the Covid-19 pandemic. This book examines different social policies, tracing their changes and outlining the implemented reforms. We can assert that they have moved along very different tracks and, overall, they suggest a significant shift in Brazil's standard of social protection.

The first question that arises is: a shift in reference to what? Chapter 2 (Sátyro) outlines the trajectory of social policies following the 1988 Federal Constitution, while Chapter 6 (Souza) illustrates the decline in poverty and income inequality from the 2000s to the mid-2010s. These changes resulted from the establishment of a more inclusive welfare state, which marked a clear departure from the era that extended until the end of the military dictatorship. This was a direct outcome of democratic consolidation in Brazil and the left-wing governments in federal executive roles. It is worth noting that inequality was significantly reduced by including outsiders (Arretche, 2018). While regional disparities decreased during the democratic period, one cannot ignore that the Brazilian social protection system is internally heterogeneous (Sátyro, 2014; Arretche, 2018). Sátyro and Cunha (2018) show that six distinct welfare regimes coexist in the Brazilian territory, each with varying levels of protection and participation from the market, state, and families.

DOI: 10.4324/9781003487777-20

The evidence presented in this book points to a significant turning point in this development, beginning in 2015. There was a drastic reversal in the previous trend of declining poverty and income inequality, as visually depicted in Chapter 6. Poverty and inequality increased, with the cost being especially higher for the poorest 20%, according to Souza (Chapter 6).

Fundamental concepts, such as dismantling and retrenchment, are discussed. Even though contributors to this book were free to define the concept of policy dismantling, they generally drew upon both Pierson's (1994) analytical framework and the definition by Bauer and Knill (2014). According to Bauer and Knill, policy dismantling refers to "a change of a direct, indirect, hidden or symbolic nature that either decreases the number of policies in a particular area or reduces the number of policy instruments used, and/or lowers their intensity. It can involve changes to these core elements of policy and/or it can be achieved by manipulating the capacities to implement and supervise them" (2014:35).

Other analytical categories should be considered. First, as emphasized since the 1990s by Esping-Andersen, the various regimes should be examined within the context of citizenship development, employing the criteria of decommodification, social stratification, and, later on, defamilialization. In a sense, this concept aligns with Green-Pedersen's (2004) discussion on the significance of increasing or diminishing commitment to equality, a topic central to the debate as mentioned in the introduction. Commitment to equality is one of the elements that make the fundamental concepts associated with institutional change in social policies less abstract. After all, while it is true that both the quantity and generosity of certain policies can be increased without a commitment to equality, particularly in dealing with highly regressive systems, the converse is also possible: scaling back a policy or system by reducing privileges while maintaining a commitment to equality. This could be seen as retrenchment, but not as dismantling. Additionally, this allows us to explore questions about who is impacted by the changes being examined, raising the well-known question "who gets less, when and how," as noted by Jordan et al. (2014). We reflect on the idea that populist radical right-wing parties (PRRPs) differ from mainstream right-wing parties in terms of their approach to social protection. They prioritize the protection of "deserving groups" while denying it to "undeserving groups." To what extent does this classification truly distinguish PRRPs from parties seen as mainstream, both on the right and left, when they implement neoliberal reforms that lead to more significant losses for less influential groups?

Another factor to consider is that much of the disagreement about conceptualization stems from the level of analysis – whether it refers to "policy dismantling/retrenchment" or "welfare state dismantling/retrenchment." Researchers may concentrate on "policy dismantling," examining a particular policy sector and analyzing a range of instruments, actions, projects, deregulations, program terminations, and internal reforms, involving the adoption of diverse strategies to reduce the scope, generosity, and eligibility criteria within that policy sector. Or they may focus on the system level, examining welfare state dismantling/retrenchment. There is a belief that the dismantling and/or retrenchment in various policy sectors can disrupt the entire system. However, we contend that this is not an inevitable outcome. The welfare state is not necessarily dismantled as a consequence of a policy dismantling process. The results in this book show that the Brazilian case involves reforms, cutbacks, (de)regulation, and efforts to contain and reduce social expenditures. When viewed collectively, there is no doubt that we are witnessing *policy dismantling and welfare retrenchment* (Pierson, 1994; Bauer and Knill, 2014).

This book contributes to both debates: firstly to the conceptual discussion and secondly to the comparison between mainstream right-wing parties and PRRPs. The book assesses various social policies, though some, such as housing and culture, were excluded. This approach moves beyond the debate about claims of dismantling. This enables a comparison between the administrations of both right-wing factions. The analysis in various chapters points to the use of different strategies in various policies, emphasizing *systematic and programmatic processes, as well as a reduced commitment to equality*.

However, is the current situation solely the responsibility of President Bolsonaro? Certainly not. The proposed timeframe allowed the authors to examine four landmark events spanning three federal administrations during the analyzed period. Dilma Rousseff was forcibly removed amid a weakened economy. The economic crisis was a significant event, as it affected her administration's budgetary and fiscal capacity. The approval of the Spending Ceiling Amendment (EC95) under Temer's government institutionalized an austerity policy that extended beyond a single administration, impacting the state as a whole and imposing constraints on future administrations, as detailed in Chapters 2 and 4. After the turbulent 2018 election, Jair Bolsonaro, previously a low-ranking congressman from a small party that, until then, held only one seat in parliament, assumed the presidency of Brazil. Midway through Bolsonaro's administration, the world was struck by a pandemic. How did these four events and the political actors involved shape the course of social policies during this period? Have they changed the underlying principles and the overall direction of social protection? Have they decreased the commitment to equality? These are our guiding questions.

A comparative evaluation: policy dismantling

How significant are the changes observed in each policy sector during the analyzed period? What is the impact of each of these landmark events? Do the changes at one landmark event resemble those from the previous one? Do Temer's actions differ from Rousseff's? And can the observed evidence provide insights into the issue of commitment to equality, for example? When examining Bolsonaro, it is important to identify the areas where he aligns and where he diverges from Temer. Given that decreasing commitment to equality leads to regressive effects within a policy or regime, let us make a comparative assessment. Using the following table, which provides a summary of the findings of the book's chapters, we will now present our analysis.

Regressive effects: a comparative analysis from the four landmark events

POLICY	Rousseff	Temer	Bolsonaro	Pandemic
Compensatory				
Social Security	No	Yes (˜=R)	Yes (=T)	No
Health	No	Yes (˜= R)	Yes (=T)	Yes+
SUAS	Yes	Yes (˜= R)	Yes (=T)	Yes
CCT	NO /YES*		Yes (=T)	Yes+
Social Investment				
Labor market	Yes	Yes (˜= R)	Yes (=T)	No
Family Policies	No	Yes	Yes (˜=T)	No
Education	No	Yes	Yes (˜=T)	-
Others				
Environment	-	-	Yes	-
Security	No	No	Yes (˜=T)	No

* Yes, because it occurred during Rousseff's term; however, since this was not her preference, but an action of the bureaucracy tasked with monitoring, it is no.

˜ = R – This is different from Roussef; = R This is similar to Rousseff; ˜ = T It is different from Temer; = T This is similar to Temer.

Compensatory policies

As seen in Chapter 2, the 1988 Brazilian Constitution established the basis for the country's welfare state with three key components: social security – pensions and retirements, funded by contributions from the beneficiaries; healthcare, as a universal right; and social assistance, which does not require contributions. These essential policies together are known as Social Welfare ("Seguridade

Social" – Social Welfare here cannot be confused with social security, which is restricted only to insurance), covering the three primary compensatory policies.

In the case of the **pension system (social security)**, regulation was the main strategy used to make changes, primarily through constitutional reforms that require a qualified majority in the National Congress (Chapter 7). Reforms occurred during the Workers' Party (PT) administrations as well, so why were they not considered cases of dismantling? Because they had a predominantly adaptive approach. For instance, a cap was imposed on public servant retirement benefits, a group often viewed as privileged and influential. This cap applied to new hires without infringing on the rights of current employees, which means passing the costs on to future generations, a classic strategy. As presented by Lanzara and Pernasetti in Chapter 7 on the pension system, reform measures led by Lula's government expanded the system's reach to include previously excluded groups. Furthermore, contribution rates were reduced, encouraging informal workers to participate and make contributions to the system.

The proposals discussed during Temer's administration – although not approved – and the reforms implemented during Bolsonaro's government have different approaches compared to previous administrations. In his first year in office, Bolsonaro successfully enacted a stringent pension reform through Constitutional Amendment 103, which was promulgated in November 2019. Much of this reform, which had been debated during the two years of Temer's administration, targeted basic pension benefits without addressing the significant privileges granted especially to the military and members of the judicial system. Starting then, beneficiaries will need to contribute for 40 years to receive the full basic benefit. In a country with high informality rates and significant job turnover, even within the formal job sector, this requirement is outrageous. Clearly, this acts as an incentive for privatizing the system, as it makes it challenging for beneficiaries to reach the maximum benefits, pushing people towards the private sector. Given the complexity of retirement and pension rules, and the absence of immediate effects on people, the severity of this reform is less evident, even for those with above-average knowledge. Both Temer, the initial proponent, and Bolsonaro claim credit for introducing a reform that they argue is central to economic recovery – and both have adopted the strategy of not highlighting the real costs for the most affected groups – obfuscation strategy, basically (Pierson, 1994). However, as mentioned in Chapter 4 on the economy, the promised results did not materialize, at least in the short term.

The 1988 Constitution recognized healthcare as a universal right, leading to the establishment of the Unified Health System (SUS). In Chapter 8, focused on **health**, Machado and Jerônimo highlight a significant shift in health policy after Temer took office. Even though the crisis initiated during Rousseff's government had already negatively impacted the financing of this policy, Temer implemented real restrictions and constraints through Constitutional Amendment 95. Austerity becomes the main lifeline. But that is not all. He promptly changed his health minister, appointing Congressman Ricardo Barros from the Progressive Party (PP), a center-right party. This change signaled a shift in policy and a break with the coalition that had supported SUS since the early 1990s. The ministry started serving the interests of private supplementary healthcare and medical corporations. The principles of universality and comprehensiveness were thus abandoned. The minister stressed the importance of "revisiting the scope of SUS" and proposed introducing affordable healthcare plans to reduce government involvement in the health sector.

In Bolsonaro's first term in office, the government continued the principles set by Temer. In 2019, two actions stood out. One involved an ordinance that introduced a new financing method for primary care services, shifting away from universalization and instead basing funding on the number of registered users. Additionally, another action affected the National Mental Health Policy, as funding from the publicly supported Psychosocial Care Networks was redirected to therapeutic communities in the private sector.

However, the pandemic brought about a change in policy tone. With the onset of the pandemic, healthcare institutions emerged as significant venues for denialist and authoritarian symbolic actions. Bolsonaro consistently denied the severity of the pandemic, referring to it as a "little flu" and advocating for herd immunity as the best way to combat it. When asked what he would do to address the pandemic and its consequences, he responded with statements like "I'm not a gravedigger."

Simultaneously, he completely undermined the autonomy of the health ministers, ordered the large-scale purchase of a proven ineffective drug (hydroxychloroquine), refused to buy vaccines, participated in numerous public gatherings, and conducted weekly live broadcasts denying the pandemic and rejecting WHO guidelines such as mask-wearing and social distancing. The widely acknowledged incident, later verified by a Parliamentary Commission of Inquiry, where Pfizer sent over 50 vaccine offers via email in August 2020 without any official response, clearly showcases the inaction of the denialist stance. In the absence of federal-level coordination, a longstanding characteristic of this policy, states and municipalities followed their own directives, depending on their alignment with the central government. The northeastern states established the Northeast Consortium, facilitating more efficient regional coordination and large-scale vaccine acquisition, for example. The successful immunization of Brazilian society was made possible by the combined efforts of governors, societal pressure, and the robust structure of SUS, with a special mention to the National Immunization Program, which marked its 50th anniversary in 2023. It stands as a benchmark of efficiency, showcasing the resilience of the established state capacity. In practice, health policy gained attention for two reasons: 1) SUS's ability to respond to the pandemic despite the president's inaction, and

2) the use of this visibility to deny science, the pandemic, and, consequently, the scientific methods to combat it.

However, Machado and Jerônymo (Chapter 8) point out that the trends of reducing the state's role, increasing commodification in healthcare, and shifting from a preventive to a supplementary model – initiated during Temer's government and reinforced in 2019 – were disrupted by the pandemic. Therefore, while SUS mitigated the impact of the pandemic, the pandemic, in turn, mitigated the dismantling of SUS. Bolsonaro followed the path laid out by Temer until the pandemic. Both adhere to a neoliberal approach, seeking to reduce the state's role, increase subsidies for the private sector, encourage the development of more accessible healthcare plans rather than fortifying SUS, and prioritize supplementary medicine over preventive measures, among other initiatives. However, Bolsonaro stood out for his denialism and symbolic fight against science particularly since the onset of the pandemic.

Social assistance was recognized as a social policy under the 1988 Federal Constitution (as seen in Chapter 2). When Brazil transitioned back to democracy, all individuals over 18 had the right to vote and access social protection. From that point onward, it took a long journey to effectively structure the National Social Assistance Policy (PNAS – 2004), ultimately leading to the creation of the Unified Social Assistance System (SUAS – 2005), inspired by SUS. In the book, we examine two policies within the SUAS framework: socio-assistance services (Chapter 9) and cash transfers (Chapter 10). Sátyro et al. (Chapter 9) emphasize a gradual decrease in SUAS funding, particularly in federal transfers to municipalities, leading to a decline in socio-assistance services from 2015 to 2022. The decrease in funding had a profound impact on service provision. Federal transfers, making up over 80% of municipal expenditures in this sector, saw a substantial reduction due to the crisis starting in 2015, reaching 10% of the value from the beginning of the historical series analyzed in 2022. The authors refer to Pierson's classic principle, "where there is no money, there is no policy," as this was the main strategy employed.

In 2015, there was a shift from the previous trajectory. Although Rousseff is blamed for the economic crisis, she did not disregard the SUAS structures as her two successors. Unlike Rousseff, Temer and Bolsonaro ignored existing structures, acting independently of SUAS: They neglected social participation spaces (including conferences and the undermining of the National Social Assistance Council – CNAS) to the forum for federative agreement (Tripartite Intermanagerial Commission – CIT). Temer created the Happy Child Program (Programa Criança Feliz – PCF) without following the institutionalized process of discussion in the CNAS and agreement in the CIT. Subsequently, the PCF started receiving a significant portion of the funds originally designated for SUAS, creating a zero-sum game. Also, the First Lady sponsored the program, a practice from a time when social assistance was seen as charity, not a right. The epistemic community saw this as a break in the policy's institutional framework. Bolsonaro took a more decisive approach, actively trying to abolish over 4,000 participatory forums in the country through a decree in his first month in office. This act was overturned by the Federal Supreme Court.

Sátyro et al. (Chapter 9) also highlight that Basic Social Protection (PSB) saw a more significant reduction in service provision compared to Special Social Protection (PSE). PSE services experienced a notably smaller reduction over time compared to PSB, and the decrease in PSE does not follow a linear trend, highlighting greater resilience in medium-complexity services. Addressing cases of rights violations and real vulnerabilities like child labor, child sexual abuse, violence, and abandonment, these services are linked to the Justice System and the Rights Guarantee System. The authors argue that, as services mandated by the Justice System, municipalities must find ways to keep them operational. The pandemic also had an impact on service indicators, pointing to a substantial increase in intra-family violence in 2021. This confirms literature findings indicating that cases of sexual abuse and violence against women, children, the elderly, and people with disabilities, among others, increased substantively as a result of isolation. Understanding these actions means acknowledging that this policy targets individuals and families in poverty and extreme poverty, whose lives are affected by various dimensions of poverty beyond the lack of income. These people embody the "underserving groups" associated with the PRRPs, as well as those who cannot mobilize and exert pressure. Political leaders will not face significant political costs if their actions lead to dissatisfaction among these groups

However, the case of **Conditional Cash Transfers (CCTs)** was more turbulent and unstable, in contrast with socio-assistance services, which are less visible. Undoubtedly, this was a site of very strong symbolic action. It is worth noting that CCTs, especially the Bolsa Família Program (PBF), were a key element in PT's fight against hunger. Even though researchers know that the reduction of poverty and inequality is primarily attributed to minimum wage valorization, job creation, and a heated economy (as discussed in Chapters 3 and 6), the public sees the PBF as the main electoral driver for Lula and the PT. And indeed, this impact, which was real, was primarily a result of an investment of less than 1% of the GDP.

Mostafa (Chapter 10) highlights that the political crisis in 2015 affected the PBF not because of Rousseff's actions, but due to the influence of federal bureaucracy. Specifically, oversight bodies such as the Office of the Comptroller General (CGU) imposed costs on the program through administrative actions. As Thelen (2006) argues, groups and individuals are not mere observers of change; they shape the power dynamics that affect them, either favoring or disfavoring their positions. They can undermine structures by creating openings and opportunities to change the political context and thus defend, maintain, or strengthen their positions. Therefore, the PFB was affected not by Rousseff herself but by the unresolved political crisis she faced. The activist stance of the political bureaucracy led to an increase in inquiries. Both Temer and Bolsonaro strategically used administrative resources and regulations within the ministry, reducing transparency in benefit allocation and verification processes. This, in turn, caused an increase in the program's waiting queue. These actions were directly carried out by both presidents, following the same approach. Mostafa showed that in the two years of Temer's administration and in Bolsonaro's first year in office (2019), the strategies for dismantling through administrative means were the same. Efforts were made to delink the Benefício de Prestação Continuada (BPC – Continuous Cash Benefit Program) from the minimum wage, but they failed in Congress due to the program's visibility in public opinion. The two strategies differ significantly from the PT administrations, which adopted the zero-queue principle to combat hunger and strengthened the BPC. They prioritized transparency in the criteria, enabling the entire epistemic community to conduct experiments and checks. Bolsonaro's strategies proved highly effective: The number of beneficiary families decreased around 1 million, reaching just over 13 million in November 2019, and the benefit value was not adjusted, reducing its effectiveness. This is objectively seen in the increased poverty and inequality, as highlighted by Souza (Chapter 6). In essence, there was an effort to reduce the scope of the PBF.

During the pandemic, CCTs were needed to address challenges arising from social isolation and its economic consequences, especially for informal workers and small entrepreneurs. The trends examined by Mostafa were entirely reversed, and CCTs served as a lifeline for the government to address the demand. Both the PBF and the BPC were maximally utilized, with legacy and installed capacity serving as determining factors. Rapidly, waiting queues disappeared. The initiative known as Emergency Aid was implemented and distributed in less than a month, making use of the existing capacity within the Ministry of Social Development. It especially relied on the Unified Registry, Caixa Econômica Federal, and municipalities, where street-level professionals are involved in registration (Chapter 10). The Emergency Aid Program initially lasted for five months but was later extended in 2021 after a period without benefits. Although both the benefit value and reach were reduced over time, this initiative significantly mitigated the impacts of the economic crisis, ranking as the seventh-largest CCT program in the world at that time. Nearly half of Brazil's population was receiving some benefit, and Bolsonaro recognized opportunities for electoral gains. In August 2021, Bolsonaro announced the end of the PBF in November, making room for the Auxílio Brasil Program. Despite reaching a much larger number of families, surpassing 20 million, Auxílio Brasil fundamentally changed the principles and guidelines of the PBF. It established an equal benefit value for all families without any equity mechanisms and introduced meritocratic, commodifying, and individual accountability principles. Concerns arise from the fact that the executive's budget bill for 2023, presented in October 2022, did not include a complete budgetary provision for the program. It appeared to be a proposal focused on the election.

Social investment policies

The book offers three analyses of traditional social investment policies: labor market policies, education, and family (care) policies. Brazil aligns with a distributive regime type characterized, according to a typology by Garritzmann, Häusermann, and Palier (2023), by substantial investment in compensatory policies and limited investment in social investment policies. In the case of education, recognized as a state obligation and a right for children and adolescents in the 1988 Federal Constitution, investment has grown substantially since 1988. However, performance in international assessments, such as the Programme for International Student Assessment (PISA), remains unsatisfactory. In any case, it is important to understand how each of these policies was implemented during the analyzed period.

Camargos and Barbosa (Chapter 13) examine **labor market** policies and demonstrate that while Rousseff may have caused some harm due to budget constraints, the true reformer was Temer. He effectively deregulated the sector by approving an extensive labor reform in 2017. According to the authors, Bolsonaro merely intensified a development that was already in progress. This chapter reveals that the significant effort of Lula's government to implement training policies did not continue under Rousseff. In Rousseff's first term, the job search policy intensified, but by 2015, it declined and did not recover in later governments. Despite Law 13,467 being approved on November 11, 2017, without sparking significant protests, Temer became the president with the lowest approval rating in history. The authors highlight the devastating effects of this reform, as it removed the state from all salary negotiations, weakened unions, suppressed collective instruments, and fragmented workers, placing them in direct negotiations with employers. The relaxation of labor market rules is tied to a populist and neoliberal discourse that proposes transforming workers into entrepreneurs. The process of "managing the informal economy" is being institutionalized. According to Camargos and Barbosa, this reform eliminates the state's protection of workers, creating a hybrid system resembling informality. It retains the controls typical of formality but lacks the formal connection to the company or organization. A side effect of this reform is that unemployment benefits become ineffective during times of crisis, as the majority of the unemployed are informal workers.

The Bolsonaro' strategies employed in family and educational policies were quite similar, characterized on the one hand by inaction or a relatively low number of concrete actions, and on the other hand by strong symbolic actions. The two chapters primarily centered on Bolsonaro's government. In the realm of family policies (Chapter 12), especially those associated with care, and educational policies (Chapter 11), the major rupture occurred at the symbolic level, marking a cultural war. This aspect represents a notable distinction from Temer's government. Bolsonaro'credit-claiming strategies were carried out through symbolic actions.

We contend that, ideologically, PRRPs align with the goals of neoliberalism and neoconservatism, as proposed by Cooper (2017). This suggests a reduced role for the state while simultaneously asserting control over moral issues such as sexuality. This is achieved through family-centric policies guided by specific religious moral values. Additionally, educational policies that strongly oppose Marxism and communism carry significant weight. The alliance between neoliberalism and neoconservatism appears to resonate with PRRPs within both family dynamics and the educational realm offered by families and schools. For example, in the neoliberal agenda, there is a push to replace public school or daycare provision with vouchers, as seen during Bolsonaro's administration. Neoconservatism, on the other hand, emphasizes family choice instead of a pluralistic system, promoting the use of the family environment to reinforce traditional roles in a patriarchal society (Brown, 2019).

We agree with Brown (2006), who argues that neoconservatism differs significantly from classical conservatism. As such, it is not simply a revival of the conservative tradition.

"neoconservatism abandons classic conservative commitments to a modest libertarianism, isolationism, frugality and fiscal tightness, belief in limits and moderation, and affinity with aristocratic virtues of refinement, rectitude, civility, education, and discipline." Unlike its predecessor, it is animated by an overtly avowed power drive, by angst about the declining or crumbling status of morality within the West, and by a concomitant moralization of a certain imaginary of the West and its values. Thus, while many neoconservatives decry the "social engineering" they attribute to socialism and liberal democratic egalitarian projects such as affirmative action, integration, and poverty reduction, neoconservatism no more rejects state-led behaviorism than neoliberalism does. Rather, it identifies the state, including law, with the task of setting the moral-religious compass for society, and indeed for the world. This endorsement of state power, and attribution of moral authority to the state, is at odds with liberalism in every sense of the word" (Brown, 2006, p. 697).

Therefore, one can say that moral and anti-identity agendas are extremely important to far-right parties. In Latin America, these parties emerged in response to the gains made by feminist and LGBTQIA+ movements in the 1990s and 2000s, constituting a movement against what is labeled as "gender ideology" (Biroli et al., 2020). The ideology of PRRPs promotes traditional values, particularly emphasizing the heteronormative and monogamous family. This perspective opposes initiatives advocating for the rights of sexual and gender minorities, for example (Mudde, 2019). In this context, the school and the family stand out as key elements in the political discourse, making public policies targeting these areas significant subjects of analysis (Biroli, 2019). In simpler terms, these are two symbolic spaces where a battle between "good" and "evil" plays out, propelled by a religiously infused populist discourse. As well highlighted by Gomes and Segatto (Chapter 11), in his inaugural speech, Bolsonaro stated: "We are going to unite the people, rescue the family, respect religions and our Judeo-Christian tradition, combat gender ideology, conserve our values" (*The Guardian*, January 2, 2019).

Concerning **care policies**, Andrade and Sátyro (Chapter 12) show that, despite substantial budgetary constraints, Rousseff implemented the Brazil Carinhoso program. She integrated it into the Brazil Without Poverty program (Brasil Sem Miséria), leveraging the pre-existing structure of the social assistance system. Temer, on the other hand, implemented a fiscal austerity policy that put pressure on discretionary spending within the Ministry of Social Development, the sole location for 100% of socio-assistance services, including those associated with care. Moreover, Temer established the Criança Feliz (Happy Child) program without consulting or obtaining approval from participatory and agreement forums. This move disregarded the service structure of SUAS and reduced federal transfers to municipalities. The Criança Feliz program took precedence over all other discretionary expenditures of the ministry. However, previous programs were not intentionally terminated; they were essentially defunded but were not formally concluded.

Indeed, Bolsonaro did terminate the Brazil Carinhoso program, but opted to retain Criança Feliz, which had already been renamed as the Primeira Infância (Early Childhood) program during Temer's administration. The primary government program, called Auxílo Criança Cidadã (Citizen Child Aid) and linked to the Auxílio Brasil (Brazil Aid) program, provided support for daycare centers targeting mothers employed in the formal labor market (as a conditionality). These daycare centers could operate privately without registering with the Ministries of Education or Social Assistance. In simpler terms, this means that mothers working informally, who make up most of the target population, are excluded from assistance provision, effectively turning the benefit into a commodity. One prominent program under Bolsonaro's government is the Qualifica Mãe program (Qualifies the mother), a component of the Mães do Brasil (Mothers of Brazil) program, which guides mothers on motherhood, promoting a vision deeply rooted in patriarchy. Terms like "gender" have also been removed from official documents, for instance. In essence, these were powerful and revealing symbolic actions.

These actions clearly extend beyond the commodification and the introduction of meritocracy in assisting families in extreme poverty, surpassing neoliberal perspectives. All the actions undertaken, including those that were left unimplemented (such as Auxílio Criança Cidadã, which did not have time to materialize), were aimed at moralizing early childhood education. This approach is grounded in religious and patriarchal values, sidelining a perspective centered on secular public education. Andrade and Sátyro show that this is more than commodification; it is conservatism and familism aimed at reinforcing traditional gender roles.

In **education**, Gomes and Segatto (Chapter 11) point out that, along with budget cuts and support for private initiatives inherited from the Temer era, one of Bolsonaro's main strategies was to disrupt established agreements on what to teach and how education should be organized. It is essentially a cultural battle to overturn policies not backed by the evangelical bloc in Congress. Anyone supporting public, universal, and secular education was treated as an adversary: trade unions, left-wing parties, social movements, etc. There was a narrative that higher education institutions were hubs of Marxist and communist ideologies and needed to be opposed. A key initiative involved an attack on public universities, encompassing not just ideological criticisms but also substantial budget reductions. University rectors faced various accusations, and there were cuts to research scholarships as well. Policies like Affirmative Action in universities and the inclusion of sexual education for children and adolescents in schools were framed as potential risks of child pornography. The idea was to eliminate the so-called "gender ideology" and initiatives recognizing LGBTQIA+ issues, contending that this could impact the innocence of children. They also had strong support from the evangelical bloc in Congress. In this context, anti-PT sentiment is reinforced through the spread of fake news, alleging that PT would distribute gay kits in schools and had manufactured a "cock-shaped baby bottle" ("*mamadeira de piroca*") (see Chapter 5).

Others policies

In Chapter 14, Silva and Medeiros illustrate how the **environmental** policy sector became a battleground during Bolsonaro's government. The authors propose that four different strategies were used simultaneously. First, the budget was reduced by one-third between 2019 and 2022, directly affecting crucial activities, particularly enforcement actions and measures to prevent and combat forest fires, which fall under the responsibilities of the Brazilian Institute for the Environment and Natural Resources (Ibama). The authors also emphasized what they refer to as the "ideological cleansing of personnel" when examining the composition of the federal bureaucracy in three key institutions: Ibama and the Chico Mendes Institute for Biodiversity Conservation (ICMBio), which are autonomous agencies and executive bodies affiliated with the Ministry of the Environment, and the ministry itself. Many top leadership positions were taken over by military personnel, and the bureaucracy, especially at the street level, faced intimidation from those in leadership roles. Civil servants who refused to attend an event with Minister Salles were threatened with administrative action. Also, the president of Ibama publicly dismissed these civil servants, labeling them as "crazy people." In essence, an atmosphere of oppression and control emerged, resulting from the imposition of discipline and loyalty inspired by military standards. The authors also highlighted a third dimension: social participation and accountability spaces were completely eliminated or reduced by 75%.

Finally, since the environmental policy is fundamentally a regulatory forum, deregulation has become one of the key strategies implemented. Most actions aimed to relax environmental legislation. In 2021, a law known as the General Environmental Licensing Law was enacted to streamline the approval of projects with potential environmental impacts by decentralizing licensing to the local level. In 2022, the Chamber of Deputies approved amendments to the 1989 General Pesticide Law, eliminating veto points for the use of these products. The executive's proposal, Bill No. 191/2020, to regulate mineral resource exploitation in indigenous lands, was not approved in the lower chamber. However, the legislature's Bill No. 2633/2020, known as the "Land Grabbing Bill" ("PL da Grilagem"), addressing land regularization in federal land, was approved. Normative instructions and a decree, which are exclusive instruments of the executive, were used to approve several changes, including alterations in policy design. Ibama was authorized to delegate environmental licensing to subnational environmental agencies, thereby shifting the responsibility of implementation away from the federal executive. Decree No. 9,760/2019 addressed the imposition of administrative sanctions on offenders, who are now judged in conciliation chambers. A policy instrument was weakened by this shift, as even clear violations now require validation by "higher authorities" before sanctions can be initiated. Silva and Medeiros (Chapter 14) conclude that "From 2019 to 2022, infralegal measures removed the discretion of environmental inspectors and granted a significant role to the private sector, particularly in licensing and the privatization of Conservation Units."

Last, but not least impactful, is the evidence brought by Ludmila et al (Chapter 15) showing the increase in new weapons since the 1980s, but which, under the Bolsonaro government, presents a strongly accentuated curve that differs from the trend of previous period as a function of its greatest slope. The deregulation promoted by Bolsonaro went beyond any administrative or political act that had previously been carried out towards the release of weapons. The ease of eligibility criteria for purchases was unprecedented both for the different weapons and for the quantity of ammunition allowed monthly, which went from 50 to 2000 units depending on the calibre. In this way, increases in the rate of new weapons registered by Hunters, Shooters, and Collectors (CACs) per 100.000 inhabitants as well as in the rate of policies killings per 100.000 inhabitants, the average growth rate of homicides and its high correlation places Brazil on another level of violence, despite historically being one of the world's most violent countries. The numbers brought by Ludmila et al are striking and if the relationship is direct, but with a delay, the years that follow will not be one of fewer deaths nor in the direction of peace. Unfortunately, even though the new government has already carried out administrative acts that partially reverse the processes that were underway, the stock of weapons in society will continue with no state capacity for supervision or control.

Can we say we are witnessing a welfare dismantling?

Certainly, throughout the analyzed period, we witnessed concurrent processes of policy dismantling. However, can we conclude that there was a dismantling of the welfare state? While the events clearly constituted a systemic action, we should be cautious when moving from individual case analyses to a broader analytical level, as it may expose us to ecological fallacy. To address this, we need to examine long-term as well as short-term spending cuts, and long-term as well as short-term consequences of all those strategies analysed, reforms, regulations, de-regulation, re-regulation, and termination. Taking this into account and acknowledging the significance of institutions, the potential responses to the question – yes and no – largely hinge on the outcome of the 2022 presidential election. Had Bolsonaro been re-elected, the processes examined here would have persisted, indicating a significant break. However, we see the election results as the first institutional response to the implemented policies. If we were to assess the election results specifically concerning social policies and their dismantling, we could argue that the public did not endorse the dismantling process, even in light of the attempts to conceal or disguise the unfolding changes and the growing influence of the right. However, we understand that Bolsonaro's defeat represents a triumph of democracy and, consequently, holds greater significance than the agenda of social policies alone. Brazilian democracy showed resilience as Bolsonaro was voted out, despite him having political control and resorting to all means, including illegal ones, to secure victory.

Even with Bolsonaro's departure, institutional changes have taken place, leading to a system less dedicated to equity. The entire process has resulted in significant social costs, including increased poverty, rising income inequality, and other social disparities, along with a surge in food insecurity to unacceptable levels (Chapter 6). In 2022, as emphasized by Sátyro et al. (Chapter 9), 58.5 million Brazilians faced varying degrees of food and nutritional insecurity. And those are just the immediate effects. In Chapter 6, Souza conducted a longitudinal analysis that clearly illustrates the consequences of the observed change in trajectory. The reduction in coverage, the diminished protective impact of Bolsa Família benefits, the restricted reach of the BPC, coupled with the discontinuation of the minimum wage valorization policy, entirely reversed the trend of poverty reduction and income distribution seen from the 2000s until the mid-2010s. In 2018, approximately 13.5 million people were in extreme poverty, a level comparable to that recorded in 2008 (Jannuzzi and Sátyro, 2023). As Souza noted, poverty and inequality decreased from 2003 to 2015, regardless of the indicators used. However, between 2015 and 2019, all these indicators showed a worsening trend. It is worth noting that the income of the wealthiest individuals did not decrease either during the period of declining poverty and inequality from 2003 and 2015 or in the subsequent period until 2022 when the indicators returned to previous levels (Souza, 2018a; 2018b).

When compared to cases involving significant changes in welfare regimes, such as Chile or New Zealand, it becomes clear that Brazil was not a case of welfare dismantling. Despite various radical policy changes, it is more accurate to characterize it as a welfare state retrenchment.

The subsequent response and interpretation result from a shift in the political landscape through the electoral process. This marks the arrival of a government that respects the establishment, led by a left-wing president. To secure victory, a broad coalition was formed with parties ranging across the entire ideological spectrum, all emphasizing a democratic discourse. Hence, with Lula's victory in 2022, the pieces on the chessboard of Brazilian politics were reshuffled. And here it is vital to understand the "distributive" nature of institutions. This allows us to see that changing institutions involves rearranging relations and power resources among actors, making it a highly contentious and dynamic process. Institutions' distributive characteristics allow for a simultaneous analysis of the agency's role and a reevaluation of the dynamic relationship between actors and structure (Mahoney and Thelen, 2010).

When a government undergoes a shift to a radical ideology, as in 2016 and again in 2022, the entire landscape sees significant rearrangements. So, we expect the current change to slow down, and some effects to be reversed depending on the extent and reversibility of the reforms. This will hinge on policy design, the nature of the observed changes, legacy, and the strength of public opinion. Policy design reveals how resistant or susceptible a given policy is to reforms, regardless of the direction it takes. The nature of these changes prompts us to consider reversibility, a concept that Pierson refers to as the lock-in effect. In this case, path dependence should be viewed as a feature of institutional evolution. Institutional adaptation and continuity over time should not overshadow how political contestation emerges in connection with the forms and functions that institutions take on in specific critical junctures (Mahoney, 2000; Thelen, 2006).

Looking at compensatory policies, health policy saw a notable decline across all analyzed indicators. This policy was marked by initiatives aiming to reduce the state's role, promoting increased market openness on the one hand, and prioritizing reduced investment in prevention and more in supplementary health on the other hand – both during Temer's government and in Bolsonaro's first year in office. Certain actions, such as implementing private healthcare plans, may be considered irreversible. However, the pandemic preserved the Unified Health System (SUS) and the understanding of the state's role, comprehensiveness, and prevention. The pandemic made the public recognize the importance of health policy, leading to an immediate increase in support for it. In 2020, Rodrigo Maia, the then-president of the Chamber of Deputies, a member of a party that, before Bolsonaro, aligned with the far-right mainstream (PFL-DEM-União Brasil), openly criticized his own stance. He publicly declared on more than one occasion that he "had a very pro-private health market view" and that the pandemic changed his perspective. Expressions like these became commonplace. In essence, the pandemic played a vital role in preserving SUS. It interrupted the privatization processes that had been ongoing since Temer's government and increased social awareness of its importance. This does not mean that changes have not occurred; it simply indicates that these changes were not significant enough to cause a fundamental shift in the nature of this policy sector.

The reversal in social assistance, encompassing both services and CCT programs, happened almost instantly. Due to insufficient federal funding, service availability was significantly reduced. However, since implementation occurs at the local level, the physical infrastructure largely endured, even though teams were demobilized. In other words, the structure was not dismantled thanks to the autonomy of federative entities. Cash transfers, on the other hand, were strengthened. In August 2021, Bolsa Família was abolished (functioning until November 2021) and replaced by the Auxílio Brasil program with a completely different profile. In a move aimed at securing electoral support, Bolsonaro preserved the benefit value set by Congress, which was more than twice the average benefit value of Bolsa Família. However, the program lost its design that generated equity, as the benefit value was the same for all families, regardless of their profile. On the other hand, he included many families, resulting in the number of beneficiaries rising from 13 million in December 2019 to over 21.6 million families in 2022. However, the budget projected for the program in 2023, submitted to Congress in October 2022, was not enough to cover its costs, with a deficit of about R$ 52 billion to fulfill the promises. Essentially, it is unclear how Bolsonaro would have tackled the issue of an insufficient budget for the program if he had been re-elected. In any case, this suggests that the policy lost its central focus in the president's agenda and was used for electoral purposes.

Following Lula's victory, the Auxílio Brasil program was swiftly terminated, preserving its positive features – the progressive character marked by a substantial benefit value and a significantly larger number of beneficiaries. These achievements, likely propelled by the pandemic's impact and its strategic use in the 2022 election, might not have been accomplished by the left otherwise. Conversely, this move entirely eradicates the meritocratic and market-oriented aspects embedded in the Auxílio Brasil program. Therefore, the policy design returns to the equitable principles of Bolsa Família, upholding a significant basic benefit value and introducing variable benefits that provide additional support to more vulnerable families based on the number of children.

The pension reform and labor market policies stand out as they introduce lasting changes – the nature of their policy design makes it challenging to reverse these changes. We highlight two important aspects. First, the pension reform required a constitutional amendment, while the labor reform was implemented through a law. Currently, we are facing a Congress even more right-leaning than the one that approved these reforms, equipped with more powerful instruments, such as the "secret budget," which did not exist previously. The era of a strong executive is over. Additionally, the results of these reforms are not immediately apparent, given the complex rules and the gradual unfolding of their effects over time. Those impacted may not immediately grasp the future costs imposed on them. Hence, we can assert that, given the design features of these policies, both the pension reform and the labor reform exhibit a significant lock-in effect, leading to the privatization of benefits and job precariousness, respectively.

In simpler terms, policies that do not rely on contributions show themselves susceptible to reversal due to their institutional designs. Moreover, under the influence of public opinion, these policies ended up being strengthened, either in practical terms, as seen in the case of CCTs, or symbolically, as observed in health policy. However, rolling back changes in contributory policies and labor law reforms will be challenging, not only because of the composition of the new government and Congress but also due to the less traceable nature of their consequences, resulting in reduced public pressure.

In domains where symbolic action has been particularly pronounced, such as in education and care policies, reversing the consequences becomes more challenging, as these initiatives have sparked changes at the societal level. As emphasized by Gomes and Segatto, long-standing consensuses have been disrupted, including the rejection of racist, sexist, and homophobic behaviors, as well as a re-valuation of the idea of a secular educational system. Part of society misconstrues the concept of freedom of expression, leading to the expression of various racist attitudes, for instance. People refer to "gender ideology" as if it were a threat to their children's safety, mistakenly fearing that "communism" would infiltrate their homes and seize their possessions, including items like cars and cattle. Cases of racism, homophobia, and other forms of discrimination have resulted in varied legal outcomes at lower courts. Nevertheless, when these cases reach the Supreme Federal Court, the responses have been exemplary, aligning with the principles of the Rule of Law.

Outside the realm of *stricto sensu* social policies, the situation is even more dire. The effects are nearly irreversible, at least in the short term, concerning environmental damage (Chapter 14) or the accumulation of weapons in society (Chapter 15). Public opinion struggles to understand the impacts of environmental policies, especially those concerning the protection of indigenous peoples and the Amazon. For the average citizen, it is hard to grasp how deforestation in the Amazon could affect the availability of water in São Paulo, despite the 4,000 km distance between them. Undoing Bolsonaro's policy of expanding access to firearms is difficult, leading to a situation where the public, including militias and organized trafficking, is now more heavily armed than the police forces. The consequences are still unclear.

Therefore, we found mixed results. On the one hand, the welfare state in Brazil has been bolstered in terms of non-contributory policies, which are more inclusive and committed to equality, at least in the short term. However, changes in contributory policies have turned the system significantly more regressive. Privileges remain unchanged, and the rules for accessing the basic benefit have become more complex. However, when it comes to education, access rights, for example, have remained the same. Moreover, labor relations have been completely relaxed, further fragmenting workers. Negotiations now occur directly between the employer and the employee without legislative protection, resulting in a decline in commitment to equality. Therefore, while it is difficult to assert a complete dismantling of the welfare state conceptually, it is clear that it has weakened. The cultural backlash, it means, the symbolic shifts in the various issues we addressed, along with the growing influence of the right, resulted in an overall decline in public support for social protection. In this context, the future does not seem promising.

So, we ask: What are the main forces driving the processes under examination?

Economic decline, rise of the far right: How did this happen?

How do institutional changes occur? This question lies at the core of political science, which has long concentrated on analyzing the stability of organizations and institutions. Two generations of theories help explain institutional change. We should extract from them what is pertinent to the phenomenon that concerns us: the dismantling of the welfare state. The theory of punctuated equilibrium posits that institutions experience extended periods of stability, occasionally "interrupted" by crises that trigger changes. In essence, institutional change could be seen as the result of a rupture or discontinuity in ideas, policies, and party coalitions. Our analysis reveals two instances of punctuated equilibrium: one in the economic sphere, triggered by the economic crisis that started to take shape in 2014 and fully unfolded in 2015, and another in the political domain, marked by a substantial reconfiguration of the Brazilian political and party system.

Regarding the political crisis in question, there is no denying that the phenomenon examined in this book arises from an instance of punctuated equilibrium, the impeachment of a president directly elected by the people. First, the ousting of Dilma Rousseff signified, in an undesirable manner, the impeachment of a politically successful project chosen by the voters, replacing it with what had been rejected. Speculating whether the documented changes in this volume would have happened without this event is an impossible counterfactual exercise. Even if not the direct cause, it does serve as a starting point. Second, starting in 2016, there was a significant reshaping of political forces in Brazil, characterized by the significant growth of a far right that was previously only figurative (Borges – Chapter 3). Political coalitions were reconstructed, and the relationship between the executive and Congress experienced a departure from its previous trajectory. According to Immergut (2002), changes in power dynamics "can cause veto points to emerge, shift, or disappear, creating strategic openings that actors can exploit to achieve their goals" (Immergut, 2002: 7). The political class knew about this when they removed Dilma Rousseff from power (Limongi, 2023).

Thelen and Steinmo (1992) identified four potential sources of institutional dynamism, where we can observe changes in how institutions operate over time within the same case. These sources of variation are empirically linked but can be analytically separated as follows: i) changes in the socio-economic and political context, capable of thrusting latent institutions to prominence, as seen in the processes analyzed in this book; ii) changes in the meaning and utility of specific institutions; iii) changes in the goals or strategies of institutions, notably the federal executive in the present case; iv) adjustments of strategies to adapt to changes, whether arising from crises, gradual maneuvers, or strategic disputes in response to institutional constraints. During the analyzed period, we identified these four sources of institutional dynamism.

Institutionalizing fiscal austerity as state policy amidst an unresponsive economy

Institutional changes within social policies cannot be analyzed without considering macroeconomic and fiscal policies. Therefore, to understand policy and regime dismantling, it is crucial to first look at the political choices related to these macroeconomic and fiscal policies. Guimarães and Resende (Chapter 4) conduct a longitudinal comparative analysis of these policies throughout the administrations of Rousseff, Temer, and Bolsonaro, highlighting the influence of neoliberal practices in the observed dynamics. According to the authors, Lula's government successfully achieved economic growth and social advancements; however, contradictions in macroeconomic policy became apparent as of 2010. Moreover, certain fundamental reforms were not implemented. Lula's second term, particularly between 2005 and 2010, "was characterized by fiscal expansion, with public investment and redistributive transfers as its main drivers" (Orair and Gobetti, 2017: p.1). Furthermore, economic performance, as assessed by Orair and Gobetti (2017) and Guimaraes and Resende, received a positive final evaluation.

Orair and Gobetti (2017) argue that Rousseff's administration, initially (2011–2014), "was characterized by a period of fiscal expansion, the fiscal space was reoriented towards tax cuts and subsidies to private investment, while public investment stagnated." However, in Rousseff's second term, there was a shift toward fiscal austerity with high costs. Guimaraes and Resende agree, contending that Rousseff struggled to navigate a challenging international environment. In January 2015, at the start of her second term, she immediately implemented a fiscal austerity measure, cutting government spending by 1.4% of the GDP. The authors argue that this decision was ill-timed because, according to Keynesian thinking, during a recession, government spending cuts can worsen economic activity by inhibiting private investment. Moreover, due to Rousseff's political ineptitude, Congress did not approve the proposed measures that year, resulting in smaller cuts than anticipated. The fact is that fiscal indicators have continued to deteriorate. In any case, the introduction of austerity measures was a catalyst for the subsequent recession or, at the very least, did not prevent it.

Rousseff's mistakes in macroeconomic policy carried a significant political and social cost. This helps us understand the impact this period had on the analyzed social policies, as public investment in all areas remained stagnant. Therefore, we can say Rousseff's second term affected various areas due to defunding. However, the analyses in this book do not offer evidence of an intentional dismantling, mostly because there was no intention to change the nature of the analyzed policies. In other words, no direct and intentional actions to dismantle the rules and designs of the policies were identified. Therefore, her action seems to have been an adaptation strategy in response to the crisis. Adopting neoliberal measures did not yield the anticipated results. Worse, these choices led to Rousseff's political downfall and further legitimized the neoliberal decisions made by Temer and Bolsonaro. However, none of them succeeded in reversing economic stagnation, even after implementing such reforms. And being left-leaning, Rousseff was penalized by the public for adopting neoliberal measures (Giger and Nelson, 2011; Klitgaard and Elmelund-Præstekær, 2014).

Both Temer and Bolsonaro adopted the neoliberal discourse and practices, centering their efforts on structural reforms, government expense reduction, privatization, and overall deregulation. In terms of macroeconomic and fiscal decisions, they maintained the same approach. In December 2016, just a few months after taking office, Temer quickly managed to pass a constitutional amendment that established a spending ceiling from 2017 to 2037. According to this amendment, the federal budget could only grow in line with the increase in GDP, as spending would be fixed in real terms. To get a sense of the effort involved, a constitutional amendment must be approved in two rounds in each legislative house by a qualified majority. Despite being a single act, this amendment embodies austerity, serving as the **institutionalization of an austerity policy** not only within a government but within the state, as it binds future administrations, as mentioned earlier. Temer also succeeded in passing a labor reform under the pretext of making labor contracts more flexible. However, according to Camargos and Barbosa (Chapter 13), this reform increases job precariousness and provides less protection for workers than it delivers positive results. In his inaugural year, Bolsonaro successfully passed the pension reform, a proposal that had been extensively debated since Temer had assumed office, undergoing various adaptations. In 2021, Congress approved the independence of the Central Bank. However, despite the pursuit of a radical liberal agenda, austerity did not define Bolsonaro's government. He succeeded in easing the spending ceiling by around R$ 795 billion over the course of four years: R$ 53.6 billion in 2019, R$ 507.9 billion in 2020, due to the pandemic, R$ 117.2 billion in 2021, and the rest in 2022[1]. In one way or another, the economy emerged from the recession but did not take off, as seen in Chapter 4; therefore, neither Temer nor Bolsonaro delivered as promised.

Rise of the right and executive-legislative relationship

It is important to remember that Temer was not elected as president. Moreover, his political agenda did not align with the one for which he was elected as vice president; instead, it was the agenda that led to Rousseff's removal from power. Upon assuming office, Temer chose not to seek re-election, allowing him to implement highly unpopular and costly reforms from an electoral standpoint. Indeed, the cost became evident, as by the conclusion of his administration, Temer held the record for the lowest approval ratings in the recent history of Brazilian democracy, as indicated by opinion polls. In the case of Rousseff, it was anticipated that she would face repercussions because of her association with a left-wing party. However, both Temer and Bolsonaro claimed credit for these neoliberal reforms. This aligns with theoretical expectations, as some authors have shown that right-wing government parties can even benefit electorally from welfare state retrenchment (Giger and Nelson, 2011; Klitgaard and Elmelund-Præstekær, 2014). According to Klitgaard and Elmelund-Præstekær (2014), such strategies are consistent with their general preferences, and they have the option of claiming credit for strategies that confront economic crises. However, for various reasons, neither of them was approved: Temer, despite not seeking re-election, concluded his term with a 5% approval rating in opinion polls, and Bolsonaro was not re-elected.

The political landscape saw a reshuffling, especially within the right. Borges (Chapter 3) highlighted the significant surge of the far right and the waning influence of the mainstream right. As Borges and Vidigal (2023) underscored, this phenomenon is connected to four primary trends: 1) the expansion of neo-pentecostalism, which extends beyond the political realm as conservatives employ non-partisan strategies to engage in a cultural war against progressive values (Smith, 2019: 2). Certainly, evangelical Christians have understood the dynamics of the electoral system, resulting in a substantial rise in the number of state and federal deputies elected from this group (Chapter 3). A right-wing faction deeply rooted in religious convictions and committed to traditional and dogmatic values. 2) Since the 2013 protests, various liberal and conservative movements, aligning with the reorganization of the right, have gained strength and organized in favor of the impeachment of Dilma Rousseff. Since then, liberal think tanks and conservative social movements have gained strength, with several leaders from this milieu being elected members of parliament. 3) The reshaping of this right-wing faction also mirrors the emergence of new options in the electoral market. Parties like the PSL, which previously held only one seat in the lower house, suddenly secured 52 seats in 2018 and 99 in 2022. This signals a substantial overhaul. Moreover, new parties were established, such as Novo and the PRB. 4) Lastly, the authors underscore the rise in ideological polarization: on the one hand, the strengthening of anti-PT sentiment, and on the other, the rise of Bolsonarism. An affective polarization, characterized by intense feelings of rejection and identification, brings with it a symbolic shift in the meaning attributed to what is labeled as right and left. Indeed, even though Lula won the 2022 presidential election in the three most populous states – Rio de Janeiro, São Paulo, and Minas Gerais – the right not only elected governors but also saw a significant increase in the number of seats in state legislatures. In simpler terms, these are lasting changes.

The change in the dynamics of the relationship between the executive and the legislative branches not only established a more right-leaning composition of the legislatures but also bolstered the role of the legislative branch. Power and Rodrigues-Silveira (2019) showed the differences and distance between the ideology of the entering presidents and the seat composition of the House of Representatives. Although their focus was on ideology at the municipal level, they graphically showed that throughout PT administrations, there was a balance between a left-leaning executive and a more right-leaning legislature. Even though Power and Rodrigues-Silveira (2019) affirmed that "over time, the left-wing PT moderated its ideology and became much closer to the national average," it always remained positioned further to the left than the national lower house, with the PMDB consistently acting as Brazil's pivotal party. We argue that the impeachment changed this composition. In the 2022 elections, both Congress and municipal executives shifted even more towards the right compared to the elections of 2016 and 2018.

We find ourselves in a paradoxical situation reminiscent of the famous phrase by Antônio Carlos Jobim (musician: 1927–1994) that "Brazil is not for beginners": Bolsonaro capitalized much less than could have been possible on the opportunities present in Congress. Despite spending three decades as a federal deputy, supposedly being knowledgeable about the Federal Constitution and the powers it grants to the president, Bolsonaro openly stated that he did not have his own agenda and would not interfere in the work of Congress. However, in March 2019, during a meeting with business leaders in the United States, he said "Brazil is not an open terrain where we intend to build things for our people. We actually have much to unbuild, much to undo. So that we can then do things. If I serve at least as an inflection point, I'll be happy,"[2] he said. In other words, he was playing a double game, declaring to Congress that he would not influence its agenda. Surprisingly, Bolsonaro failed to capitalize on his substantial majority in Congress. Despite holding a qualified majority in terms of ideological alignment, he ended up becoming the president with the lowest approval rate of executive bills sent to Congress in the history of Brazilian democracy (Limongi et al., 2022). As highlighted by Limongi et al. (2022), Bolsonaro secured approval for legislative bills at a rate of less than 10%, indicating an overall legislative approval rate of only 50% for his initiatives. In contrast, Lula achieved over 75% approval in both of his terms. Even Rousseff, accused of political ineptitude, garnered an approval rate of over 70%. This suggests that if Bolsonaro had genuinely prioritized a specific agenda, the dismantling could have been even more significant. In many situations, he appears more inclined towards inaction than effective action. This implies that the observed backward movement could have been much worse. However, as we are aware, there is no void in power, and the leader of Congress has become a sort of "head of a parallel government." His influence arises from his significant control over the "secret budget," a type of budget ratified by Congress in 2019 for parliamentary amendments that evade the scrutiny of fiscal responsibility or any form of accountability, lacking a prior designation or assured allocation.

Populism, fake news, and authoritarian and systemic vision

While Temer is associated with austerity, Bolsonaro is labeled as populist, anti-systemic, and authoritarian. He gains strength in the context of the aforementioned rise of the right (Borges – Chapter 3). Borges underscored the surge in recent years of a radical and populist far right, simultaneously noting the waning influence of the old right (referred to here as mainstream). He highlighted that these two groups do not differ significantly in terms of their economic and social agendas. However, Borges pointed out that the far right introduces a cultural agenda, heavily grounded in neopentecostalism, and is characterized by an anti-systemic and apolitical stance.

While the term populism is quite controversial, the concept fundamentally revolves around a style of communication in which the populist leader establishes a direct connection with the public, often bypassing various institutions. As emphasized in Chapter 13, Heller (2020), in an analysis of cases in Brazil and India, uses what he calls "populism as retrenchment to underscore its distinct social base and the fact that it has a relatively well-defined project of rolling back expansions of social rights and asserting traditional socio-cultural hierarchies" (2020: 592). According to the author, "beyond an erosion of democratic institutions and norms, retrenchment populism has included open efforts to repress civil society, policies to de-certify specific socio-cultural groups and the use of state-sponsored vigilantism." (2020: 591). These concepts directly align with the notion of "authoritarian populism" as described by Urbinati (2019). In this framework, Urbinati characterizes governments that were elected through democratic processes but adopt anti-systemic and authoritarian positions and discourses, leading to a weakening of democracy.

Nunes and Traumann (2023) emphasized that, in the eyes of Brazilian voters, particularly those who align themselves either for or against PT, roughly corresponding to left and right mainstreams, opinions on economic and social issues are quite similar. However, these groups diverge significantly when it comes to moral, traditional, and cultural agendas. Borges (Chapter 3) found a similar result in the case of federal deputies. The far right skillfully exploited this specific segment. Bolsonaro seized upon this opening: On the one hand, he took a confrontational moral stance against groups supporting LGBTQIA+ rights, feminists, leftists, and all minorities; on the other hand, he embraced an anti-systemic discourse, opposing electronic voting machines and criticizing traditional politics, presenting himself as if he were not a professional politician. However, as explored in Chapter 5 on disinformation and democracy, it is not merely about outdated discursive strategies. Bolsonaro set up a highly effective "machine" of fake news that played a crucial role in this cultural battle, exploiting distorted and antagonistic identities. Concurrently, he implemented measures to curtail rights, in a fashion reminiscent of experiences observed in various other countries, such as the United States and India (Hacker and Pierson, 2020; Heller, 2020). Santana and Mitozo (Chapter 5) show the daily influx of over 400 pieces of fake news in WhatsApp groups.

Concerning the anti-systemic, apolitical, and authoritarian agenda, along with the discursive strategy to erode trust in the party system, judiciary, and electoral system, especially electronic voting machines, Bolsonaro declared he would not follow the bargaining logic typical of coalition politics in presidential systems. For example, he explicitly stated that he would not engage in negotiations involving political positions and ministries (Limongi et al., 2022). Indeed, he appointed several military figures as ministers, alongside individuals characterized by the Brazilian media as "ideological." These individuals were known for openly supporting agendas such as anti-vaccination, the denial of science (including the idea that the Earth is flat), and the rejection of climate change, for instance. Additionally, Bolsonaro also appointed economists with ultra-liberal inclinations (Limongi et al., 2022). Neo-Pentecostal religious fervor was another characteristic of the selected profile. These choices would not be an issue if these individuals were committed to democratic principles and political or administrative experience. However, the ministers lacked political connections or involvement with the epistemic communities of the policy sectors for which they were responsible. In simpler terms, they could be seen as inexperienced individuals with far-right leanings, as noted by Limongi et al. (2022).

In this context, the pandemic unfolds, becoming a significant arena for denial, as documented by Machado and Jerônymo. Although Jair Bolsonaro's administration declared that the pandemic represented a national health emergency, he resisted measures to prevent the spread of the virus. Municipal governments had to intervene and implement social distancing measures and restrictions on public services. At the same time, they focused their efforts on health care. Various industries halted their operations, leading to a surge in the demand for non-contributory social protection. Moreover, soaring inflation rates eroded the purchasing power of families. All of this had an impact on the economy, especially on services provided by informal workers, increasing pre-existing social vulnerabilities and creating new ones, mainly due to workers' inability to earn income while exposing themselves to the virus. Society exerted significant pressure, primarily through the media and civil society organizations, urging the federal government to take action. This pressure was complemented by an unprecedented move by Congress, resulting in the creation of an emergency support program targeting individuals facing vulnerability and social risks, known as Emergency Aid. The primary concern was to ensure access to food for families who lost their source of income due to work restrictions – additionally, there was the issue of comorbidities caused by poor nutrition, which aggravated the health issues of those who contracted the virus.

As we reach the end of our journey, let us take a moment to ponder the insights offered by the second generation of institutional change theorists. They do not see the connection between stability and change as something static or discontinuous, but rather as interconnected and dynamic. This approach brings fresh perspectives to the ongoing debate about how agency, structure, and political contexts are intertwined in processes of change. In exploring these dynamics, we refine our critiques of institutional legacies, recognizing that they might conceal meaningful disagreements and political conflicts related to a policy or institution. An economy experiencing decline or stagnation, coupled with the widespread adoption of fiscal austerity measures as if no alternative political options existed for macroeconomics, has led to political instability. This was exacerbated by the enforced removal of a president, attributed to both economic incompetence and anti-corruption efforts, as emphasized by Limongi (2023). Additionally, the rise of an extreme populist and radical right-wing movement, leveraging a fake news apparatus to disseminate discourse against identity minorities and the established system, has further contributed to a significant weakening of the social welfare state. Paradoxically, amid the pandemic and political strategies centered on elections, cash transfers have gained prominence, while the healthcare system, although suffering setbacks, maintained its core. The future cost implications of pension policy are expected to be substantial. This will pose a significant obstacle to accessing essential benefits, prompting individuals to turn to private pension plans. Furthermore, given the high rates of informality, it is likely that upcoming cohorts will lack social security protection. Therefore, there has been welfare retrenchment, even though the system has not been privatized or transformed into a residual model, and despite social security having not undergone a process of capitalization. The shift in society, influenced by symbolic discourses on the traditional family, gender issues, and educational content, indicates reduced support for social policies. Continuous monitoring will be required to assess the long-term consequences of this situation.

In a recent book addressing crises in democracy, Adam Przeworski (2020) examined two examples where democracy showed resilience during crises – France and the USA – and two examples where systems succumbed, namely Chile and the Weimar Republic. Brazil appears to be a compelling case of resilience worth considering, as its institutions have endured. Despite the less-than-optimal state of Brazilian democracy, it has resisted a violent and explicit attack. More time will be needed to assess the resilience of the system as a whole and the consequences of all these processes analyzed here.

Notes

1 www.bbc.com/portuguese/brasil-63653642#:~:text=Bolsonaro%20furou%20t eto%20de%20gastos,de%20governo%20%2D%20BBC%20News%20Brasil
2 See on Twitter the video of Jair Bolsonaro's son, Eduardo Bolsonaro: https://twitter. com/BolsonaroSP/status/1107596301133406209
  Or in the news article: https://veja.abril.com.br/politica/temos-de-desconstruir-muita-coisa-diz-bolsonaro-a-americanos-de-direita

References

Arretche, Marta. (2018). Democracia e Redução Da Desigualdade Econômica No Brasil: A Inclusão Dos Outsiders. *Revista Brasileira de Ciências Sociais, 33*(96), 1–23.
Bauer, Michael. W. and Knill, Christoph. (2014). A conceptual framework for the comparative analysis of policy change: Measurement, explanation and strategies of policy dismantling. *Journal of Comparative Policy Analysis: Research and Practice, 16*(1), 28–44.

Biroli, Flávia. (2019). A reação contra o gênero e a democracia. *Nueva Sociedad*, *23*(65), 76–87.

Biroli, Flávia, Machado, Maria das D., and Vaggione, Juan. (2020). Introdução: Matrizes do neoconservadorismo religioso na América Latina. In: Flávia Biroli, Maria Machado, and Juan Vaggione (eds.), *Gênero, neoconservadorismo e democracia*. São Paulo: Boitempo, pp. 13–40.

Borges, André and Vidigal, Robert. (2023). *Para entender a nova direita brasileira: polarização, populismo, antipetismo*. Porto Alegre: Editora Zouk.

Brown, Wendy. (2006). American nightmare: Neoliberalism, neoconservatism, and de-democratization. *Political Theory*, *34*(6), 690–714.

Brown, Wendy. (2019). *In the ruins of neoliberalism: the rise of antidemocratic politics in the West*. Nova York: Columbia University Press.

Cooper, Melinda. (2017). *Family values: Between neoliberalism and the new social conservatism*. New York: MIT Press.

Garritzmann, Julian L., Häusermann, Silja, and Palier, Bruno. (2023). Social investments in the knowledge economy: The politics of inclusive, stratified, and targeted reforms across the globe. *Social Policy & Administration*, *57*(1), 87–101.

Giger, Nathalie and Nelson, Moira. (2011). The electoral consequences of welfare state retrenchment: Blame avoidance or credit claiming in the era of permanent austerity? *European Journal of Political Research*, *50*(1), 1–23.

Green-Pedersen, Christoffer. (2004). The dependent variable problem within the study of welfare state retrenchment: Defining the problem and looking for solutions. *Journal of Comparative Policy Analysis: Research and Practice*, *6*(1), 3–14.

The Guardian. (2019). www.theguardian.com/world/2019/jan/01/jair-bolsonaro-inauguration-brazil-president

Hacker, Jacob and Pierson, Paul. (2020). *Let them eat tweets: How the right rules in an age of extreme inequality*. New York: Liveright Publishing.

Heller, Patrick. (2020). The age of reaction: Retrenchment populism in India and Brazil. *International Sociology*, *35*(6), 590–609.

Immergut, Ellen. M. (2002). The Rule of the Game: the logic of health policy-making in France, Switzerland and Sweden. In: Sven Steimo and Kathleen, T. Thelen (eds.), *Structuring politics – Historical institutionalism in comparative analysis*. Nova York: Cambrigde, pp. 57–89.

Jannuzzi, Paulo and Sátyro, Natália. (2023). Social policies, poverty, and hunger in Brazil: The social and institutional legacy of the Lula/Dilma governments. In: Richard Bourne (ed.), *Brazil After Bolsonaro: The comeback of the Lula da Silva*. 1ed. Nova Iorque: Routledge, Vol. 1, pp. 67–79.

Jordan, Andrew, Green-Pedersen, Christoffer, and Turnpenny, Jordan. (2014). Policy dismantling: An introduction. In: Michael W.Bauer, Andrew Jordan, Christoffer Green-Pedersen, and Adrienne Heritier (eds.), *Dismantling public policy: Preferences, strategies, and effects*. Oxford: Oxford University Press, pp. 3–29.

Klitgaard, Michael B. and Elmelund-Præstekær, Christian. (2014). The partisanship of systemic retrenchment: tax policy and welfare reform in Denmark 1975–2008. *European Political Science Review*, *6*(1), 1–19.

Limongi, Fernando. (2023). *Operação impeachment: Dilma Rousseff e o Brasil da Lava Jato*. São Paulo: Todavia.

Limongi, Fernando, Freitas, Andrea, Medeiros, Danilo, and Luz, Joice. (2022). Government and Congress. Brazil under Bolsonaro. How endangered is democracy.

In: Peter Birle and Bruno Speck (eds.), *Brazil under Bolsonaro. How endangered is democracy?* Berlin: Ibero-Amerikanisches Institut Preußischer Kulturbesitz, pp. 30–43.

Mahoney, James. (2000). Analyzing path dependence: Lessons from the social sciences. In: Andrew Wimmer and Reinhart Kossler (eds.), *Understanding change: Models, methodologies, and metaphors*. Basingstoke: Palgrave Macmillan. pp. 129-139

Mahoney, James and Thelen, Kathleen. (2010). A theory of gradual institutional change. In: James Mahoney and Kathleen Thelen (eds.). *Explaining institutional change: Ambiguity, agency, and power*. Cambridge: Cambridge University Press, pp. 1–37.

Mudde, Cas. (2019). *The far right today*. Cambridge: Polity Press.

Nunes, Felipe and Traumann, Thomas. (2023). *Biografia do Abismo: Como a polarização divide famílias, desafia empresas e compromete o futuro do Brasil*. Rio de Janeiro: Harper Collins.

Orair, Rodrigo Octávio and Gobetti, Sergio Wulff. (2017). *Brazilian fiscal policy in perspective: from expansion to austerity. Paper presented at the 45° Encontro Nacional de Economia-ANPEC*. Natal: Brasil.

Pierson, Paul. (1994). *Dismantling the welfare state? Reagan, Thatcher, and the politics of retrenchment*. Cambridge: Cambridge University.

Power, Timothy J. and Rodrigues-Silveira, Rodrigo. (2019). Mapping ideological preferences in Brazilian elections, 1994-2018: A municipal-level study. *Brazilian Political Science Review*, *13*(1), e0001. https://doi.org/10.1590/1981-382120190 0010001

Przeworski, Adam. (2020). *As crises da Democracia*. São Paulo: Editora Zahar.

Sátyro, Natália. (2014). Padrões distintos de bem-estar no Brasil: uma análise temporal. *Opinião Pública (UNICAMP. Impresso)*, *20*, 219–251.

Sátyro, Natália and Cunha, Pedro S. (2018). The coexistence of different welfare regimes in the same country: a comparative analysis of the Brazilian municipalities heterogeneity. *Journal of Comparative Policy Analysis: Research and Practice*, *21*(1), 65–89.

Smith, Amy Erica. (2019). *Religion and Brazilian democracy: Mobilizing the people of God*. Cambridge University Press. England.

Souza, Pedro H. G. F. (2018a). A history of inequality: Top incomes in Brazil, 1926–2015. *Research in Social Stratification and Mobility*, *57*, 35–45.

Souza, Pedro H. G. F. (2018b). *Uma História de Desigualdade: A Concentração de Renda Entre Os Ricos, 1926-2013*. Hucitec Editora; ANPOCS, São Paulo.

Thelen, Kathleen. (2006). Institutions and social change: The evolution of vocational training in Germany. In: Ian Shapiro, Stephen Skowronek, and Daniel Galvin (eds.), *Rethinking political institutions: The art of the state*. New York: New York University Press, pp. 135–170.

Thelen, Kathleen and Steinmo, Sven. (1992). Historical institutionalism in comparative politics. In: Sven Steinmo, Kathleen Thelen and Frank Longstreth. *Structuring politics: Historical institutionalism in comparative analysis*. Cambridge: Cambridge University Press, pp. 1–33.

Urbinati. Nadia. (2019). *Me the people. How populism transforms democracy*. Cambridge, London: Harvard University Press.

INDEX

Note: Endnotes are indicated by the page number followed by "n" and the note number e.g., 253n1 refers to note 1 on page 253. Page numbers in **bold** and *italics* refer to tables and figures, respectively.

For Product Safety Concerns and Information please contact our EU
representative GPSR@taylorandfrancis.com Taylor & Francis Verlag GmbH,
Kaufingerstraße 24, 80331 München, Germany

Printed and bound by CPI Group (UK) Ltd, Croydon, CR0 4YY
05/02/2025
01832129-0008